CÉSAR VALLEJO

The publisher gratefully acknowledges the generous contribution to this book provided by the Ahmanson Foundation Humanities Endowment Fund of the University of California Press Foundation.

The publisher also gratefully acknowledges the generous contribution toward the publication of this book provided by the Director's Circle of the University of California Press Foundation, whose members are:

ROBERT & ALICE BRIDGES FOUNDATION

EARL & JUNE CHEIT

LLOYD COTSEN

SONIA H. EVERS

ORVILLE & ELLINA GOLUB

ANN GIVEN HARMSEN & BILL HARMSEN

DANIEL HEARTZ

LEO & FLORENCE HELZEL

MRS. CHARLES HENRI HINE

PATRICK KING

RUTH A. SOLIE

THE COMPLETE POETRY

A BILINGUAL EDITION

CÉSAR VALLEJO

EDITED AND TRANSLATED BY
CLAYTON ESHLEMAN

WITH A FOREWORD BY
MARIO VARGAS LLOSA

AN INTRODUCTION BY
EFRAÍN KRISTAL

AND A CHRONOLOGY BY
STEPHEN M. HART

UNIVERSITY OF CALIFORNIA PRESS
BERKELEY   LOS ANGELES   LONDON

University of California Press, one of the most distinguished university presses in the United States, enriches lives around the world by advancing scholarship in the humanities, social sciences, and natural sciences. Its activities are supported by the UC Press Foundation and by philanthropic contributions from individuals and institutions. For more information, visit www.ucpress.edu.

University of California Press
Berkeley and Los Angeles, California

University of California Press, Ltd.
London, England

Library of Congress Cataloging-in-Publication Data

Vallejo, César, 1892–1938.
  [Poems. English & Spanish]
  The complete poetry : a bilingual edition / César Vallejo ; edited and translated by Clayton Eshleman ; with a foreword by Mario Vargas Llosa ; an introduction by Efraín Kristal ; and a chronology by Stephen M. Hart.
    p.   cm.
  Includes bibliographical references and index.
  Contents: Los heraldos negros = The black heralds — Trilce — Poemas humanos = Human Poems — España, aparta de mí este cáliz = Spain, take this cup from me.
  ISBN-13: 978-0-520-24552-5 (cloth : alk. paper)
  ISBN-10: 0-520-24552-0 (cloth : alk. paper).
  1. Vallejo, César, 1892–1938—Translations into English.   I. Eshleman, Clayton.   II. Title.

PQ8497.V35A2   2007
861'.62 — dc22
                                             2006045620

Manufactured in the United States of America

16 15 14 13 12 11 10 09 08 07
10 9 8 7 6 5 4 3 2

This book is printed on New Leaf EcoBook 50, a 100% recycled fiber of which 50% is de-inked post-consumer waste, processed chlorine-free. EcoBook 50 is acid-free and meets the minimum requirements of ANSI/ASTM D5634-01 (*Permanence of Paper*).

In memory of José Rubia Barcia (1914–1997),
dear friend and early collaborator

CÉSAR VALLEJO. *Photograph taken by Juan Domingo Córdoba Vargas in Versailles, 1929.*

CONTENTS

NOTE: In the poems and their translations the symbol >, placed in the right margin at the foot of the page and the left margin on the following page, signals the continuation of a poem (to distinguish from the first line of an untitled poem). Asterisks that appear in the right margin of the translation indicate a word or phrase discussed in the Notes to the Poems.

FOREWORD
MARIO VARGAS LLOSA

There are poets whose work can be explained, and there are inexplicable poets, like César Vallejo. But being unable to explain does not mean being unable to understand, or that his poems are incomprehensible, totally hermetic. It means that, contrary to our reading of explicable poets, even after we have studied everything about his poems that rational knowledge has to offer—his sources, his techniques, his unique vocabulary, his subjects, his influences, the historical circumstances surrounding the creation of his poems—we remain in the dark, unable to penetrate that mysterious aureole that we feel to be the secret of this poetry's originality and power.

Whether or not a poet is rationally explicable implies nothing about the depth or the excellence of his poetry. Neruda is a great and original poet, and his poetry, even the most obscure, that of *Residencia en la tierra,* is accessible through logical analysis by perceptive critics who know how to follow the text down to its roots, to its deepest core. With Vallejo the opposite happens. Even the poems of his youth— those of *The Black Heralds,* strongly marked by modernism and the avant-garde schools that came after it—have, within their seeming transparency, a nucleus irreducible to pure reason, a secret heart that eludes every effort the rational mind makes to hear it beat.

Vallejo's poetry, for all its references to familiar landscapes and a social and historical milieu, transcends those coordinates of time and space and positions the reader on a more permanent and profound plane: that of the human condition. Which is to say, the existential reality of which the lives of men and women are made: the uncertainty about our origin and our future beyond this earth; the extremes of suffering and desperation that human beings can reach; and also the intensity of our emotions when we are overcome by love, excitement, pity, or nostalgia. But the mystery in his poetry resides not in those existential subjects or states but, rather, in how they take shape in a language that communicates them to the reader directly, more through a sort of osmosis or contagion than through any intelligible discourse.

Vallejo's is a poetry that makes us feel the very fibers of existence, that strips us of all that is incidental and transitory, and confronts us with the essence we have within us: our mortality, the desperate wish to achieve transcendence and somehow to survive death, the skein of absurdities, errors, and confusions that determine our individual destinies.

Clayton Eshleman discovered Vallejo in 1957, while still in college and not yet fluent in Spanish. As he himself recounts, he has spent a good part of his life reading, studying, and trying to render this poetry in English. He was never satisified with the results; again and again he revised and polished his versions to achieve an elusive perfection. There is a sort of heroism in his undertaking, like that of those creators in pursuit of a work as beautiful as it is impossible. His case reveals an admirable fidelity to a poet who no doubt changed his life. His tireless loyalty and determination have made possible this edition of the complete poetry of Vallejo in English, perhaps the one that comes closest to the texts of the poet's own hand. Only the dauntless perseverance and the love with which the translator has dedicated so many years of his life to this task can explain why the English version conveys, in all its boldness and vigor, the unmistakable voice of César Vallejo.

TRANSLATED BY ROSE VEKONY

ACKNOWLEDGMENTS

Over the many years that I have been involved in translating Vallejo, a number of people have been extraordinarily generous with their time in response to my questions and research needs. I want especially to thank Cid Corman, Maureen Ahern, Octavio Corvalán, Julio Ortega, Américo Ferrari, José Cerna Bazán, and Efraín Kristal, who were, in their individual ways, instrumental in clarifying translation quandaries. All these people worked through at least one version of one of Vallejo's individual books with me. I would also like to thank Eliot Weinberger, Cecilia Vicuña, Walter Mignolo, Esther Allen, Jill Suzanne Levine, Theodoro Maus, Mónica de la Torre, Susan Briante, Jorge Guzmán, and Stephen Hart for their responsive readings and suggestions. My gratitude as well goes to Eastern Michigan University for two research fellowships (1989 and 1997) and to the Wheatland Foundation and the National Translation Center for grants.

In 1980 I wrote a note about co-translating Vallejo's European poetry with José Rubia Barcia in Los Angeles in the 1970s. In one paragraph I tried to get at what often appeared to be an impossible task:

> A marvelous complex of emotions is stirred when I think back to our work together. We were like two beavers, both working at different angles into the Vallejo tree, hoping it would fall at the angle each of us was setting it up to fall, but unsure if it would fall at all. Does this line really mean anything? It reads like nonsense but doesn't feel like nonsense. Have we simply not found its uncommon sense? There was always the risk of making sense of what was actually poised on the edge of sense and nonsense.

José and I worked together, always at his home in Westwood, several times a week, for around five years. During this period I came to terms with Vallejo and gained the ground necessary for going ahead, on my own, to translate *Trilce* and *Los heraldos negros*. José's honesty, intelligence, and stubborn scrupulousness coincided beautifully with the texts we were working on. Whatever I have ultimately managed to accomplish in this book I owe to having worked with him.

Versions of my Vallejo translations and co-translations, almost always in nonfinal form, appeared between 1960 and 2005 in the following magazines: *American Poetry Review, Antaeus, Arson, Bezoar, Boundary 2, Burning Water, Camels Coming, Caterpillar, Caw!, Choice, Contemporary Literature in Translation, El Corno Emplumado, Denver Quarterly, East Village Other, Ecuatorial, Evergreen Review, Folio,*

Grand Street, Hunger, Impact, Kulchur, Mandorla, Maps, Mid-American Review, Monte-mora, The Nation, New American Writing, Oasis (London), *oblēk, Omega 5, origin, Partisan Review, Pequod, Potpourri, Prairie Schooner, Quark, Review, River Styx, Spar-row, Sulfur, Text, Tish, Tri-Quarterly,* and *Ygdrasil.* Two of the translations appeared as Ta-wil and Bellevue Press broadsides. Several translations appeared as a Back-woods Broadside.

My translations of individual Vallejo collections have also appeared in different versions: *Human Poems* was first published in 1968 by Grove Press, which brought out my co-translation with José Rubia Barcia of *Spain, Take This Cup from Me* in 1974. Both these collections, retranslated with Barcia, appeared in 1978 as *César Vallejo: The Complete Posthumous Poetry,* published by University of California Press. Forty-three poems from *The Complete Posthumous Poetry* appeared, again in differing translations, in my *Conductors of the Pit: Major Works by Rimbaud, Vallejo, Césaire, Artaud, Holan* (Paragon House, 1988). Marsilio published my translation of *Trilce* in 1992, and Wesleyan University Press brought out a new, slightly revised edition of *Trilce* in 2000, with an introduction by Américo Ferrari. Trans-lations of four Vallejo prose poems were included in a revised and expanded ver-sion of *Conductors of the Pit,* published by Soft Skull Press in 2005. In the same year, Letters Bookshop in Toronto brought out *Telluric & Magnetic,* a booklet con-taining thirteen poems.

INTRODUCTION

EFRAÍN KRISTAL

The emotional rawness of César Vallejo's poetry stretched the Spanish language beyond grammar and lexicon into compelling dissonances and asymmetries, unprecedented and unsurpassed in the history of Hispanic poetry.[1] His affecting directness makes him immediately accessible, even while his poems can defy interpretation. Like Paul Celan, Vallejo has presented daunting perplexities to his readers and translators: his language, fraught with inner tensions, generates false starts, fragmentations, silences, and paradoxes.[2] His poetry cannot be analyzed within a single register because he writes in multiple ones, and can shift from one to another, or operate simultaneously within several in the same poem. In Vallejo, oral expression and the conventions of written language are often in conflict, as are memory and the passing of time, but his distortions can be moving, and his visual configurations are often arresting, as are his auditory effects. His ambiguities and ambivalences, made up of embers and auras of meaning, an affront to reductive paraphrase, are charged with pathos, even when pitched as parody. He is not immune to sentimentalism, or even bathos, but his blemishes are those of an inspired poet who unsettled and reoriented the local and cosmopolitan literary traditions on which he drew.

Vallejo's poetry is imbued with feelings of guilt, trepidation, and uncertainty and with intimations that satisfying one's own needs can feel shameful when confronted with the suffering of others. In *The Black Heralds* (1918), his first book of poems, Vallejo confronts his theological demons, expressing a tragic vision in which sexuality and sin are one and the same. With *Trilce* (1922) he still longs for attachment and is nostalgic for family bonds but no longer relies on the rhetoric of religion to address his angst, reaching his most persuasive experimental heights. In his posthumous poetry, the *Human Poems* and *Spain, Take This Cup from Me*, his feelings of collective anguish and compassion are expressed with a keener historical awareness and a nettled attentiveness to cosmopolitan concerns.

While some have branded Vallejo's most difficult poetry as either densely hermetic or as a challenge to the logos of Western culture, others have argued that his difficulties are a window into the indigenous soul of the Andean peoples. José María Arguedas, the most celebrated novelist of the Andes, made this point:

> Vallejo carried the anguished and tortured sensibility of a great people in his heart and in his spirit. This accounts for the immense depth, the human palpitation of his oeuvre, his undeniable universal value. With Vallejo, Peruvian

poetry soars above the lyrical heights of Latin America. Rubén Darío was prob-
ably a greater master of versification, but his voice is always the voice of an indi-
vidual man; he always speaks of his personal destiny. Vallejo feels the guilt of
the pain and destiny of humanity; he speaks and protests in the name of us all.[3]

DARÍO, NERUDA, AND VALLEJO

Like Rubén Darío (1867–1916) and Pablo Neruda (1904–1973), César Vallejo is a
towering figure of Hispanic poetry, and like them he was born far away in the
periphery, both in geographical and social terms: Darío was an illegitimate child
from a remote Nicaraguan village, Neruda was the son of a railroad operator in the
rainy southernmost regions of Chile, and Vallejo grew up in Santiago de Chuco, an
isolated hamlet in the northern Andes of Peru ten thousand feet above sea level. All
three left the confines of their provincial birthplaces, attracted by larger cities and
international hubs of cultural life; but Vallejo did not receive either the social recog-
nition or the financial rewards of his counterparts, and his fame was posthumous.
His literary merits did not go unnoticed in Peru, where local luminaries, including
José María Eguren, Abraham Valdelomar, and José Carlos Mariátegui recognized
the significance of his poetry, or in Spain, where poets like Gerardo Diego, Juan
Larrea, and José Bergamín discovered and championed him in the 1930s. But he
lived a life of financial penury, serious illnesses, and distressing encounters with
the law, including imprisonment in Peru and deportation from France.

According to Ricardo González Vigil, Darío was Vallejo's favorite poet in the
Spanish language.[4] Vallejo called him "Darío of the Americas!" in an early poem;
and even as he and other poets distanced themselves from the ornamental excesses
and mellifluous rhythms of the Nicaraguan poet, Vallejo continued to defend his
legacy. "Darío, el cósmico" ("Darío the cosmic one"), the title of an article Vallejo
wrote in 1927, five years after the publication of his *Trilce*—the masterpiece of
avant-garde poetry in the Hispanic world—is sufficient testimony to Vallejo's
appreciation of his predecessor.[5]

In the two centuries before Darío the conventions of Spanish poetry were so
codified and petrified that even the most daring of the Romantics were limited to
a handful of poetic forms. With Darío, Spanish prosody ceases to be normative and
becomes descriptive, as poets assume responsibility for inventing the forms and
motifs of their works. His *Prosas profanas* (1896) was studied by many Spanish
American poets as a virtual manual of formal possibilities; and in *Songs of Life and
Hope* (1905) his formal magic takes on an earnest confessional tone, espousing
political and spiritual ideals aiming to unite Latin America, and even the Hispanic
world, in the aftermath of the Spanish War of 1898.[6] Darío's impact, felt through-
out Spanish America, gave rise to *modernismo*, the first literary movement gener-
ated locally yet diffused widely throughout the Spanish-speaking world. After
Darío, Spanish American poets such as Jorge Luis Borges, Gabriela Mistral, and

Octavio Paz shared the Nicaraguan writer's confidence that European literature would no longer fix the parameters of their creativity. Spanish literature itself entered a rich period of renewal, in which poets such as Juan Ramón Jiménez, Pedro Salinas, Jorge Guillén, and Federico García Lorca acknowledged their debt to developments in Spanish America and worked to establish the fraternal environment of literary relations in which Spain embraced Neruda and Vallejo.

Pablo Neruda—whose beginnings were as marked by Darío as Vallejo's—is the most internationally celebrated Latin American poet, recipient of both the Lenin and the Nobel Prize during the cold war, and a player in the political developments of his nation. His remarkable ability to write in a seamless, flowing verse with a distinctive music of earnest pathos, or to sing a simple ode to the most elemental object of everyday life, has been widely acclaimed.

Neruda reinvented the language of love in Spanish America with his *Twenty Love Poems and a Song of Despair* (1924), expressing sensual longing and fulfillment with a directness that had eluded Darío. In his early masterpiece, the two volumes of *Residence on Earth* (1933, 1935), Neruda observes, sometimes with sadness, the inevitable triumphs of unfeeling nature over human mortality. When he became a socialist, Neruda was eager to follow Whitman with an invigorated voice confident in a political vision. In his later books Neruda meditated, now with calm resignation, on the return of living beings to a state of matter. The vastness of his poetic universe was always grounded in the material world. Disdainful of abstractions and metaphysical speculations, Neruda could write a poem about anything his five senses might encounter. His voice did not question language's ability to mirror reality. In contrast, Vallejo's vision is often vexed: he struggled with language itself as he tested his own emotional resources.

It is instructive to compare the poetry of Vallejo and Neruda written as the Spanish Civil War was unfolding. Neruda expresses pain and outrage but also certainty about the ultimate outcome. After describing the fires of fascist bombings, the death of his friend Lorca, and the blood of Spain flowing through the streets of Madrid, he strikes a defiant stance:

> But from each hole in Spain
> Spain emerges
> but from each dead child a rifle with eyes emerges,
> but from each crime bullets are born
> which will one day find the right spot
> in your hearts.

("I EXPLAIN A FEW THINGS," *ESPAÑA EN EL CORAZÓN*, 1937)

Vallejo's poetic response to the same events is more anguished and uncertain, even though he was no less committed than Neruda to the armed response in favor of the Spanish Republic:

Spanish volunteer, civilian-fighter
of veritable bones, when your heart marches to die,
when it marches to kill with its worldwide
agony, I don't know truly
what to do, where to place myself; I run, write, applaud,
weep, glimpse, destroy, they extinguish, I say
to my chest that it should end, to the good, that it should come,
and I want to ruin myself [. . .]

("HYMN TO THE VOLUNTEERS FOR THE REPUBLIC,"
SPAIN, TAKE THIS CUP FROM ME)

[. . .] if mother
Spain falls—I mean, it's just a thought—
go out, children of the world, go look for her! . . .

("SPAIN, TAKE THIS CUP FROM ME," *SPAIN, TAKE THIS CUP FROM ME*)

Their differences can also be appreciated in their poems of human solidarity. In "Heights of Machu Picchu," the epiphanous tour de force of his *Canto general*, Neruda vows to become the voice of the disenfranchised. Neruda's poetic persona moves from a valley to reach the summit of Machu Picchu, where his metaphors pile one on another, like the stones of the Incan ruins. The poem's steady crescendo culminates as the poet becomes one with the common man:

Give me your hand from the deep
zone of your disseminated pain
. . . .
Look at me from the depths of the earth,
farmer, weaver, silent shepherd:
trainer of tutelary guanacos:
bricklayer of the daring scaffold:
water-carrier of the Andean tears:
jeweler of the crushed fingers:
agriculturist trembling in the seed:
potter in your spilled clay:
bring the cup of this new life
your ancient and buried pains.
Show me your blood and your furrow,
tell me: here I was punished.
. . . .
Tell me everything, chain by chain,
link by link, and step by step,

sharpen the knives you kept hidden
and place them in my breast and in my hand.
. . . .
Speak through my words and my blood.

("HEIGHTS OF MACHU PICCHU," *CANTO GENERAL*)

In "Telluric and Magnetic," his comparable statement, Vallejo adheres to what he takes to be the soul of the Andes with a contrapuntal contempt for everything outside its aura:

Cavess or cavy to be eaten fried
with the hot bird pepper from the templed valleys!
(Condors? Screw the condors!)
Christian logs by the grace of
a happy trunk and a competent stalk!
Family of lichens,
species in basalt formation that I
respect
from this most modest paper!
Four operations, I subtract you
to save the oak and sink it in sterling!
Slopes caught in the act!
Tearful Auchenia, my own souls!
Sierra of my Peru, Peru of the world,
and Peru at the foot of the globe: I adhere!
. . . .
Indian after man and before him!
I understand all of it on two flutes
and I make myself understood on a quena!
As for the others, they can jerk me off! . . .

("TELLURIC AND MAGNETIC," *HUMAN POEMS*)

In this poem, whose tone can suddenly shift from the cosmic to the vulgar, Vallejo's invectives—including "Condors? Screw the condors!"—were intended to knock José Santos Chocano (1875–1934) from his pedestal. Chocano's star has long since fallen, but in Vallejo's lifetime he was the most celebrated Peruvian poet, best known for his invocations of condors and other images of the Andean environment in his self-appointed role as spokesman of the Peruvian nation. Vallejo is derisive of Chocano, and more guarded than Neruda in his attitude toward the indigenous world. He does not attempt to become the voice of the Sierra (as the Andean region is called in Peru). His yearnings are more challenging: to alter his own consciousness by engaging with the indigenous world on terms other than his own.

Vallejo's multilayered world of imagery is less expansive than Neruda's but more inventive and unpredictable, denser and more emotionally intense. Neruda draws on the natural world for metaphors that can inspire political rallies; Vallejo's metaphors evince a sometimes perplexing tension between the natural, political, linguistic, and spiritual realms. His struggles with language are at times a stirring articulation of his anger and subversion, and he often communicates the frustration that linguistic expression may be too ephemeral to withstand human sorrow:

> And if after so many words,
> the word itself does not survive!
>
> . . . .
>
> It will be said that we have
> in one eye much sorrow
> and also in the other, much sorrow
> and in both, when they look, much sorrow . . .
> Then! . . . Of course! . . . Then . . . not a word!
>
> ("AND IF AFTER SO MANY WORDS," *HUMAN POEMS*)

VALLEJO'S PERUVIAN PERIOD (1892–1923)

Vallejo's first forays into the literary world took place in the provincial city of Trujillo, where he graduated from the local university in 1915 with a thesis on Romantic poetry in the Spanish language. He singles out two Peruvians, Carlos Augusto Salaverry and José Arnaldo Márquez, for special praise ("every time I read them I am deeply moved");[7] traces of their concerns emerge in the sentimental moments of Vallejo's early poetry. His encounter with Spanish Golden Age poetry, however, was more fruitful. His friend Antenor Orrego remembered a notebook in which Vallejo had rehearsed variations on Spanish classics, including imitations of Quevedo and Lope de Vega, and indicated that echoes of these exercises reverberate through *The Black Heralds* and *Trilce*.[8] Antonio Armisén has shown that Vallejo's engagements with Golden Age poetry are also evident in the *Human Poems*. Armisén demonstrated that "Intensity and Height," which begins "I want to write, but out comes foam," is not just a variation on a sonnet by Lope that begins "I want to write, but my tears won't let me" but is also a "deconstruction of poetic and religious language," including that of St. John of the Cross.[9]

Vallejo's early poetry draws directly on Darío's symbolist aesthetic, nuanced by inflections of Peruvian poets of his time: Abraham Valdelomar's *modernismo*, respectful of Catholicism; José María Eguren's dreamy symbolism, with nods to the Germanic lyrical tradition; and the anticlerical anarchist virility of Manuel González Prada. As André Coyne and Américo Ferrari have shown, Vallejo was also influenced by the poetry of two Latin American contemporaries: the Uruguayan José Herrera y Reisig and the Argentine Leopoldo Lugones.

In Peru Baudelaire, discovered in the 1890s, became a contemporary of Darío.[10] Indeed, some of the versions that Vallejo read came from Eduardo Marquina's 1905 translation of *Les fleurs du mal*, which evince a sensibility closer to Vallejo than to the French original: *vagabond* becomes *mendigo* (beggar), *misère* (misery) and *horreur* (horror) become *dolor* (pain), and *ma Douleur* (my pain) becomes *tú, Dolor mío, humano* (you, my human Pain). The often-debated Gallicisms in Vallejo's poetry, such as the adjective *pluvioso* (for *rainy*, instead of the everyday Spanish *lluvioso*) in *Trilce* XV, also appear in Marquina's translation of Baudelaire. José Pascual Buxó intimated that Vallejo's engagements with French poetry in Spanish translation were decisive in his own movement from the stylized conventions of symbolism to "the unmasked solitude of the individual in agony."[11]

Tensions between religion and sexuality in various permutations were recurrent in Spanish and Spanish American Romantic poetry; but it was Rubén Darío, in "Lo fatal" ("The inevitable"), who best expressed erotic apprehensions by addressing the conflict between sexuality and religion in an agnostic vein:

> To be, without knowing a thing, and to be, without a certain course,
> and the fear of having been, and a terror looming in the future . . .
> And the certain trepidation of being dead tomorrow,
> and to suffer for life and for the shadow and for
>
> what we don't know and hardly suspect,
> and the flesh that tempts with its tender fruits,
> and not knowing where we are going
> or from where we've come! . . .

Darío's poem was the benchmark for any Spanish American poet who addressed sexual anxieties using the rhetoric of Christian sin, but Vallejo is to Darío what Darío was to his own Romantic antecedents. Vallejo's erotically mangled poetry traces imaginal contours that relegate Darío's poem, which once felt disarmingly contemporary, to the search for honest expression in a dated past:

> Slop of maximum ablution.
> Voyaging boilers
> that crash and spatter with unanimous fresh
> shadow, the color, the fraction, the hard life,
>   the hard life eternal.
> Let's not be afraid. Death is like that.
>
> Sex blood of the beloved who moans
> ensweetened, at bearing so much

at such a ludicrous spot.
And the circuit
between our poor day and the great night,
at two in the immoral afternoon.

(*TRILCE* XXX)

THE BLACK HERALDS (1918)

The Black Heralds is a landmark in Spanish-language poetry. The title of the collection pays homage to Darío's poem "Los heraldos" ("The heralds") and to the darkness of Baudelaire. In *The Black Heralds* the symbolist idiom of Rubén Darío and the early Juan Ramón Jiménez gives way to a new aesthetic whose intensity is palpable from the first line, one of the most memorable in Latin American poetry:

> *Hay golpes en la vida, tan fuertes . . . Yo no sé!*
>
> There are blows in life, so powerful . . . I don't know!

The full pathos is not in the words that can be recited, but in the silence of the ellipsis. One feels the breath knocked out of the poetic voice, or at least the poet's inability to finish a sentence expressing the impotence of a suffering humanity. This is a world in which love is miserable, and no God can save or console.

In his most intimate writings, the "blows" of the poem were integral to Vallejo's vocabulary. During a hospitalization Vallejo wrote a despairing letter to his friend Pablo Abril de Vivero:

> In life, Pablo, there is a dark blackness that is closed to all consolation. There are hours that are more sinister and agonizing than one's grave . . . . In my convalescence I often cry for the slightest cause. A childlike propensity for tears has saturated me with an immense pity for things. I often think of my home, my parents, and lost affection. Some day I will be able to die in the course of the risky life that has been my lot, and then, like now, will find myself alone, an orphan without family or even love. . . . In a few days I will leave the hospital, according to the doctor. In the street life awaits me ready to strike its blows at will.[12]

This heart-wrenching letter offers intimations of Vallejo's propensity to transform his own pain into pity for the collective. As in the letter, the "blows" of the poem are those of "destiny," but they are also compared to the "hatred of God." It is not the soul of man that falls within a Christian framework, but Christianity itself within a humanistic one, for the blows of suffering are themselves "the deep falls of the Christs of the soul,/of some adored faith blasphemed by Destiny." In Vallejo's religious rhetoric, humanity is not awaiting Christ's salvation. On the contrary, and with intended blasphemy, a Christ "falls" each time the soul is battered by the blows of life. José Carlos Mariátegui, who set the tone for Vallejo's reception, offers a précis of his early poetry:

> The pessimism is full of tenderness and compassion, because it is not engendered by egocentricity and narcissism, disenchanted and exacerbated, as is the case almost throughout the Romantic school. Vallejo feels all human suffering. His grief is not personal. His soul is "sad unto death" with the sorrow of all men, and with the sorrow of God, because for the poet it is not only men who are sad.[13]

The opening poem is followed by a few lyrical exercises in which Vallejo has not yet found his own voice, but these hesitations are left behind with his remarkable poem "The Spider," and with many other poems in which he moves into uncharted territories that would be reached, decades later, by some of the representative writers of the twentieth century. Vallejo's closest analogue in world literature is not Samuel Beckett, whose compassion for human suffering is expressed with personal detachment, but rather Beckett's character Lucky, who gives the longest speech in any of his plays. Lucky is both a victim of brutality and a compassionate observer of human quandaries:

> Given the existence [. . .] of a personal God [. . .] who from the heights of divine apathia [. . .] loves us dearly with some exceptions for reasons unknown but time will tell and suffers like the divine Miranda with those who for reasons unknown but time will tell are plunged in torment [. . .] and considering what is more that as a result of the labors left unfinished [. . .] that man in brief in spite of the strides of alimentation and defecation wastes and pines [. . .] and considering [. . .] that in the plains in the mountains [. . .] the air is the same and then the earth namely the air and then the earth in the great cold the great dark the air and the earth abode of stones [. . .] the tears the stones so blue so calm alas alas on on the skull the skull the skull the skull [. . .] alas the stones.[14]

Lucky's philosophical reflections on bodily functions, human predicaments, and theological apprehensions are central in Vallejo's poetry. His God, distant and personal, who can love, suffer, and become indifferent to human torment, corresponds to the complex and paradoxical conception of God in Vallejo's early poetry:

> I consecrate you God, because you love so much;
> because you never smile; because your heart
> must always ache so much.
>
> ("GOD," *THE BLACK HERALDS*)

> My God [. . .] you, who were always fine,
> feel nothing for your own creation.
>
> ("THE ETERNAL DICE," *THE BLACK HERALDS*)

The grim image of heavy, colored skulls used to refer to humanity was so central to Vallejo that the provisional title of *Trilce* (1922) was "Cráneos de bronce" ("Bronze skulls"). The mention of skulls, as blue suffering stones, with which Lucky's speech comes to an abrupt end when he is assaulted by Vladimir, Estragon, and Pozzo, is akin to Vallejo's "The Stones":

> Stones do not offend; they
> covet nothing. They solely ask
> love of everybody, and they ask
> love of even Nothingness.
>
> And if some of them go away
> crestfallen, or leave
> ashamed, it is because
> they must do something human . . .
>
> [. . .] this morning
> I have aligned myself with the ivy,
> on seeing the blue caravan
> of the stones,
> of the stones,
> of the stones . . .

Even the situation of Lucky, who is pulled by a rope and beaten with it by those who punish him without cause, could have been inspired by another one of Vallejo's most anthologized poems in which he forecasts his own death:

> César Vallejo has died, they beat him,
> all of them, without him doing anything to them;
> they gave it to him hard with a stick and hard
>
> likewise with a rope; witnesses are
> the Thursdays and the humerus bones,
> the loneliness, the rain, the roads . . .
>
> ("BLACK STONE ON A WHITE STONE," HUMAN POEMS)

When writing *Waiting for Godot,* Samuel Beckett worked as a translator for UNESCO in Paris. One of his assignments was to translate Latin American poetry into English for Octavio Paz.[15] It is appropriate that Beckett should have turned to the forms and images of a Latin American poet in composing a speech that expresses commiseration with the miserable fate of the tormented.

In his own Peruvian context, Vallejo's religious poems corrected the writings of his most celebrated contemporaries, even those he admired. Unlike Manuel González Prada—who railed against priests and Catholicism, and to whom Vallejo dedicated "The Eternal Dice," one of his poems of deicide—Vallejo does not attack the institutions of the Church. Instead, he deploys the very concepts and categories of Catholic dogma in quarreling with his waning Christian faith.

This is a tragic vision—perhaps the only one in the canon of Spanish-language literature—in which salvation and sin are one and the same ("Lover, on this night you have been crucified on/the two curved beams of my kiss"). Vallejo's protests against our fate are nuanced by alternating feelings of pity, isolation, and guilt: responses to the affliction his poetic voice might have witnessed or caused, for he is not innocent and does not feel blameless. In "Dregs," in *The Black Heralds*, the poet laments the consequences of his anger:

> [. . .] And I recall
> the cruel caverns of my ingratitude;
> my block of ice over her poppy,
> stronger than her "Don't be this way!"
>
> My violent black flowers; and the barbaric
> and terrible stoning; and the glacial distance.
> And the silence of her dignity
> with burning holy oils will put an end to it.

This poem is an inspired rewriting of Lope de Vega's sonnet "¿Qué tengo yo que mi amistad procuras?" ("Why do you seek my friendship?"), in which the poetic voice recalls his undeserved mistreatment by a lover.

A misogynistic streak manifests itself in some of Vallejo's erotic poetry. Intermittent expressions of contempt for the objects of his sexual desire ("The tomb is still/woman's sex that draws man in!") resonate with letters that blame women for the consequences of his own actions: "How easily one catches one of these infections, and how difficult it is to get rid of them. Believe me, I sometimes have such anger toward women."[16]

In *The Black Heralds* Vallejo's poetic voice seeks but fails to find salvation in sexuality, or in his commiseration with the hungry and the indigenous peoples of the Andes. Anticipating Kafka, Vallejo projects the inner struggles of a human being into an order that exceeds his individuality but cannot save him: "I was born on a day/when God was sick." With the emphatic repetition of this line at the end of *The Black Heralds*, the omnipotent deity has been purged from Vallejo's poetry.

TRILCE (1922)

Trilce, Vallejo's second book of poems, is widely considered a masterpiece of avant-garde poetry. Here there is no divinity against which to argue, and the tragic vision subsides, but the malaise that informed his deicide in *The Black Heralds* intensifies. Most of the poems that make up the volume were conceived between 1919 and 1922, a stormy period of Vallejo's life during which he attempted suicide, Abraham Valdelomar (one of his most influential literary supporters in Peru) died, and Vallejo was jailed in Trujillo for four months for his alleged participation in social unrest.

Trilce includes not only jaggedly abstract writing full of non sequiturs (undoubtedly received as nonsensical babble by many of its first readers) but also poems in which capitalized consonants are repeated within a word, spaces of various lengths separate words, and words are written vertically rather than horizontally or are grouped in geometrical patterns. Vallejo creates neologisms to a much more daring degree in this book than he did in *The Black Heralds,* uses numbers as symbols, and turns nouns into verbs and verbs into adjectives. *Trilce*'s originality, both surprising and transgressive, resonates with the gestures and sensibilities of Ron Silliman, Charles Bernstein, Lyn Hejinian, and other poets associated with the American Language Poetry movement of the 1970s.[17]

Some distinguished Peruvian critics wrote early reviews of *Trilce* they would later regret. Luis Alberto Sánchez called it "incomprehensible and outlandish," and Clemente Palma wondered if its unaccountable title and style were an affront to good taste. Others, however, recognized *Trilce* as a great work beyond their grasp: "*Trilce* is incomprehensible, because it is strange, unique, and strong. To understand it one needs a spontaneous critical attitude and an exceptional psychological endowment."[18]

A humorous haughtiness in *Trilce* camouflages irreverent gestures, confounding readers' expectations, in a collection that shifts gears as it moves from the experimental to the sentimental to the realistic. Compare the following stanzas, two pages apart, which seem to have been written by two different poets. The first is from a poem in which a troubled adult consciousness evokes childhood memories, and the second from a poem that generates apprehension by endowing numbers with symbolic force:

> Aguedita, Nativa, Miguel?
> I call out, I grope in the dark.
> They can't have left me all alone,
> the only prisoner can't be me.
>
> (TRILCE III)

> So don't strike 1, which will echo into infinity.
> And don't strike 0, which will be so still,
> until it wakes the 1 and makes it stand.
>
> (TRILCE V)

Vallejo's *ars poetica, Trilce* XXXVI, is an explicit response to Darío's *ars poetica,* a poem titled "Yo persigo una forma" ("I'm searching for a form"). In Darío's poem the intractable search for poetic harmony is signaled by the image of the "impossible embrace of Venus de Milo." In *Trilce* XXXVI Vallejo dissects Darío's image, shunning his harmonies and symmetries in the name of an existence, odd and imperfect:

> Are you that way, Venus de Milo?
> You hardly act crippled, pullulating
> enwombed in the plenary arms
> of existence,
> of this existence that neverthelessez
> perpetual imperfection.
> . . . .
>
> Refuse, all of you, to set foot
> on the double security of Harmony.
> Truly refuse symmetry.

Vallejo's poetry offers sustained reflections on time and memory, with inflections that honor Quevedo's engagements with human temporality and his masterful effects that seem to slow the passing of time or speed it up. Vallejo redirects Quevedo's attainments in poems such as in *Trilce* LXIV, in which a whirlwind of remembrances are capped by a disquieting ordering of temporal labels:

> Oh voices and cities that pass galloping on a finger pointed at bald Unity. While, from much to much, farmhands of a great wise lineage pass, behind the three tardy dimensions.
>
> Today   Tomorrow   Yesterday
>
> (No way!)

Vallejo's tendency to create dramatic links between events that may have taken place at different times informs his rewriting of Abraham Valdelomar's poem "El hermano ausente en la cena de Pascua" ("The absent brother at the Christmas meal"). Valdelomar's poem captures the anguish of a mother at a family meal after the death of her son:

> There is an empty place toward which
> my mother turns her gaze of honey
> and the name of the absent one is whispered
> but he will not come today to the paschal table.

In *Trilce* XXVIII, Vallejo's variation on this poem, a mother is absent, and the despondent poetic persona longs for a family meal:

> I've had lunch alone now, and without any
> mother, or may I have, or help yourself, or water,

or father who, over the eloquent offertory
of ears of corn, asks for his postponed
image, between the greater clasps of sound.

Four stanzas down, on another occasion he is invited to dine at a friend's home, where the mother is also absent; and yet there is a sense of communion. Vallejo's poetic persona feels even more bereft in the company of those who were able to mourn and move on:

Viandry at such tables, where one tastes
someone else's love instead of one's own,
turns into earth the mouthful not offered by
　　　MOTHER,
makes the hard degllusion a blow; the dessert,
bile; the coffee, funereal oil.

THE EUROPEAN PERIOD (1923–1938)

In 1923 Vallejo traveled to Europe, never to return to Peru. His exhilaration and excitement on his arrival in France ("Paris! Oh what a wonder! I have realized the greatest yearning that every cultured man feels when gazing at the globe of the earth!")[19] was soon to dissolve into disappointment. For a period of some six years he felt unsettled and paralyzed. In a letter he recounts

the long years of worthless and perhaps injurious optimism in which I have lived in Europe . . . I'm sunk in a provisional parenthesis, on the threshold of another form of existence that never comes. I take everything as provisional. And so have transpired almost five years in Paris. Five years of waiting, without being able to do anything seriously, nothing in a state of rest, nothing definitive; agitated in a continuous economic stress that does not allow me to undertake or treat anything too deeply.[20]

Vallejo's correspondence can be painful to read. He is continually requesting loans, payments, fellowships, governmental support, and even monetary gifts from friends and acquaintances in order to stay afloat. He entered a short period of relative financial ease in 1929 with Georgette Philippart, his companion and future wife, thanks to a small inheritance she had received. This period coincided with his political radicalization, which began in 1928, when he traveled to the Soviet Union on the first of three trips. He aroused suspicion from French immigration authorities, who tagged him as a potential subversive and deported him from the country in 1930 for his communist sympathies. He moved to Madrid, and returned to Paris two years later.

Some of the prose poems that appear in *Human Poems* were written between

1923 and 1927, and even though Vallejo possibly had intended to publish them under the title "Nómina de huesos," ("Roster of bones"), the project never materialized. He published many articles—one of his few sources of income—in newspapers and journals. *Tungsten* (1930), his novel of social protest, set in a mining town in Peru, was published with some success, as were his accounts of his travel to the Soviet Union. In the 1930s he worked on plays that were not produced or published in his lifetime.[21]

When the Spanish Civil War broke out in 1936 Vallejo participated in the Committees in Defense of the Spanish Republic. He was a Peruvian delegate to the Second International Congress of Anti-Fascist Writers in Defense of Culture in Spain. The congress was a momentous political and literary event. It was the only time that César Vallejo, Pablo Neruda, Octavio Paz, Vicente Huidobro, Nicolás Guillén, and Alejo Carpentier (to mention just some of the Latin American participants) were in the same place at the same time.[22] In 1937 Vallejo enjoyed one of his most productive years, writing some fifty poems to be included in the *Human Poems* and *Spain, Take This Cup from Me*. The following year, his health failed, and he died without seeing a new book of his poems in print since *Trilce* was published in 1922.

As Clayton Eshleman points out in his notes to this volume, the editorial problems associated with the posthumous poetry are insurmountable. We will never know with certainty which of the poems were actually finished and which Vallejo might have discarded. Nor will we know how he would have organized them into collections or if he had envisaged some poems that would give others their raison d'être. And we will never know how many poems or drafts may have been lost or destroyed.

Many thoughtful critics and editors of Vallejo, including Roberto Paoli and Ricardo González Vigil, have argued that the title *Human Poems* is an acceptable compromise for grouping most of the posthumous work, not just because this is how many of Vallejo's best poems have been known since 1939, when his widow first gave them that title, but also because the adjective *human* is an apt one for Vallejo. Other distinguished Vallejo critics and editors, including Ricardo Silva-Santisteban, disagree, arguing that the rubric is misleading because it groups many poems written from 1923 until 1938 that do not necessarily belong together.

Eshleman decided to follow González Vigil's critical edition and call the posthumous poems *Human Poems*, while acknowledging that informed discussions and fresh research may yield results that affect the organization of future editions. Eshleman also followed editorial convention in considering the fifteen poems of *Spain, Take This Cup from Me* a separate entity.

HUMAN POEMS AND SPAIN, TAKE THIS CUP FROM ME

Many scholars, including Stephen M. Hart, believe that the posthumous work includes the most mature and enduring of Vallejo's poetry. Although parts of *Human*

Poems exemplify an aesthetic akin to that of his first two books, most of the poems evince an attentiveness to history with a myriad of cultural and geographical references unavailable to Vallejo in his Peruvian years—including poems in which he expresses the outrageous discrepancy between intellectuality and human experience:

> A man walks by with a baguette on his shoulder
> Am I going to write, after that, about my double?
>
> Another sits, scratches, extracts a louse from his armpit, kills it
> How dare one speak about psychoanalysis?
> . . . .
>
> A cripple passes by holding a child's hand
> After that I'm going to read André Breton?
> . . . .
>
> Another searches in the muck for bones, rinds
> How to write, after that, about the infinite?
>
> ("A MAN WALKS BY . . . ," HUMAN POEMS)

Collective angst and compassion epitomize much of the later posthumous verse, including poems in which Vallejo's expressions of concern are not intended to single out individuals but to convey representative types:

> Beloved be the one who works by the day, by the month, by the hour,
> the one who sweats from pain or from shame,
> . . . .
> the one who pays with what he lacks,
> the one who sleeps on his back,
> the one who no longer remembers his childhood [. . .]
>
> ("STUMBLE BETWEEN TWO STARS," HUMAN POEMS)

Vallejo's religious language resurfaces in some of these poems, but now he is indifferent to the hereafter and in no mood to quarrel with supernatural entities. In this poetry, religious imagery is at the service of empathy, solidarity, and redemption in the here and now, as in the following poem in which Vallejo remembers his deceased friend Alfonso, a musician:

> today I suffer bitterly sweet,
> I drink your blood as to Christ the hard,
> I eat your bone as to Christ the soft,
> because I love you, two by two, Alfonso,
> and could almost say so, eternally.
>
> ("ALFONSO: YOU ARE LOOKING AT ME, I SEE," HUMAN POEMS)

In *Spain, Take This Cup from Me,* as a Christ-like figure the atheist poet expresses his anguish over and solidarity with the Republicans in the heat of the Spanish Civil War, announcing his hope that human solidarity can enact the Resurrection:

> Then, all the inhabitants of the earth
> surrounded him; the corpse looked at them sadly, deeply moved;
> he got up slowly,
> embraced the first man; started to walk . . .
>
> ("MASS," SPAIN, TAKE THIS CUP FROM ME)

It was because of Vallejo's commitment to the Republican cause as a Latin American Marxist that Louis Aragon gave a moving speech at his funeral that began the process of his gaining posthumous literary fame.

ON ESHLEMAN'S TRANSLATION

In recent years the English-reading public has been fortunate that some of the major corpuses of Hispanic poetry have become available in translation. Christopher Maurer's edition of the complete poetry of Federico García Lorca is a great achievement in Hispanism; and thanks to Eliot Weinberger, a beautiful edition of the collected poetry of Octavio Paz is available. Neruda has also been graced by splendid translations, including those by Alastair Reid. Eshleman's own accomplishment as a translator takes a special place in this felicitous context. His Vallejo marks the first time that the complete poetry of a great Spanish-language poet has been translated in a volume by a single translator who is also a celebrated poet in his own right. Eshleman has been reading and translating Vallejo for almost five decades. The engaging account of this experience included as an appendix to this volume, his "Translator's Memoir," should be expanded into a book: it only hints at the considerable work, persistence, and personal sacrifice required to bring this book to completion, not to mention the many literary rewards that justified this rich odyssey. It has taken the prolonged concentration of a resourceful poet, devoted to the work of his counterpart, a poet who can see into the potentialities and attainments, and even the shortcomings, of the original work.

In his foreword to this volume Mario Vargas Llosa rightly places Vallejo in the category of wondrous, inexplicable poets. Better than anyone else, Eshleman knows that Vallejo can be impossible to paraphrase, interpret, or explain, but he also knows that his task as translator is not to resolve or simplify these perplexities but to transpose them with accuracy, if possible, or to find equivalences and invent parallels.

Eshleman renders Vallejo's paradoxes with ease and his linguistic unconventionalities with instinctual acumen. Thanks to Eshleman's successful translations, it has not been necessary for me to quote Vallejo in the Spanish in order to discuss the poems' complexities. Some of Vallejo's geometrical patterns can be reproduced as a matter of course, but the handling of his neologisms, and his arcane or coined words, is hardly straightforward and has defeated others who have tried. Eshleman invents equivalents that might enrich the English language itself, as when he translates Vallejo's neologism *corazonmente* (in "One pillar supporting solace") as "hearterially." When he translates *espergesia* as "epexegesis," he captures the power of this impossible word, which some interpreters have considered a neologism and others an elusive archaism.

Eshleman delivers, in an American idiom, Vallejo's impulse for verbal play. His onomatopoeic equivalences are often as stunning as his replication of Vallejo's shifting spellings and visual dispositions in a poem. In *Trilce* XXXII, Vallejo captures bodily and sensory functions through a combination of onomatopoeias, visual metaphors, and the distortion of conventional spelling. Eshleman matches Vallejo's original inventiveness:

> 999 calories.
> Roombbb ... Hulllablll llust ... ster
> Serpenteenic **e** of the sweet roll vendor
> engyrafted to the eardrum.

Eshleman's formal achievements as a translator are all the more admirable given his search for a persuasive English version that can rise to Vallejo's humanity. One finds in these translations a sense of friendship and camaraderie that honors those poems by Vallejo in which the human will can bring those who have died back to life.

NOTES

1   I would like to express my heartfelt gratitude to Clayton Eshleman, Romy Sutherland, and Michael Bell for careful readings of drafts and for their splendid suggestions in the preparation of this introduction. The Spanish sources for this edition come mostly from the splendid critical edition by Ricardo González Vigil, in César Vallejo, *Obras completas,* vol. 1, *Obra poética* (Lima: Banco de Crédito del Perú, 1991). The other indispensable edition is the four-volume *Poesía completa,* edited by Ricardo Silva-Santisteban (Lima: Pontificia Universidad Católica del Perú, 1997). This remarkable volume includes photographic reproductions of many of Vallejo's manuscripts and materials that are invaluable in reconstructing the gestation and reception of the poems. Stephen M. Hart's bibliography is also indispensable to any Vallejo scholar, as is his book on Vallejo and religion. See Stephen M. Hart (in collaboration with Jorge Cornejo Polar), *César Vallejo: A Critical Biography of Research* (London: Tamesis, 2002). The books, essays, and editions by André Coyné, Américo Ferrari, Saúl Yurkiévich, Julio Ortega, Jean Franco, James Higgins, William Rowe, and Roberto Paoli are considered landmarks in Vallejo studies.

2   Rafael Gutiérrez Girardot is the pioneer in the comparative study of Vallejo and Paul

Celan. See his "Génesis y recepción de la poesía de César Vallejo," in *César Vallejo. Obra poética,* ed. Américo Ferrari (Madrid: Archivos, 1988), 523.

3 José María Arguedas, "César Vallejo, el más grande poeta del Perú," in *César Vallejo: Al pie del orbe,* ed. Nestor Tenorio Requejo (Lambayeque, Peru: Universidad Nacional Pedro Ruiz Gallo, 1992), 11–12. All translations in this introduction, except for Clayton Eshleman's translations of Vallejo's poetry, are mine.

4 Ricardo González Vigil, *César Vallejo* (Lima: Editorial Brasa, 1995), 55.

5 According to some literary critics, Vicente Huidobro's *Altazor* is *Trilce*'s only rival as the high point of the avant-garde in the Spanish language.

6 It has been argued that Darío's poetic revolution involved the transfer of French literary trends to Spanish America. But this is a misleading claim, for Darío's poetic innovations bred new forms that are unique to the Spanish language. Darío found harmonies and dissonances in his poetic lines that revolutionized the way poetry could be written in the idiom. See Rubén Darío's *Selected Writings,* edited by Ilán Stavans (New York: Penguin, 2005); and *Songs of Life and Hope. Cantos de vida y esperanza,* a bilingual edition, edited and translated by Will Derusha and Alberto Acereda (Durham: Duke University Press, 2004).

7 César Vallejo, *El romanticismo en la poesía castellana* (Lima: Juan Mejía Baca, 1954), 61.

8 Ricardo Silva-Santisteban quotes Orrego's recollection, underscoring the importance of exploring the connections between Vallejo and Golden Age poetry; see "Dos posibles reminiscencias en un poema de Vallejo," in *Escrito en el agua* (Lima: Editorial Colmillo Blanco, 1989).

9 Antonio Armisén, "Intensidad y altura: Lope de Vega, César Vallejo y los problemas de la escritura poética," *Bulletin Hispanique,* 88, nos. 3–4 (July–December, 1985): 297.

10 See Estuardo Núñez, "Charles Baudelaire y el Perú," *Alma Mater* 13–14 (1997): 57–62.

11 José Pascual Buxó, *César Vallejo. Crítica y contracrítica* (Mexico City: UNAM, 1992), 23. See also Enrique Diez Canedo and Fernando Fortún's anthology *La poesía francesa moderna* (Madrid: Renacimiento), 1913.

12 César Vallejo, letter to Pablo Abril de Vivero, October 19, 1924, in Vallejo, *Correspondencia completa,* ed. Jesús Cabel (Lima: Pontificia Universidad Católica del Perú, 2002), 87.

13 José Carlos Mariategui, *Seven Interpretive Essays on Peruvian Reality* (Austin: University of Texas Press, 1971), 254.

14 Samuel Beckett, *Waiting for Godot* (New York: Grove Press, 1982), 28–29. In 1941, two years after the first publication of Vallejo's complete poetry, Octavio Paz co-edited an anthology including a respectable selection of Vallejo's poems, which would have been sufficient to inform Lucky's speech in *Waiting for Godot.* See Emilio Prados, Xavier Villaurrutia, Juan Gil Albert, and Octavio Paz, eds., *Laurel* (Mexico City: Séneca, 1941).

15 The only publication that came out of this collaboration, as far as I know, is Octavio Paz, ed., and Samuel Beckett, trans., *Anthology of Mexican Poetry* (Bloomington: Indiana University Press, 1958).

16 César Vallejo, letter to Pablo Abril de Vivero February 8, 1926, in Vallejo, *Correspondencia completa,* 147.

17 I thank Clayton Eshleman for this point.

18 Luis Alberto Sánchez's note was published in *Mundial*, no. 129 (Nov. 3, 1922): 5; Clemente Palma's note in *Variedades*, no. 768 (Nov. 18, 1922): 6668. The last commentary is from the lesser-known C. Alberto Espinosa Bravo, published in *Mundial*, no. 270 (Aug. 14, 1925): 33. These three reviews are reproduced in the rich dossier of documents included in Ricardo Silva-Santisteban's edition of *Trilce*. See César Vallejo, *Poesía Completa II* (Lima: Pontificia Universidad Católica del Perú, 1997).

19 César Vallejo, letter to his brother, Victor Clemente, July 14, 1923, in Vallejo, *Correspondencia completa*, 57.

20 César Vallejo, letter to Pablo Abril de Vivero, September 12, 1927, in Vallejo, *Correspondencia completa*, 252–53.

21 See César Vallejo's three-volume *Teatro completo* (Lima: Pontificia Universidad Católica del Perú, 1999).

22 González Vigil offers an account of these events in his *César Vallejo*, 105.

CÉSAR VALLEJO

LOS HERALDOS NEGROS (1918)

Qui potest capere capiat

EL EVANGELIO

THE BLACK HERALDS

He who is able to receive it, let him receive it.

THE GOSPEL

*

Hay golpes en la vida, tan fuertes . . . Yo no sé!
Golpes como del odio de Dios; como si ante ellos,
la resaca de todo lo sufrido
se empozara en el alma . . . Yo no sé!

Son pocos; pero son . . . Abren zanjas oscuras
en el rostro más fiero y en el lomo más fuerte.
Serán talvez los potros de bárbaros atilas;
o los heraldos negros que nos manda la Muerte.

Son las caídas hondas de los Cristos del alma,
de alguna fe adorable que el Destino blasfema.
Esos golpes sangrientos son las crepitaciones
de algún pan que en la puerta del horno se nos quema.

Y el hombre . . . Pobre . . . pobre! Vuelve los ojos, como
cuando por sobre el hombro nos llama una palmada;
vuelve los ojos locos, y todo lo vivido
se empoza, como charco de culpa, en la mirada.

Hay golpes en la vida, tan fuertes . . . Yo no sé!

THE BLACK HERALDS

There are blows in life, so powerful . . . I don't know!
Blows as from the hatred of God; as if, facing them,
the undertow of everything suffered
welled up in the soul . . . I don't know!

They are few; but they are . . . They open dark trenches
in the fiercest face and in the strongest back.
Perhaps they are the colts of barbaric Attilas;
or the black heralds sent to us by Death.

They are the deep falls of the Christs of the soul,
of some adored faith blasphemed by Destiny.
Those bloodstained blows are the crackling of
bread burning up at the oven door.

And man . . . Poor . . . poor! He turns his eyes, as
when a slap on the shoulder summons us;
turns his crazed eyes, and everything lived
wells up, like a pool of guilt, in his look.

There are blows in life, so powerful . . . I don't know!

PLAFONES ÁGILES

DESHOJACIÓN SAGRADA

Luna! Corona de una testa inmensa,
que te vas deshojando en sombras gualdas!
Roja corona de un Jesús que piensa
trágicamente dulce de esmeraldas!

Luna! Alocado corazón celeste
¿por qué bogas así, dentro la copa
llena de vino azul, hacia el oeste,
cual derrotada y dolorida popa?

Luna! Y a fuerza de volar en vano,
te holocaustas en ópalos dispersos:
tú eres talvez mi corazón gitano
que vaga en el azul llorando versos! . . .

AGILE SOFFITS

SACRED DEFOLIACITY

Moon! Crown of an immense head,
which you keep shedding in golden shadows!
Red crown of a Jesus who thinks
tragically sweet of emeralds!

Moon! Maddened celestial heart
—why are you rowing like this, inside the cup
full of blue wine, toward the west,
such a defeated and aching stern?

Moon! And by flying off in vain,
you holocaust into scattered opals:
perhaps you are my gypsy heart
wandering the blue weeping verses!

COMUNIÓN

Linda Regia! Tus venas son fermentos
de mi noser antiguo y del champaña
negro de mi vivir!

Tu cabello es la ignota raicilla
del árbol de mi vid.
Tu cabello es la hilacha de una mitra
de ensueño que perdí!

Tu cuerpo es la espumante escaramuza
de un rosado Jordán;
y ondea, como un látigo beatífico
que humillara a la víbora del mal!

Tus brazos dan la sed de lo infinito,
con sus castas hespérides de luz,
cual dos blancos caminos redentores,
dos arranques murientes de una cruz.
Y están plasmados en la sangre invicta
de mi imposible azul!

Tus pies son dos heráldicas alondras
que eternamente llegan de mi ayer!
Linda Regia! Tus pies son las dos lágrimas
que al bajar del Espíritu ahogué,
un Domingo de Ramos que entré al Mundo,
ya lejos para siempre de Belén!

COMMUNION

Fair queenly one! Your veins are the ferment
of my ancient nonbeing and of the black
champagne of my life!

Your hair is the undiscovered rootlet
of the tree of my vine.
Your hair is the strand from a miter
of fantasy that I lost!

Your body is the bubbly skirmish
of a pink Jordan;
and it ripples, like a beatific whip
that would have put the viper of evil to shame!

Your arms create a thirst for the infinite,
with their hesperidian castes of light,
like two white redeeming roads,
two dying wrenchings of a cross.
And they are molded in the unconquered blood of
my impossible blue!

Your feet are two heraldic larks
eternally arriving from my yesterday!
Fair queenly one! Your feet are the two tears
I choked back, descending from the Spirit
one Palm Sunday when I entered the World,
already forever distant from Bethlehem!

NERVAZÓN DE ANGUSTIA

Dulce hebrea, desclava mi tránsito de arcilla;
desclava mi tensión nerviosa y mi dolor . . .
Desclava, amada eterna, mi largo afán y los
dos clavos de mis alas y el clavo de mi amor!

Regreso del desierto donde he caído mucho;
retira la cicuta y obséquiame tus vinos:
espanta con un llanto de amor a mis sicarios,
cuyos gestos son férreas cegueras de Longinos!

Desclávame mis clavos ¡oh nueva madre mía!
¡Sinfonía de olivos, escancia tu llorar!
Y has de esperar, sentada junto a mi carne muerta,
cuál cede la amenaza, y la alondra se va!

Pasas . . . vuelves . . . Tus lutos trenzan mi gran cilicio
con gotas de curare, filos de humanidad,
la dignidad roquera que hay en tu castidad,
y el judithesco azogue de tu miel interior.

Son las ocho de una mañana en crema brujo . . .
Hay frío . . . Un perro pasa royendo el hueso de otro
perro que fue . . . Y empieza a llorar en mis nervios
un fósforo que en cápsulas de silencio apagué!

Y en mi alma hereje canta su dulce fiesta asiática
un dionisíaco hastío de café . . . !

Sweet Jewess, unnail my clay transit;
unnail my nerve tension and my pain . . .
Unnail, eternal lover, my protracted anxiety and
the two nails from my wings and the nail from my love!

I am back from the desert where I have often fallen;
put away the hemlock and regale me with your wines:
scare off my assassins with a love sob,
their grimaces are the iron blindness of Longinus!

Pull out my nails, oh my new mother!
Symphony of olives, decant your tears!
And wait, seated next to my dead flesh,
as the menace subsides, and the lark ascends!

You go . . . return . . . Your mourning plaits my great cilice
with drops of curare, sharp edges of humanity,
the rocky dignity there in your chastity,
and the Judithesque mercury of your inner honey.

It is eight o'clock on a creamy, bewitched morning . . .
And it is cold . . . A dog goes by gnawing the bone of another
dog that was . . . And the match that I extinguished
in capsules of silence starts crying in my nerves!

And in my heretic soul, coffee's Dionysian spleen
sings its sweet Asiatic feast . . . !

BORDAS DE HIELO

Vengo a verte pasar todos los días,
vaporcito encantado siempre lejos . . .
Tus ojos son dos rubios capitanes;
tu labio es un brevísimo pañuelo
rojo que ondea en un adiós de sangre!

Vengo a verte pasar; hasta que un día,
embriagada de tiempo y de crueldad,
vaporcito encantado siempre lejos,
la estrella de la tarde partirá!

Las jarcias; vientos que traicionan; vientos
de mujer que pasó!
Tus fríos capitanes darán orden;
y quien habrá partido seré yo . . .

MAINSAILS OF ICE

I come to watch you go by every day,
enchanted little steamer always distant . . .
Your eyes are two blond captains;
your lip is a fleeting red
handkerchief fluttering a blood good-bye!

I come to watch you go by; until one day,
intoxicated with time and with cruelty,
enchanted little steamer always distant,
the evening star will fade away!

The rigging; winds that betray; winds
from a woman who passed by!
Your cold captains will give the order;
and the one who will have faded will be I . . .

NOCHEBUENA

Al callar la orquesta, pasean veladas
sombras femeninas bajo los ramajes,
por cuya hojarasca se filtran heladas
quimeras de luna, pálidos celajes.

Hay labios que lloran arias olvidadas,
grandes lirios fingen los ebúrneos trajes.
Charlas y sonrisas en locas bandadas
perfuman de seda los rudos boscajes.

Espero que ría la luz de tu vuelta;
y en la epifanía de tu forma esbelta
cantará la fiesta en oro mayor.

Balarán mis versos en tu predio entonces,
canturreando en todos sus místicos bronces
que ha nacido el niño-jesús de tu amor.

CHRISTMAS EVE

As the orchestra falls silent, veiled feminine
shadows pass beneath the branches
through whose dry leaves filter icy
chimeras of moonlight, pale varicolored clouds.

There are lips that weep forgotten arias,
ivory gowns feigning huge lilies.
Chatter and smiles in wild flocks
perfume the rugged woods with silk.

I hope the light of your return laughs;
and in the epiphany of your graceful form
the holy day will rejoice in gold major.

On your estate my verses will then bleat,
humming with all their mystical bronze
that the baby-jesus of your love has been born.

ASCUAS

Para Domingo Parra del Riego

Luciré para Tilia, en la tragedia,
mis estrofas en ópimos racimos;
sangrará cada fruta melodiosa,
como un sol funeral, lúgubres vinos.
     Tilia tendrá la cruz
que en la hora final será de luz!

Prenderé para Tilia, en la tragedia,
la gota de fragor que hay en mis labios;
y el labio, al encresparse para el beso,
se partirá en cien pétalos sagrados.
     Tilia tendrá el puñal,
el puñal floricida y auroral!

Ya en la sombra, heroína, intacta y mártir,
tendrás bajo tus plantas a la Vida;
mientras veles, rezando mis estrofas,
mi testa, como una hostia en sangre tinta!
     Y en un lirio, voraz,
mi sangre, como un virus, beberás!

EMBERS

For Domingo Parra del Riego

In the tragedy, I will display for Tilia
my stanzas in abundant clusters;
each melodious fruit will bleed,
like a funereal sun, doleful wines.
        Tilia will hold the cross
that in the final hour will be of light!

In the tragedy, I will capture for Tilia
the drop of uproar that is on my lips;
and the lip, tightening for the kiss,
will break into a hundred holy petals.
        Tilia will hold the dagger,
the floricidal and auroral dagger!

Now in shadow, heroine, virgin and martyr,
you will feel Life under your soles;
while, praying my stanzas, you hold vigil over
my head, like a Host in blood ink!
        And you will drink my blood,
like a virus, from a lily, voraciously!

MEDIALUZ

He soñado una fuga. Y he soñado
tus encajes dispersos en la alcoba.
A lo largo de un muelle, alguna madre;
y sus quince años dando el seno a una hora.

He soñado una fuga. Un "para siempre"
suspirado en la escala de una proa;
he soñado una madre;
unas frescas matitas de verdura,
y el ajuar constelado de una aurora.

A lo largo de un muelle . . .
Y a lo largo de un cuello que se ahoga!

HALF-LIGHT

I have dreamed of a flight. And I have dreamed of
your silks strewn about the bedroom.
Along a pier, some mother;
and her fifteen years breast-feeding an hour.

I have dreamed of a flight. A "forever and ever"
whispered on the ladder to a prow;
I have dreamed of a mother;
some fresh sprigs of greenery,
and the aurora-constellated trousseau.

Along a pier . . .
And along a throat that is drowning!

SAUCE

Lirismo de invierno, rumor de crespones,
cuando ya se acerca la pronta partida;
agoreras voces de tristes canciones
que en la tarde rezan una despedida.

Visión del entierro de mis ilusiones
en la propia tumba de mortal herida.
Caridad verónica de ignotas regiones,
donde a precio de éter se pierda la vida.

Cerca de la aurora partiré llorando;
y mientras mis años se vayan curvando,
curvará guadañas mi ruta veloz.

Y ante fríos óleos de luna muriente,
con timbres de aceros en tierra indolente,
cavarán los perros, aullando, un adiós!

WILLOW

Lyricism of winter, rustle of crepe,
now when the hasty departure nears;
oracular voices of plaintive songs
that in the evening pray for a farewell.

Vision of the burial of my illusions
in the very tomb of the mortal wound.
Veronican charity from unknown regions,
where at the price of ether life is lost.

Near dawn I will depart in tears;
and while my years go on curving,
my swift course will curve scythes.

And under the cold holy oils of a dying moon,
with the timbre of steel in the indolent earth,
dogs, howling, will dig a good-bye.

AUSENTE

Ausente! La mañana en que me vaya
más lejos de lo lejos, al Misterio,
como siguiendo inevitable raya,
tus pies resbalarán al cementerio.

Ausente! La mañana en que a la playa
del mar de sombra y del callado imperio,
como un pájaro lúgubre me vaya,
será el blanco panteón tu cautiverio.

Se habrá hecho de noche en tus miradas;
y sufrirás, y tomarás entonces
penitentes blancuras laceradas.

Ausente! Y en tus propios sufrimientos
ha de cruzar entre un llorar de bronces
una jauría de remordimientos!

ABSENT

Absent! The morning when I go away
farther than far, to the Mystery,
as if following the inevitable ray,
your feet will slide into the cemetery.

Absent! The morning when, like a rueful bird,
I go away to the shore of
the sea of shadow and silent empire,
the white pantheon will be your captivity.

Night will have fallen in your glances;
and you will suffer, and then acquire
penitent lacerated whitenesses.

Absent! And in your own suffering
amid a wail of bronzes
a pack of remorse will lope by!

AVESTRUZ

Melancolía, saca tu dulce pico ya;
no cebes tus ayunos en mis trigos de luz.
Melancolía, basta! Cuál beben tus puñales
la sangre que extrajera mi sanguijuela azul!

No acabes el maná de mujer que ha bajado;
yo quiero que de él nazca mañana alguna cruz,
mañana que no tenga yo a quien volver los ojos,
cuando abra su gran O de burla el ataúd.

Mi corazón es tiesto regado de amargura;
hay otros viejos pájaros que pastan dentro de él . . .
Melancolía, deja de secarme la vida,
y desnuda tu labio de mujer . . . !

OSTRICH

Melancholy, pull out your sweet beak now;
don't batten your fasting on my wheat of light.
Melancholy, enough! As your daggers drink
the blood my blue leech would suck out!

Do not finish off the fallen woman's manna;
I want some cross to be born of it tomorrow,
tomorrow when I will have no one to turn my eyes to,
when the coffin opens its great sneering O.

My heart is a potsherd sprinkled with gall;
there are other old birds who graze inside it . . .
Melancholy, stop drying up my life,
and bare your woman's lip . . . !

BAJO LOS ÁLAMOS

Para José Eulogio Garrido

Cual hieráticos bardos prisioneros,
los álamos de sangre se han dormido.
Rumian arias de yerba al sol caído,
las greyes de Belén en los oteros.

El anciano pastor, a los postreros
martirios de la luz estremecido,
en sus pascuales ojos ha cogido
una casta manada de luceros.

Labrado en orfandad baja el instante
con rumores de entierro, al campo orante;
y se otoñan de sombra las esquilas.

Supervive el azul urdido en hierro,
y en él, amortajadas las pupilas,
traza su aullido pastoral un perro.

UNDER THE POPLARS

For José Eulogio Garrido

Like imprisoned hieratic bards,
the poplars of blood have gone to sleep.
On the knolls the flocks of Bethlehem
ruminate arias of grass in the setting sun.

The ancient shepherd, shaken by
the last martyrdoms of light,
has caught in his paschal eyes
a chaste cluster of brilliant stars.

Wrought by orphanhood he descends the instant
with rumors of burial, to the praying field;
the cattle-bells are autumn-cast with shadow.

The blue survives warped in iron,
and in it, eyeballs shrouded,
a dog traces its bucolic howl.

BUZOS

LA ARAÑA

Es una araña enorme que ya no anda;
una araña incolora, cuyo cuerpo,
una cabeza y un abdomen, sangra.

Hoy la he visto de cerca. Y con qué esfuerzo
hacia todos los flancos
sus pies innumerables alargaba.
Y he pensado en sus ojos invisibles,
los pilotos fatales de la araña.

Es una araña que temblaba fija
en un filo de piedra;
el abdomen a un lado,
y al otro la cabeza.

Con tantos pies la pobre, y aún no puede
resolverse. Y, al verla
atónita en tal trance,
hoy me ha dado qué pena esa viajera.

Es una araña enorme, a quien impide
el abdomen seguir a la cabeza.
Y he pensado en sus ojos
y en sus pies numerosos . . .
¡Y me ha dado qué pena esa viajera!

DIVERS

THE SPIDER

It is an enormous spider that now cannot move;
a colorless spider, whose body,
a head and an abdomen, bleeds.

Today I watched it up close. With what effort
toward every side
it extended its innumerable legs.
And I have thought about its invisible eyes,
the spider's fatal pilots.

It is a spider that tremored caught
on the edge of a rock;
abdomen on one side,
head on the other.

With so many legs the poor thing, and still unable
to free itself. And, on seeing it
confounded by its fix
today, I have felt such sorrow for that traveler.

It is an enormous spider, impeded by
its abdomen from following its head.
And I have thought about its eyes
and about its numerous legs . . .
And I have felt such sorrow for that traveler!

BABEL

Dulce hogar sin estilo, fabricado
de un solo golpe y de una sola pieza
de cera tornasol. Y en el hogar
ella daña y arregla; a veces dice:
"El hospicio es bonito; aquí no más!"
¡Y otras veces se pone a llorar!

BABEL

Sweet styleless home, built
with a single blow and with a single bit
of sunflower wax. And in the home
she damages and repairs; at times says:
"The hospice is nice; no need to look further!"
At other times she breaks into tears!

ROMERÍA

Pasamos juntos. El sueño
lame nuestros pies qué dulce;
y todo se desplaza en pálidas
renunciaciones sin dulce.

Pasamos juntos. Las muertas
almas, las que, cual nosotros,
cruzaron por el amor,
con enfermos pasos ópalos,
salen en sus lutos rígidos
y se ondulan en nosotros.

Amada, vamos al borde
frágil de un montón de tierra.
Va en aceite ungida el ala,
y en pureza. Pero un golpe,
al caer yo no sé dónde,
afila de cada lágrima
un diente hostil.

Y un soldado, un gran soldado,
heridas por charreteras,
se anima en la tarde heroica,
y a sus pies muestra entre risas,
como una gualdrapa horrenda,
el cerebro de la Vida.

Pasamos juntos, muy juntos,
invicta Luz, paso enfermo;
pasamos juntos las lilas
mostazas de un cementerio.

PILGRIMAGE

We walk together. Sleep
gently laps at our feet;
and everything is displaced by wan
harsh renunciations.

We walk together. Dead
souls, who, like us,
crossed for love,
appear in stiff shrouds
with sick opal footsteps
and undulate within us.

My love, we go to the fragile
edge of a mound of earth.
A wing passes anointed in oil
and in purity. But a blow,
falling I know not where,
sharpens each tear into
a hostile tooth.

And a soldier, a great soldier,
wounds for epaulets,
cheered by the heroic evening,
displays at his feet, laughing,
like a hideous rag,
the brain of Life.

We walk together, closer together,
victorious Light, sick footstep;
together we pass the mustard-yellow
lilacs of a graveyard.

Más acá, más acá. Yo estoy muy bien.
Llueve; y hace una cruel limitación.
Avanza, avanza el pie.

Hasta qué hora no suben las cortinas
esas manos que fingen un zarzal?
Ves? Los otros, qué cómodos, qué efigies.
Más acá, más acá!

Llueve. Y hoy tarde pasará otra nave
cargada de crespón;
será como un pezón negro y deforme
arrancado a la esfíngica Ilusión.

Más acá, más acá. Tú estás al borde
y la nave arrastrarte puede al mar.
Ah, cortinas inmóviles, simbólicas . . .
Mi aplauso es un festín de rosas negras:
cederte mi lugar!
Y en el fragor de mi renuncia,
un hilo de infinito sangrará.

Yo no debo estar tan bien;
avanza, avanza el pie!

THE NARROW THEATER BOX

Closer, closer. I am feeling great.
It is raining; and that is a cruel restriction.
Move it, move that foot.

How long before those hands pretending to be
a thicket raise the curtain?
You see? The others, how comfortable, what effigies.
Closer, closer!

It is raining. And later today another ship will pass
loaded with crepe;
it will be like a nipple black and deformed
torn out of a sphinxine Illusion.

Closer, closer! You are at the edge
and the ship may haul you out to sea.
Ah, unmoving, symbolic curtains . . .
My applause is a festival of black roses:
you can have my seat!
And in the clamor of my renunciation,
a thread of infinity will bleed.

I must not be feeling so great;
move it, move that foot!

DE LA TIERRA

¿ . . . .

—Si te amara . . . qué sería?
—Una orgía!
—Y si él te amara?
Sería
todo rituario, pero menos dulce.

Y si tú me quisieras?
La sombra sufriría
justos fracasos en tus niñas monjas.

Culebrean latigazos,
cuando el can ama a su dueño?
—No; pero la luz es nuestra.
Estás enfermo . . . Vete . . . Tengo sueño!

(Bajo la alameda vesperal
se quiebra un fragor de rosa).
—Idos, pupilas, pronto . . .
Ya retoña la selva en mi cristal!

OF THE EARTH

. . . . ?

    —If I loved you . . . what then?
—An orgy!
—And if he loved you?
It would be
all rituary, but not as sweet.

    And if you loved me?
The shadow would suffer
a deserved defeat by your little nuns.

    Do whiplashes serpentize,
when the dog loves its master?
—No; but the light is ours.
You're sick . . . Go away . . . I need to sleep!

    (Under the vesperal poplar grove
the blare of roses is stifled).
—Off you go, girls, quickly . . .
Already the forest is luxuriating in my windowpane!

*

EL POETA A SU AMADA

Amada, en esta noche tú te has crucificado
sobre los dos maderos curvados de mi beso;
y tu pena me ha dicho que Jesús ha llorado,
y que hay un viernesanto más dulce que ese beso.

En esta noche rara que tanto me has mirado,
la Muerte ha estado alegre y ha cantado en su hueso.
En esta noche de Setiembre se ha oficiado
mi segunda caída y el más humano beso.

Amada, moriremos los dos juntos, muy juntos;
se irá secando a pausas nuestra excelsa amargura;
y habrán tocado a sombra nuestros labios difuntos.

Y ya no habrá reproches en tus ojos benditos;
ni volveré a ofenderte. Y en una sepultura
los dos nos dormiremos, como dos hermanitos.

THE POET TO HIS LOVER

My love, on this night you have been crucified on
the two curved beams of my kiss;
your torment has told me that Jesus wept,
that there is a goodfriday sweeter than that kiss.

On this strange night when you looked at me so,
Death was happy and sang in his bone.
On this September night my second fall
and the most human kiss have been presided over.

My love, we two will die together, close together;
our sublime bitterness will slowly dry up;
and our defunct lips will have touched in shadow.

There will be no more reproach in your holy eyes;
nor will I offend you ever again. In one grave
we two will sleep, as two siblings.

VERANO

Verano, ya me voy. Y me dan pena
las manitas sumisas de tus tardes.
Llegas devotamente; llegas viejo;
y ya no encontrarás en mi alma a nadie.

Verano! Y pasarás por mis balcones
con gran rosario de amatistas y oros,
como un obispo triste que llegara
de lejos a buscar y bendecir
los rotos aros de unos muertos novios.

Verano, ya me voy. Allá, en Setiembre
tengo una rosa que te encargo mucho;
la regarás de agua bendita todos
los días de pecado y de sepulcro.

Si a fuerza de llorar el mausoleo,
con luz de fe su mármol aletea,
levanta en alto tu responso, y pide
a Dios que siga para siempre muerta.
Todo ha de ser ya tarde;
y tú no encontrarás en mi alma a nadie.

Ya no llores, Verano! En aquel surco
muere una rosa que renace mucho . . .

SUMMER

Summer, I am leaving now. The submissive
little hands of your evenings pain me.
You arrive devoutly; you arrive old;
and now you will not find anyone in my soul.

Summer! And you will pass by my balconies
with a great rosary of amethyst and gold,
like a sad bishop who would come
from afar to seek and to bless
the broken rings of some dead sweethearts.

Summer, I am leaving now. Over there, in September
I have a rose that I will entrust to you completely;
you will sprinkle it with holy water all
the days of sin and of tomb.

If from crying the mausoleum,
in the light of faith, should flutter its marble wings,
raise on high your response, and pray
to God that such light remains dead forever.
It is way too late now;
you will not find anyone in my soul.

Cry no more, Summer! In that furrow
a rose dies to be reborn evermore . . .

SETIEMBRE

Aquella noche de Setiembre, fuiste
tan buena para mí . . . hasta dolerme!
Yo no sé lo demás; y para eso,
no debiste ser buena, no debiste.

Aquella noche sollozaste al verme
hermético y tirano, enfermo y triste.
Yo no sé lo demás . . . y para eso,
yo no sé por qué fui triste . . . tan triste . . . !

Sólo esa noche de Setiembre dulce,
tuve a tus ojos de Magdala, toda
la distancia de Dios . . . y te fui dulce!

Y también fue una tarde de Setiembre
cuando sembré en tus brasas, desde un auto,
los charcos de esta noche de diciembre.

SEPTEMBER

You were so good to me
that September night . . . even to hurting me!
I do not know about the rest; and for that matter,
you shouldn't have been so good, you shouldn't have.

You sobbed that night upon finding me
hermetic and tyrannical, ill and sad.
I do not know about the rest . . . and for that matter,
I do not know why I was sad . . . so sad . . . !

Solely on that sweet September night
did I possess in your Magdalene eyes, all
the distance of God . . . and I was sweet to you!

Likewise it was a September evening
when I sowed in your embers, as decreed,
the puddles of this December night.

HECES

Esta tarde llueve, como nunca; y no
tengo ganas de vivir, corazón.

Esta tarde es dulce. Por qué no ha de ser?
Viste gracia y pena; viste de mujer.

Esta tarde en Lima llueve. Y yo recuerdo
las cavernas crueles de mi ingratitud;
mi bloque de hielo sobre su amapola,
más fuerte que su "No seas así!"

Mis violentas flores negras; y la bárbara
y enorme pedrada; y el trecho glacial.
Y pondrá el silencio de su dignidad
con óleos quemantes el punto final.

Por eso esta tarde, como nunca, voy
con este búho, con este corazón.

Y otras pasan; y viéndome tan triste,
toman un poquito de ti
en la abrupta arruga de mi hondo dolor.

Esta tarde llueve, llueve mucho. ¡Y no
tengo ganas de vivir, corazón!

DREGS

This afternoon it is raining, as never before; and I
have no desire to live, my heart.

This afternoon is sweet. Why should it not be?
Dressed in grace and pain; dressed like a woman.

This afternoon in Lima it is raining. And I recall
the cruel caverns of my ingratitude;
my block of ice over her poppy,
stronger than her "Don't be this way!"

My violent black flowers; and the barbaric
and terrible stoning; and the glacial distance.
And the silence of her dignity
with burning holy oils will put an end to it.

So this afternoon, as never before, I am
with this owl, with this heart.

Other women go by; and seeing me so sad,
they take on a bit of you
in the abrupt wrinkle of my deep remorse.

This afternoon it is raining, raining hard. And I
have no desire to live, my heart!

IMPÍA

Señor! Estabas tras los cristales
humano y triste de atardecer;
y cuál lloraba tus funerales
      esa mujer!

Sus ojos eran el jueves santo,
dos negros granos de amarga luz!
Con duras gotas de sangre y llanto
      clavó tu cruz!

Impía! Desde que tú partiste,
Señor, no ha ido nunca al Jordán,
en rojas aguas su piel desviste,
y al vil judío le vende pan!

IMPIOUS WOMAN

Lord! You were behind the window
human and sad as dusk approached;
and how that woman was bewailing
      your funeral!

Her eyes were Holy Thursday,
two black grains of embittered light!
With stony drops of blood and tears
      she nailed your cross!

Impious woman! Since you departed,
Lord, she has never returned to the Jordan,
in red waters she exposes her flesh,
and to the vile Jew she sells bread!

LA COPA NEGRA

La noche es una copa de mal. Un silbo agudo
del guardia la atraviesa, cual vibrante alfiler.
Oye, tú, mujerzuela, ¿cómo, si ya te fuiste,
la onda aún es negra y me hace aún arder?

La Tierra tiene bordes de féretro en la sombra.
Oye, tú, mujerzuela, no vayas a volver.

Mi carne nada, nada
en la copa de sombra que me hace aún doler;
mi carne nada en ella,
como en un pantanoso corazón de mujer.

Ascua astral . . . He sentido
secos roces de arcilla
sobre mi loto diáfano caer.
Ah, mujer! Por ti existe
la carne hecha de instinto. Ah, mujer!

Por eso ¡oh, negro cáliz! aun cuando ya te fuiste,
me ahogo con el polvo,
y piafan en mis carnes más ganas de beber!

THE BLACK CUP

Night is a cup of evil. Shrilly a police
whistle pierces it, like a vibrating pin.
Listen, bitch, how come if you are gone now
the flicker is still black and still makes me burn?

The Earth has coffinesque edges in the dark.
Listen, bitch, don't come back.

My flesh swims, swims
in the cup of darkness still aching me;
my flesh swims in her,
in the marshy heart of woman.

Astral ember . . . I have felt
dry scrapes of clay
fall upon my diaphanous lotus.
Ah, woman! Flesh formed of instinct
exists because of you. Ah, woman!

That is why—oh, black chalice! even after you left
I am choking on dust,
and more urges to drink paw at my flesh!

DESHORA

Pureza amada, que mis ojos nunca
llegaron a gozar. Pureza absurda!

Yo sé que estabas en la carne un día,
cuando yo hilaba aún mi embrión de vida.

Pureza en falda neutra de colegio;
y leche azul dentro del trigo tierno

a la tarde de lluvia, cuando el alma
ha roto su puñal en retirada,

cuando ha cuajado en no sé qué probeta
sin contenido una insolente piedra,

cuando hay gente contenta; y cuando lloran
párpados ciegos en purpúreas bordas.

Oh, pureza que nunca ni un recado
me dejaste, al partir del triste barro

ni una migaja de tu voz; ni un nervio
de tu convite heroico de luceros.

Alejaos de mí, buenas maldades,
dulces bocas picantes . . .

Yo la recuerdo al veros ¡oh, mujeres!
Pues de la vida en la perenne tarde,
nació muy poco ¡pero mucho muere!

INOPPORTUNELY

Beloved purity, that my eyes never
came to enjoy. Absurd purity!

I know that you were in the flesh one day,
when I was still spinning my embryo of life.

Purity in a neutral school skirt;
and the blue milk inside tender wheat

on a rainy afternoon, when the soul
while withdrawing has broken its dagger,

when an insolent stone has jelled in
who knows what empty test tube,

when there are content people; and when
blind eyelids cry in purple rims.

Oh, purity you never left me even
one message, on leaving the sad clay

nor one crumb of your voice; nor one nerve
of your heroic banquet of brilliant stars.

Get away from me, good evils,
sweet hot mouths . . .

I remember her when I see you, oh women!
For out of life in the perpetual afternoon,
so little was born, but so much is dying!

FRESCO

Llegué a confundirme con ella,
tanto . . .! Por sus recodos
espirituales, yo me iba
jugando entre tiernos fresales,
entre sus griegas manos matinales.

Ella me acomodaba después los lazos negros
y bohemios de la corbata. Y yo
volvía a ver la piedra
absorta, desairados los bancos, y el reloj
que nos iba envolviendo en su carrete,
al dar su inacabable molinete.

Buenas noches aquellas,
que hoy la dan por reír
de mi extraño morir,
de mi modo de andar meditabundo.
Alfeñiques de oro,
joyas de azúcar
que al fin se quiebran en
el mortero de losa de este mundo.

Pero para las lágrimas de amor,
los luceros son lindos pañuelitos
lilas,
naranjas,
verdes,
que empapa el corazón.
Y si hay ya mucha hiel en esas sedas,
hay un cariño que no nace nunca,
que nunca muere,
vuela otro gran pañuelo apocalíptico,
la mano azul, inédita de Dios!

FRESCO

I came to confuse myself with her,
so much . . . ! Through her spiritual
twists and turns, I kept
playing among the tender strawberry beds,
between her matinal Greek hands.

Later she would arrange the black
and bohemian loops of my tie. Once again
I would see the absorbed
stone, the spurned benches, and the clock
winding us up on its reel
to the stroke of its interminable wheel.

How good those nights were,
that today make her laugh
at my strange dying,
at my pensive way of wandering.
Golden sugar pastes,
sugar jewels
that in the end shatter on
the tombstone mortar of this world.

But for the tears of love,
stars are lovely little handkerchiefs,
lilac,
orange,
and green,
which the heart soaks through.
And if now there is thick bile in these silks,
there is a tenderness that is never born,
that never dies,
another great apocalyptic handkerchief is flying,
the blue, unpublished hand of God!

YESO

Silencio. Aquí se ha hecho ya de noche,
ya tras del cementerio se fue el sol;
aquí se está llorando a mil pupilas:
no vuelvas; ya murió mi corazón.
Silencio. Aquí ya todo está vestido
de dolor riguroso; y arde apenas,
como un mal kerosene, esta pasión.

Primavera vendrá. Cantarás "Eva"
desde un minuto horizontal, desde un
hornillo en que arderán los nardos de Eros.
¡Forja allí tu perdón para el poeta,
que ha de dolerme aún,
como clavo que cierra un ataúd!

Mas . . . una noche de lirismo, tu
buen seno, tu mar rojo
se azotará con olas de quince años,
al ver lejos, aviado con recuerdos
mi corsario bajel, mi ingratitud.

Después, tu manzanar, tu labio dándose,
y que se aja por mí por la vez última,
y que muere sangriento de amar mucho,
como un croquis pagano de Jesús.

Amada! Y cantarás;
y ha de vibrar el femenino en mi alma,
como en una enlutada catedral.

PLASTER

Silence. Here night has now fallen,
the sun has gone down behind the graveyard;
here a thousand pupils are weeping:
do not return; my heart is already dead.
Silence. Everything here is now clothed
in strict grief; and this passion,
like bad kerosene, barely burns.

Spring will come. You will sing "Eve"
from a horizontal minute, from a
furnace in which the spikenards of Eros burn.
Forge there for the poet your pardon,
that will grieve for me still,
like a nail closing a coffin!

And yet . . . one night of lyricism, your
marvelous breast, your red sea
will flog itself with the waves of fifteen years,
on seeing far off, freighted with memories,
my corsair, my ingratitude.

Afterward, your apple orchard, your tendered lip
that humbles itself to me one last time,
and that dies bloody from so much loving,
like a pagan sketch of Jesus.

My love! And you will sing;
and the feminine in my soul will vibrate,
as inside a cathedral in mourning.

NOSTALGIAS IMPERIALES

NOSTALGIAS IMPERIALES

I

En los paisajes de Mansiche labra
imperiales nostalgias el crepúsculo;
y lábrase la raza en mi palabra,
como estrella de sangre a flor de músculo.

El campanario dobla . . . No hay quien abra
la capilla . . . Diríase un opúsculo
bíblico que muriera en la palabra
de asiática emoción de este crepúsculo.

Un poyo con tres potos, es retablo
en que acaban de alzar labios en coro
la eucaristía de una chicha de oro.

Más allá, de los ranchos surge al viento
el humo oliendo a sueño y a establo,
como si se exhumara un firmamento.

II

La anciana pensativa, cual relieve
de un bloque pre-incaico, hila que hila;
en sus dedos de Mama el huso leve
la lana gris de su vejez trasquila.

Sus ojos de esclerótica de nieve
un ciego sol sin luz guarda y mutila . . . !
Su boca está en desdén, y en calma aleve
su cansancio imperial talvez vigila.

Hay ficus que meditan, melenudos
trovadores incaicos en derrota,
la rancia pena de esta cruz idiota,

>

IMPERIAL NOSTALGIAS

IMPERIAL NOSTALGIAS

I

In the landscapes of Mansiche the twilight
fashions imperial nostalgias;
and the race takes shape in my word,
a star of blood on the surface of muscle.

The bell tower tolls . . . There is no one to open
the chapel . . . One could say that
a biblical opuscule died in the words of
this twilight's Asiatic emotion.

A stone bench with three gourd pots, is an altarpiece
on which a chorus of lips have just raised
the Eucharist of golden chicha.

Beyond, smoke smelling of sleep and stable
rises on the wind from the farms,
as if a firmament were being exhumed.

II

Like a relief on a pre-Incan block,
the pensive old woman spins and spins;
in her Mama fingers the thin spindle
shears the gray wool of her old age.

A blind, unlit sun guards and mutilates
her sclerotic snowy eyes . . . !
Her mouth is scornful, and with a deceptive calm
her imperial weariness perhaps holds vigil.

There are meditating ficuses, routed
shaggy Incan troubadours,
the rancid pain of this idiotic cross,

>

> en la hora en rubor que ya se escapa,
y que es lago que suelda espejos rudos
donde náufrago llora Manco-Cápac.

III
Como viejos curacas van los bueyes
camino de Trujillo, meditando . . .
Y al hierro de la tarde, fingen reyes
que por muertos dominios van llorando.

En el muro de pie, pienso en las leyes
que la dicha y la angustia van trocando:
ya en las viudas pupilas de los bueyes
se pudren sueños que no tienen cuándo.

La aldea, ante su paso, se reviste
de un rudo gris, en que un mugir de vaca
se aceita en sueño y emoción de huaca.

Y en el festín del cielo azul yodado
gime en el cáliz de la esquila triste
un viejo corequenque desterrado.

IV
La Grama mustia, recogida, escueta
ahoga no sé qué protesta ignota:
parece el alma exhausta de un poeta,
arredrada en un gesto de derrota.

La Ramada ha tallado su silueta,
cadavérica jaula, sola y rota,
donde mi enfermo corazón se aquieta
en un tedio estatual de terracota.

Llega el canto sin sal del mar labrado
en su máscara bufa de canalla
que babea y da tumbos, ahorcado!

La niebla hila una venda al cerro lila
que en ensueños miliarios se enmuralla,
como un huaco gigante que vigila.

in the shameful hour that now escapes,
and is a lake soldering crude mirrors
where shipwrecked Manco Capac weeps.

III

Like old caciques the oxen walk
the road to Trujillo, meditating . . .
And in the iron of the evening, they feign kings
who wander dead domains sobbing.

Standing on the wall, I ponder the laws
happiness and anguish keep exchanging:
already in the oxen's widowed pupils
dreams that have no when are rotting.

The village, as they pass, is dressed in
harsh gray, where a cow's mooing
is oiled with dreams and huaca emotion.

And in the banquet of the blue iodized sky
an ancient exiled corequenque moans in
the chalice of a melancholy cattle-bell.

IV

La Grama—gloomy, secluded, unadorned—
stifles I don't know what unknown protest:
it resembles the exhausted soul of a poet,
withdrawn in an expression of defeat.

La Ramada has carved its silhouette,
a cadaverous cage, alone and broken,
where my sick heart calms itself in
a statuesque tedium of terra-cotta.

The song saltlessly arrives from the sea
fitted out in the farcical mask of a thug
who drools and staggers, hanged!

The fog weaves a bandage about the lilac hill
enwalled with milliary dreams,
like a gigantic huaco holding vigil.

HOJAS DE ÉBANO

Fulge mi cigarrillo;
su luz se limpia en pólvoras de alerta.
Y a su guiño amarillo
entona un pastorcillo
el tamarindo de su sombra muerta.

Ahoga en una enérgica negrura
el caserón entero
la mustia distinción de su blancura.
Pena un frágil aroma de aguacero.

Están todas las puertas muy ancianas,
y se hastía en su habano carcomido
una insomne piedad de mil ojeras.
Yo las dejé lozanas;
y hoy ya las telarañas han zurcido
hasta en el corazón de sus maderas,
coágulos de sombra oliendo a olvido.
La del camino, el día
que me miró llegar, trémula y triste,
mientras que sus dos brazos entreabría,
chilló como en un llanto de alegría.
Que en toda fibra existe,
para el ojo que ama, una dormida
novia perla, una lágrima escondida.

Con no sé qué memoria secretea
mi corazón ansioso.
—Señora? . . . —Sí, señor; murió en la aldea;
aún la veo envueltita en su rebozo . . .

Y la abuela amargura
de un cantar neurasténico de paria
¡oh, derrotada musa legendaria!
afila sus melódicos raudales
bajo la noche oscura;
como si abajo, abajo,
en la turbia pupila de cascajo
de abierta sepultura,
celebrando perpetuos funerales,
se quebrasen fantásticos puñales.

>

EBONY LEAVES

My cigarette sparkles;
its light cleansed by gunpowder alerts.
And to its yellow wink
a little shepherd intones
the tamarind of his dead shadow.

The whole ramshackle house drowns in
an energetic blackness
the faded distinction of its whiteness.
A delicate odor of downpour lingers.

All the doors are very old,
and a sleepless piety of a thousand hollow eyes
sickens in their worm-eaten Havana brown.
I left them robust;
today spiderwebs have already woven into
the very heart of their wood,
clots of shadow smelling of neglect.
The day the woman by the road
saw me arrive, she shrieked
as if crying for joy, tremulous and sad,
while half-opening her two arms.
For in every fiber there dwells,
for the loving eye, a sleeping
bridal pearl, a hidden tear.

My anxious heart
whispers with I don't know what recollection.
—Señora? . . . —Yes, señor; she died in the village;
I still see her wrapped in her shawl . . .

And the grandmotherly bitterness
of an outcast's neurasthenic song
—oh defeated legendary muse!—
sharpens its melodious outpouring
under the dark night;
as if below, below,
in an open grave's
muddy gravel eye,
celebrating perpetual funerals,
fantastic daggers were shattering.   >

> Llueve … llueve … Sustancia el aguacero,
reduciéndolo a fúnebres olores,
el humor de los viejos alcanfores
que velan *tahuashando* en el sendero
con sus ponchos de hielo y sin sombrero.

>   It's raining . . . raining . . . The downpour condenses,
reducing itself to funereal odors,
the mood of ancient camphors
that hold vigil *tahuashando* down the path   *
with their ponchos of ice and no sombreros.

TERCETO AUTÓCTONO

I

El puño labrador se aterciopela,
y en cruz en cada labio se aperfila.
Es fiesta! El ritmo del arado vuela;
y es un chantre de bronce cada esquila.

Afílase lo rudo. Habla escarcela . . .
En las venas indígenas rutila
un yaraví de sangre que se cuela
en nostalgias de sol por la pupila.

Las pallas, aquenando hondos suspiros,
como en raras estampas seculares,
enrosarian un símbolo en sus giros.

Luce el Apóstol en su trono, luego;
y es, entre inciensos, cirios y cantares,
el moderno dios-sol para el labriego.

II

Echa una cana al aire el indio triste.
Hacia el altar fulgente va el gentío.
El ojo del crepúsculo desiste
de ver quemado vivo el caserío.

La pastora de lana y llanque viste,
con pliegues de candor en su atavío;
y en su humildad de lana heroica y triste,
copo es su blanco corazón bravío.

Entre músicas, fuegos de bengala,
solfea un acordeón! Algún tendero
da su reclame al viento: "Nadie iguala!"

Las chispas al flotar lindas, graciosas,
son trigos de oro audaz que el chacarero
siembra en los cielos y en las nebulosas.

>

AUTOCHTHONOUS TERCET

I

The laborer fist velvetizes
and outlines itself as a cross on every lip.
It's feast day! The plow's rhythm takes wing;
and every cowbell is a bronze precentor.

What's crude is sharpened. Talk pouched . . .
In indigenous veins gleams
a yaraví of blood filtered   *
through pupils into nostalgias of sun.

Quenaing deep sighs, the Pallas,   * *
as in rare century-old prints, enrosarize
a symbol in their gyrations.

On his throne the Apostle shines, then;
and he is, amid incense, tapers, and songs,
a modern sun-god for the peasant.

II

The sad Indian is living it up.
The crowd heads toward the resplendent altar.
The eye of twilight desists
from watching the hamlet burned alive.

The shepherdess wears wool and sandals,
with pleats of candor in her finery;
and in her humbleness of sad and heroic wool,
her feral white heart is a tuft of flax.

Amid the music, Bengal lights,
an accordion sol-fas! A shopkeeper
shouts to the wind: "Nobody can match that!"

The floating sparks—lovely and charming—
are wheats of audacious gold sown by
the farmer in the skies and in the nebulae.   >

   Madrugada. La chicha al fin revienta
en sollozos, lujurias, pugilatos;
entre olores de úrea y de pimienta
traza un ebrio al andar mil garabatos.

   "Mañana que me vaya . . ." se lamenta
un Romeo rural cantando a ratos.
Caldo madrugador hay ya de venta;
y brinca un ruido aperital de platos.

   Van tres mujeres . . . silba un golfo . . . Lejos
el río anda borracho y canta y llora
prehistorias de agua, tiempos viejos.

   Y al sonar una *caja* de Tayanga,
como iniciando un *huaino* azul, remanga
sus pantorrillas de azafrán la Aurora.

Daybreak. The chicha finally explodes
into sobs, lust, fistfights;
amid the odors of urine and pepper
a wandering drunk traces a thousand scrawls.

"Tomorrow when I go away . . ." a rural
Romeo bewails, singing at times.
Now there is early-riser soup for sale;
and an aperitive sound of clinking plates.

Three women go by . . . an urchin whistles . . . Distantly
the river flows along drunkenly, singing and weeping
prehistories of water, olden times.

And as a *caja* from Tayanga sounds,   *
as if initiating a blue *huaino,* Dawn   *
tucks up her saffron-colored calves.

ORACIÓN DEL CAMINO

Ni sé para quién es esta amargura!
Oh, Sol, llévala tú que estás muriendo,
y cuelga, como un Cristo ensangrentado,
mi bohemio dolor sobre su pecho.
    El valle es de oro amargo;
    y el viaje es triste, es largo.

Oyes? Regaña una guitarra. Calla!
Es tu raza, la pobre viejecita
que al saber que eres huésped y que te odian,
se hinca la faz con una roncha lila.
    El valle es de oro amargo,
    y el trago es largo . . . largo . . .

Azulea el camino; ladra el río . . .
Baja esa frente sudorosa y fría,
fiera y deforme. Cae el pomo roto
de una espada humanicida!

Y en el mómico valle de oro santo,
la brasa de sudor se apaga en llanto!

Queda un olor de tiempo abonado de versos,
para brotes de mármoles consagrados que hereden
la aurífera canción
de la alondra que se pudre en mi corazón!

PRAYER ON THE ROAD

I don't even know who this bitterness is for!
Oh Sun, you who are dying, take it away
and hang, like a bloody Crucifix,
my bohemian pain on their breast.
    The valley is full of bitter gold;
    and the journey is sad, is long.

Do you hear? A guitar scolds. Be quiet!
It is your race, the poor little old woman who,
on learning that you're a guest and that they hate you,
picks at her face with its lilac-colored weal.
    The valley is full of bitter gold,
    and the drink is long . . . long . . .

The road shines blue; the river barks . . .
That forehead, sweaty and cold, bestial and deformed,
is bowed. The broken pommel of
a humanicidal sword falls!

And in the mummyesque valley of sacred gold,
an ember of sweat is extinguished with tears!

An odor of time lingers fertilized by verses,
for the shoots of consecrated marble that would inherit
the auriferous song
of the lark rotting in my heart!

HUACO

Yo soy el corequenque ciego
que mira por la lente de una llaga,
y que atado está al Globo,
como a un huaco estupendo que girara.

Yo soy el llama, a quien tan sólo alcanza
la necedad hostil a trasquilar
volutas de clarín,
volutas de clarín brillantes de asco
y bronceadas de un viejo yaraví.

Soy el pichón de cóndor desplumado
por latino arcabuz;
y a flor de humanidad floto en los Andes
como un perenne Lázaro de luz.

Yo soy la gracia incaica que se roe
en áureos coricanchas bautizados
de fosfatos de error y de cicuta.
A veces en mis piedras se encabritan
los nervios rotos de un extinto puma.

Un fermento de Sol;
¡levadura de sombra y corazón!

HUACO

I am the blind corequenque
who sees through the lens of a wound,
and who is bound to the Globe
as to a stupendous huaco spinning.

I am the llama, whose hostile stupidity
is only grasped when sheared by
volutes of a bugle,
volutes of a bugle glittering with disgust
and bronzed with an old yaraví.

I am the fledgling condor plucked
by a Latin harquebus;
and flush with humanity I float in the Andes
like an everlasting Lazarus of light.

I am Incan grace, gnawing at itself
in golden coricanchas baptized
with phosphates of error and hemlock.
At times the shattered nerves of an extinct puma
rear up in my stones.

A ferment of Sun;
yeast of darkness and the heart!

*

MAYO

Vierte el humo doméstico en la aurora
su sabor a rastrojo;
y canta, haciendo leña, la pastora
un salvaje aleluya!
                    Sepia y rojo.

Humo de la cocina, aperitivo
de gesta en este bravo amanecer.
El último lucero fugitivo
lo bebe, y, ebrio ya de su dulzor,
¡oh celeste zagal trasnochador!
se duerme entre un jirón de rosicler.

Hay ciertas ganas lindas de almorzar,
y beber del arroyo, y chivatear!
Aletear con el humo allá, en la altura;
o entregarse a los vientos otoñales
en pos de alguna Ruth sagrada, pura,
que nos brinde una espiga de ternura
bajo la hebraica unción de los trigales!

Hoz al hombro calmoso,
acre el gesto brioso,
va un joven labrador a Irichugo.
Y en cada brazo que parece yugo
se encrespa el férreo jugo palpitante
que en creador esfuerzo cuotidiano
chispea, como trágico diamante,
a través de los poros de la mano
que no ha bizantinado aún el guante.
Bajo un arco que forma verde aliso,
¡oh cruzada fecunda del andrajo!
pasa el perfil macizo
de este Aquiles incaico del trabajo.

La zagala que llora
su yaraví a la aurora,
recoge ¡oh Venus pobre!
frescos leños fragantes
en sus desnudos brazos arrogantes

>

MAY

Household smoke pours into the dawn
its haulm savor;
and, gathering kindling, the shepherdess lets loose
a wild hallelujah!
                    Sepia and red.

Smoke from the kitchen, an epic
apertif on this sumptuous dawn.
The last fleeting star
drinks it, and, now high on its sweetness
—oh celestial all-night shepherd!—
falls asleep in a wisp of rosy hue.

There are certain lovely desires to eat lunch,
to drink from the arroyo, and to kid around!
To soar with the smoke beyond, on high;
or to surrender oneself to autumnal winds
in pursuit of some pure, holy Ruth
who offers us a spike of tenderness
under the Hebraic unction of wheat fields!

Sickle on sluggish shoulder,
his lively countenance bitter,
a young farmhand goes to Irichugo.
And in each yokelike arm
the iron juice agitates, throbbing,
and in a daily creative effort
sparkles, like a tragic diamond,
through the pores of a hand
no glove has ever byzantinized.
Under an archway formed by green alders
—oh fecund crossing of a man in rags!—
the massive profile of
this Incan Achilles of labor passes.

The young shepherdess crying
her yaraví into the dawn
gathers—oh poor Venus!—
fresh fragrant kindling
in her proud naked arms   >

> esculpidos en cobre.
En tanto que un becerro,
perseguido del perro,
por la cuesta bravía
corre, ofrendando al floreciente día
un himno de Virgilio en su cencerro!

Delante de la choza
el indio abuelo fuma;
y el serrano crepúsculo de rosa,
el ara primitiva se sahúma
en el gas del tabaco.
Tal surge de la entraña fabulosa
de epopéyico huaco,
mítico aroma de broncíneos lotos,
el hilo azul de los alientos rotos!

> sculpted of copper.
While a calf
chased by a dog
runs across the uncultivated
hill, offering to the flowering day
a Virgilian hymn in his cowbell!

In front of the hut
the Indian grandfather smokes;
and the pink highland dusk,
the primitive altar is scented
with tobacco fumes.
Thus from the fabulous entrails
of an epic huaco surges
a mythic aroma of bronzine lotuses,
the blue thread of severed breaths!

ALDEANA

Lejana vibración de esquilas mustias
en el aire derrama
la fragancia rural de sus angustias.
En el patio silente
sangra su despedida el sol poniente.
El ámbar otoñal del panorama
toma un frío matiz de gris doliente!

Al portón de la casa
que el tiempo con sus garras torna ojosa,
asoma silenciosa
y al establo cercano luego pasa,
la silueta calmosa
de un buey color de oro,
que añora con sus bíblicas pupilas,
oyendo la oración de las esquilas,
su edad viril de toro!

Al muro de la huerta,
aleteando la pena de su canto,
salta un gallo gentil, y, en triste alerta,
cual dos gotas de llanto,
tiemblan sus ojos en la tarde muerta!

Lánguido se desgarra
en la vetusta aldea
el dulce yaraví de una guitarra,
en cuya eternidad de hondo quebranto
la triste voz de un indio dondonea,
como un viejo esquilón de camposanto.

De codos yo en el muro,
cuando triunfa en el alma el tinte oscuro
y el viento reza en los ramajes yertos
llantos de quenas, tímidos, inciertos,
suspiro una congoja,
al ver que en la penumbra gualda y roja
llora un trágico azul de idilios muertos!

VILLAGE SCENE

The distant vibration of melancholy cowbells
pours the rural
fragrance of their anguish into the air.
Onto the silent patio
the setting sun bleeds its farewell.
The autumnal amber of the panorama
takes on a cold hue of aching gray!

At the house's front door
that time with its talons turns holey,
the sluggish silhouette of
a gold-colored ox
silently looms
and then passes into the nearby barn;
hearing cowbell prayers
he yearns with biblical pupils
for his virile bull years!

Onto the garden wall
an elegant cock leaps, fluttering
the pain of his song, and, in sad alarm,
like two teardrops,
his eyes tremble in the dead afternoon!

Languidly through
the decrepit village
rends a guitar's sweet yaraví,
in whose eternity of deep affliction
the sad voice of an Indian dronedongs   *
like a big, old cemetery bell.

My elbows on the wall,
while a dark stain triumphs in the soul
and the wind sheds in motionless branches
tears of timid, uncertain quenas,
I sigh a torment,
on seeing how in the golden red penumbra
a tragic blue of dead idylls weeps!

IDILIO MUERTO

Qué estará haciendo esta hora mi andina y dulce Rita
de junco y capulí;
ahora que me asfixia Bizancio, y que dormita
la sangre, como flojo coñac, dentro de mí.

Dónde estarán sus manos que en actitud contrita
planchaban en las tardes blancuras por venir;
ahora, en esta lluvia que me quita
las ganas de vivir.

Qué será de su falda de franela; de sus
afanes; de su andar;
de su sabor a cañas de Mayo del lugar.

Ha de estarse a la puerta mirando algún celaje,
y al fin dirá temblando: "Qué frío hay . . . Jesús!".
Y llorará en las tejas un pájaro salvaje.

DEAD IDYLL

What would she be doing now, my sweet Andean Rita
of rush and tawny berry;
now when Byzantium asphyxiates me, and my blood
dozes, like thin cognac, inside of me.

Where would her hands, that showing contrition
ironed in the afternoon whitenesses yet to come,
be now, in this rain that deprives me of
my desire to live.

What has become of her flannel skirt; of her
toil; of her walk;
of her taste of homemade May rum.

She must be at the door watching some cloudscape,
and at length she'll say, trembling: "Jesus . . . it's so cold!"
And on the roof tiles a wild bird will cry.

TRUENOS

EN LAS TIENDAS GRIEGAS

Y el Alma se asustó
a las cinco de aquella tarde azul desteñida.
El labio entre los linos la imploró
con pucheros de novio para su prometida.

El Pensamiento, el gran General se ciñó
de una lanza deicida.
El Corazón danzaba; mas, luego sollozó:
¿la bayadera esclava estaba herida?

Nada! Fueron los tigres que la dan por correr
a apostarse en aquel rincón, y tristes ver
los ocasos que llegan desde Atenas.

No habrá remedio para este hospital de nervios,
para el gran campamento irritado de este atardecer!
Y el General escruta volar siniestras penas
allá.....................................
en el desfiladero de mis nervios!

THUNDERCLAPS

IN THE GREEK TENTS

And the Soul was alarmed
at five o'clock that faded blue afternoon.
The lip implored it between the linens
pouting like a bridegroom to his betrothed.

Thought, the great General, girded himself
with a deicidal lance.
The Heart was dancing; but then it sobbed:
was the bayadere slave wounded?

Not at all! It was just tigers given to running
so as to post themselves in that corner, and sadly watch
the sunsets arrive from Athens.

There will be no cure for this hospital of nerves,
for the great vexed encampment of this late afternoon!
And the General inspects sinister pains spreading swiftly
there. . . . .
in the narrow pass of my nerves!

AGAPE

Hoy no ha venido nadie a preguntar;
ni me han pedido en esta tarde nada.

No he visto ni una flor de cementerio
en tan alegre procesión de luces.
Perdóname, Señor: qué poco he muerto!

En esta tarde todos, todos pasan
sin preguntarme ni pedirme nada.

Y no sé qué se olvidan y se queda
mal en mis manos, como cosa ajena.

He salido a la puerta,
y me da ganas de gritar a todos:
Si echan de menos algo, aquí se queda!

Porque en todas las tardes de esta vida,
yo no sé con qué puertas dan a un rostro,
y algo ajeno se toma el alma mía.

Hoy no ha venido nadie;
y hoy he muerto qué poco en esta tarde!

AGAPE

Today no one has come to inquire;
nor have they asked me for anything this afternoon.

I have not seen a single cemetery flower
in such a happy procession of lights.
Forgive me, Lord: how little I have died!

On this afternoon everybody, everybody passes by
without inquiring or asking me for anything.

And I do not know what they forget and feels
wrong in my hands, like something that is not mine.

I have gone to the door,
and feel like shouting at everybody:
If you are missing something, here it is!

Because in all the afternoons of this life,
I do not know what doors they slam in a face,
and my soul is seized by someone else's thing.

Today no one has come;
and today I have died so little this afternoon!

Así pasa la vida, como raro espejismo.
¡La rosa azul que alumbra y da el ser al cardo!
Junto al dogma del fardo
matador, el sofisma del Bien y la Razón!

Se ha cogido, al acaso, lo que rozó la mano;
los perfumes volaron, y entre ellos se ha sentido
el moho que a mitad de la ruta ha crecido
en el manzano seco de la muerta Ilusión.

Así pasa la vida,
con cánticos aleves de agostada bacante.
Yo voy todo azorado, adelante . . . adelante,
rezongando mi marcha funeral.

Van al pie de brahacmánicos elefantes reales
y al sórdido abejeo de un hervor mercurial,
parejas que alzan brindis esculpidos en roca,
y olvidados crepúsculos una cruz en la boca.

Así pasa la vida, vasta orquesta de Esfinges
que arrojan al Vacío su marcha funeral.

THE VOICE IN THE MIRROR

So life goes, like a bizarre mirage.
The blue rose that sheds light, giving the thistle its being!
Together with the dogma of the murderous
burden, the sophism of Good and Reason!

What the hand grazed, by chance, has been grasped;
perfumes drifted, and among them the scent of
mold that halfway down the path has grown
on the withered apple tree of dead Illusion.

So life goes,
with the treacherous canticles of a shriveled bacchante.
Completely rattled, I push onward . . . onward,
growling my funeral march.

Walking at the feet of royal Brahacmanic elephants   *
and to the sordid buzzing of a mercurial boiling,
couples raise toasts sculpted in rock,
and forgotten twilights a cross to their lips.

So life goes, a vast orchestra of Sphinxes
belching out its funeral march into the Void.

ROSA BLANCA

Me siento bien. Ahora
brilla un estoico hielo
en mí.
Me da risa esta soga
rubí
que rechina en mi cuerpo.

Soga sin fin,
como una
voluta
descendente
de
mal . . .
soga sanguínea y zurda
formada de
mil dagas en puntal.

Que vaya así, trenzando
sus rollos de crespón;
y que ate el gato trémulo
del Miedo al nido helado,
al último fogón.

Yo ahora estoy sereno,
con luz.
Y maya en mi Pacífico
un náufrago ataúd.

WHITE ROSE

I feel fine. A stoic
ice glistens in
me now.
This ruby rope creak-
ing in
my body makes me laugh.

Unending rope,
like a
volute
descending
from
evil . . .
rope bloodied and left-handed
formed by
a thousand daggers pounded in.

So let it go, plaiting
its rolls of crepe;
and let it tie the trembling cat
of Fear to the frozen nest,
to the final hearth.

I am serene now,
with light.
Mewing on my Pacific:
a shipwrecked coffin.

LA DE A MIL

El suertero que grita "La de a mil",
contiene no sé qué fondo de Dios.

Pasan todos los labios. El hastío
despunta en una arruga su yanó.
Pasa el suertero que atesora, acaso
nominal, como Dios,
entre panes tantálicos, humana
impotencia de amor.

Yo le miro al andrajo. Y él pudiera
darnos el corazón;
pero la suerte aquella que en sus manos
aporta, pregonando en alta voz,
como un pájaro cruel, irá a parar
adonde no lo sabe ni lo quiere
este bohemio dios.

Y digo en este viernes tibio que anda
a cuestas bajo el sol:
¡por qué se habrá vestido de suertero
la voluntad de Dios!

THE BIG ONE

The lottery vendor who shouts "The big one"
possesses I don't know what depths of God.

The lips all pass by. In a wrinkle
tedium sprouts its notthistime.
The vendor passes by hoarding, perhaps
in name only, like God,
among Tantalic loaves, the human
impotence of love.

I see him in this wretch. And he could have
given us heart;
but whatever luck he holds out in
his hands, hawking loudly,
like a cruel bird, will end up
somewhere this bohemian god neither
knows nor cares about.

And I say on this tepid Friday that bears
the sun downhill on its back:
why would God's volition have dressed up
as a lottery vendor!

EL PAN NUESTRO

Para Alejandro Gamboa

Se bebe el desayuno . . . Húmeda tierra
de cementerio huele a sangre amada.
Ciudad de invierno . . . La mordaz cruzada
de una carreta que arrastrar parece
una emoción de ayuno encadenada!

Se quisiera tocar todas las puertas
y preguntar por no sé quién; y luego
ver a los pobres, y, llorando quedos,
dar pedacitos de pan fresco a todos.
Y saquear a los ricos sus viñedos
con las dos manos santas
que a un golpe de luz
volaron desclavadas de la Cruz!

Pestaña matinal, no os levantéis!
¡El pan nuestro de cada día dánoslo,
Señor . . . !

Todos mis huesos son ajenos;
yo talvez los robé!
Yo vine a darme lo que acaso estuvo
asignado para otro;
y pienso que, si no hubiera nacido,
otro pobre tomara este café!
Yo soy un mal ladrón . . . A dónde iré!

Y en esta hora fría, en que la tierra
trasciende a polvo humano y es tan triste,
quisiera yo tocar todas las puertas,
y suplicar a no sé quién, perdón,
y hacerle pedacitos de pan fresco
aquí, en el horno de mi corazón . . . !

OUR BREAD

For Alejandro Gamboa

One drinks one's breakfast . . . The damp graveyard
earth smells of beloved blood.
City of winter . . . Mordant crusade
of a cart that seems to drag along
a feeling of fasting in chains!

One wants to knock on each door
and ask for who knows who; and then
see to the poor, and, crying softly,
give morsels of bread to everybody.
And to strip the rich of their vineyards
with the two saintly hands
that with a blast of light
flew off unnailed from the Cross!

Matinal eyelash, don't raise up!
Our daily bread—give it to us,
Lord . . . !

All my bones belong to others;
maybe I stole them!
I took for my own what was perhaps
meant for another;
and I think that, had I not been born,
another poor man would be drinking this coffee!
I'm a lousy thief . . . Where will I go?

And in this cold hour, when the earth
smells of human dust and is so sad,
I want to knock on every door
and beg who knows who, forgive me,
and bake him morsels of fresh bread
here, in the oven of my heart . . . !

ABSOLUTA

Color de ropa antigua. Un Julio a sombra,
y un Agosto recién segado. Y una
mano de agua que injertó en el pino
resinoso de un tedio malas frutas.

Ahora que has anclado, oscura ropa,
tornas rociada de un suntuoso olor
a tiempo, a abreviación . . . Y he cantado
el proclive festín que se volcó.

Mas ¿no puedes, Señor, contra la muerte,
contra el límite, contra lo que acaba?
Ay! la llaga en color de ropa antigua,
cómo se entreabre y huele a miel quemada!

Oh unidad excelsa! Oh lo que es uno
por todos!
Amor contra el espacio y contra el tiempo!
Un latido único de corazón;
un solo ritmo: Dios!

Y al encogerse de hombros los linderos
en un bronco desdén irreductible,
hay un riego de sierpes
en la doncella plenitud del 1.
¡Una arruga, una sombra!

ABSOLUTE

The color of old clothes. Shadowed July,
and just-harvested August. And one
coat of water that onto the resinous
pine of boredom grafted evil fruit.

Now that you have dropped anchor, dark clothing,
you return dampened with a sumptuous fragrance
in time, in abbreviation . . . And I have sung
the inclined feast that overturned.

But, have you no power, Lord, against death,
against the limit, against that which ends?
Ay! wound the color of old clothes,
how it slightly opens and smells of burnt honey!

Oh exalted unity! Oh that which is one
for all!
Love against space and against time!
A single heartbeat;
a single rhythm: God!

And as the boundaries in surly irreducible
disdain shrug their shoulders,
there is a pouring forth of serpents
onto the virgin plenitude of 1.
A crease, a shade!

DESNUDO EN BARRO

Como horribles batracios a la atmósfera,
suben visajes lúgubres al labio.
Por el Sahara azul de la Substancia
camina un verso gris, un dromedario.

Fosforece un mohín de sueños crueles.
Y el ciego que murió lleno de voces
de nieve. Y madrugar, poeta, nómada,
al crudísimo día de ser hombre.

Las Horas van febriles, y en los ángulos
abortan rubios siglos de ventura.
¡Quién tira tanto el hilo; quién descuelga
sin piedad nuestros nervios,
cordeles ya gastados, a la tumba!

Amor! Y tú también. Pedradas negras
se engendran en tu máscara y la rompen.
¡La tumba es todavía
un sexo de mujer que atrae al hombre!

NAKED IN CLAY

Like horrible batrachians in the atmosphere,
lugubrious smirks rise to the lip.
Through the blue Sahara of Substance
walks a gray verse, a dromedary.

A grimace of cruel dreams phosphoresces.
And the blind man who died full of the voices
of snow. Rise at dawn, poet, nomad,
to the rawest day of being man.

The Hours feverishly go by, and in the corners
blond centuries of happiness abort.
Who spins out so much thread; who ruthlessly
lowers our nerves, cords
already frayed, into the tomb!

Love! And you too. Black stonings
breed in your mask and smash it.
The tomb is still
woman's sex that draws man in!

CAPITULACIÓN

Anoche, unos abriles granas capitularon
ante mis mayos desarmados de juventud;
los marfiles histéricos de su beso me hallaron
muerto; y en un suspiro de amor los enjaulé.

Espiga extraña, dócil. Sus ojos me asediaron
una tarde amaranto que dije un canto a sus
cantos; y anoche, en medio de los brindis, me hablaron
las dos lenguas de sus senos abrasadas de sed.

Pobre trigueña aquella; pobres sus armas; pobres
sus velas cremas que iban al tope en las salobres
espumas de un marmuerto. Vencedora y vencida,

se quedó pensativa y ojerosa y granate.
Yo me partí de aurora. Y desde aquel combate,
de noche entran dos sierpes esclavas a mi vida.

CAPITULATION

Last night, some April grain capitulated
before my disarmed youthful Mays;
the hysterical ivories of her kiss found me
dead; and with a love sigh I caged them.

Strange, docile spike. Her eyes besieged me
one amaranthine evening when I recited a song to her
songs; and last night, during the toasts, the two
tongues of her thirst-inflamed breasts spoke to me.

Swarthy poor she was; poor her weapons; poor
her cream-colored sails pushed to the hilt over the salt
spray of a deadsea. Conquering and conquered,

she was left pensive, hollow-eyed and garnet.
I took off at dawn. Ever since that battle,
at night two serpent slaves go into my life.

LÍNEAS

Cada cinta de fuego
que, en busca del Amor,
arrojo y vibra en rosas lamentables,
me da a luz el sepelio de una víspera.
Yo no sé si el redoble en que lo busco,
será jadear de roca,
o perenne nacer de corazón.

Hay tendida hacia el fondo de los seres,
un eje ultranervioso, honda plomada.
¡La hebra del destino!
Amor desviará tal ley de vida,
hacia la voz del Hombre;
y nos dará la libertad suprema
en transubstanciación azul, virtuosa,
contra lo ciego y lo fatal.

¡Que en cada cifra lata,
recluso en albas frágiles,
el Jesús aún mejor de otra gran Yema!

Y después . . . La otra línea . . .
Un Bautista que aguaita, aguaita, aguaita . . .
Y, cabalgando en intangible curva,
un pie bañado en púrpura.

LINES

Each ribbon of fire
that, in quest of Love,
I fling and vibrates in pitiful roses,
births me to the burial of a day before.
I do not know if the drumroll in which I seek it
will be the gasping of a rock
or the perennial birth of heart.

Extended toward the depth of beings
is an ultranervous axis, a deep plumb line.
Thread of destiny!
Love will divert such a law of life
toward the voice of Man;
and will give us a supreme liberty
in blue, virtuous transubstantiation,
against what is blind and what is fatal.

Let there palpitate in each cipher,
imprisoned in the frail dawns,
an even better Jesus from another great Yolk!

And afterward . . . The other line . . .
A Baptist who keeps watch, keeps watch, keeps watch . . .
And, riding on an intangible curve,
one foot bathed in purple.

AMOR PROHIBIDO

Subes centelleante de labios y ojeras!
Por tus venas subo, como un can herido
que busca el refugio de blandas aceras.

Amor, en el mundo tú eres un pecado!
Mi beso es la punta chispeante del cuerno
del diablo; mi beso que es credo sagrado!

Espíritu es el horópter que pasa
        ¡puro en su blasfemia!
¡el corazón que engendra al cerebro!
que pasa hacia el tuyo, por mi barro triste.
        ¡Platónico estambre
que existe en el cáliz donde tu alma existe!

¿Algún penitente silencio siniestro?
Tú acaso lo escuchas? Inocente flor!
. . . Y saber que donde no hay un Padrenuestro,
el Amor es un Cristo pecador!

FORBIDDEN LOVE

You rise sparkling from lips and dark-circled eyes!
Through your veins I rise, like an injured dog
seeking the refuge of soft pavements.

Love, in this world you are a sin!
My kiss is the sparking point of the devil's
horn; my kiss that is a sacred creed!

Spirit is the horopter that passes
         —pure in its blasphemy!
the heart that begets the brain!—
that passes toward yours, through my sad clay.
         Platonic stamen
that dwells in the calyx where your soul dwells!

Some sinister silent penitent?
Do you by chance hear him? Innocent flower!
. . . And to know that where there is no Paternoster,
Love is a sinning Christ!

Hasta cuándo estaremos esperando lo que
no se nos debe . . . Y en qué recodo estiraremos
nuestra pobre rodilla para siempre! Hasta cuándo
la cruz que nos alienta no detendrá sus remos.

Hasta cuándo la Duda nos brindará blasones
por haber padecido . . .
                       Ya nos hemos sentado
mucho a la mesa, con la amargura de un niño
que a media noche, llora de hambre, desvelado . . .

Y cuándo nos veremos con los demás, al borde
de una mañana eterna, desayunados todos.
Hasta cuándo este valle de lágrimas, a donde
yo nunca dije que me trajeran.
                          De codos,
todo bañado en llanto, repito cabizbajo
y vencido: hasta cuándo la cena durará.

Hay alguien que ha bebido mucho, y se burla,
y acerca y aleja de nosotros, como negra cuchara
de amarga esencia humana, la tumba . . .
                           Y menos sabe
ese oscuro hasta cuándo la cena durará!

THE MISERABLE SUPPER

How long will we have to wait for what is
not owed to us . . . And in what corner will
we kick our poor sponge forever! How long before   *
the cross that inspires us does not rest its oars.

How long before Doubt toasts our nobility for
having suffered . . .
                        We have already sat so
long at this table, with the bitterness of a child
who at midnight, cries from hunger, wide awake . . .

And when will we join all the others, at the brink
of an eternal morning, everybody breakfasted.
For just how long this vale of tears, into which
I never asked to be led.
                              Resting on my elbows,
all bathed in tears, I repeat head bowed
and defeated: how much longer will this supper last.

There's someone who has drunk too much, and he mocks us,
and offers and withdraws from us—like a black spoonful
of bitter human essence—the tomb . . .
                              And this abstruse one knows
even less how much longer this supper will last!

PARA EL ALMA IMPOSIBLE DE MI AMADA

Amada: no has querido plasmarte jamás
como lo ha pensado mi divino amor.
    Quédate en la hostia,
    ciega e impalpable,
    como existe Dios.

Si he cantado mucho, he llorado más
por ti ¡oh mi parábola excelsa de amor!
    Quédate en el seso,
    y en el mito inmenso
    de mi corazón!

Es la fe, la fragua donde yo quemé
el terroso hierro de tanta mujer;
y en un yunque impío te quise pulir.
    Quédate en la eterna
    nebulosa, ahí,
en la multicencia de un dulce noser.

Y si no has querido plasmarte jamás
en mi metafísica emoción de amor
    deja que me azote,
    como un pecador.

FOR THE IMPOSSIBLE SOUL OF MY LOVER

My love: you have never wanted to shape yourself
as my divine love has devised.
> Remain in the Host,
> blind and impalpable,
> the way God exists.

If I have sung a lot, I have cried even more
for you—oh my sublime parable of love!
> Remain in the brain,
> and in the immense myth
> of my heart!

It is faith, the forge where I burned
the earthy iron of so much woman;
and on an unholy anvil I wanted to refine you.
> Remain in the eternal
> nebula, there,
in the polyessence of a sweet nonbeing.

And if you have never wanted to shape yourself
into my metaphysical love emotion,
> let me flog myself,
> like a sinner.

EL TÁLAMO ETERNO

Sólo al dejar de ser, Amor es fuerte!
Y la tumba será una gran pupila,
en cuyo fondo supervive y llora
la angustia del amor, como en un cáliz
de dulce eternidad y negra aurora.

Y los labios se encrespan para el beso,
como algo lleno que desborda y muere;
y, en conjunción crispante,
cada boca renuncia para la otra
una vida de vida agonizante.

Y cuando pienso así, dulce es la tumba
donde todos al fin se compenetran
en un mismo fragor;
dulce es la sombra, donde todos se unen
en una cita universal de amor.

Only when it ceases to be, is Love strong!
And the tomb will be a huge eyeball,
in whose depths the anguish of love
survives and weeps, as in a chalice
of sweet eternity and black dawn.

And lips curl up for the kiss,
as when something full overflows and dies;
and, in convulsed conjunction,
each mouth renounces for the other
a life of moribund life.

And when I think this way, sweet is the tomb
where everybody finally interpenetrates
in a single roar;
sweet is the shadow, where everybody unites
in a universal assignation of love.

LAS PIEDRAS

Esta mañana bajé
a las piedras ¡oh las piedras!
Y motivé y troquelé
un pugilato de piedras.

Madre nuestra, si mis pasos
en el mundo hacen doler,
es que son los fogonazos
de un absurdo amanecer.

Las piedras no ofenden; nada
codician. Tan sólo piden
amor a todos, y piden
amor aun a la Nada.

Y si algunas de ellas se
van cabizbajas, o van
avergonzadas, es que
algo de humano harán . . .

Mas, no falta quien a alguna
por puro gusto golpee.
Tal, blanca piedra es la luna
que voló de un puntapié . . .

Madre nuestra, esta mañana
me he corrido con las hiedras,
al ver la azul caravana
de las piedras,
de las piedras,
de las piedras . . .

THE STONES

This morning I went down
to the stones, oh the stones!
And I encouraged and coined
a brawl of stones.

Our Mother, if my footsteps
in the world cause pain,
it is because they are the flashes
of an absurd daybreak.

Stones do not offend; they
covet nothing. They solely ask
love of everybody, and they ask
love of even Nothingness.

And if some of them go away
crestfallen, or leave
ashamed, it is because
they must do something human . . .

But there are always those who
for the fun of it will strike one.
Thus, the moon is a white stone
sent flying by a kick. . .

Our Mother, this morning
I have aligned myself with the ivy,
on seeing the blue caravan
of the stones,
of the stones,
of the stones . . .

RETABLO

Yo digo para mí: por fin escapo al ruido;
nadie me ve que voy a la nave sagrada.
Altas sombras acuden,
y Darío que pasa con su lira enlutada.

Con paso innumerable sale la dulce Musa,
y a ella van mis ojos, cual polluelos al grano.
La acosan tules de éter y azabaches dormidos,
en tanto sueña el mirlo de la vida en su mano.

Dios mío, eres piadoso, porque diste esta nave,
donde hacen estos brujos azules sus oficios.
Darío de las Américas celestes! Tal ellos se parecen
a ti! Y de tus trenzas fabrican sus cilicios.

Como ánimas que buscan entierros de oro absurdo,
aquellos arciprestes vagos del corazón,
se internan, y aparecen . . . y, hablándonos de lejos,
nos lloran el suicidio monótono de Dios!

ALTARPIECE

I tell myself: at last I have escaped the noise;
no one sees me on my way to the sacred nave.
Tall shades attend,
and Darío who passes with lyre in mourning.

With innumerable steps the gentle Muse emerges,
and my eyes go to her, like chicks to corn.
Ethereal tulles and sleeping titmice harass her,
while the blackbird of life dreams in her hand.

My God, you are merciful, for you have bestowed this nave
where these blue sorcerers perform their duties.
Darío of celestial Americas! They are so much
like you! And from your braids they make their hair shirts.

Like souls seeking burials of absurd gold,
these wayward archpriests of the heart,
probe deeper, and appear . . . and, addressing us from afar,
bewail the monotonous suicide of God!

PAGANA

Ir muriendo y cantando. Y bautizar la sombra
con sangre babilónica de noble gladiador.
Y rubricar los cuneiformes de la áurea alfombra
con la pluma del ruiseñor y la tinta azul del dolor.

La Vida? Hembra proteica. Contemplarla asustada
escaparse en sus velos, infiel, falsa Judith;
verla desde la herida, y asirla en la mirada,
incrustando un capricho de cera en un rubí.

Mosto de Babilonia, Holofernes sin tropas,
en el árbol cristiano yo colgué mi nidal;
la viña redentora negó amor a mis copas;
Judith, la vida aleve, sesgó su cuerpo hostial.

Tal un festín pagano. Y amarla hasta en la muerte,
mientras las venas siembran rojas perlas de mal;
y así volverse al polvo, conquistador sin suerte,
dejando miles de ojos de sangre en el puñal.

PAGAN WOMAN

To go along dying and singing. And to baptize shadow
with the Babylonian blood of a noble gladiator.
And to initial the gold carpet's cuneiforms
with a nightingale quill and the blue ink of sorrow.

Life? A protean female. To contemplate her alarmed
escaping in her veils, a heathen, deceitful Judith;
to see her from the wound, and to seize her with a look,
inlaying a ruby with a wax caprice.

The must of Babylon, a Holofernes without troops,
I hung my nest in the Christian tree;
the redeeming vineyard denied love to my cups;
Judith, perfidious life, slanted her sacrificial body.

What a pagan feast. And to love her unto death,
while my veins sow the red pearls of wickedness;
in this way to return to dust, a luckless conquistador,
leaving thousands of eyes of blood on the dagger.

LOS DADOS ETERNOS

PARA MANUEL GONZÁLEZ PRADA,
esta emoción bravía y selecta,
una de las que, con más entusiasmo,
me ha aplaudido el gran maestro.

Dios mío, estoy llorando el ser que vivo;
me pesa haber tomádote tu pan;
pero este pobre barro pensativo
no es costra fermentada en tu costado:
tú no tienes Marías que se van!

Dios mío, si tú hubieras sido hombre,
hoy supieras ser Dios;
pero tú, que estuviste siempre bien,
no sientes nada de tu creación.
Y el hombre sí te sufre: el Dios es él!

Hoy que en mis ojos brujos hay candelas,
como en un condenado,
Dios mío, prenderás todas tus velas,
y jugaremos con el viejo dado . . .
Talvez ¡oh jugador! al dar la suerte
del universo todo,
surgirán las ojeras de la Muerte,
como dos ases fúnebres de lodo.

Dios mío, y esta noche sorda, oscura,
ya no podrás jugar, porque la Tierra
es un dado roído y ya redondo
a fuerza de rodar a la aventura,
que no puede parar sino en un hueco,
en el hueco de inmensa sepultura.

THE ETERNAL DICE

FOR MANUEL GONZÁLEZ PRADA,
this wild, choice emotion, one for
which the great master has most
enthusiastically applauded me.

My God, I am crying over the being I live;
it grieves me to have taken your bread;
but this poor thinking clay
is no scab fermented in your side:
you do not have Marys who leave you!

My God, had you been a man,
today you would know how to be God;
but you, who were always fine,
feel nothing for your own creation.
Indeed, man suffers you; God is he!

Today there are candles in my sorcerer eyes,
as in those of a condemned man—
my God, you will light all of your candles
and we will play with the old die . . .
Perhaps, oh gambler, throwing for the fate of
the whole universe,
Death's dark-circled eyes will come up,
like two funereal snake eyes of mud.

My God, and this deaf, gloomy night,
you will not be able to gamble, for the Earth
is a worn die now rounded from
rolling at random,
it cannot stop but in a hollow,
the hollow of an immense tomb.

LOS ANILLOS FATIGADOS

Hay ganas de volver, de amar, de no ausentarse,
y hay ganas de morir, combatido por dos
aguas encontradas que jamás han de istmarse.

Hay ganas de un gran beso que amortaje a la Vida,
que acaba en el áfrica de una agonía ardiente,
suicida!

Hay ganas de . . . no tener ganas, Señor;
a ti yo te señalo con el dedo deicida:
hay ganas de no haber tenido corazón.

La primavera vuelve, vuelve y se irá. Y Dios,
curvado en tiempo, se repite, y pasa, pasa
a cuestas con la espina dorsal del Universo.

Cuando las sienes tocan su lúgubre tambor,
cuando me duele el sueño grabado en un puñal,
¡hay ganas de quedarse plantado en este verso!

WEARY RINGS

There are desires to return, to love, to not disappear,
and there are desires to die, fought by two
opposing waters that have never isthmused.

There are desires for a great kiss that would shroud Life,
one that ends in the Africa of a fiery agony,
a suicide!

There are desires to . . . have no desires, Lord;
I point my deicidal finger at you:
there are desires to not have had a heart.

Spring returns, returns and will depart. And God,
bent in time, repeats himself, and passes, passes
with the spinal column of the Universe on his back.

When my temples beat their lugubrious drum,
when the dream engraved on a dagger aches me,
there are desires to be left standing in this verse!

SANTORAL

(Parágrafos)

Viejo Osiris! Llegué hasta la pared
de enfrente de la vida.

Y me parece que he tenido siempre
a la mano esta pared.

Soy la sombra, el reverso: todo va
bajos mis pasos de columna eterna.

Nada he traído por las trenzas; todo
fácil se vino a mí, como una herencia.

Sardanápalo. Tal, botón eléctrico
de máquinas de sueño fue mi boca.

Así he llegado a la pared de enfrente;
y siempre esta pared tuve a la mano.

Viejo Osiris! Perdónote! Que nada
alcanzó a requerirme, nada, nada . . .

SANCTOLOGY

(Paragraphs)

Old Osiris! I came as far as the wall
facing life.

And it seems to me that I have always had
this wall within reach.

I am the shadow, the reverse: everything passes
under the steps of my eternal column.

I have dragged in nothing by its hair; everything
came easily to me, like an inheritance.

Sardanapalus. So, my mouth was
the electric button of a dream machine.

Thus have I arrived at the wall facing me,
a wall always within reach.

Old Osiris! I forgive you! For nothing
ever needed anything from me, nothing, nothing . . .

LLUVIA

En Lima . . . En Lima está lloviendo
el agua sucia de un dolor
qué mortífero. Está lloviendo
de la gotera de tu amor.

No te hagas la que está durmiendo,
recuerda de tu trovador;
que yo ya comprendo . . . comprendo
la humana ecuación de tu amor.

Truena en la mística dulzaina
la gema tempestuosa y zaina,
la brujería de tu "sí".

Más, cae, cae el aguacero
al ataúd de mi sendero,
donde me ahueso para ti . . .

RAIN

In Lima . . . In Lima it is raining
the dirty water of a pain
so deadly. It is raining
through the leak in your love.

Don't pretend to be sleeping,
remember your troubadour;
for I now understand . . . understand
the human equation of your love.

Tempestuous and meretricious gem,
the witchery of your "yes"
thunders on the mystical flageolet.

More, the downpour resounds
the coffin of my path,
where I ossify for you . . .

AMOR

Amor, ya no vuelves a mis ojos muertos;
y cuál mi idealista corazón te llora.
Mis cálices todos aguardan abiertos
tus hostias de otoño y vinos de aurora.

Amor, cruz divina, riega mis desiertos
con tu sangre de astros que sueña y que llora.
¡Amor, ya no vuelves a mis ojos muertos
que temen y ansían tu llanto de aurora!

Amor, no te quiero cuando estás distante
rifado en afeites de alegre bacante,
o en frágil y chata facción de mujer.

Amor, ven sin carne, de un icor que asombre;
y que yo, a manera de Dios, sea el hombre
que ama y engendra sin sensual placer!

LOVE

Love, no longer do you return to my dead eyes;
and how my idealistic heart weeps for you.
All my chalices openly await
your autumnal Hosts and dawn wines.

Love, cross divine, water my deserts
with your astral blood that dreams and that cries.
Love, no longer do you return to my dead eyes
that dread and long for your dawn tears.

Love, I do not desire you when you are distant
raffled off in the make-up of a tipsy bacchante,
or in the weak and pug-nosed features of a woman.

Love, come without flesh, from an astonishing ichor,
so that I, in the manner of God, may be a man
who loves and begets without sensual pleasure!

DIOS

Siento a Dios que camina
tan en mí, con la tarde y con el mar.
Con él nos vamos juntos. Anochece.
Con él anochecemos. Orfandad . . .

Pero yo siento a Dios. Y hasta parece
que él me dicta no sé qué buen color.
Como un hospitalario, es bueno y triste;
mustia un dulce desdén de enamorado:
debe dolerle mucho el corazón.

Oh, Dios mío, recién a ti me llego,
hoy que amo tanto en esta tarde; hoy
que en la falsa balanza de unos senos,
mido y lloro una frágil Creación.

Y tú, cuál llorarás . . . tú, enamorado
de tanto enorme seno girador . . .
Yo te consagro Dios, porque amas tanto;
porque jamás sonríes; porque siempre
debe dolerte mucho el corazón.

GOD

I feel God who walks
so inside me, with the evening and with the sea.
With him we go away together. Night falls.
With him we darken. Orphanhood . . .

But I feel God. And it even seems
that he dictates to me I don't know what good color.
Like a hospitaler, he is kind and sad;
he languishes with a lover's sweet disdain:
how much his heart must ache.

Oh, my God, I have only just approached you,
now when I love so much this evening; now
when on the fraudulent scales of someone's breasts
I weigh and weep for a fragile Creation.

And you, how you will cry . . . you, so in love
with such an enormous rotating breast . . .
I consecrate you God, because you love so much;
because you never smile; because your heart
must always ache so much.

UNIDAD

En esta noche mi reloj jadea
junto a la sien oscurecida, como
manzana de revólver que voltea
bajo el gatillo sin hallar el plomo.

La luna blanca, inmóvil, lagrimea,
y es un ojo que apunta . . . Y siento cómo
se acuña el gran Misterio en una idea
hostil y ovóidea, en un bermejo plomo.

¡Ah, mano que limita, que amenaza
tras de todas las puertas, y que alienta
en todos los relojes, cede y pasa!

Sobre la araña gris de tu armazón,
otra gran Mano hecha de luz sustenta
un plomo en forma azul de corazón.

UNITY

Tonight my clock gasps
next to my darkened temple, like
the apple of a revolver that turns
under the trigger without finding the bullet.

The moon white, immobile, shows tears,
and is an eye that aims . . . And I sense how
the great Mystery is locked up in a hostile
and ovoid idea, in a vermilion bullet.

Ah, hand that limits, that threatens
behind every door, and that breathes
in every clock, yield and transfer!

Over the gray spider of your frame,
another great Hand made of light sustains
a bullet in a heart's blue shape.

LOS ARRIEROS

Arriero, vas fabulosamente vidriado de sudor.
La hacienda Menocucho
cobra mil sinsabores diarios por la vida.
Las doce. Vamos a la cintura del día.
El sol que duele mucho.

Arriero, con tu poncho colorado te alejas,
saboreando el romance peruano de tu coca.
Y yo desde una hamaca,
desde un siglo de duda,
cavilo tu horizonte, y atisbo lamentado
por zancudos y por el estribillo gentil
y enfermo de una "paca-paca".
Al fin tú llegarás donde debes llegar,
arriero, que, detrás de tu burro santurrón,
te vas . . . .
te vas . . . .

Feliz de ti, en este calor en que se encabritan
todas las ansias y todos los motivos;
cuando el espíritu que anima al cuerpo apenas,
va sin coca, y no atina a cabestrar
su bruto hacia los Andes
oxidentales de la Eternidad.

MULETEERS

Muleteer, you walk fabulously glazed in sweat.
Menocucho hacienda
charges a thousand displeasures a day for life.
It is noon. We've arrived at the waist of the day.
The sun that hurts so much.

Muleteer, with your beet-red poncho you depart,
savoring the Peruvian romance of your coca.
And, from a hammock,
from a century of doubt,
I ponder your horizon and observe, deploring
the long-shanked mosquitoes and the charming feeble
refrain of a "paca-paca."   *
In the end you will arrive where you should arrive,
muleteer, you who, behind your sanctimonious burro,
trudge on. . . . . . .
trudge on. . . . .

Lucky you, in this heat in which all anxieties,
all motives rear up;
when the spirit that barely animates the body
goes without coca, and does not manage to halter
its beast toward the oxidental   *
Andes of Eternity.

CANCIONES DE HOGAR

ENCAJE DE FIEBRE

Por los cuadros de santos en el muro colgados
mis pupilas arrastran un ay! de anochecer;
y en un temblor de fiebre, con los brazos cruzados,
mi ser recibe vaga visita del Noser.

Una mosca llorona en los muebles cansados
yo no sé qué leyenda fatal quiere verter:
una ilusión de Orientes que fugan asaltados;
un nido azul de alondras que mueren al nacer.

En un sillón antiguo sentado está mi padre.
Como una Dolorosa, entra y sale mi madre.
Y al verlos siento un algo que no quiere partir.

Porque antes de la oblea que es hostia hecha de Ciencia,
está la hostia, oblea hecha de Providencia.
Y la visita nace, me ayuda a bien vivir . . . .

SONGS OF HOME

FEVER LACE

Through the pictures of saints hung on the wall
my eyeballs drag an ay! of nightfall;
and in a fever shudder, arms crossed,
my being receives a nebulous visit from Nonbeing.

A crying fly on the tired furniture
wants to spill I do not know what ghastly legend:
an illusion of Orients that flee assaulted;
a blue nest of skylarks that die while being born.

An old armchair holds my father.
Like Our Lady of Sorrows my mother comes and goes.
Seeing them I feel something that does not want to go away.

Because before the wafer, host made of Science,
there is the Host, wafer made of Providence.
And the visit is born, it helps me to live right . . . .

LOS PASOS LEJANOS

Mi padre duerme. Su semblante augusto
figura un apacible corazón;
está ahora tan dulce . . .
si hay algo en él de amargo, seré yo.

Hay soledad en el hogar; se reza;
y no hay noticias de los hijos hoy.
Mi padre se despierta, ausculta
la huida a Egipto, el restañante adiós.
Está ahora tan cerca;
si hay algo en él de lejos, seré yo.

Y mi madre pasea allá en los huertos,
saboreando un sabor ya sin sabor.
Está ahora tan suave,
tan ala, tan salida, tan amor.

Hay soledad en el hogar sin bulla,
sin noticias, sin verde, sin niñez.
Y si hay algo quebrado en esta tarde,
y que baja y que cruje,
son dos viejos caminos blancos, curvos.
Por ellos va mi corazón a pie.

DISTANT FOOTSTEPS

My father is asleep. His august face
expresses a peaceful heart;
he is now so sweet . . .
if there is anything bitter in him, it must be me.

There is loneliness in the house; there is prayer;
and no news of the children today.
My father stirs, sounding
the flight into Egypt, the styptic farewell.
He is now so near;
if there is anything distant in him, it must be me.

My mother walks in the orchard,
savoring a savor now without savor.
She is so soft,
so wing, so gone, so love.

There is loneliness in the house with no bustle,
no news, no green, no childhood.
And if there is something broken this afternoon,
something that descends and that creaks,
it is two old white, curved roads.
Down them my heart makes its way on foot.

A MI HERMANO MIGUEL

In memoriam

Hermano, hoy estoy en el poyo de la casa,
donde nos haces una falta sin fondo!
Me acuerdo que jugábamos esta hora, y que mamá
nos acariciaba: "Pero, hijos . . ."

Ahora yo me escondo,
como antes, todas estas oraciones
vespertinas, y espero que tú no des conmigo.
Por la sala, el zaguán, los corredores.
Después, te ocultas tú, y yo no doy contigo.
Me acuerdo que nos hacíamos llorar,
hermano, en aquel juego.

Miguel, tú te escondiste
una noche de Agosto, al alborear;
pero, en vez de ocultarte riendo, estabas triste.
Y tu gemelo corazón de esas tardes
extintas se ha aburrido de no encontrarte. Y ya
cae sombra en el alma.

Oye, hermano, no tardes
en salir. Bueno? Puede inquietarse mamá.

TO MY BROTHER MIGUEL

In memoriam

Brother, today I am on the stone bench by the door,
where we miss you terribly!
I recall how we would play at this hour, and Mama
would caress us: "Now, boys . . ."

Now I go hide,
as before, all those evening
prayers, and hope you do not find me.
Through the living room, the hall, the corridors.
Then, you hide, and I cannot find you.
I recall that we made each other cry,
brother, with that game.

Miguel, you hid
one night in August, at dawn;
but, instead of hiding laughing, you were sad.
And your twin heart of those extinct
evenings has grown weary from not finding you. And now
shadow falls into the soul.

Hey, brother, don't take so long
to come out. Okay? Mama might get worried.

ENEREIDA

Mi padre, apenas,
en la mañana pajarina, pone
sus setentiocho años, sus setentiocho
ramos de invierno a solear.
El cementerio de Santiago, untado
en alegre año nuevo, está a la vista.
Cuántas veces sus pasos cortaron hacia él,
y tornaron de algún entierro humilde.

Hoy hace mucho tiempo que mi padre no sale!
Una broma de niños se desbanda.

Otras veces le hablaba a mi madre
de impresiones urbanas, de política;
y hoy, apoyado en su bastón ilustre
que sonara mejor en los años de la Gobernación,
mi padre está desconocido, frágil,
mi padre es una víspera.
Lleva, trae, abstraído, reliquias, cosas,
recuerdos, sugerencias.
La mañana apacible le acompaña
con sus alas blancas de hermana de caridad.

Día eterno es éste, día ingenuo, infante,
coral, oracional;
se corona el tiempo de palomas,
y el futuro se puebla
de caravanas de inmortales rosas.
Padre, aún sigue todo despertando;
es Enero que canta, es tu amor
que resonando va en la Eternidad.
Aún reirás de tus pequeñuelos,
y habrá bulla triunfal en los Vacíos.

Aún será año nuevo. Habrá empanadas;
y yo tendré hambre, cuando toque a misa
en el beato campanario
el buen ciego mélico con quien
departieron mis sílabas escolares y frescas,
mi inocencia rotunda.

>

My father can hardly,
in the bird-borne morning, get
his seventy-eight years, his seventy-eight
winter branches, out into the sunlight.
The Santiago graveyard, anointed
with Happy New Year, is in view.
How many times his footsteps have cut over toward it,
then returned from some humble burial.

Today it's a long time since my father went out!
A hubbub of kids breaks up.

Other times he would talk to my mother
about city life, politics;
today, supported by his distinguished cane
(which sounded better during his years in office),
my father is unknown, frail,
my father is a vesper.
He carries, brings, absentmindedly, relics, things,
memories, suggestions.
The placid morning accompanies him
with its white Sister of Charity wings.

This is an eternal day, an ingenuous, childlike,
choral, prayerful day;
time is crowned with doves
and the future is filled with
caravans of immortal roses.
Father, yet everything is still awakening;
it is January that sings, it is your love
that keeps resonating in Eternity.
You will laugh with your little ones,
and there will be a triumphant racket in the Void.

It will still be New Year. There will be empanadas;
and I will be hungry, when Mass is rung
in the pious bell tower by
the kind melic blind man with whom
my fresh schoolboy syllables, my rotund
innocence, chatted.   >

> Y cuando la mañana llena de gracia,
desde sus senos de tiempo
que son dos renuncias, dos avances de amor
que se tienden y ruegan infinito, eterna vida,
cante, y eche a volar Verbos plurales,
girones de tu ser,
a la borda de sus alas blancas
de hermana de caridad ¡oh, padre mío!

>   And when the morning full of grace,
from its breasts of time,
which are two renunciations, two advances of love
which stretch out and plead for infinity, eternal life,
sings, and lets fly plural Words,
tatters of your being,
at the edge of its white
Sister of Charity wings, oh! my father!

ESPERGESIA

Yo nací un día
que Dios estuvo enfermo.

Todos saben que vivo,
que soy malo; y no saben
del Diciembre de ese Enero.
Pues yo nací un día
que Dios estuvo enfermo.

Hay un vacío
en mi aire metafísico
que nadie ha de palpar:
el claustro de un silencio
que habló a flor de fuego.

Yo nací un día
que Dios estuvo enfermo.

Hermano, escucha, escucha . . . .
Bueno. Y que no me vaya
sin llevar diciembres,
sin dejar eneros.
Pues yo nací un día
que Dios estuvo enfermo.

Todos saben que vivo,
que mastico . . . Y no saben
por qué en mi verso chirrían,
oscuro sinsabor de féretro,
luyidos vientos
desenroscados de la Esfinge
preguntona del Desierto.

Todos saben . . . Y no saben
que la Luz es tísica,
y la Sombra gorda . . . .
Y no saben que el Misterio sintetiza . . . .
que él es la joroba

>

I was born on a day
when God was sick.

Everybody knows that I am alive,
that I am bad; and they do not know
about the December of that January.
For I was born on a day
when God was sick.

There is a void
in my metaphysical air
that no one is going to touch:
the cloister of a silence
that spoke flush with fire.

I was born on a day
when God was sick.

Brother, listen, listen . . . .
Okay. And do not let me leave
without bringing Decembers,
without leaving Januaries.
For I was born on a day
when God was sick.

Everybody knows that I am alive,
that I chew . . . And they do not know
why in my poetry galled winds,
untwisted from the inquisitive
Sphinx of the Desert,
screech an obscure
coffin anxiety.

Everybody knows . . . And they do not know
that the Light is consumptive,
and the Shadow fat. . . . .
And they do not know how the Mystery synthesizes. . . . .
how it is the sad musical   >

> musical y triste que a distancia denuncia
el paso meridiano de las lindes a las Lindes.

    Yo nací un día
que Dios estuvo enfermo,
grave.

> humpback who denounces from afar
the meridional step from the limits to the Limits.

I was born on a day
when God was sick,
gravely.

TRILCE (1922)

TRILCE

I

Quién hace tánta bulla, y ni deja
testar las islas que van quedando.

Un poco más de consideración
en cuanto será tarde, temprano,
y se aquilatará mejor
el guano, la simple calabrina tesórea
que brinda sin querer,
en el insular corazón,
salobre alcatraz, a cada hialóidea
    grupada.

Un poco más de consideración,
y el mantillo líquido, seis de la tarde
   DE LOS MAS SOBERBIOS BEMOLES

Y la península párase
por la espalda, abozaleada, impertérrita
en la línea mortal del equilibrio.

I

Who's making all that racket, and not even letting   *
the islands that linger make a will.

A little more consideration
as it will be late, early,
and easier to assay
the guano, the simple fecapital ponk   * * *
a brackish gannet
toasts unintentionally,
in the insular heart, to each hyaloid
    squall.

A little more consideration,
and liquid muck, six in the evening
OF THE MOST GRANDIOSE B-FLATS

And the peninsula raises up
from behind, muzziled, imperturbable   *
on the fatal balance line.

II

Tiempo Tiempo.

Mediodía estancado entre relentes.
Bomba aburrida del cuartel achica
tiempo tiempo tiempo tiempo.

Era Era.

Gallos cancionan escarbando en vano.
Boca del claro día que conjuga
era era era era.

Mañana Mañana.

El reposo caliente aún de ser.
Piensa el presente guárdame para
mañana mañana mañana mañana.

Nombre Nombre.

¿Qué se llama cuanto heriza nos?
Se llama Lomismo que padece
nombre nombre nombre nombrE.

II

Time Time.

Noon dammed up in night damp.
Bored pump in the cell block bailing out
time   time   time   time.

Was Was.

Cocks song on scratching in vain.   *
Mouth of the bright day that conjugates
was   was   was   was.

Tomorrow Tomorrow.

The repose in being still warm.
The present thinks keep me for
tomorrow   tomorrow   tomorrow   tomorrow.

Name Name.

What call all that stands our end on hAIR?   *
It's called Thesame as suffers
name   name   name   namE.

III

Las personas mayores
¿a qué hora volverán?
Da la seis el ciego Santiago,
y ya está muy oscuro.

Madre dijo que no demoraría.

Aguedita, Nativa, Miguel,
cuidado con ir por ahí, por donde
acaban de pasar gangueando sus memorias
dobladoras penas,
hacia el silencioso corral, y por donde
las gallinas que se están acostando todavía,
se han espantado tanto.
Mejor estemos aquí no más.
Madre dijo que no demoraría.

Ya no tengamos pena. Vamos viendo
los barcos ¡el mío es más bonito de todos!
con los cuales jugamos todo el santo día,
sin pelearnos, como debe de ser:
han quedado en el pozo de agua, listos,
fletados de dulces para mañana.

Aguardemos así, obedientes y sin más
remedio, la vuelta, el desagravio
de los mayores siempre delanteros
dejándonos en casa a los pequeños,
como si también nosotros
                        no pudiésemos partir.

Aguedita, Nativa, Miguel?
Llamo, busco al tanteo en la oscuridad.
No me vayan a haber dejado solo,
y el único recluso sea yo.

III

The grown-ups
—when are they coming back?
Blind Santiago is ringing six o'clock,   *
and it's already pretty dark.

Mother said she wouldn't be late.

Aguedita, Nativa, Miguel,   *
be careful going around there, where
stooped souls in torment   *
have just passed twanging their memories,
toward the silent barnyard, and where
the hens still getting settled,
had been so frightened.
We'd better stay right here.
Mother said she wouldn't be late.

We shouldn't fret. Let's keep looking at
the boats—mine's the nicest of all!—
that we play with the whole day long,
without fighting, how it should be:
they've stayed on the well water, ready,
loaded with candy for tomorrow.

So let's wait, obedient and with no
other choice, for the return, the apologies
of the grown-ups always in front
leaving us the little ones at home,
as if we too couldn't

                          go away.

Aguedita, Nativa, Miguel?
I call out, I grope in the dark.
They can't have left me all alone,
the only prisoner can't be me.

IV

Rechinan dos carretas contra los martillos
hasta los lagrimales trifurcas,
cuando nunca las hicimos nada.
A aquella otra sí, desamada,
amargurada bajo túnel campero
por lo uno, y sobre duras áljidas
pruebas   espiritivas.

Tendime en són de tercera parte,
mas la tarde—qué la bamos a hhazer—
se anilla en mi cabeza, furiosamente
a no querer dosificarse en madre. Son
                 los anillos.
Son los nupciales trópicos ya tascados.
El alejarse, mejor que todo,
rompe a Crisol.

Aquel no haber descolorado
por nada. Lado al lado al destino y llora
y llora. Toda la canción
cuadrada en tres silencios.

Calor. Ovario. Casi transparencia.
Háse llorado todo.   Háse entero velado
en plena izquierda.

IV

Two carts grind against the hammers
until trifurca lachrymals,   *
when we never did anything to them.
To that other one yes, unloved,
embitternessed under an exposed shelter   *
by the first one, and over tough aljid   *
spiritive   ordeals.   *

I stretched out as a third part,
but the evening—nuthin to ddo about it   *
rings around in my head, furiously
not wanting to dose itself into a mother. It is
                    the rings.
It is the nuptial tropics already champed.
The parting, best of all,
breaks into Crucible.

That one that nothing had
discolored. Side to side to destiny and cries
and cries. The whole song
squared by three silences.

Heat. Ovary. Almost transparency.
All has been cried out.   Has been completely waked
in deep left.

V

Grupo dicotiledón. Oberturan
desde él petreles, propensiones de trinidad,
finales que comienzan, ohs de ayes
creyérase avaloriados de heterogeneidad.
¡Grupo de los dos cotiledones!

A ver. Aquello sea sin ser más.
A ver. No trascienda hacia afuera,
y piense en són de no ser escuchado,
y crome y no sea visto.
Y no glise en el gran colapso.

La creada voz rebélase y no quiere
ser malla, ni amor.
Los novios sean novios en eternidad.
Pues no deis 1, que resonará al infinito.
Y no deis 0, que callará tánto,
hasta despertar y poner de pie al 1.

Ah grupo bicardiaco.

V

Dicotyledonous group. From it petrels
overture, propensities for trinity,
finales that begin, ohs of ayes
believed to be rhinestoned with heterogeneity.   *
Group of two cotyledons!

Let's see. That one could be without being more.
Let's see. Don't let it transcend outward,
and think as if it's not being listened to,
and chrome and not be seen.
And not glise on the great collapse.   *

The created voice rebels and doesn't want
to be meshwork, or amour.
Let the newlyweds be newlyweds in eternity.
So don't strike 1, which will echo into infinity.
And don't strike 0, which will be so still,
until it wakes the 1 and makes it stand.

Ah bicardiac group.

VI

El traje que vestí mañana
no lo ha lavado mi lavandera:
lo lavaba en sus venas otilinas,
en el chorro de su corazón, y hoy no he
de preguntarme si yo dejaba
el traje turbio de injusticia.

A hora que no hay quien vaya a las aguas,
en mis falsillas encañona
el lienzo para emplumar, y todas las cosas
del velador de tánto qué será de mí,
todas no están mías
a mi lado.
                        Quedaron de su propiedad,
fratesadas, selladas con su trigueña bondad.

Y si supiera si ha de volver;
y si supiera qué mañana entrará
a entregarme las ropas lavadas, mi aquella
lavandera del alma. Qué mañana entrará
satisfecha, capulí de obrería, dichosa
de probar que sí sabe, que sí puede
                ¡COMO NO VA A PODER!
azular y planchar todos los caos.

VI

The suit I wore tomorrow
my laundress has not laundered it:
she used to launder it in her Otilian veins,   *
in the gush of her heart, and today I don't
have to wonder if I left
the suit muddy with injustice.

Now that there's no one who goes to the waters,
the linen for feathering
fledges in my underlining, and all the things
on the nightstand from so much what'll become of me,
all don't feel mine
at my side.
                    They remained her property,
lustred, sealed with her olive-skinned goodness.   *

And if only I knew she'd come back;
and if only I knew what morning she'd come in
to hand me my laundered clothes, my own that
laundress of the soul. What morning she'd come in
satisfied, tawny berry of handiwork, happy   *
to prove that yes she does know, that yes she can
                    HOW COULD SHE NOT!
blue and iron all the chaoses.

VII

Rumbé sin novedad por la veteada calle
que yo me sé. Todo sin novedad,
de veras. Y fondeé hacia cosas así,
y fui pasado.

Doblé la calle por la que raras
veces se pasa con bien, salida
heroica por la herida de aquella
esquina viva, nada a medias.

Son los grandores,
el grito aquel, la claridad de careo,
la barreta sumersa en su función de
                    ¡ya!
Cuando la calle está ojerosa de puertas,
y pregona desde descalzos atriles
trasmañanar las salvas en los dobles.

Ahora hormigas minuteras
se adentran dulzoradas, dormitadas, apenas
dispuestas, y se baldan,
quemadas pólvoras, altos de a 1921.

VII

I headed as usual down the veined street
I know so well. Everything as usual,
really. And I sounded toward things in this way,
and was past.

I turned onto the street on which one
rarely fares well, a heroic
exit through the wound of that
raw corner, nothing halfway.

It is the magnitudes,
that shout, the clarity of facing off,
the barret plunged into its function of   *
                      now!
When the street is hollow-eyed with doors,
and proclaims from barefoot lecterns
procrastinating the salvos in the knells.

Now minute hand ants
penetrate deep ensweetened, drowsy, barely
willing to, and spend themselves,
burnt-out powder, the upstairs price 1921.

VIII

Mañana esotro día, alguna
vez hallaría para el hifalto poder,
entrada eternal.

Mañana algún día,
sería la tienda chapada
con un par de pericardios, pareja
de carnívoros en celo.

Bien puede afincar todo eso.
Pero un mañana sin mañana,
entre los aros de que enviudemos,
margen de espejo habrá
donde traspasaré mi propio frente
hasta perder el eco
y quedar con el frente hacia la espalda.

VIII

Tomorrow that other day, some-
time I might find for the saltatory power,
eternal entrance.   *

Tomorrow someday,
it would be the shop plated
with a pair of pericardia, paired
carnivores in rut.

Could very well take root all this.
But one tomorrow without tomorrow,
between the rings of which we become widowers,
a margin of mirror there will be
where I run through my own front
until the echo is lost
and I'm left with my front toward my back.

IX

Vusco volvvver de golpe el golpe.
Sus dos hojas anchas, su válvula
que se abre en suculenta recepción
de multiplicando a multiplicador,
su condición excelente para el placer,
todo avía verdad.

Busco volvver de golpe el golpe.
A su halago, enveto bolivarianas fragosidades
a treintidós cables y sus múltiples,
se arrequintan pelo por pelo
soberanos belfos, los dos tomos de la Obra,
y no vivo entonces ausencia,
                    ni al tacto.

Fallo bolver de golpe el golpe.
No ensillaremos jamás el toroso Vaveo
de egoísmo y de aquel ludir mortal
de sábana,
desque la mujer esta
                    ¡cuánto pesa de general!

Y hembra es el alma de la ausente.
Y hembra es el alma mía.

IX   *

I sdrive to dddeflect at a blow the blow.
Her two broad leaves, her valve
opening in succulent reception
from multiplicand to multiplier,
her condition excellent for pleasure,
all readies truth   *

I strive to ddeflect at a blow the blow.
To her flattery, I transasfixiate Bolivarian asperities   *
at thirty-two cables and their multiples,
hair for hair majestic thick lips,
the two tomes of the Work, constringe,
and I do not live absence then,
                not even by touch.

I fail to teflect at a blow the blow.
We will never saddle the torose Trool
of egotism or of that mortal chafe
of the bedsheet,
since this here woman
                —how she weighs being general!

And female is the soul of the absent-she.
And female is my own soul.

X

Prístina y última piedra de infundada
ventura, acaba de morir
con alma y todo, octubre habitación y encinta.
De tres meses de ausente y diez de dulce.
Cómo el destino,
mitrado monodáctilo, ríe.

Cómo detrás desahucian juntas
de contrarios. Cómo siempre asoma el guarismo
bajo la línea de todo avatar.

Cómo escotan las ballenas a palomas.
Cómo a su vez éstas dejan el pico
cubicado en tercera ala.
Cómo arzonamos, cara a monótonas ancas.

Se remolca diez meses hacia la decena,
hacia otro más allá.
Dos quedan por lo menos todavía en pañales.
Y los tres meses de ausencia.
Y los nueve de gestación.

No hay ni una violencia.
El paciente incorpórase
y sentado empavona tranquilas misturas.

X

The pristine and last stone of groundless
fortune, has just died
with soul and all, October bedroom and pregnant.
Of three months of absent and ten of sweet.
How destiny,
mitered monodactyl, laughs.

How at the rear conjunctions of contraries
destroy all hope. How under every avatar's lineage
the number always shows up.

How whales cut doves to fit.
How these in turn leave their beak
cubed as a third wing.
How we saddleframe, facing monotonous croups.   *

Ten months are towed toward the tenth,
toward another beyond.
Two at least are still in diapers.
And the three months of absence.
And the nine of gestation.

There's not even any violence.
The patient raises up
and seated enpeacocks tranquil nosegays.   *

XI

He encontrado a una niña
en la calle, y me ha abrazado.
Equis, disertada, quien la halló y la halle,
no la va a recordar.

Esta niña es mi prima. Hoy, al tocarle
el talle, mis manos han entrado en su edad
como en par de mal rebocados sepulcros.
Y por la misma desolación marchóse,
      delta al sol tenebloso,
      trina entre los dos.

      "Me he casado",
me dice. Cuando lo que hicimos de niños
en casa de la tía difunta.
      Se ha casado.
      Se ha casado.

Tardes años latitudinales,
qué verdaderas ganas nos ha dado
de jugar a los toros, a las yuntas,
pero todo de engaños, de candor, como fue.

XI

I have met a girl
in the street, and she has embraced me.
X, expounded, whoever found her and finds her,
will not remember her.

This girl is my cousin. Today, on touching
her waist, my hands have entered her age
as into a pair of badly bitewashed sepulchers.   *
And for that very desolation she left,
        the delta in a teneblearic sun,   *
        a trine between the two.

        "I got married,"
she tells me. In spite of what we did as kids
in the house of the dead aunt.
        She's married.
        She's married.

Late latitudinal years,
how much it made us want
to play bulls, yoked oxen,
but just fooling, in candor, like it was.

XII

Escapo de una finta, peluza a peluza.
Un proyectil que no sé dónde irá a caer.
Incertidumbre. Tramonto. Cervical coyuntura.

Chasquido de moscón que muere
a mitad de su vuelo y cae a tierra.
¿Qué dice ahora Newton?
Pero, naturalmente, vosotros sois hijos.

Incertidumbre. Talones que no giran.
Carilla en nudo, fabrida
cinco espinas por un lado
y cinco por el otro: Chit! Ya sale.

XII

I escape with a feint, fluf by fluf.
A projectile I know not where it will fall.
Incertitude. Tramontation. Cervical articulation. *

Zap of a horsefly that dies
in midair and drops to earth.
What would Newton say now?
But, naturally, you're all sons.

Incertitude. Heels that don't spin.
The page knotted, factures *
five thorns on one side
and five on the other: Ssh! Here it comes.

XIII

Pienso en tu sexo.
Simplificado el corazón, pienso en tu sexo,
ante el hijar maduro del día.
Palpo el botón de dicha, está en sazón.
Y muere un sentimiento antiguo
degenerado en seso.

Pienso en tu sexo, surco más prolífico
y armonioso que el vientre de la Sombra,
aunque la Muerte concibe y pare
de Dios mismo.
Oh Conciencia,
pienso, sí, en el bruto libre
que goza donde quiere, donde puede.

Oh, escándalo de miel de los crepúsculos.
Oh estruendo mudo.

¡Odumodneurtse!

XIII

I think about your sex.
My heart simplified, I think about your sex,
before the ripe daughterloin of day.   *
I touch the bud of joy, it is in season.
And an ancient sentiment dies
degenerated into brains.

I think about your sex, furrow more prolific
and harmonious than the belly of the Shadow,
though Death conceives and bears
from God himself.
Oh Conscience,
I am thinking, yes, about the free beast
who takes pleasure where he wants, where he can.

Oh, scandal of the honey of twilights.
Oh mute thunder.

Rednuhtetum!

XIV

Cual mi explicación.
Esto me lacera de tempranía.

Esa manera de caminar por los trapecios.

Esos corajosos brutos como postizos.

Esa goma que pega el azogue al adentro.

Esas posaderas sentadas para arriba.

Ese no puede ser, sido.

Absurdo.

Demencia.

Pero he venido de Trujillo a Lima.
Pero gano un sueldo de cinco soles.

XIV

As for my explanation.
This lacerates me with earliness.

That way of traveling through trapezes.

Those ill-tempered loutlike fakes.

That rubber that sticks the quicksilver inside.   *

Those buttocks seated upward.

That cannot be, been.

Absurd.

Dementia.

But I have come from Trujillo to Lima.
But I earn a wage of five soles.   *

XV

En el rincón aquel, donde dormimos juntos
tantas noches, ahora me he sentado
a caminar. La cuja de los novios difuntos
fue sacada, o talvez qué habrá pasado.

Has venido temprano a otros asuntos,
y ya no estás. Es el rincón
donde a tu lado, leí una noche,
entre tus tiernos puntos,
un cuento de Daudet. Es el rincón
amado. No lo equivoques.

Me he puesto a recordar los días
de verano idos, tu entrar y salir,
poca y harta y pálida por los cuartos.

En esta noche pluviosa,
ya lejos de ambos dos, salto de pronto . . .
Son dos puertas abriéndose cerrándose,
dos puertas que al viento van y vienen
sombra   a   sombra.

XV

In that corner, where we slept together
so many nights, I've now sat down
to wander. The deceased newlyweds' bed   *
was taken out, or who knows what might've happened.

You've come early on other matters,
and now you're not around. It is the corner
where at your side, I read one night,
between your tender points,
a story by Daudet. It is the corner   *
we loved. Don't mistake it.

I've started to remember the days
of summer gone, your entering and leaving,
little and burdened and pale through the rooms.

On this rainy night,
now far from both, I suddenly start . . .
Two doors are opening closing,
two doors that in the wind come and go
shadow   to   shadow.

XVI

    Tengo fe en ser fuerte.
Dame, aire manco, dame ir
galoneándome de ceros a la izquierda.
Y tú, sueño, dame tu diamante implacable,
tu tiempo de deshora.

    Tengo fe en ser fuerte.
Por allí avanza cóncava mujer,
cantidad incolora, cuya
gracia se cierra donde me abro.

    Al aire, fray pasado. Cangrejos, zote!
Avístase la verde bandera presidencial,
arriando las seis banderas restantes,
todas las colgaduras de la vuelta.

    Tengo fe en que soy,
y en que he sido menos.

    Ea! Buen primero!

XVI

I have faith in being strong.
Give me, armless air, give me leave
to galloon myself with zeros on the left.
And you, dream, give me your implacable diamond,
your untimely time.

I have faith in being strong.
Over there advances a concave woman,
a colorless quantity, whose
grace closes where I open.

Into the air, friar past. Crabs, dolt!
The green presidential flag is glimpsed,
lowering the six remaining flags,
all the hangings of the return.

I have faith that I am,
and that I've been less.

Hey! A good start!

*

XVII

Destílase este 2 en una sola tanda,
y entrambos lo apuramos.
Nadie me hubo oído. Estría urente
abracadabra civil.

La mañana no palpa cual la primera,
cual la última piedra ovulandas
a fuerza de secreto. La mañana descalza.
El barro a medias
entre sustancias gris, más y menos.

Caras no saben de la cara, ni de la
marcha a los encuentros.
Y sin hacia cabecee el exergo.
Yerra la punta del afán.

Junio, eres nuestro. Junio, y en tus hombros
me paro a carcajear, secando
mi metro y mis bolsillos
en tus 21 uñas de estación.

Buena! Buena!

XVII

This 2 distills in a single batch,
and together we'll finish it off.
No one'd heard me. Striate urent
civil abracadabra.

The morning doesn't touch like the first,
like the last stone ovulatable
by force of secrecy. The barefoot morning.
The clay halfway
between gray matters, more and less.

Faces do not know of the face, nor of the
walk to the encounters.
And without a toward the exergue may nod.
The tip of fervor wanders.

June, you're ours. June, and on your shoulders
I stand up to guffaw, drying
my meter and my pockets
on your 21 seasonal fingernails.

Good! Good!

*

XVIII

Oh las cuatro paredes de la celda.
Ah las cuatro paredes albicantes
que sin remedio dan al mismo número.

Criadero de nervios, mala brecha,
por sus cuatro rincones cómo arranca
las diarias aherrojadas extremidades.

Amorosa llavera de innumerables llaves,
si estuvieras aquí, si vieras hasta
qué hora son cuatro estas paredes.
Contra ellas seríamos contigo, los dos,
más dos que nunca. Y ni lloraras,
di, libertadora!

Ah las paredes de la celda.
De ellas me duelen entre tanto, más
las dos largas que tienen esta noche
algo de madres que ya muertas
llevan por bromurados declives,
a un niño de la mano cada una.

Y sólo yo me voy quedando,
con la diestra, que hace por ambas manos,
en alto, en busca de terciario brazo
que ha de pupilar, entre mi donde y mi cuando,
esta mayoría inválida de hombre.

XVIII

Oh the four walls of the cell.
Ah the four whitening walls
that inevitably add up to the same number.

Breeding place for nerves, foul breach,
through its four corners how it snatches at
the daily shackled extremities.

Loving keeper of innumerable keys,
if only you were here, if you could only see unto
what hour these walls remain four.
Against them we would be with you, the two of us,
more two than ever. And you wouldn't even cry,
no, liberator?

Ah the walls of the cell.
Meanwhile of those that hurt me, most
the two long ones that tonight are
somehow like mothers now dead
leading a child through
bromidic inclines by the hand.

And only I hang on,
with my right, serving for both hands,
raised, in search of a tertiary arm
to pupilize, between my where and my when,
this invalid coming of age.

XIX

A trastear, Hélpide dulce, escampas,
cómo quedamos de tan quedarnos.

Hoy vienes apenas me he levantado.
El establo está divinamente meado
y excrementado por la vaca inocente
y el inocente asno y el gallo inocente.

Penetra en la maría ecuménica.
Oh sangabriel, haz que conciba el alma,
el sin luz amor, el sin cielo,
lo más piedra, lo más nada,
            hasta la ilusión monarca.

Quemaremos todas las naves!
Quemaremos la última esencia!

Mas si se ha de sufrir de mito a mito,
y a hablarme llegas masticando hielo,
mastiquemos brasas,
ya no hay donde bajar,
ya no hay donde subir.

Se ha puesto el gallo incierto, hombre.

XIX

To rummage, sweet Hélpide, you clear,   *
how we remain from so remaining ourselves.

Today you came when I just got up.
The stable has been divinely pissed
and excreted by the innocent cow
and the innocent ass and the innocent cock.

Penetrate the ecumenical mary.
Oh saintgabriel, make the soul conceive,
the lightless love, the heavenless,
that most stone, that most nothing,
       even the monarch illusion.

We will burn all the bridges!
We will burn the ultimate essence!

But if one is to suffer from myth to myth,
and to speak to me you arrive chewing ice,
let's chew embers,
now there is nowhere to descend,
now there is nowhere to rise.

The cock has become uncertain, man.

XX

Al ras de batiente nata blindada
de piedra ideal. Pues apenas
acerco el 1 al 1 para no caer.

Ese hombre mostachoso. Sol,
herrada su única rueda, quinta y perfecta,
y desde ella para arriba.
Bulla de botones de bragueta,
                        libres,
bulla que reprende A vertical subordinada.
El desagüe jurídico. La chirota grata.

Mas sufro. Allende sufro. Aquende sufro.

Y he aquí se me cae la baba, soy
una bella persona, cuando
el hombre guillermosecundario
puja y suda felicidad
a chorros, al dar lustre al calzado
de su pequeña de tres años.

Engállase el barbado y frota un lado.
La niña en tanto pónese el índice
en la lengua que empieza a deletrear
los enredos de enredos de los enredos,
y unta el otro zapato, a escondidas,
con un poquito de saliba y tierra,
                        pero con un poquito
                        no má-
                        .s.

XX

Flush with the bubbling milk scum buttressed
by ideal stone. Thus barely do
I bring 1 up to 1 so as to not fall.

That mustachioed man. Sun,
its only wheel iron-rimmed, fifth and perfect,
and from it on upward.
Bustle of crotch buttons,
    free,
bustle that reprimands A subordinate vertical.
Juridical drainage. Grateful gullery.   *

But I suffer. Hither I suffer. Thither I suffer.

And behold I am a doting fool, I am
a beautiful person, when
the williamthesecondary man
strains, drip-happy
with sweat, while putting a shine
on his little three-year-old's shoe.

Whiskers puffs himself up and rubs one side.
The girl meanwhile puts her forefinger
on her tongue which starts spelling
the tangles of the tangles of the tangles,
and dabs the other shoe, secretly,
with a bit of siliva and dirt,
    but just a bit,
     no mor-
      .e.

XXI

En un auto arteriado de círculos viciosos,
torna diciembre qué cambiado,
con su oro en desgracia. Quién le viera:
diciembre con sus 31 pieles rotas,
                    el pobre diablo.

Yo le recuerdo. Hubimos de esplendor,
bocas ensortijadas de mal engreimiento,
todas arrastrando recelos infinitos.
Cómo no voy a recordarle
al magro señor Doce.

Yo le recuerdo. Y hoy diciembre torna
qué cambiado, el aliento a infortunio,
helado, moqueando humillación.

Y a la ternurosa avestruz
como que la ha querido, como que la ha adorado.
Pero ella se ha calzado todas sus diferencias.

XXI

In an auto arteried with vicious circles,   *
December returns so changed,
with his gold in disgrace. Who'd believe it:
December with his 31 skins torn,
                    the poor devil.

I remember him. We had to splendor,   *
mouths twisted from being so spoiled,
all of them pulling infinite distrust.
How can I not remember
the gaunt Mr. Twelve.

I remember him. And today December returns
so changed, his breath of misfortune,
frozen, blubbering humiliation.

And to the tenderlovin' ostrich   *
as if he had loved her, as if he had adored her.
But she has put on all his differences.

XXII

Es posible me persigan hasta cuatro
magistrados vuelto. Es posible me juzguen pedro.
¡Cuatro humanidades justas juntas!
Don Juan Jacobo está en hacerio,
y las burlas le tiran de su soledad,
como a un tonto. Bien hecho.

Farol rotoso, el día induce a darle algo,
y pende
a modo de asterisco que se mendiga
a sí propio quizás qué enmendaturas.

Ahora que chirapa tan bonito
en esta paz de una sola línea,
aquí me tienes,
aquí me tienes, de quien yo penda,
para que sacies mis esquinas.
Y si, éstas colmadas,
te derramases de mayor bondad,
sacaré de donde no haya,
forjaré de locura otros posillos,
insaciables ganas
de nivel y amor.

Si pues siempre salimos al encuentro
de cuanto entra por otro lado,
ahora, chirapado eterno y todo,
heme, de quien yo penda,
estoy de filo todavía. Heme!

XXII

Possibly up to four magistrates
pursue me returned. Possibly they'll judge me Peter.
Four joined just humanities!
M. Jean Jacques is in the black books,   *
and the jeers draw him out of his solitude,
like a fool. Well done.

A cracked lantern, the day induces to give it something,
and it hangs
like an asterisk begging
from itself who knows what emendations.

Now that it rainshines so pretty   *
in this peace of a single line,
here you have me,
here you have me, from whom I might hang,
so that you may satiate my corners.
And if, these brimming,
you overflow with greater kindness,
I'll draw from where there may not be,
I'll forge from madness other sumpage   *
insatiable urges
to level and love.

If then we always turn to oppose
whatever enters from the other side,
now, rainshined eternal and all,
here I am, from whom I might hang,
I'm edgewise still. Here I am!

XXIII

Tahona estuosa de aquellos mis bizcochos
pura yema infantil innumerable, madre.

Oh tus cuatro gorgas, asombrosamente
mal plañidas, madre: tus mendigos.
Las dos hermanas últimas, Miguel que ha muerto
y yo arrastrando todavía
una trenza por cada letra del abecedario.

En la sala de arriba nos repartías
de mañana, de tarde, de dual estiba,
aquellas ricas hostias de tiempo, para
que ahora nos sobrasen
cáscaras de relojes en flexión de las 24
en punto parados.

Madre, y ahora! Ahora, en cuál alvéolo
quedaría, en qué retoño capilar,
cierta migaja que hoy se me ata al cuello
y no quiere pasar. Hoy que hasta
tus puros huesos estarán harina
que no habrá en qué amasar
¡tierna dulcera de amor,
hasta en la cruda sombra, hasta en el gran molar
cuya encía late en aquel lácteo hoyuelo
que inadvertido lábrase y pulula ¡tú lo viste tánto!
en las cerradas manos recién nacidas.

Tal la tierra oirá en tu silenciar,
cómo nos van cobrando todos
el alquiler del mundo donde nos dejas
y el valor de aquel pan inacabable.
Y nos lo cobran, cuando, siendo nosotros
pequeños entonces, como tú verías,
no se lo podíamos haber arrebatado
a nadie; cuando tú nos lo diste,
¿di, mamá?

XXIII

Estuous oven of those my sweet rolls
pure infantile innumerable yolk, mother.

Oh your four gorges, astoundingly
mislamented, mother: your beggars.
The two youngest sisters, Miguel who has died
and me still pulling
one braid for each letter in the primer.

In the room upstairs you handed out to us
in the morning, in the evening, from a dual stowage,
those delicious hosts of time, so
that now we'd have more than enough
clock husks in flexion of 24 hours
stopped on the dot.

Mother, and now! Now, in which alveolus
might remain, on what capillary sprout,
a certain crumb that today perplexed in my throat
doesn't want to go down. Today when even
your pure bones might be flour
with nowhere to knead
—tender confectioner of love,
even in raw shade, even in the great molar
whose gum throbs on that lacteal dimple
which unseen builds and abounds—you saw it so often!
in closed hands newborn.

So the earth will hear in your silencing,
how they keep charging us all
rent on the world in which you leave us
and the cost of that interminable bread.
And they charge us for it, when, being only
children then, as you could see,
we couldn't have snatched it
from anyone; when you gave it to us,
no, mama?

XXIV

Al borde de un sepulcro florecido
transcurren dos marías llorando,
llorando a mares.

El ñandú desplumado del recuerdo
alarga su postrera pluma,
y con ella la mano negativa de Pedro
graba en un domingo de ramos
resonancias de exequias y de piedras.

Del borde de un sepulcro removido
se alejan dos marías cantando.

Lunes.

XXIV

By the edge of a flowered tomb
two marys pass weeping,
weeping passionately.

The deplumed nandu of memory
extends its hindmost plume,
and with it Peter's negative hand
engraves on a palm sunday
echoes of exequies and stones.

From the edge of a disturbed tomb
two marys go off singing.

Monday.

XXV

Alfan alfiles a adherirse
a las junturas, al fondo, a los testuces,
al sobrelecho de los numeradores a pie.
Alfiles y cadillos de lupinas parvas.

Al rebufar el socaire de cada caravela
deshilada sin ameracanizar,
ceden las estevas en espasmo de infortunio,
con pulso párvulo mal habituado
a sonarse en el dorso de la muñeca.
Y la más aguda tiplisonancia
se tonsura y apeálase, y largamente
se ennazala hacia carámbanos
de lástima infinita.

Soberbios lomos resoplan
al portar, pendientes de mustios petrales
las escarapelas con sus siete colores
bajo cero, desde las islas guaneras
hasta las islas guaneras.
Tal los escarzos a la intemperie de pobre
fe.
Tal el tiempo de las rondas. Tal el del rodeo
para los planos futuros,
cuando innánima grifalda relata sólo
fallidas callandas cruzadas.

Vienen entonces alfiles a adherirse
hasta en las puertas falsas y en los borradores.

XXV

Thrips uprear to adhere
to joints, to the base, to napes,
to the underface of numerators on foot.
Thrips and thrums from lupine heaps.

As the lee of each caravel, unraveled
without Ameracanizing, snorts loudly,
plow handles give way in a calamitous spasm,
with a puny pulse unfortunately given
to blowing its nose on the back of its wrist.
And the most high-pitched sopraneity
tonsures and hobbles itself, and gradually
ennazals toward icicles
of infinite pity.

Spirited loins wheeze hard
on bearing, dangling from musty breastplates,
cockades with their seven colors
below zero, from the guano islands
to the guano islands.
Thus the dirty honeycombs in the open air of little
faith.
Thus the hour of the rounds. Thus the one with a detour
to future planes,
when the innanimous gerfalcon reports solely
failed silence-deserving crusades.

Then thrips end up adhering
even in trapdoors and in rough drafts.

*

*

*

XXVI

El verano echa nudo a tres años
que, encintados de cárdenas cintas, a todo
      sollozo,
aurigan orinientos índices
de moribundas alejandrías,
de cuzcos moribundos.

Nudo alvino deshecho, una pierna por allí,
más allá todavía la otra,
      desgajadas,
      péndulas.
Deshecho nudo de lácteas glándulas
de la sinamayera,
bueno para alpacas brillantes,
para abrigo de pluma inservible
¡más piernas los brazos que brazos!

Así envérase el fin, como todo,
como polluelo adormido saltón
de la hendida cáscara,
a luz eternamente polla.
Y así, desde el óvalo, con cuatros al hombro,
      ya para qué tristura.

Las uñas aquellas dolían
retesando los propios dedos hospicios.
De entonces crecen ellas para adentro,
      mueren para afuera,
      y al medio ni van ni vienen,
      ni van ni vienen.

Las uñas. Apeona ardiente avestruz coja,
desde perdidos sures,
flecha hasta el estrecho ciego
      de senos aunados.

Al calor de una punta
de pobre sesgo ESFORZADO,

>

XXVI

Summer knots three years
that, beribboned with purplish ribbons, at full
            sob,
chariot the rusty indices   *
of moribund alexandrias,
of cuzcos moribund.

Alvine knot undone, one leg there,
the other even further,
            torn off,
            pendulous.
Undone knot of the sinamayera's   *
lacteal glands,
good for brilliant alpacas,
for a coat of useless feather
—arms more legs than arms!

So the end shows color, like everything,
like a drowsy chick hopping
from the cracked shell,
into light eternally pullet.
And so, after the ovum, shouldering fours,
            now no point in sorrow.

Those fingernails ached
tautening their own asylum fingers.
From then on they grow inward,
            die outward,
            and in between neither come nor go,
            neither come nor go.

The fingernails. An ardent crippled ostrich darts,
from lost sures,   *
an arrow into the blind strait
            of fused breasts.

In the heat of a point
of VIGOROUS humble obliquity,   >

> la griega sota de oros tórnase
morena sota de islas,
cobriza sota de lagos
en frente a moribunda alejandría,
a cuzco moribundo.

> the greek jack of diamonds turns into
a swarthy jack of islands,
a coppery jack of lakes
facing moribund alexandria,
cuzco moribund.

XXVII

Me da miedo ese chorro,
buen recuerdo, señor fuerte, implacable
cruel dulzor. Me da miedo.
Esta casa me da entero bien, entero
lugar para este no saber dónde estar.

No entremos. Me da miedo este favor
de tornar por minutos, por puentes volados.
Yo no avanzo, señor dulce,
recuerdo valeroso, triste
esqueleto cantor.

Qué contenido, el de esta casa encantada,
me da muertes de azogue, y obtura
con plomo mis tomas
a la seca actualidad.

El chorro que no sabe a cómo vamos,
dame miedo, pavor.
Recuerdo valeroso, yo no avanzo.
Rubio y triste esqueleto, silba, silba.

XXVII

That spurt frightens me,
good memory; powerful master, implacable
cruel sweetness. It frightens me.
This house pleases me perfectly, a perfect
spot for this not knowing where to be.

Let's not go in. It frightens me, this permission
to return by the minute, across exploded bridges.
I push no further, sweet master,
courageous memory, sad
songskeleton.

How the content, that of this enchanted house,
gives me quicksilver deaths, and plugs
with lead my outlets
to dry actuality.

The spurt that doesn't know what we're up to,
frightens me, terrifies me.
Courageous memory, I push no further.
Blond and sad skeleton, whistle, whistle.

XXVIII

He almorzado solo ahora, y no he tenido
madre, ni súplica, ni sírvete, ni agua,
ni padre que, en el facundo ofertorio
de los choclos, pregunte para su tardanza
de imagen, por los broches mayores del sonido.

Cómo iba yo a almorzar. Cómo me iba a servir
de tales platos distantes esas cosas,
cuando habráse quebrado el propio hogar,
cuando no asoma ni madre a los labios.
Cómo iba yo a almorzar nonada.

A la mesa de un buen amigo he almorzado
con su padre recién llegado del mundo,
con sus canas tías que hablan
en tordillo retinte de porcelana,
bisbiseando por todos sus viudos alvéolos;
y con cubiertos francos de alegres tiroriros,
porque estánse en su casa. Así, qué gracia!
Y me han dolido los cuchillos
de esta mesa en todo el paladar.

El yantar de estas mesas así, en que se prueba
amor ajeno en vez del propio amor,
torna tierra el bocado que no brinda la
                    MADRE,
hace golpe la dura deglusión; el dulce,
hiel; aceite funéreo, el café.

Cuando ya se ha quebrado el propio hogar,
y el sírvete materno no sale de la
tumba,
la cocina a oscuras, la miseria de amor.

XXVIII

I've had lunch alone now, and without any
mother, or may I have, or help yourself, or water,
or father who, over the eloquent offertory
of ears of corn, asks for his postponed
image, between the greater clasps of sound.

How could I have had lunch. How served myself
these things from such distant plates,
when my own home will have broken up,
when not even mother appears at my lips.
How could I have had a nothing lunch.

At the table of a good friend I've had lunch
with his father just arrived from the world,
with his white-haired aunts who speak
in dapple-gray tinkle of porcelain,
mumbling through all their widow alveoli;
and with generous place settings of lively tootlings,
because they're in their own home. What a snap!
And the knives on this table
have hurt me all over my palate.

Viandry at such tables, where one tastes   *
someone else's love instead of one's own,
turns into earth the mouthful not offered by
        MOTHER,
makes the hard degllusion a blow; the dessert,   *
bile; the coffee, funereal oil.

Now when my own home has broken up,
and the maternal help yourself does not leave the
tomb,
the kitchen in darkness, the misery of love.

XXIX

Zumba el tedio enfrascado
bajo el momento improducido y caña.

Pasa una paralela a
ingrata línea quebrada de felicidad.
Me extraña cada firmeza, junto a esa agua
que se aleja, que ríe acero, caña.

Hilo retemplado, hilo, hilo binómico
¿por dónde romperás, nudo de guerra?

Acoraza este ecuador, Luna.

XXIX

Bottled tedium buzzes
under the moment unproduced and cane.

A parallel turns into
an ungrateful broken line of joy.
Each steadiness surprises me, next to that water
that recedes, that laughs steel, cane.

Retempered thread, thread, binomic thread
—where will you break, knot of war?

Armor-plate this equator, Moon.

XXX

Quemadura del segundo
en toda la tierna carnecilla del deseo,
picadura de ají vagoroso,
a las dos de la tarde inmoral.

Guante de los bordes borde a borde.
Olorosa verdad tocada en vivo, al conectar
la antena del sexo
con lo que estamos siendo sin saberlo.

Lavaza de máxima ablución.
Calderas viajeras
que se chocan y salpican de fresca sombra
unánime, el color, la fracción, la dura vida,
              la dura vida eterna.
No temamos. La muerte es así.

El sexo sangre de la amada que se queja
dulzorada, de portar tánto
por tan punto ridículo.
Y el circuito
entre nuestro pobre día y la noche grande,
a las dos de la tarde inmoral.

XXX

Burn of the second
throughout the tender fleshbud of desire,
sting of vagurant chili   *
at two in the immoral afternoon.

Glove of the edges edge to edge.
Aromatic truth touched to the quick, on connecting
the sexual antenna
to what we are being without knowing it.

Slop of maximum ablution.
Voyaging boilers
that crash and spatter with unanimous fresh
shadow, the color, the fraction, the hard life,
        the hard life eternal.
Let's not be afraid. Death is like that.

Sex blood of the beloved who moans
ensweetened, at bearing so much   *
at such a ludicrous spot.
And the circuit
between our poor day and the great night,
at two in the immoral afternoon.

XXXI

Esperanza plañe entre algodones.

Aristas roncas uniformadas
de amenazas tejidas de esporas magníficas
y con porteros botones innatos.
¿Se luden seis de sol?
Natividad. Cállate, miedo.

Cristiano espero, espero siempre
de hinojos en la piedra circular que está
en las cien esquinas de esta suerte
tan vaga a donde asomo.

Y Dios sobresaltado nos oprime
el pulso, grave, mudo,
y como padre a su pequeña,
        apenas,
pero apenas, entreabre los sangrientos algodones
y entre sus dedos toma a la esperanza.

Señor, lo quiero yo . . .
Y basta!

XXXI

Hope wails cotton coddled.   *

Arris bellings uniformed
in threats woven of magnificent spores
and with inborn doorman buttons.
Are the six rubbing by sun?
Nativity. Be quiet, fear.

A Christian I hope, hope always
kneeling on the circular stone that is
on the hundred corners of this luck
so vague where I appear.

And God startled presses our
pulse, grave, mute,
and like a father to his little girl,
         just,
but just, opens slightly the bloodied cotton
and takes the hope between his fingers.

Lord, I want it . . .
And that's enough!

XXXII

999 calorías
Rumbbb . . . Trrraprrrr rrach . . . chaz
Serpentínica **u** del bizcochero
engirafada al tímpano.

Quién como los hielos. Pero no.
Quién como lo que va ni más ni menos.
Quién como el justo medio.

1,000 calorías.
Azulea y ríe su gran cachaza
el firmamento gringo. Baja
el sol empavado y le alborota los cascos
al más frío.

Remeda al cuco; Roooooooeeeis . . . . . .
tierno autocarril, móvil de sed,
que corre hasta la playa.

Aire, aire! Hielo!
Si al menos el calor (——Mejor
                no digo nada.

Y hasta la misma pluma
con que escribo por último se troncha.

Treinta y tres trillones trescientos treinta
y tres calorías.

XXXII

999 calories.
Roombbb . . . Hulllablll llust . . . ster   *
Serpenteenic **e** of the sweet roll vendor   *
engyrafted to the eardrum.   *

Lucky are the ices. But no.
Lucky that which moves neither more nor less.
Lucky the golden mean.

1,000 calories.
The gringo firmament looks blue
and chuckles up its hocker. The razzed
sun sets and scrambles the brains
even of the coldest.

It mimics the bogeyman: Weeeeeetrozzz . . . . . .
the tender railcar, rolling from thirst,
that runs up to the beach.

Air, air! Ice!
If at least the calor (——Better
        I say nothing.

And even the very pen
with which I write finally cracks up.

Thirty-three trillion three hundred thirty-
three calories.

XXXIII

Si lloviera esta noche, retiraríame
de aquí a mil años.
Mejor a cien no más.
Como si nada hubiese ocurrido, haría
la cuenta de que vengo todavía.

O sin madre, sin amada, sin porfía
de agacharme a aguaitar al fondo, a puro
pulso,
esta noche así, estaría escarmenando
la fibra védica,
la lana védica de mi fin final, hilo
del diantre, traza de haber tenido
por las narices
a dos badajos inacordes de tiempo
                    en una misma campana.

Haga la cuenta de mi vida
o haga la cuenta de no haber aún nacido
no alcanzaré a librarme.

No será lo que aún no haya venido, sino
lo que ha llegado y ya se ha ido,
sino lo que ha llegado y ya se ha ido.

XXXIII

If it should rain tonight, I'd withdraw
from here a thousand years.
Maybe just a hundred.
As if nothing had happened, I'd
imagine that I'm still coming.

Or without mother, without lover, without persistence
in crouching down to spy at the bottom, with my own
bare hands,
on a night like this, I'd be carding
the Vedic fiber,
the Vedic wool of my endmost end, deuce
of a thread, sign of having led
by their noses
two incordant clappers of time   *
           in the same bell.

However I imagine my life
or imagine not having yet been born,
I will not succeed in freeing myself.

It will not be what is yet to come, but
that which came and has already left,
but that which came and has already left.

XXXIV

Se acabó el extraño, con quien, tarde
la noche, regresabas parla y parla.
Ya no habrá quien me aguarde,
dispuesto mi lugar, bueno lo malo.

Se acabó la calurosa tarde;
tu gran bahía y tu clamor, la charla
con tu madre acabada
que nos brindaba un té lleno de tarde.

Se acabó todo al fin: las vacaciones,
tu obediencia de pechos, tu manera
de pedirme que no me vaya fuera.

Y se acabó el diminutivo, para
mi mayoría en el dolor sin fin,
y nuestro haber nacido así sin causa.

XXXIV

That's it for the stranger, with whom, late
at night, you would return in endless chatter.
Now there will be no one waiting for me,
my place set, what is bad good.

That's it for the ardent evening;
your spacious bay and your outcry; the prattle
with your mother ended
who would offer us a tea full of evening.

That's it for everything at last: the holidays,
your breast-fed obedience, your way
of asking me not to go out.

And that's it for the diminutive, for
my coming of age in unending pain,
and our having been born thus for no reason.

XXXV

El encuentro con la amada
tánto alguna vez, es un simple detalle,
casi un programa hípico en violado,
que de tan largo no se puede doblar bien.

El almuerzo con ella que estaría
poniendo el plato que nos gustara ayer
y se repite ahora,
pero con algo más de mostaza;
el tenedor absorto, su doneo radiante
de pistilo en mayo, y su verecundia
de a centavito, por quítame allá esa paja.
Y la cerveza lírica y nerviosa
a la que celan sus dos pezones sin lúpulo,
y que no se debe tomar mucho!

Y los demás encantos de la mesa
que aquella núbil campaña borda
con sus propias baterías germinales
que han operado toda la mañana,
según me consta, a mí,
amoroso notario de sus intimidades,
y con las diez varillas mágicas
de sus dedos pancreáticos.

Mujer que, sin pensar en nada más allá,
suelta el mirlo y se pone a conversarnos
sus palabras tiernas
como lancinantes lechugas recién cortadas.

Otro vaso, y me voy. Y nos marchamos,
ahora sí, a trabajar.

Entre tanto, ella se interna
entre los cortinajes y ¡oh aguja de mis días
desgarrados! se sienta a la orilla
de una costura, a coserme el costado
a su costado,
a pegar el botón de esa camisa,
que se ha vuelto a caer. Pero hase visto!

XXXV

An hour with one's lover
so much once, is a single detail,
nearly a violet racing-form,
so long that it is hard to fold.

Lunch with her who might be
serving the dish that we liked yesterday
and is repeated today,
but with a bit more mustard;
the absorbed fork, her coquettish radiance
of a pistil in May, and her worthless
modesty, for no reason at all.
And the lyric and nervous beer
watched over by her two nipples without hops,
of which you shouldn't drink so much!

And the other bewitchments of the table
which that nubile campaign embroiders
with her own germinal weapons
in operation all morning long,
according to my account, my own,
the amorous notary of her intimacies,
and with the ten magic wands
of her pancreatic fingers.

A woman who without a further thought,
starts chattering and begins to engage us
her words tender
as lancinating freshly cut lettuce.

Another glass, and I'm off. And we leave,
now for sure, to work.

Meanwhile, she disappears
behind the curtains and—oh needle of my ripped
days!—sits down at the edge
of a seam, to sew my side
to her side,
to stick the button on that shirt,
that's fallen off again. Why fancy that!

XXXVI

Pugnamos ensartarnos por un ojo de aguja,
enfrentados, a las ganadas.
Amoniácase casi el cuarto ángulo del círculo.
¡Hembra se continúa el macho, a raíz
de probables senos, y precisamente
a raíz de cuanto no florece.

¿Por ahí estás, Venus de Milo?
Tú manqueas apenas, pululando
entrañada en los brazos plenarios
de la existencia,
de esta existencia que todaviiza
perenne imperfección.
Venus de Milo, cuyo cercenado, increado
brazo revuélvese y trata de encodarse
a través de verdeantes guijarros gagos,
ortivos nautilos, aunes que gatean
recién, vísperas inmortales.
Laceadora de inminencias, laceadora
del paréntesis.

Rehusad, y vosotros, a posar las plantas
en la seguridad dupla de la Armonía.
Rehusad la simetría a buen seguro.
Intervenid en el conflicto
de puntas que se disputan
en la más torionda de las justas
el salto por el ojo de la aguja!

Tal siento ahora al meñique
demás en la siniestra. Lo veo y creo
no debe serme, o por lo menos que está
en sitio donde no debe.
Y me inspira rabia y me azarea
y no hay cómo salir de él, sino haciendo
la cuenta de que hoy es jueves.

¡Ceded al nuevo impar
                    potente de orfandad!

XXXVI

We struggle to thread ourselves through a needle's eye,
face to face, hell-bent on winning.   *
The fourth angle of the circle ammoniafies almost.   *
Female is continued the male, on the basis
of probable breasts, and precisely
on the basis of how much does not flower.

Are you that way, Venus de Milo?
You hardly act crippled, pullulating
enwombed in the plenary arms
of existence,
of this existence that neverthelessez   *
perpetual imperfection.
Venus de Milo, whose cut-off, increate
arm swings round and tries to elbow
across greening stuttering pebbles,
ortive nautili, recently crawling
evens, immortal on the eves of.
Lassoer of imminences, lassoer
of the parenthesis.

Refuse, all of you, to set foot
on the double security of Harmony.
Truly refuse symmetry.
Intervene in the conflict
of points that contend
in the most rutty of jousts
for the leap through the needle's eye!

So now I feel my little finger
in excess on my left. I see it and think
it shouldn't be me, or at least that it's
in a place where it shouldn't be.
And it inspires me with rage and alarms me
and there is no way out of it, except by
imagining that today is Thursday.

Make way for the new odd number
                    potent with orphanhood!

XXXVII

He conocido a una pobre muchacha
a quien conduje hasta la escena.
La madre, sus hermanas qué amables y también
aquel su infortunado "tú no vas a volver".

Como en cierto negocio me iba admirablemente,
me rodeaban de un aire de dinasta florido.
La novia se volvía agua,
y cuán bien me solía llorar
su amor mal aprendido.

Me gustaba su tímida marinera
de humildes aderezos al dar las vueltas,
y cómo su pañuelo trazaba puntos,
tildes, a la melografía de su bailar de juncia.

Y cuando ambos burlamos al párroco,
quebróse mi negocio y el suyo
y la esfera barrida.

XXXVII

I used to know a poor girl
who I brought onto the scene.
The mother, her sisters so nice and likewise
that unfortunate "you're not coming back" of hers.

As I was doing splendidly in a certain business,
they surrounded me with airs of an affluent dynast.
My girlfriend turned to water,
and how well she used to sob for me
her half-learned love.

I enjoyed her bashful marinera   *
of humble adornments circling about,
and how her kerchief would sketch dots,
accents, to the melography of her sedgelike sway.

And when we both sidestepped the priest,
my business failed as did hers
and the sphere swept away.

XXXVIII

Este cristal aguarda ser sorbido
en bruto por boca venidera
sin dientes. No desdentada.
Este cristal es pan no venido todavía.

Hiere cuando lo fuerzan
y ya no tiene cariños animales.
Mas si se le apasiona, se melaría
y tomaría la horma de los sustantivos
que se adjetivan de brindarse.

Quienes lo ven allí triste individuo
incoloro, lo enviarían por amor,
por pasado y a lo más por futuro:
si él no dase por ninguno de sus costados;
si él espera ser sorbido de golpe
y en cuanto transparencia, por boca ve-
nidera que ya no tendrá dientes.

Este cristal ha pasado de animal,
y márchase ahora a formar las izquierdas,
los nuevos Menos.
Déjenlo solo no más.

XXXVIII

This crystal waits to be sipped
in the rough by a future mouth
without teeth. Not toothless.
This crystal is bread yet to come.

It wounds when they force it
and no longer shows animal affection.
But if it gets excited, it could deposit honey
and become a sugar mold for nouns
which adjectivize in self-offerings.

Those who see it there a sad colorless
individual, could dispatch it for love,
through the past and at most into the future:
if it does not surrender any of its sides;
if it waits to be sipped in a gulp
and as transparence, by a future mou-
th at will no longer have teeth.

This crystal has passed from animal,
and now goes off to form lefts,
the new Minuses.
Just leave it alone.

XXXIX

Quién ha encendido fósforo!
Mésome. Sonrío
a columpio por motivo.
Sonrío aún más, si llegan todos
a ver las guías sin color
y a mí siempre en punto. Qué me importa.

Ni ese bueno del Sol que, al morirse de gusto,
lo desposta todo para distribuirlo
entre las sombras, el pródigo,
ni él me esperaría a la otra banda.
Ni los demás que paran solo
entrando y saliendo.

Llama con toque de retina
el gran panadero. Y pagamos en señas
curiosísimas el tibio valor innegable
horneado, trascendiente.
Y tomamos el café, ya tarde,
con deficiente azúcar que ha faltado,
y pan sin mantequilla. Qué se va a hacer.

Pero, eso sí, los aros receñidos, barreados.
La salud va en un pie. De frente: marchen!

XXXIX

Who's lit a match!
I rock. Smile   *
on a swing for a reason.
I smile even more, if all come
to see the colorless guides
and to me always on the dot. What do I care.

Not even that good old Sun that, dying of delight,
butchers everything to distribute it
among the shadows, the prodigal,
not even he would await me on the other shore.
Nor the others who end up solely
entering and leaving.

The great baker calls with a tap
on the retina. And we pay with most
curious signs the warm undeniable baked,
transcendentary price.   *
And we take our coffee, now late,
with deficient sugar that's run out,
and bread without butter. What can one do.

But, of course, the regirded, barred hoops.
Health goes on one foot. Forward: march!

XL

Quién nos hubiera dicho que en domingo
así, sobre arácnidas cuestas
se encabritaría la sombra de puro frontal.
(Un molusco ataca yermos ojos encallados,
a razón de dos o más posibilidades tantálicas
contra medio estertor de sangre remordida).

Entonces, ni el propio revés de la pantalla
deshabitada enjugaría las arterias
trasdoseadas de dobles todavías.
Como si nos hubiesen dejado salir! Como
si no estuviésemos embrazados siempre
a los dos flancos diarios de la fatalidad!

Y cuánto nos habríamos ofendido.
Y aún lo que nos habríamos enojado y peleado
y amistado otra vez
y otra vez.

Quién hubiera pensado en tal domingo,
cuando, a rastras, seis codos lamen
de esta manera, hueras yemas lunesentes.

Habríamos sacado contra él, de bajo
de las dos alas del Amor,
lustrales plumas terceras, puñales,
nuevos pasajes de papel de oriente.
Para hoy que probamos si aún vivimos,
casi un frente no más.

XL

Who would have told us that on a Sunday
like this, over arachnoid slopes
the shadow would rear completely frontal.
(A mollusk is attacking barren foundered eyes,
at the rate of two or more tantalean possibilities
against a half death rattle of remorseful blood).

Then, not even the very back of the uninhabited
screen could wipe dry the arteries
extradosed with double neverthelesses.
As if they would have let us leave! As
if we weren't always clasping shields
at the two daily flanks of fatality!

And how much we might have offended each other.
And yet how much we might have annoyed each other and
fought and made up again
and again.

Who would have thought of such a Sunday,
when, dragging, six elbows are licking
this way, addled Mondayescent yolks.   *

We might have pulled out against it, from under
the two wings of Love,
lustral third feathers, daggers,
new passages on oriental paper.
For today when we test if we even live,
almost a front at the most.

XLI

La Muerte de rodillas mana
su sangre blanca que no es sangre.
Se huele a garantía.
Pero ya me quiero reír.

Murmúrase algo por allí. Callan.
Alguien silba valor de lado,
y hasta se contaría en par
veintitrés costillas que se echan de menos
entre sí, a ambos costados; se contaría
en par también, toda la fila
de trapecios escoltas.

En tanto, el redoblante policial
(otra vez me quiero reír)
se desquita y nos tunde a palos,
dale y dale,
de membrana a membrana,
tas
con
tas.

XLI

Death kneeling spills
its white blood that's not blood.
It smells of guarantee.
But now I want to laugh.

Something is being murmured over there. They quiet.
Someone whistles courage from the side,
and one could even count as a pair
the twenty-three ribs that are missing
among themselves, on both sides; one could also
count as a pair, the entire file
of trapezius escorts.

Meanwhile, the policial snare drummer
(again I want to laugh)
gets even and beats us with a stick,
over and over,
from membrane to membrane,
slap   *
for
swap.

XLII

Esperaos. Ya os voy a narrar
todo. Esperaos sossiegue
este dolor de cabeza. Esperaos.

¿Dónde os habéis dejado vosotros
que no hacéis falta jamás?

Nadie hace falta! Muy bien.

Rosa, entra del último piso.
Estoy niño. Y otra vez rosa:
ni sabes a dónde voy.

¿Aspa la estrella de la muerte?
O son extrañas máquinas cosedoras
dentro del costado izquierdo.
Esperaos otro momento.

No nos ha visto nadie. Pura
búscate el talle.
¡A dónde se han saltado tus ojos!

Penetra reencarnada en los salones
de ponentino cristal. Suena
música exacta casi lástima.

Me siento mejor. Sin fiebre, y ferviente.
Primavera. Perú. Abro los ojos.
Ave! No salgas. Dios, como si sospechase
algún flujo sin reflujo ay.

Paletada facial, resbala el telón
cabe las conchas.

Acrisis. Tilia, acuéstate.

XLII

Wait, all of you. Now I'm going to tell you
everything. All of you wait this headache
may subsside. Wait.

Where have you left yourselves
that you're never needed?

No one's needed! Very good.

Rosa, entering from the top floor.
I feel like a child. And again rosa:
you don't even know where I'm going.

Is the death star reeling?
Or are strange sewing machines
inside the left side.
All of you wait one moment more.

No one has seen us. Pure one
search for your waist.
Where have your eyes popped!

 Enter reincarnated the parlors
of western crystal. Exact
music plays almost a pity.

I feel better. Without fever, and fervent.
Spring. Peru. I open my eyes.
Ave! Don't leave. God, as if suspecting
some ebbless flow ay.

A facial shovelful, the curtain sweeps
nigh to the prompt boxes.

Acrisia. Tilia, go to bed.

XLIII

Quién sabe se va a ti. No le ocultes.
Quién sabe madrugada.
Acaríciale. No le digas nada. Está
duro de lo que se ahuyenta.
Acaríciale. Anda! Cómo le tendrías pena.

Narra que no es posible
todos digan que bueno,
cuando ves que se vuelve y revuelve,
animal que ha aprendido a irse . . . No?
Sí! Acaríciale. No le arguyas.

Quién sabe se va a ti madrugada.
¿Has contado qué poros dan salida solamente,
y cuáles dan entrada?
Acaríciale. Anda! Pero no vaya a saber
que lo haces porque yo te lo ruego.
Anda!

XLIII

Who knows parts toward you. Don't thwart it.
Who knows daybreak.
Caress it. Say nothing to it. It is
hard from what flees from it.
Caress it. Come on! How you could feel for it.

Convey that it is not possible
all will say that it's fine,
when you see that it returns again and again,
an animal that has learned to part . . . No?
Yes! Caress it. Don't hassle it.

Who knows parts toward you daybreak.
Have you counted which pores solely allow exit,
and which ones allow entrance?
Caress it. Come on! But it should not know
you're doing this because I beg you to.
Come on!

XLIV

Este piano viaja para adentro,
viaja a saltos alegres.
Luego medita en ferrado reposo,
clavado con diez horizontes.

Adelanta. Arrástrase bajo túneles,
más allá, bajo túneles de dolor,
bajo vértebras que fugan naturalmente.

Otras veces van sus trompas,
lentas asias amarillas de vivir,
van de eclipse,
y se espulgan pesadillas insectiles,
ya muertas para el trueno, heraldo de los génesis.

Piano oscuro ¿a quién atisbas
con tu sordera que me oye,
con tu mudez que me asorda?

Oh pulso misterioso.

XLIV

This piano travels within,
travels by joyful leaps.
Then meditates in ferrate repose,
nailed with ten horizons.

It advances. Drags itself under tunnels,
beyond, under tunnels of pain,
under vertebrae naturally fugacious.

At times its tubes go,
slow asias yellow with living,
they go in eclipse,
and insectile nightmares delouse,
now dead to thunder, the herald of geneses.

Dark piano, on whom do you spy
with your deafness that hears me,
with your muteness that deafens me?

Oh mysterious pulse.

XLV

Me desvinculo del mar
cuando vienen las aguas a mí.

Salgamos siempre. Saboreemos
la canción estupenda, la canción dicha
por los labios inferiores del deseo.
Oh prodigiosa doncellez.
Pasa la brisa sin sal.

A lo lejos husmeo los tuétanos
oyendo el tanteo profundo, a la caza
de teclas de resaca.

Y si así diéramos las narices
en el absurdo,
nos cubriremos con el oro de no tener nada,
y empollaremos el ala aún no nacida
de la noche, hermana
de esta ala huérfana del día,
que a fuerza de ser una ya no es ala.

XLV

I lose contact with the sea
when the waters come to me.

Let us always depart. Let us savor
the stupendous song, the song expressed
by the lower lips of desire.
Oh prodigious maidenhood.
The saltless breeze passes.

In the distance I scent the pith
listening to the deep sounding, in search
of undertow keys.

And if in this way we bang head-on
into the absurd,
we'll cover ourselves with the gold of having nothing,
and will hatch the yet unborn wing
of night, the sister
of this orphan wing of day,
that by dint of being one no longer is a wing.

XLVI

La tarde cocinera se detiene
ante la mesa donde tú comiste;
y muerta de hambre tu memoria viene
sin probar ni agua, de lo puro triste.

Mas, como siempre, tu humildad se aviene
a que le brinden la bondad más triste.
Y no quieres gustar, que ves quien viene
filialmente a la mesa en que comiste.

La tarde cocinera te suplica
y te llora en su delantal que aún sórdido
nos empieza a querer de oírnos tánto.

Yo hago esfuerzos también; porque no hay
valor para servirse de estas aves.
Ah! qué nos vamos a servir ya nada.

The evening a cook lingers
before the table where you ate;
and starved to death your memory comes
without even sipping, utterly sad.

But, as usual, your humility agrees
to receive the saddest goodness.
And you refuse to taste, seeing who's coming
filially to the table at which you ate.

The evening a cook implores you
and weeps for you in her apron which even if sordid
starts to love us having heard us so much.

I too make an effort; for there is no
courage to help oneself to these birds.
Ah! how can we help ourselves to anything.

XLVII

Ciliado arrecife donde nací,
según refieren cronicones y pliegos
de labios familiares historiados
en segunda gracia.

Ciliado archipiélago, te desislas a fondo,
                            a fondo, archipiélago mío!
Duras todavía las articulaciones
al camino, como cuando nos instan,
y nosotros no cedemos por nada.

Al ver los párpados cerrados,
implumes mayorcitos, devorando azules bombones,
se carcajean pericotes viejos.
Los párpados cerrados, como si, cuando nacemos,
siempre no fuese tiempo todavía.

Se va el altar, el cirio para
que no le pasase nada a mi madre,
y por mí que sería con los años, si Dios
quería, Obispo, Papa, Santo, o talvez
sólo un columnario dolor de cabeza.

Y las manitas que se abarquillan
asiéndose de algo flotante,
a no querer quedarse.
Y siendo ya la 1.

XLVII

Ciliate reef where I was born,
according to the brief chronicles and papers
of family lips historicized
in second grace.

Ciliate archipelago, you deisland thoroughly,   *
                        deeply, my archipelago!
Hard still the articulations
to the road, as when they press us,
and we do not yield at all.

On seeing the closed eyelids,
featherless young men, devouring blue bonbons,
burst out laughing old mice.   *
The closed eyelids, as if, when we are born
it was always not yet time.

The altar goes, the taper so
that nothing happens to my mother,
and so that in time to come I might be, God
willing, a Bishop, a Pope, a Saint, or maybe
only a columnar headache.

And the little hands that curl about
grabbing something floating,
not wanting to be left.
It being already 1 o'clock.

XLVIII

Tengo ahora 70 soles peruanos.
Cojo la penúltima moneda, la que sue-
na 69 veces púnicas.
Y he aquí, al finalizar su rol,
quémase toda y arde llameante,
      llameante,
redonda entre mis tímpanos alucinados.

 Ella, siendo 69, dase contra 70;
luego escala 71, rebota en 72.
Y así se multiplica y espejea impertérrita
en todos los demás piñones.

 Ella, vibrando y forcejeando,
pegando grittttos,
soltando arduos, chisporroteantes silencios,
orinándose de natural grandor,
en unánimes postes surgentes,
acaba por ser todos los guarismos,
     la vida entera.

XLVIII

I now have 70 Peruvian soles.
I clutch the penultimate coin, which sound
s 69 punic times.
And behold, on finalizing its role,
it burns completely and blazes flaming,
                    flaming,
round between my deluded eardrums.

This coin, being 69, bumps into 70;
then scales 71, bounces on 72.
And so it multiplies and shines unshaken
in all its other pinions.

Vibrating and struggling,
letting out yelllls,
unleashing arduous, scintillating silences,
urinating out of natural grandeur,
on unanimous spouting posts,
it ends up being all numbers,
                    the whole of life.

XLIX

Murmurado en inquietud, cruzo,
el traje largo de sentir, los lunes
                de la verdad.
Nadie me busca ni me reconoce,
y hasta yo he olvidado
                de quien seré.

    Cierta guardarropía, sólo ella, nos sabrá
a todos en las blancas hojas
                de las partidas.
Esa guardarropía, ella sola,
al volver de cada facción,
                de cada candelabro
                ciego de nacimiento.

    Tampoco yo descubro a nadie, bajo
este mantillo que iridice los lunes
                de la razón;
y no hago más que sonreír a cada púa
de las verjas, en la loca búsqueda
                del conocido.

    Buena guardarropía, ábreme
                tus blancas hojas:
quiero reconocer siquiera al 1,
quiero el punto de apoyo, quiero
                saber de estar siquiera.

    En los bastidores donde nos vestimos,
no hay, no Hay nadie: hojas tan sólo
                de par en par.
Y siempre los trajes descolgándose
por sí propios, de perchas
como ductores índices grotescos,
y partiendo sin cuerpos, vacantes,
                hasta el matiz prudente
de un gran caldo de alas con causas
y lindes fritas.
Y hasta el hueso!

XLIX

Muttered in anxiety, my suit
long with feeling, I cross the Mondays
                    of truth.
No one looks for me or recognizes me,
and even I have forgotten
                    whose I will be.

A certain wardrobe, only it, will know
all of us in the white leaves
                    of certificates.
That wardrobe, it alone,
on returning from each faction,
                    from each candelabrum
                    blind from birth.

Nor do I discover anyone, under
this muck that irisizes the Mondays
                    of reason;
and I no more than smile at each spike
of the gratings, in the insane search
                    for the known one.

Good wardrobe, open for me
                    your white leaves;
I want to recognize at least the 1,
I want a fulcrum, I want to know about
                    being here at least.

Offstage where we dress,
there's—there Is nobody: only leaves
                    wide open.
And always costumes slipping down,
by themselves, off coat hooks
like grotesque ductor forefingers,
and departing without bodies, vacant,
                    right into the prudent nuance
of a great stock of wings with mashed causes
and fried boundaries.
Right down to the bone!

L

El cancerbero cuatro veces
al día maneja su candado, abriéndonos
cerrándonos los esternones, en guiños
que entendemos perfectamente.

Con los fundillos lelos melancólicos,
amuchachado de trascendental desaliño,
parado, es adorable el pobre viejo.
Chancea con los presos, hasta el tope
los puños en las ingles. Y hasta mojarrilla
les roe algún mendrugo; pero siempre
cumpliendo su deber.

Por entre los barrotes pone el punto
fiscal, inadvertido, izándose en la falangita
del meñique,
a la pista de lo que hablo,
lo que como,
lo que sueño.
Quiere el corvino ya no hayan adentros,
y cómo nos duele esto que quiere el cancerbero.

Por un sistema de relojería, juega
el viejo inminente, pitagórico!
a lo ancho de las aortas. Y sólo
de tarde en noche, con noche
soslaya alguna su excepción de metal.
Pero, naturalmente,
siempre cumpliendo su deber.

L

    Cerberus four times
a day wields his padlock, opening
closing our breastbones, with winks
we understand perfectly.

    With his sad, baggy-assed pants,
boyish in transcendental scruffiness,
standing up, the poor old man is adorable.
He jokes with the prisoners, his fists
jammed into their groins. And even jolly
he gnaws some crust for them; but always
doing his duty.

    In between the bars he pokes the fiscal
point, unnoticed, hoisting on the third phalanx
of his little finger,
on the trail of what I say,
what I eat,
what I dream.
This corvine one doesn't want any inwardness,   *
and how much pain for us is in what Cerberus wants.

    Through a clockwork system, the imminent,
Pythagorean! old man plays
as he pleases with our aortas. And solely
from time to night, at night
he somewhat ignores his exception from metal.
But, naturally,
always doing his duty.

Mentira. Si lo hacía de engaños,
y nada más. Ya está. De otro modo,
también tú vas a ver
cuánto va a dolerme el haber sido así.

Mentira. Calla.
Ya está bien.
Como otras veces tú me haces esto mismo,
por eso yo también he sido así.

A mí, que había tánto atisbado si de veras
llorabas,
ya que otras veces sólo te quedaste
en tus dulces pucheros,
a mí, que ni soñé que los creyeses,
me ganaron tus lágrimas.
Ya está.

Mas ya lo sabes: todo fue mentira.
Y si sigues llorando, bueno, pues!
Otra vez ni he de verte cuando juegues.

LI

Just joking. I was only pretending,
that's all. And that's it. Otherwise,
you're also going to see
how much acting up that way's going to hurt me.

Just joking. Ssh.
So there.
Like before you're doing the same thing to me,
therefore I've also acted up.

Me, always spying to see if you really
were crying,
because at other times you'd go off alone
for your sweet little pouts,
me, who never even dreamed you believed them,
your tears won me over.
S'there.

So now you know: it was all a game.
And if you keep on crying—fine by me!
Next time I won't even watch you when you play.

LII

Y nos levantaremos cuando se nos dé
la gana, aunque mamá toda claror
nos despierte con cantora
y linda cólera materna.
Nosotros reiremos a hurtadillas de esto,
mordiendo el canto de las tibias colchas
de vicuña ¡y no me vayas a hacer cosas!

Los humos de los bohíos ¡ah golfillos
en rama! madrugarían a jugar
a las cometas azulinas, azulantes,
y, apañuscando alfarjes y piedras, nos darían
su estímulo fragante de boñiga,
                             para sacarnos
al aire nene que no conoce aún las letras,
a pelearles los hilos.

Otro día querrás pastorear
entre tus huecos onfalóideos
                        ávidas cavernas,
                  meses nonos,
                        mis telones.
O querrás acompañar a la ancianía
a destapar la toma de un crepúsculo,
para que de día surja
toda el agua que pasa de noche.

Y llegas muriéndote de risa,
y en el almuerzo musical,
cancha reventada, harina con manteca,
con manteca,
le tomas el pelo al peón decúbito
que hoy otra vez olvida dar los buenos días,
esos sus días, buenos con b de baldío,
que insisten en salirle al pobre
por la culata de la v
dentilabial que vela en él.

LII

And we'll get up when we feel
like it, even though mama all luminosity
rouses us with melodious
and charming maternal anger.
We'll laugh in secret about this,
biting the edge of the warm vicuña
quilts—and don't do that to me!

Fumes from thatched huts—ah bunch
of scamps!—rising early to play
with bluish, bluing kites,
and, copping grinders and stones, they'd
pungently incite us with cow dung,
                                to draw us out
into the baby air that doesn't know its letters yet,
to struggle over the strings.

Another time you'll want to pasture
between your omphaloid hollows
                        avid caverns,
                ninth months,
                        my drop curtains.
Or you'll want to accompany the elders
to unplug the tap of a dusk,
so that all the water slipping away by night
surges during the day.

And you arrive dying of laughter,
and at the musical lunch,
popped roasted corn, flour with lard,
with lard,
you tease the decubital peasant
who today once again forgets to say buenos días,
those días of his, buenos with the b of barrens,
that keep backfiring for the poor guy
through the dentilabial
v that holds vigil in him.

LIII

Quién clama las once no son doce!
Como si las hubiesen pujado, se afrontan
de dos en dos las once veces.

Cabezazo brutal. Asoman
las coronas a oír,
pero sin traspasar los eternos
trescientos sesenta grados, asoman
y exploran en balde, dónde ambas manos
ocultan el otro puente que les nace
entre veras y litúrgicas bromas.

Vuelve la frontera a probar
las dos piedras que no alcanzan a ocupar
una misma posada a un mismo tiempo.
La frontera, la ambulante batuta, que sigue
inmutable, igual, sólo
más ella a cada esguince en alto.

Veis lo que es sin poder ser negado,
veis lo que tenemos que aguantar,
mal que nos pese.
¡Cuánto se aceita en codos
que llegan hasta la boca!

LIII

Who cries out eleven o'clock is not twelve!
As if they'd been bid up, the hands confront
two by two eleven times.

    Brutal head butt. Crowns
peer out to hear,
but without violating the eternal
three hundred sixty degrees, they peer out
and explore in vain, where both hands
hide the other bridge born to them
between the truth and liturgical jokes.

    Again the border tests
two stones that don't manage to occupy
the same spot at the same time.
The border, the ambulant baton, that thrusts on
immutable, the same, only
more itself with each swerve on high.

    You see what is powerless to be denied,
you see what we have to endure,
like it or not.
How much is oiled in elbows
that reach to the mouth!

LIV

Forajido tormento, entra, sal
por un mismo forado cuadrangular.
Duda. El balance punza y punza
hasta las cachas.

A veces doyme contra todas las contras,
y por ratos soy el alto más negro de los ápices
en la fatalidad de la Armonía.
Entonces las ojeras se irritan divinamente,
y solloza la sierra del alma,
se violentan oxígenos de buena voluntad,
arde cuanto no arde y hasta
el dolor dobla el pico en risa.

Pero un día no podrás entrar
ni salir, con el puñado de tierra
que te echaré a los ojos, forajido!

LIV

Outcast torment, enter, leave
through a single quadrangular outlet.
Doubt. Oscillation pricks and pricks
up to the hilt.

Sometimes I hit against all the againsts,
and for moments I'm the blackest height of the apexes
in the fatality of Harmony.
Then the circles under my eyes irritate divinely,
and the sierra of my soul sobs,
the oxygens of good will force their way,
what does not burn burns and even
pain doubles up dead with laughter.

But one day you won't be able to enter
or to leave, with the fistful of dirt
I'll fling into your eyes, outcast!

LV

Samain diría el aire es quieto y de una contenida tristeza.

Vallejo dice hoy la Muerte está soldando cada lindero a cada hebra de cabello perdido, desde la cubeta de un frontal, donde hay algas, toronjiles que cantan divinos almácigos en guardia, y versos antisépticos sin dueño.

El miércoles, con uñas destronadas se abre las propias uñas de alcanfor, e instila por polvorientos harneros, ecos, páginas vueltas, sarros,
                    zumbidos de moscas
cuando hay muerto, y pena clara esponjosa y cierta esperanza.

Un enfermo lee La Prensa, como en facistol.
Otro está tendido palpitante, longirrostro,
cerca a estarlo sepulto.
Y yo advierto un hombro está en su sitio
todavía y casi queda listo tras de éste, el otro lado.

Ya la tarde pasó diez y seis veces por el subsuelo empatrullado,
y se está casi ausente
en el número de madera amarilla
de la cama que está desocupada tanto tiempo
                    allá . . . .
                                        enfrente.

LV

Samain would say the air is calm and of a contained sadness. *

Vallejo says today Death is soldering each limit to each strand of lost hair, from the bucket of a frontal, where there is seaweed, lemon balm that sings of divine seedbeds on the alert, and antiseptic verses with no master.

Wednesday, with dethroned fingernails peels back its own nails of camphor, and instills through dusty sieves, echoes, turned pages, incrustations,
                    the buzzings of flies
when there is corpse, and clear spongy suffering and some hope.

A sickman reads La Prensa, as if at a lectern. *
Another is laid out palpitating, longirostrine,
about to be buried.
And I notice a shoulder is still in place
and almost stays ready behind this one, the other side.

The afternoon has now passed sixteen times through the
empatrolled subsoil, *
and is almost absent
in the yellow wood number
on the bed that's been unoccupied for so long
                    over there . . . .
                                        in front.

LVI

Todos los días amanezco a ciegas
a trabajar para vivir; y tomo el desayuno,
sin probar ni gota de él, todas las mañanas.
Sin saber si he logrado, o más nunca,
algo que brinca del sabor
o es sólo corazón y que ya vuelto, lamentará
hasta dónde esto es lo menos.

El niño crecería ahito de felicidad
                    oh albas,
ante el pesar de los padres de no poder dejarnos
de arrancar de sus sueños de amor a este mundo;
ante ellos que, como Dios, de tanto amor
se comprendieron hasta creadores
y nos quisieron hasta hacernos daño.

Flecos de invisible trama,
dientes que huronean desde la neutra emoción,
                    pilares
libres de base y coronación,
en la gran boca que ha perdido el habla.

Fósforo y fósforo en la oscuridad,
lágrima y lágrima en la polvareda.

LVI

Everyday I wake blindly
to work so as to live; and I eat breakfast,
not tasting a bit of it, every morning.
Not knowing if I have achieved, or even more, never,
something that explodes with flavor
or is merely the heart and that returned now, will lament
to what extent this is the least.

A child could grow up bloated with happiness
                    oh dawns,
before the grief of parents unable to avoid
wrenching us from their dreams of love into this world;
before those who, like God, from so much love
understood themselves even as creators
and loved us even to doing us harm.

Fringes of an invisible weft,
teeth that ferret from neuter emotion,
                    pillars
free of base and crown,
in the great mouth that has lost speech.

Match after match in the blackness,
tear after tear in clouds of dust.

LVII

Craterizados los puntos más altos, los puntos
del amor, de ser mayúsculo, bebo, ayuno ab-
sorbo heroína para la pena, para el latido
lacio y contra toda corrección.

¿Puedo decir que nos han traicionado? No.
¿Qué todos fueron buenos? Tampoco. Pero
allí está una buena voluntad, sin duda,
y sobre todo, el ser así.

Y qué quien se ame mucho! Yo me busco
en mi propio designio que debió ser obra
mía, en vano: nada alcanzó a ser libre.

Y sin embargo, quién me empuja.
A que no me atrevo a cerrar la quinta ventana.
Y el papel de amarse y persistir, junto a las
horas y a lo indebido.

Y el éste y el aquél.

LVII

The highest points craterized, the points
of love, of capital being, I drink, I fast, I ab-
sorb heroin for the sorrow, for the languid
throb and against all correction.

Can I say that they've betrayed us? No.
That all were good? Neither. But
good will exists there, no doubt,
and above all, being so.

And so what who loves himself so! I seek myself
in my own design which was to be a work
of mine, in vain: nothing managed to be free.

And yet, who pushes me.
I bet I don't dare shut the fifth window.
And the role of loving oneself and persisting, close to the
hours and to what is undue.

And this and that.

LVIII

En la celda, en lo sólido, también
se acurrucan los rincones.

Arreglo los desnudos que se ajan,
se doblan, se harapan.

Apéome del caballo jadeante, bufando
líneas de bofetadas y de horizontes;
espumoso pie contra tres cascos.
Y le ayudo: Anda, animal!

Se tomaría menos, siempre menos, de lo
que me tocase erogar,
en la celda, en lo líquido.

El compañero de prisión comía el trigo
de las lomas, con mi propia cuchara,
cuando, a la mesa de mis padres, niño,
me quedaba dormido masticando.

Le soplo al otro:
Vuelve, sal por la otra esquina;
apura . . . aprisa, . . . apronta!

E inadvertido aduzco, planeo,
cabe camastro desvencijado, piadoso:
No creas. Aquel médico era un hombre sano.

Ya no reiré cuando mi madre rece
en infancia y en domingo, a las cuatro
de la madrugada, por los caminantes,
encarcelados,
enfermos
y pobres.

En el redil de niños, ya no le asestaré
puñetazos a ninguno de ellos, quien, después,
todavía sangrando, lloraría: El otro sábado
te daré de mi fiambre, pero

>

LVIII

In the cell, in what's solid, the
corners are huddling too.

I straighten up the nudes that're crumpling,
doubling over, stripshredding.   *

I dismount the panting horse, snorting
lines of slaps and horizons;
lathered foot against three hoofs.
And I help him along: Move, animal!

Less could be taken, always less, from what
I'm obliged to distribute,
in the cell, in what's liquid.

The prison mate used to eat wheat
from the hills, with my spoon,
when, at my parents' table, a child,
I'd fall asleep chewing.

I whisper to the other:
Come back, go out by the other corner;
hurry up . . . hurry . . . hasten!

And unnoticed I adduce, I plan,
nigh to the broken-down makeshift bed, pious:
Don't think so. That doctor was a healthy man.

I'll no longer laugh when my mother prays
in childhood and on Sunday, at four o'clock
in the morning, for travelers,
the imprisoned,
the sick
and the poor.

In the sheepfold of children, I'll no longer aim
punches at anyone, who, afterward,
still bleeding, might whimper: Next Saturday
I'll give you some of my lunch meat, but   >

> no me pegues!
Ya no le diré que bueno.

En la celda, en el gas ilimitado
hasta redondearse en la condensación,
¿quién tropieza por afuera?

> don't hit me!
Now I won't tell him OK.

In the cell, in the gas boundless
until balling in condensation,
who's stumbling outside?

LIX

La esfera terrestre del amor
que rezagóse abajo, da vuelta
y vuelta sin parar segundo,
y nosotros estamos condenados a sufrir
como un centro su girar.

Pacífico inmóvil, vidrio, preñado
de todos los posibles.
Andes frío, inhumanable, puro.
Acaso. Acaso.

Gira la esfera en el pedernal del tiempo,
y se afila,
y se afila hasta querer perderse;
gira forjando, ante los desertados flancos,
aquel punto tan espantablemente conocido,
porque él ha gestado, vuelta
y vuelta,
el corralito consabido.

Centrífuga que sí, que sí,
que Sí,
que sí, que sí, que sí, que sí: no!
Y me retiro hasta azular, y retrayéndome
endurezco, hasta apretarme el alma!

LIX

The terrestrial sphere of love
left behind below, goes round
and round not stopping a second,
and we are condemned as a center
to suffer its spinning.

Motionless Pacific, glass, pregnant
with all potentials.
Cold Andes, inhumanable, pure.
Could be. Could be.

The sphere spins on the flint of time,
and sharpens itself
so sharply it wants to disappear;
it spins forging, before deserted flanks,
that point so terrifyingly familiar,
because it has gestated, round
and round,
the celebrated "tender trap."   *

Centrifugally yes, yes,
say Yes,
yes, yes, yes, yes: NO!
And I retreat until I turn blue, and retracting myself
harden, until I clench my soul!

LX

Es de madera mi paciencia,
sorda, vejetal.

Día que has sido puro, niño, inútil,
que naciste desnudo, las leguas
de tu marcha, van corriendo sobre
tus doce extremidades, ese doblez ceñudo
que después deshiláchase
en no se sabe qué últimos pañales.

Constelado de hemisferios de grumo,
bajo eternas américas inéditas, tu gran plumaje,
te partes y me dejas, sin tu emoción ambigua,
sin tu nudo de sueños, domingo.

Y se apolilla mi paciencia,
y me vuelvo a exclamar: ¡Cuándo vendrá
el domingo bocón y mudo del sepulcro;
cuándo vendrá a cargar este sábado
de harapos, esta horrible sutura
del placer que nos engendra sin querer,
y el placer que nos DestieRRa!

LX

Of wood is my patience,
deaf, vegetold.   *

Day you who've been pure, a child, a good-for-nothing,
you were born naked, the leagues
of your march, keep running across
your twelve extremities, that frowning fold
which later frays
into who knows what final diapers.

Constellated of grumose hemispheres,
under eternal unknown americas, your great plumage,
you depart and leave me, without your ambiguous emotion,
without your knot of dreams, Sunday.

And my patience is eaten away,
and I turn to exclaim: When will Sunday,
big-mouthed and mute, emerge from the sepulcher;
when will it come to load up this Saturday
of rags, this horrible suture
of the pleasure that begets us accidentally,
and the pleasure that BaniSHEs us.

LXI

Esta noche desciendo del caballo,
ante la puerta de la casa, donde
me despedí con el cantar del gallo.
Está cerrada y nadie responde.

El poyo en que mamá alumbró
al hermano mayor, para que ensille
lomos que había yo montado en pelo,
por rúas y por cercas, niño aldeano;
el poyo en que dejé que se amarille al sol
mi adolorida infancia . . . ¿Y este duelo
que enmarca la portada?

Dios en la paz foránea,
estornuda, cual llamando también, el bruto;
husmea, golpeando el empedrado. Luego duda,
relincha,
orejea a viva oreja.

Ha de velar papá rezando, y quizás
pensará se me hizo tarde.
Las hermanas, canturreando sus ilusiones
sencillas, bullosas,
en la labor para la fiesta que se acerca,
y ya no falta casi nada.
Espero, espero, el corazón
un huevo en su momento, que se obstruye.

Numerosa familia que dejamos
no ha mucho, hoy nadie en vela, y ni una cera
puso en el ara para que volviéramos.

Llamo de nuevo, y nada.
Callamos y nos ponemos a sollozar, y el animal
relincha, relincha más todavía.

Todos están durmiendo para siempre,
y tan de lo más bien, que por fin
mi caballo acaba fatigado por cabecear
a su vez, y entre sueños, a cada venia, dice
que está bien, que todo está muy bien.

Tonight I get down from my horse,
before the door of the house, where
I said farewell with the cock's crowing.
It is shut and no one responds.

The stone bench on which mama gave birth
to my older brother, so he could saddle
backs I had ridden bare,
through lanes, past hedges, a village boy;
the bench on which I left my heartsick childhood
yellowing in the sun . . . And this mourning
that frames the portal?

God in alien peace,
the beast sneezes, as if calling too;
noses about, prodding the cobbles. Then doubts,
whinnies,
his ears all ears.

Papa must be up praying, and perhaps
he will think I am late.
My sisters, humming their simple,
bubblish illusions,   *
preparing for the approaching holy day,
and now it's almost here.
I wait, I wait, my heart
an egg at its moment, that gets blocked.

Large family that we left
not long ago, no one awake now, and not even a candle
placed on the altar so that we might return.

I call again, and nothing.
We fall silent and begin to sob, and the animal
whinnies, keeps on whinnying.

They're all sleeping forever,
and so nicely, that at last
my horse dead-tired starts nodding
in his turn, and half-asleep, with each pardon, says
it's all right, everything is quite all right.

LXII

Alfombra
Cuando vayas al cuarto que tú sabes,
entra en él, pero entorna con tiento la mampara
que tánto se entreabre,
cása bien los cerrojos, para que ya no puedan
volverse otras espaldas.

Corteza
Y cuando salgas, di que no tardarás
a llamar al canal que nos separa:
fuertemente cojido de un canto de tu suerte,
te soy inseparable,
y me arrastras de borde de tu alma.

Almohada
Y sólo cuando hayamos muerto ¡quién sabe!
Oh nó. Quién sabe!
entonces nos habremos separado.
Mas si, al cambiar el paso, me tocase a mí
la desconocida bandera, te he de esperar allá;
en la confluencia del soplo y el hueso,
como antaño,
como antaño en la esquina de los novios
ponientes de la tierra.

Y desde allí te seguiré a lo largo
de otros mundos, y siquiera podrán
servirte mis nós musgosos y arrecidos,
para que en ellos poses las rodillas
en las siete caídas de esa cuesta infinita,
y así te duelan menos.

LXII

Carpet
Whenever you go to the room that you know,
enter it, but carefully half-close the screen
that so often is slightly open,
tighten the bolts, so that other backs
no longer can turn.

Rind
And when you leave, say that you'll not delay
in calling the canal that separates us:
powerfully kaught on an edge of your fate,
I am to you inseparable,
and you drag me brinkwise with your soul.

Pillow
And only when we have died—who knows!
Oh no. Who knows!
will we then have separated.
But if, on changing step, I am handed
the unknown flag, I will wait for you there,
at the confluence of breath and bone,
as in olden days,
as in olden days on the corner of the western
bride and groom of the earth.

And from there I'll follow you along
other worlds, and at least my mossy
and cold-benumbed nos will serve you,
so you may rest your knees on them
in the seven falls of that infinite slope,
and thus they will hurt you less.

LXIII

Amanece lloviendo. Bien peinada
la mañana chorrea el pelo fino.
Melancolía está amarrada;
y en mal asfaltado oxidente de muebles hindúes,
vira, se asienta apenas el destino.

Cielos de puna descorazonada
por gran amor, los cielos de platino, torvos
de imposible.

Rumia la majada y se subraya
de un relincho andino.

Me acuerdo de mí mismo. Pero bastan
las astas del viento, los timones quietos hasta
hacerse uno,
y el grillo del tedio y el jiboso codo inquebrantable.

Basta la mañana de libres crinejas
de brea preciosa, serrana,
cuando salgo y busco las once
y no son más que las doce deshoras.

LXIII

Day breaks raining. Combed through
morning drips fine hair.
Melancholy is lashed fast;
and on the misasphalted oxident of Hindu furniture,   *
veering, destiny hardly settles.

Skies of the puna disheartened
by great love, platinum skies, torvous
with impossibility.

The flock ruminates and is underscored
by an Andean whinny.

I remember myself. But the staves
of the wind suffice, the rudders so still
they appear one,
and the cricket of tedium and the jibbous unbreakable elbow.

The morning suffices with loose tresses
of precious, sierran tar,
when I go out and look for eleven o'clock
and it is only an untimely twelve.

LXIV

Hitos vagarosos enamoran, desde el minuto montuoso que obstetriza y fécha los amotinados nichos de la atmósfera.

Verde está el corazón de tánto esperar; y en el canal de Panamá ¡hablo con vosotras, mitades, bases, cúspides! retoñan los peldaños, pasos que suben, pasos que baja-
n.
Y yo que pervivo,
y yo que sé plantarme.

Oh valle sin altura madre, donde todo duerme horrible mediatinta, sin ríos frescos, sin entradas de amor. Oh voces y ciudades que pasan cabalgando en un dedo tendido que señala a calva Unidad. Mientras pasan, de mucho en mucho, gañanes de gran costado sabio, detrás de las tres tardas dimensiones.

Hoy   Mañana   Ayer

(No, hombre!)

LXIV

Wandering landmarks enamor, since the mountainous minute that midwives and dates the insurgent niches of the atmosphere.

The heart is green from so much waiting; and in the Panama Canal—I'm speaking to you, middles, bases, cusps!—stairsteps sprout, steps going up, steps going dow-
n.
And I who liveforever,
and I who know to stand firm.

Oh valley without mother height, where everything sleeps a horrible halftone, without refreshing rivers, without beginnings of love. Oh voices and cities that pass galloping on a finger pointed at bald Unity. While, from much to much, farmhands of a great wise lineage pass, behind the three tardy dimensions.

Today   Tomorrow   Yesterday

(No way!)

LXV

Madre, me voy mañana a Santiago,
a mojarme en tu bendición y en tu llanto.
Acomodando estoy mis desengaños y el rosado
de llaga de mis falsos trajines.

Me esperará tu arco de asombro,
las tonsuradas columnas de tus ansias
que se acaban la vida. Me esperará el patio,
el corredor de abajo con sus tondos y repulgos
de fiesta. Me esperará mi sillón ayo,
aquel buen quijarudo trasto de dinástico
cuero, que pára no más rezongando a las nalgas
tataranietas, de correa a correhuela.

Estoy cribando mis cariños más puros.
Estoy ejeando ¿no oyes jadear la sonda?
                    ¿no oyes tascar dianas?
estoy plasmando tu fórmula de amor
para todos los huecos de este suelo.
Oh si se dispusieran los tácitos volantes
para todas las cintas más distantes,
para todas las citas más distintas.

Así, muerta inmortal. Así.
Bajo los dobles arcos de tu sangre, por donde
hay que pasar tan de puntillas, que hasta mi padre
para ir por allí,
humildóse hasta menos de la mitad del hombre,
hasta ser el primer pequeño que tuviste.

Así, muerta inmortal.
Entre la columnata de tus huesos
que no puede caer ni a lloros,
y a cuyo lado ni el Destino pudo entrometer
ni un solo dedo suyo.

Así, muerta inmortal.
Así.

LXV

Mother, tomorrow I am going to Santiago,
to dip myself in your blessing and in your tears.
I am taking on my disillusions and the rosy
sore of my pointless tasks.

Your arch of astonishment will await me,
the tonsured columns of your longings
that exhaust life. The patio will await me,
the downstairs corridor with its tori and festive   *
pie edgings. My tutorial armchair will await me,
that solid bigjawed piece of dynastic
leather, forever grumbling at the great-great-grandchild
rumps, from strap to strand.

I am sifting my purest affections.
I am axling—don't you hear the plummet gasping?   *
              —don't you hear the reveilles champing?   *
I am molding your love formula
for all the hollows of this ground.
Oh if only tacit volantes were available
for all the most distant ribbons,
for all the most diverse appointments.

There, there, immortal dead one. There, there.
Under the double arches of your blood, where
one can only pass on tiptoes, even my father
to go through there,
humblest himself until less than half a man,   *
until being the first child that you had.

There, there, immortal dead one.
In the colonnade of your bones
which not even sobs can topple,
and in whose side not even Destiny could intrude
even one of his fingers.

There, there, immortal dead one.
There, there.

LXVI

Dobla el dos de Noviembre.

Estas sillas son buenas acojidas.
La rama del presentimiento
va, viene, sube, ondea sudorosa,
fatigada en esta sala.
Dobla triste el dos de Noviembre.

Difuntos, qué bajo cortan vuestros dientes
abolidos, repasando ciegos nervios,
sin recordar la dura fibra
que cantores obreros redondos remiendan
con cáñamo inacabable, de innumerables nudos
latientes de encrucijada.

Vosotros, difuntos, de las nítidas rodillas
puras a fuerza de entregaros,
cómo aserráis el otro corazón
con vuestras blancas coronas, ralas
de cordialidad. Sí. Vosotros, difuntos.

Dobla triste el dos de Noviembre.
Y la rama del presentimiento
se la muerde un carro que simplemente
rueda por la calle.

The Second of November tolls.

These chairs are truly welkoming.
The branch of forebodings
goes, comes, rises, undulates, sweaty,
wearied in this sitting room.
Sadly the Second of November tolls.

Souls, how low your abolished teeth
cut, scanning blind nerves,
without recalling the tough fiber
rotund singing workers are mending
with unending hemp, of innumerable knots
throbbing with crossroads.

You, souls, of the limpid knees
pure after so many surrenderings,
how you saw at the other heart
with your white crowns, sparse
in cordiality. Yes. You, souls.

Sadly the Second of November tolls.
And the branch of forebodings is
bitten by a wagon that simply
rolls through the street.

LXVII

Canta cerca el verano, y ambos
diversos erramos, al hombro
recodos, cedros, compases unípedos,
espatarrados en la sola recta inevitable.

Canta el verano, y en aquellas paredes
endulzadas de marzo,
lloriquea, gusanea la arácnida acuarela
              de la melancolía.

Cuadro enmarcado de trisado anélido, cuadro
que faltó en ese sitio para donde
pensamos que vendría el gran espejo ausente.
Amor, éste es el cuadro que faltó.

Mas, para qué me esforzaría
por dorar pajilla para tal encantada aurícula,
si, a espaldas de astros queridos,
se consiente el vacío, a pesar de todo.

Cuánta madre quedábase adentrada
siempre, en tenaz atavío de carbón, cuando
el cuadro faltaba, y para lo que crecería
al pie de ardua quebrada de mujer.

Así yo me decía: Si vendrá aquel espejo
que de tan esperado, ya pasa de cristal.
Me acababa la vida, ¿para qué?
Me acababa la vida, para alzarnos

              sólo de espejo a espejo.

LXVII

Summer sings near, and we both
wander diverse, shouldering
curves, cedars, uniped compasses,
straddling the inevitable single straight line.

Summer sings, and on those sweetened
walls of March,
the arachnoid aquarelle of melancholy
        snivels, swarms.

A picture framed with cracked annelid, a picture
missing from that spot where
we thought the great absent mirror should go.
Love, this is the picture that was missing.

But, why exert myself
to gild straws for such an enchanted auricle,
if, on the back of beloved stars,
emptiness is tolerated, despite everything.

How much mother remained inside
always, in tenacious carbon attire, when
the painting was missing, and for what could grow
at the foot of woman's arduous ravine.

So I told myself: If that mirror ever arrives
having been so awaited, now it's more than glass.
I was wasting my life—to what end?
I was wasting my life, to raise us

        only from mirror to mirror.

LXVIII

Estamos a catorce de Julio.
Son las cinco de la tarde. Llueve en toda
una tercera esquina de papel secante.
Y llueve más de abajo ay para arriba.

Dos lagunas las manos avanzan
de diez en fondo,
desde un martes cenagoso que ha seis días
está en los lagrimales helado.

Se ha degollado una semana
con las más agudas caídas; hase hecho
todo lo que puede hacer miserable genial
en gran taberna sin rieles. Ahora estamos
bien, con esta lluvia que nos lava
y nos alegra y nos hace gracia suave.

Hemos a peso bruto caminado, y, de un solo
                    desafío,
blanqueó nuestra pureza de animales.
Y preguntamos por el eterno amor,
por el encuentro absoluto,
por cuanto pasa de aquí para allá.
Y respondimos desde dónde los míos no son los tuyos
desde qué hora el bordón, al ser portado,
sustenta y no es sustentado. (Neto.)

Y era negro, colgado en un rincón,
sin proferir ni jota, mi paletó,
a
t
o
d
a
s
t
A

LXVIII

It is the Fourteenth of July.
Five in the evening. It's raining all over
a blotting paper's third corner.
And it rains more from below ay upward.

Two lagoons the hands advance
ten abreast,
out of a muddy Tuesday that has for six days
in the lachrymals been frozen.

A week has slashed its throat
with the sharpest falls; everything
haz been done to make the miserable genial
in a big tavern without rails. Now we're
OK, given this rain which washes us
and cheers us up and softly pleases us.

We've walked with our gross weight, and, with a single
                           defiance,
our animal purity whitened.
And we ask for eternal love,
for the absolute encounter,
for what goes on from here to there.
And we responded from where mine are not yours,
from the time that the pilgrim's staff, on being carried,
supports and is not supported. (Net).

And my greatcoat, it was black,
hanging in a corner, not uttering a sound,

a
t
f
u
l
m
a
s
T

                                                                    *

LXIX

Qué nos buscas, oh mar, con tus volúmenes
docentes! Qué inconsolable, qué atroz
estás en la febril solana.

Con tus azadones saltas,
con tus hojas saltas,
hachando, hachando en loco sésamo,
mientras tornan llorando las olas, después
de descalcar los cuatro vientos
y todos los recuerdos, en labiados plateles
de tungsteno, contractos de colmillos
y estáticas eles quelonias.

Filosofía de alas negras que vibran
al medroso temblor de los hombros del día.

El mar, y una edición en pie,
en su única hoja el anverso
de cara al reverso.

LXIX

What in us do you seek, oh sea, with your docent
volumes! How inconsolable, how atrocious
you are in the feverish sunshine.

With your mattocks you leap,
with your leaves you leap,
hacking, hacking in maddened sesame,
while the waves return weeping, after
uncaulking the four winds
and all memories, in labiate platters
of tungsten, contracted by tusks
and static chelonian Ls.

Philosophy of black wings vibrating
to the timid tremor of the shoulders of day.

The sea, and an edition standing,
in its single leaf the recto
facing the verso.

LXX

Todos sonríen del desgaire con que voyme a fondo, celular de comer bien y bien beber.

Los soles andan sin yantar? O hay quien les da granos como a pajarillos? Francamente, yo no sé de esto casi nada.

Oh piedra, almohada bienfaciente al fin. Amémonos los vivos a los vivos, que a las buenas cosas muertas será después. Cuánto tenemos que quererlas y estrecharlas, cuánto. Amemos las actualidades, que siempre no estaremos como estamos. Que interinos Barrancos no hay en los esenciales cementerios.

El porteo va en el alfar, a pico. La jornada nos da en el cogollo, con su docena de escaleras, escaladas, en horizontizante frustración de pies, por pávidas sandalias vacantes.

Y temblamos avanzar el paso, que no sabemos si damos con el péndulo, o ya lo hemos cruzado.

LXX

Everyone smiles at the nonchalance with which I sink to the bottom, cellular from eating right and drinking well.

Do suns move without purveyance? Or is there someone who offers them grain as if to little birds? Frankly, I know almost nothing about this.

Oh stone, benefacient pillow at last. Let us the living love the living, since gratefully dead things will be later. How much we must love them and hug them, how much. Let us love actualities, for we won't always be as we are. For there are no interim Barrancos in the essential cemeteries.   *

The transport takes place on the clay, edgily. The working day hits us in our core, with its dozen stairways, scaled, in a horizonifying frustration of feet, by pavid   *
vacant sandals.

And we tremble to take another step, for we don't know if we bang into the pendulum, or have already crossed it.

LXXI

Serpea el sol en tu mano fresca,
y se derrama cauteloso en tu curiosidad.

Cállate. Nadie sabe que estás en mí,
toda entera. Cállate. No respires. Nadie
sabe mi merienda suculenta de unidad:
legión de oscuridades, amazonas de lloro.

Vanse los carros flajelados por la tarde,
y entre ellos los míos, cara atrás, a las riendas
fatales de tus dedos.
Tus manos y mis manos recíprocas se tienden
polos en guardia, practicando depresiones,
y sienes y costados.

Calla también, crepúsculo futuro,
y recójete a reír en lo íntimo, de este celo
de gallos ajisecos soberbiamente,
soberbiamente ennavajados
de cúpulas, de viudas mitades cerúleas.
Regocíjate, huérfano; bebe tu copa de agua
desde la pulpería de una esquina cualquiera.

LXXI

The sun coils in your fresh hand,
and spreads cautious in your curiosity.

Hush. No one knows that you are in me,
all of you. Hush. Don't breathe. No one
knows of my succulent snack of unity:
the legion of obscurities, the amazons of crying.

The carts leave flajellated by evening,
and among them my own, face backward, toward the fatal
reins of your fingers.
Reciprocal your hands and mine stretch forth
poles on guard, practicing depressions,
and temples and sides.

Hush too, future dusk,
and retyre to laugh intimately, at this rut
of purple-reddish gamecocks magisterially,   *
magisterially fitted out with demilune
spurs, with cerulean widow halves.
Rejoice, orphan; down your shot of water
from the general store on any corner.

LXXII

Lento salón en cono, te cerraron, te cerré,
aunque te quise, tú lo sabes,
y hoy de qué manos penderán tus llaves.

Desde estos muros derribamos los últimos
escasos pabellones que cantaban.
Los verdes han crecido. Veo labriegos trabajando,
los cerros llenos de triunfo.
Y el mes y medio transcurrido alcanza
para una mortaja, hasta demás.

Salón de cuatro entradas y sin una salida,
hoy que has honda murria, te hablo
por tus seis dialectos enteros.
Ya ni he de violentarte a que me seas,
de para nunca; ya no saltaremos
ningún otro portillo querido.

Julio estaba entonces de nueve. Amor
contó en sonido impar. Y la dulzura
dió para toda la mortaja, hasta demás.

LXXII

Slow conical salon, they closed you, I closed you,
although I loved you, as you know,
and from whose hands will your keys dangle today.

From these walls we tore down the last
few pavilions that sang.
The fodder is in leaf. I see peasants working,
the hills filled with triumph.
And the elapsed month and a half is enough
for a shroud, even too much.

Salon with four entrances and without an exit,
since you are deeply morose today, I speak to you
using your six entire dialects.
No longer will I force you to be for me,
for fornever; no longer will we leap
any other beloved wicket.

July was then in its ninth. Love
counted in an uneven sound. And there was enough
sweetness for the whole shroud, even too much.

LXXIII

Ha triunfado otro ay. La verdad está allí.
Y quien tal actúa ¿no va a saber
amaestrar excelentes dijitígrados
para el ratón Sí . . . No . . . ?

Ha triunfado otro ay y contra nadie.
Oh exósmosis de agua químicamente pura.
Ah míos australes. Oh nuestros divinos.
        Tengo pues derecho
a estar verde y contento y peligroso, y a ser
el cincel, miedo del bloque basto y vasto;
a meter la pata y a la risa.

Absurdo, sólo tú eres puro.
Absurdo, este exceso sólo ante ti se
suda de dorado placer.

LXXIII

Another ay has triumphed. The truth is there.
And whoever acts that way, won't he know
how to train excellent dijitigrades
for the mouse Yes . . . No . . . ?

Another ay has triumphed and against no one.
Oh exosmosis of water chemically pure.
Ah my southerns. Oh our divines.
                    I have the right then
to be green and happy and dangerous, and to be
the chisel, what the coarse colossal block fears;
to make a false step and to my laughter.

Absurdity, only you are pure.
Absurdity, only facing you does this ex-
cess sweat golden pleasure.

LXXIV

Hubo un día tan rico el año pasado . . . !
que ya ni sé qué hacer con él.

Severas madres guías al colegio,
asedian las reflexiones, y nosotros enflechamos
la cara apenas. Para ya tarde saber
que en aquello gozna la travesura
y se rompe la sien.
Qué día el del año pasado,
que ya ni sé qué hacer con él,
rota la sien y todo.

Por esto nos separarán,
por eso y para ya no hagamos mal.
Y las reflexiones técnicas aún dicen
¿no las vas a oír?
que dentro de dos gráfilas oscuras y aparte,
por haber sido niños y también
por habernos juntado mucho en la vida,
reclusos para siempre nos irán a encerrar.

Para que te compongas.

LXXIV

One day last year was so rich . . . !
that now I don't know what to do with it.

Stern mother guides to school,
harass our reflections, and we hardly let
fly our faces. Only to later discover
the hanky-panky hinges on that
and breaks our temples.
What a day that was last year,
right now, I don't know what to do with it,
cracked temple and all.

For this they'll separate us,
for that and so we'll no longer act up.
And our technical reflections still say
—aren't you going to hear them?
that inside two dark and apart milled edges,
for having been children and likewise
for having gotten together so much in life,
they're going to lock us up captives forever.

So that you'll compose yourself.

LXXV

Estáis muertos.

Qué extraña manera de estarse muertos. Quienquiera diría no lo estáis. Pero, en verdad, estáis muertos.

Flotáis nadamente detrás de aquesa membrana que, péndula del zenit al nadir, viene y va de crepúsculo a crepúsculo, vibrando ante la sonora caja de una herida que a vosotros no os duele. Os digo, pues, que la vida está en el espejo, y que vosotros sois el original, la muerte.

Mientras la onda va, mientras la onda viene, cuán impunemente se está uno muerto. Sólo cuando las aguas se quebrantan en los bordes enfrentados, y se doblan y doblan, entonces os transfiguráis y creyendo morir, percibís la sexta cuerda que ya no es vuestra.

Estáis muertos, no habiendo antes vivido jamás. Quienquiera diría que, no siendo ahora, en otro tiempo fuisteis. Pero, en verdad, vosotros sois los cadáveres de una vida que nunca fue. Triste destino. El no haber sido sino muertos siempre. El ser hoja seca, sin haber sido verde jamás. Orfandad de orfandades.

Y sinembargo, los muertos no son, no pueden ser cadáveres de una vida que todavía no han vivido. Ellos murieron siempre de vida.

Estáis muertos.

You're all dead.

What a strange way of being dead. Anyone would say you aren't. But, truly, you're all dead.

You float nothingly behind that membrane that, pendant from zenith to nadir, comes and goes from dusk to dusk, vibrating before the sonorous box of a wound that hurts none of you. Verily, I say unto you, then, that life is in the mirror, and that you are the original, death.

While the wave goes, while the wave comes, with what impunity does one stay dead. Only when the waters crash against facing banks, folding and doubling, do you then transfigure yourselves and believing you are dying, perceive the sixth string that no longer is yours.

You're all dead, not having lived before ever. Anyone would say that, not existing now, in another time you might have. But, verily, you are the cadavers of a life that never was. A sad fate. The not having been but always dead. Being a dry leaf, without ever having been green. Orphanhood of orphanhoods.

How ever, the dead are not, cannot be cadavers of a life they have not yet lived. They always died of life.

You're all dead.

LXXVI

De la noche a la mañana voy
sacando lengua a las más mudas equis.

En nombre de esa pura
que sabía mirar hasta ser 2.

En nombre de que la fui extraño,
llave y chapa muy diferentes.

En nombre della que no tuvo voz
ni voto, cuando se dispuso
esta su suerte de hacer.

Ebullición de cuerpos, sinembargo,
aptos; ebullición que siempre
tan sólo estuvo a 99 burbujas.

¡Remates, esposados en naturaleza,
de dos días que no se juntan,
que no se alcanzan jamás.

LXXVI

All night long I keep drawing
language out of the mutest Xs.

In the name of that pure one
who knew how to watch until she was 2.

In the name of that to her I was a stranger,
key and lock very different.

In the name o'her who had no voice
nor vote, when this
her fate to make was determined.

Ebullition of bodies, never the less,
apt; ebullition that always
stayed at just 99 bubbles.

Endings! married in nature,
of two days that do not come together,
that do not reach each other ever.

LXXVII

Graniza tánto, como para que yo recuerde
y acreciente las perlas
que he recogido del hocico mismo
de cada tempestad.

No se vaya a secar esta lluvia.
A menos que me fuese dado
caer ahora para ella, o que me enterrasen
mojado en el agua
que surtiera de todos los fuegos.

¿Hasta dónde me alcanzará esta lluvia?
Temo me quede con algún flanco seco;
temo que ella se vaya, sin haberme probado
en las sequías de increíbles cuerdas vocales,
por las que,
para dar armonía,
hay siempre que subir ¡nunca bajar!
¿No subimos acaso para abajo?

Canta, lluvia, en la costa aún sin mar!

LXXVII

It hails so much, as if to make me recall
and increase the pearls
that I've gathered from the very snout
of every storm.

May this rain not dry up.
Unless I am permitted
to fall now for it, or unless they bury me
drenched in the water
that would surge from all fires.

This rain, how far will it reach me?
I'm afraid I'm left with one flank dry;
afraid that it's ending, without having tested me
in droughts of incredible vocal cords,
by which,
to create harmony,
one must always rise—never descend!
Don't we rise in fact downward?

Sing, rain, on the coast still without sea!

POEMAS HUMANOS (1939)

HUMAN POEMS

I

EL BUEN SENTIDO

—Hay, madre, un sitio en el mundo, que se llama París. Un sitio muy grande y lejano y otra vez grande.

Mi madre me ajusta el cuello del abrigo, no porque empieza a nevar, sino para que empiece a nevar.

La mujer de mi padre está enamorada de mí, viniendo y avanzando de espaldas a mi nacimiento y de pecho a mi muerte. Que soy dos veces suyo: por el adiós y por el regreso. La cierro, al retornar. Por eso me dieran tánto sus ojos, justa de mí, infraganti de mí, aconteciéndose por obras terminadas, por pactos consumados.

Mi madre está confesa de mí, nombrada de mí. ¿Cómo no da otro tanto a mis otros hermanos? A Víctor, por ejemplo, el mayor, que es tan viejo ya, que las gentes dicen: ¡Parece hermano menor de su madre! ¡Fuere porque yo he viajado mucho! ¡Fuere porque yo he vivido más!

Mi madre acuerda carta de principio colorante a mis relatos de regreso. Ante mi vida de regreso, recordando que viajé durante dos corazones por su vientre, se ruboriza y se queda mortalmente lívida, cuando digo, en el tratado del alma: Aquella noche fui dichoso. Pero, más se pone triste; más se pusiera triste.

—Hijo, ¡cómo estás viejo!

Y desfila por el color amarillo a llorar, porque me halla envejecido, en la hoja de espada, en la desembocadura de mi rostro. Llora de mí, se entristece de mí. ¿Qué falta hará mi mocedad, si siempre seré su hijo? ¿Por qué las madres se duelen de hallar envejecidos a sus hijos, si jamás la edad de ellos alcanzará a la de ellas? ¿Y por qué, si los hijos, cuanto más se acaban, más se aproximan a los padres? ¡Mi madre llora porque estoy viejo de mi tiempo y porque nunca llegaré a envejecer del suyo!

Mi adiós partió de un punto de su ser, más externo que el punto de su ser al que retorno. Soy, a causa del excesivo plazo de mi vuelta, más el hombre ante mi madre

I

GOOD SENSE

—There is, mother, a place in the world called Paris. A very big place and far off and once again big.

My mother turns up the collar of my overcoat, not because it is beginning to snow, but so it can begin to snow.

My father's wife is in love with me, coming and advancing backward toward my birth and chestward toward my death. For I am hers twice: by the farewell and by the return. I close her, on coming back. That is why her eyes would have given so much to me, brimming with me, caught red-handed with me, manifesting herself through finished tasks, through consummated pacts.

*

My mother is confessed by me, named by me. Why doesn't she give as much to my other brothers? To Victor, for example, the eldest, who is so old now that people say: He looks like his mother's younger brother! Perhaps because I have traveled so much! Perhaps because I have lived more!

My mother grants a charter of colorful beginnings to my stories of return. Before my life of returnings, remembering that I traveled during two hearts through her womb, she blushes and remains mortally livid when I say, in the treatise of the soul: That night I was happy. But the more she becomes sad; the more she would become sad.

*

—My son, you look so old!

And files along the yellow color to cry, for she finds me aged, in the sword blade, in the outlet of my face. She cries over me, saddens over me. What need will there be for my youth, if I am always to be her son? Why do mothers ache finding their sons old, if the age of the sons never reaches that of their mothers? And why, if the children, the more they are used up, come nearer to their parents? My mother cries because I am old from my time and because never will I grow old from hers!

My farewell set off from a point in her being more external than the point in her being to which I return. I am, because of the excessive time in my return, more the que el hijo ante mi madre. Allí reside el candor que hoy nos alumbra con tres llamas. Le digo entonces hasta que me callo:

—Hay, madre, en el mundo un sitio que se llama París. Un sitio muy grande y muy lejano y otra vez grande.

La mujer de mi padre, al oírme, almuerza y sus ojos mortales descienden suavemente por mis brazos.

[1923]

man before my mother than the child before my mother. There resides the candor   *
which today makes us glow with three flames. I say to her then until I hush:

—There is, mother, in the world, a place called Paris. A very big place and very
far off and once again big.

My father's wife, on hearing me, eats her lunch and her mortal eyes descend
softly down my arms.

LA VIOLENCIA DE LAS HORAS

Todos han muerto.

Murió doña Antonia, la ronca, que hacía pan barato en el burgo.

Murió el cura Santiago, a quien placía le saludasen los jóvenes y las mozas, respondiéndoles a todos, indistintamente: "Buenos días, José! Buenos días, María!"

Murió aquella joven rubia, Carlota, dejando un hijito de meses, que luego también murió, a los ocho días de la madre.

Murió mi tía Albina, que solía cantar tiempos y modos de heredad, en tanto cosía en los corredores, para Isidora, la criada de oficio, la honrosísima mujer.

Murió un viejo tuerto, su nombre no recuerdo, pero dormía al sol de la mañana, sentado ante la puerta del hojalatero de la esquina.

Murió Rayo, el perro de mi altura, herido de un balazo de no se sabe quién.

Murió Lucas, mi cuñado en la paz de las cinturas, de quien me acuerdo cuando llueve y no hay nadie en mi experiencia.

Murió en mi revólver mi madre, en mi puño mi hermana y mi hermano en mi víscera sangrienta, los tres ligados por un género triste de tristeza, en el mes de agosto de años sucesivos.

Murió el músico Méndez, alto y muy borracho, que solfeaba en su clarinete tocatas melancólicas, a cuyo articulado se dormían las gallinas de mi barrio, mucho antes de que el sol se fuese.

Murió mi eternidad y estoy velándola.

[1924]

All are dead.

Doña Antonia died, the hoarse one, who made cheap bread in the hamlet.

The priest Santiago died, who liked to be greeted by the young men and the girls, acknowledging everyone indiscriminately: "Good morning, José! Good morning, María!"

That young blonde, Carlota, died, leaving a very young son, who then also died, eight days after his mother.

My Aunt Albina died, who used to sing inherited tenses and moods, while she sewed in the interior corridors, for Isidora, the maidservant by trade, that most   *
honorable woman.

An old one-eyed died, I don't remember his name, but he slept in the morning sun, seated before the corner tinsmith's door.

Rayo died, the dog as tall as me, shot by lord-knows-who.

Lucas died, my brother-in-law in the peace of the waists, who I remember when it rains and there is no one in my experience.   *

My mother died in my revolver, my sister in my fist and my brother in my bloody viscera, the three bound by a sad kind of sadness, in the month of August of successive years.

The musician Méndez died, tall and very drunk, who used to sol-fa melancholy toccatas on his clarinet, at whose articulation the hens in my neighborhood would go to sleep, long before the sun went down.

My eternity has died and I am waking it.

Las ventanas se han estremecido, elaborando una metafísica del universo. Vidrios han caído. Un enfermo lanza su queja: la mitad por su boca lenguada y sobrante, y toda entera, por el ano de su espalda.

Es el huracán. Un castaño del jardín de las Tullerías habráse abatido, al soplo del viento, que mide ochenta metros por segundo. Capiteles de los barrios antiguos, habrán caído, hendiendo, matando.

¿De qué punto, interrogo, oyendo a ambas riberas de los océanos, de qué punto viene este huracán, tan digno de crédito, tan honrado de deuda, derecho a las ventanas del hospital? ¡Ay! las direcciones inmutables, que oscilan entre el huracán y esta pena directa de toser o defecar! ¡Ay! las direcciones inmutables, que así prenden muerte en las entrañas del hospital y despiertan células clandestinas, a deshora, en los cadáveres.

¿Qué pensaría de sí el enfermo de enfrente, ése que está durmiendo, si hubiera percibido el huracán? El pobre duerme, boca arriba, a la cabeza de su morfina, a los pies de toda su cordura. Un adarme más o menos en la dosis y le llevarán a enterrar, el vientre roto, la boca arriba, sordo al huracán, sordo a su vientre roto, ante el cual suelen los médicos dialogar y cavilar largamente, para, al fin, pronunciar sus llanas palabras de hombres.

La familia rodea al enfermo agrupándose ante sus sienes regresivas, indefensas, sudorosas. Ya no existe hogar sino en torno al velador del pariente enfermo, donde montan guardia impaciente, sus zapatos vacantes, sus cruces de repuesto, sus píldoras de opio. La familia rodea la mesita por espacio de un alto dividendo. Una mujer acomoda en el borde de la mesa, la taza, que casi se ha caído.

Ignoro lo que será del enfermo esta mujer, que le besa y no puede sanarle con el beso, le mira y no puede sanarle con los ojos, le habla y no puede sanarle con el verbo. ¿Es su madre? ¿Y cómo, pues, no puede sanarle? ¿Es su amada? ¿Y cómo, pues, no puede sanarle? ¿Es su hermana? ¿Y cómo, pues, no puede sanarle? ¿Es, simplemente, una mujer? ¿Y cómo, pues, no puede sanarle? Porque esta mujer le ha besado, le ha mirado, le ha hablado y hasta le ha cubierto mejor el cuello al enfermo y ¡cosa verdaderamente asombrosa! no le ha sanado.

El paciente contempla su calzado vacante. Traen queso. Llevan tierra. La muerte se acuesta al pie del lecho, a dormir en sus tranquilas aguas y se duerme. Entonces, los libres pies del hombre enfermo, sin menudencias ni pormenores innecesarios, se estiran en acento circunflejo, y se alejan, en una extensión de dos cuerpos de novios, del corazón.   >

The windows shuddered, elaborating a metaphysic of the universe. Glass fell. A   *
sick man lets loose his complaint: half of it through his tongued and remaining
mouth, and the whole thing, through the anus in his back.

It is the hurricane. A chestnut tree in the Tuileries garden must have been toppled,
by the blowing of the wind which attained eighty meters a second. Capitals in the
old quarters, must have fallen, splitting, killing.

From what point, do I question, listening to both shores of the oceans, from what
point does the hurricane come, so worthy of credit, so honest in debt, straight at
the hospital windows? Ay the immutable directions, that oscillate between the hur-   *
ricane and this direct weariness of coughing or defecating! Ay the immutable direc-
tions, that thus entrap death in the entrails of the hospital and awaken clandestine
cells, untimely, in the cadavers.

What would the sick man in front of me, the one sleeping, think of himself if he
had noticed the hurricane? The poor guy sleeps, on his back, at the head of his
morphine, at the foot of all of his sanity. A half drachm more or less in the dose and
they will carry him away to be buried, belly torn open, mouth up, deaf to the hur-
ricane, deaf to his torn belly, over which the doctors are accustomed to debate and
ponder at great lengths, to finally pronounce their plain and human words.

The family surrounds the sick man clustering before his regressive, defenseless,
sweaty temples. Home no longer exists except around the sick relative's night table,
where his unoccupied shoes, his spare crosses, his opium pills impatiently mount
guard. The family surrounds the small table during a high dividend. At the edge of
the table, a woman sets back the cup, which had almost fallen.

I don't know who this woman could be to this sick man, who kisses him and can-
not heal him with her kiss, who looks at him and cannot heal him with her eyes,
who talks to him and cannot heal him with her word. Is she his mother? And why,
then, can't she heal him? Is she his lover? And why, then, can't she heal him? Is she
his sister? And why, then, can't she heal him? Is she, simply, a woman? And why,
then, can't she heal him? For this woman has kissed him, has watched over him,
has talked to him and has even carefully covered the sick man's neck and—what
is truly astonishing!—she has not healed him.

The patient contemplates his unoccupied shoes. They bring in cheese. They carry
out dirt. Death lies down at the foot of the bed, to sleep in its quiet waters and goes
to sleep. Then, the freed feet of the sick man, without trifles or unnecessary details,
stretch out in a circumflex accent, and pull away, the distance of two sweethearts'
bodies, from his heart.   >

> El cirujano ausculta a los enfermos, horas enteras. Hasta donde sus manos cesan de trabajar y empiezan a jugar, las lleva a tientas, rozando la piel de los pacientes, en tanto sus párpados científicos vibran, tocados por la indocta, por la humana flaqueza del amor. Y he visto a esos enfermos morir precisamente del amor desdoblado del cirujano, de los largos diagnósticos, de las dosis exactas, del riguroso análisis de orinas y excrementos. Se rodeaba de improviso un lecho con un biombo. Médicos y enfermeros cruzaban delante del ausente, pizarra triste y próxima, que un niño llenara de números, en un gran monismo de pálidos miles. Cruzaban así, mirando a los otros, como si más irreparable fuese morir de apendicitis o neumonía, y no morir al sesgo del paso de los hombres.

Sirviendo a la causa de la religión, vuela con éxito esta mosca, a lo largo de la sala. A la hora de la visita de los cirujanos, sus zumbidos no perdonan el pecho, ciertamente, pero desarrollándose luego, se adueñan del aire, para saludar con genio de mudanza, a los que van a morir. Unos enfermos oyen a esa mosca hasta durante el dolor y de ellos depende, por eso, el linaje del disparo, en las noches tremebundas.

¿Cuánto tiempo ha durado la anestesia, que llaman los hombres? ¡Ciencia de Dios, Teodicea! ¡si se me echa a vivir en tales condiciones, anestesiado totalmente, volteada mi sensibilidad para adentro! ¡Ah doctores de las sales, hombres de las esencias, prójimos de las bases! ¡Pido se me deje con mi tumor de conciencia, con mi irritada lepra sensitiva, ocurra lo que ocurra, aunque me muera! Dejadme dolerme, si lo queréis, mas dejadme despierto de sueño, con todo el universo metido, aunque fuese a las malas, en mi temperatura polvorosa.

En el mundo de la salud perfecta, se reirá por esta perspectiva en que padezco; pero, en el mismo plano y cortando la baraja del juego, percute aquí otra risa de contrapunto.

En la casa del dolor, la queja asalta síncopes de gran compositor, golletes de carácter, que nos hacen cosquillas de verdad, atroces, arduas, y, cumpliendo lo prometido, nos hielan de espantosa incertidumbre.

En la casa del dolor, la queja arranca frontera excesiva. No se reconoce en esta queja de dolor, a la propia queja de la dicha en éxtasis, cuando el amor y la carne se eximen de azor y cuando, al regresar, hay discordia bastante para el diálogo.   >

> The surgeon auscultates the sick, for hours on end. Up to the point when his hands quit working, and begin to play, he uses them gropingly, grazing the patients' skin, while his scientific eyebrows vibrate, touched by the untaught, by the human weakness of love. And I have seen these sick die precisely from the unfolded love of the surgeon, from the lengthy diagnoses, from the exact doses, from the rigorous analysis of urine and excrement. A bed was suddenly encircled with a folding screen. Doctors and nurses were crossing in front of the absent one, sad and nearby blackboard, the kind that a child would fill with numbers, in a great monism of pallid thousands. They kept on crossing, looking at each other, as if it were more irreparable to die from appendicitis or pneumonia, than to die aslant the step of men.

Serving the cause of religion, this fly zooms successfully all around the hospital ward. Certainly, during the surgeons' visiting hours, its buzzings surely do not forgive our chests, but expanding then they take over the air, to salute in the spirit of   *
change, those who are about to die. Some of the sick hear this fly even in their pain and on them depends, for this reason, the lineage of the gunshot in the dreadful nights.

How long has anesthesia, as men call it, lasted? Science of God, Theodicy! if I am forced to live under such circumstances, totally anesthetized, my sensitivity turned outside in! Ah doctors of the salts, men of the essences, fellowmen of the bases! I beg to be left with my tumor of consciousness, with my sensitive irritated leprosy, no matter what happens, even if I die! Allow me to feel my pain, if you wish, but leave me awake from sleep, with all the universe embedded, even if by force, in my dusty temperature.

In the world of perfect health, the perspective on which I suffer will be mocked; but, on the same plane and cutting the deck for the game, another laugh percusses here in counterpoint.

In the house of pain, the moans assault the syncopes of a great composer, gullets of character, which make us feel real, arduous, atrocious tickles, and, fulfilling what they promised, freeze us in terrifying uncertainty.

In the house of pain, the moan uproots the excessive frontier. In this moan of pain, one cannot recognize one's own moan of happiness in ecstasy, when love and flesh are free from the goshawk and when, upon coming back, there is enough discord for dialogue.   >

> ¿Dónde está, pues, el otro flanco de esta queja de dolor, si, a estimarla en conjunto, parte ahora del lecho de un hombre?

De la casa del dolor parten quejas tan sordas e inefables y tan colmadas de tanta plenitud que llorar por ellas sería poco, y sería ya mucho sonreír.

Se atumulta la sangre en el termómetro.

¡No es grato morir, señor, si en la vida nada se deja y si en la muerte nada es posible, sino sobre lo que se deja en la vida!
¡No es grato morir, señor, si en la vida nada se deja y si en la muerte nada es posible, sino sobre lo que se deja en la vida!
¡No es grato morir, señor, si en la vida nada se deja y si en la muerte nada es posible, sino sobre lo que pudo dejarse en la vida!

[1924]

Where then is the other flank of this painful moan if, to consider it as a whole, it now comes from the bed of a man?

From the house of pain there come moans so muffled and ineffable and so overflowing with so much fullness that to weep for them would be too little, and yet to smile would be too much.

Blood runs wild in the thermometer.   *

It is not pleasant to die, lord, if one leaves nothing in life and if nothing is possible in death, except for that which is left in life!
It is not pleasant to die, lord, if one leaves nothing in life and if nothing is possible in death, except for that which is left in life!
It is not pleasant to die, lord, if one leaves nothing in life and if nothing is possible in death, except for that which one could have left in life!

EL MOMENTO MÁS GRAVE DE LA VIDA

Un hombre dijo:

—El momento más grave de mi vida estuvo en la batalla del Marne, cuando fui herido en el pecho.

Otro hombre dijo:

—El momento más grave de mi vida, ocurrió en un maremoto de Yokohama, del cual salvé milagrosamente, refugiado bajo el alero de una tienda de lacas.

Y otro hombre dijo:

—El momento más grave de mi vida acontece cuando duermo de día.

Y otro dijo:

—El momento más grave de mi vida ha estado en mi mayor soledad.

Y otro dijo:

—El momento más grave de mi vida fue mi prisión en una cárcel del Perú.

Y otro dijo:

—El momento más grave de mi vida es el haber sorprendido de perfil a mi padre.

Y el último hombre dijo:

—El momento más grave de mi vida no ha llegado todavía.

*

A man said:

—The low point in my life took place in the battle of the Marne, when I was wounded in the chest.

Another man said:

— The low point in my life occurred during a tsunami in Yokohama, from which I was miraculously saved, sheltered under the eaves of a lacquer shop.

And another man said:

— The low point in my life happens when I sleep during the day.

And another said:

— The low point in my life has been during my greatest loneliness.

And another said:

— The low point in my life was my imprisonment in a Peruvian jail.

And another said:

— The low point in my life is having surprised my father in profile.

And the last man said:

— The low point of my life hasn't happened yet.

NÓMINA DE HUESOS

Se pedía a grandes voces:
—Que muestre las dos manos a la vez.
Y esto no fue posible.
—Que, mientras llora, le tomen la medida de sus pasos.
Y esto no fue posible.
—Que piense un pensamiento idéntico, en el tiempo en que un cero permanece inútil.
Y esto no fue posible.
—Que haga una locura.
Y esto no fue posible.
—Que entre él y otro hombre semejante a él, se interponga una muchedumbre de hombres como él.
Y esto no fue posible.
—Que le comparen consigo mismo.
Y esto no fue posible.
—Que le llamen, en fin, por su nombre.
Y esto no fue posible.

[1924/1925]

They demanded shouting:
—Let him show both hands at once.
And this was not possible.
—Let them, while he's crying, take the measure of his steps.
And this was not possible.
—Let him think an identical thought, in the time that a zero remains useless.
And this was not possible.
—Let him do something crazy.
And this was not possible.
—Between him and another man similar to him, let a crowd of men like him
interpose themselves.
And this was not possible.
—Let them compare him with himself.
And this was not possible.
—Let them call him, finally, by his name.
And this was not possible.

Yo no sufro este dolor como César Vallejo. Yo no me duelo ahora como artista, como hombre ni como simple ser vivo siquiera. Yo no sufro este dolor como católico, como mahometano ni como ateo. Hoy sufro solamente. Si no me llamase César Vallejo, también sufriría este mismo dolor. Si no fuese artista, también lo sufriría. Si no fuese hombre ni ser vivo siquiera, también lo sufriría. Si no fuese católico, ateo ni mahometano, también lo sufriría. Hoy sufro desde más abajo. Hoy sufro solamente.

Me duelo ahora sin explicaciones. Mi dolor es tan hondo, que no tuvo ya causa ni carece de causa. ¿Qué sería su causa? ¿Dónde está aquello tan importante, que dejase de ser su causa? Nada es su causa; nada ha podido dejar de ser su causa. ¿A qué ha nacido este dolor, por sí mismo? Mi dolor es del viento del norte y del viento del sur, como esos huevos neutros que algunas aves raras ponen del viento. Si hubiera muerto mi novia, mi dolor sería igual. Si me hubieran cortado el cuello de raíz, mi dolor sería igual. Si la vida fuese, en fin, de otro modo, mi dolor sería igual. Hoy sufro desde más arriba. Hoy sufro solamente.

Miro el dolor del hambriento y veo que su hambre anda tan lejos de mi sufrimiento, que de quedarme ayuno hasta morir, saldría siempre de mi tumba una brizna de yerba al menos. Lo mismo el enamorado. ¡Qué sangre la suya más engendrada, para la mía sin fuente ni consumo!

Yo creía hasta ahora que todas las cosas del universo eran, inevitablemente, padres o hijos. Pero he aquí que mi dolor de hoy no es padre ni es hijo. Le falta espalda para anochecer, tanto como le sobra pecho para amanecer y si lo pusiesen en una estancia obscura, no daría luz y si lo pusiesen en una estancia luminosa, no echaría sombra. Hoy sufro suceda lo que suceda. Hoy sufro solamente.

I AM GOING TO SPEAK OF HOPE

I do not suffer this pain as César Vallejo. I do not ache now as an artist, as a man or even as a simple living being. I do not suffer this pain as a Catholic, as a Mohammedan or as an atheist. Today I simply suffer. If my name were not César Vallejo, I would still suffer this very same pain. If I were not an artist, I would still suffer it. If I were not a man or even a living being, I would still suffer it. If I were not a Catholic, atheist or Muhammadan, I would still suffer it. Today I suffer from further below. Today I simply suffer.

I ache now without any explanation. My pain is so deep, that it never had a cause nor does it lack a cause now. What could have been its cause? Where is that thing so important, that it might stop being its cause? Its cause is nothing; nothing could have stopped being its cause. For what has this pain been born, for itself? My pain is from the north wind and from the south wind, like those neuter eggs certain rare birds lay in the wind. If my bride were dead, my pain would be the same. If they slashed my throat all the way through, my pain would be the same. If life were, in short, different, my pain would be the same. Today I suffer from further above. Today I simply suffer.   *

I look at the hungry man's pain and see that his hunger is so far away from my suffering, that were I to fast unto death, at least a blade of grass would always sprout from my tomb. The same with the lover. How engendered his blood is, in contrast to mine without source or consumption!

I believed until now that all things of the universe were, inevitably, parents or offsprings. But behold that my pain today is neither parent nor offspring. It lacks a back to darken, as well as having too much chest to dawn and if they put it in a dark room, it would not give light and if they put it in a brightly lit room, it would cast no shadow. Today I suffer come what may. Today I simply suffer.   *

¡Señores! Hoy es la primera vez que me doy cuenta de la presencia de la vida. ¡Señores! Ruego a ustedes dejarme libre un momento, para saborear esta emoción formidable, espontánea y reciente de la vida, que hoy, por la primera vez, me extasía y me hace dichoso hasta las lágrimas.

Mi gozo viene de lo inédito de mi emoción. Mi exultación viene de que antes no sentí la presencia de la vida. No la he sentido nunca. Miente quien diga que la he sentido. Miente y su mentira me hiere a tal punto que me haría desgraciado. Mi gozo viene de mi fe en este hallazgo personal de la vida, y nadie puede ir contra esta fe. Al que fuera, se le caería la lengua, se le caerían los huesos y correría el peligro de recoger otros, ajenos, para mantenerse de pie ante mis ojos.

Nunca, sino ahora, ha habido vida. Nunca, sino ahora, han pasado gentes. Nunca, sino ahora, ha habido casas y avenidas, aire y horizonte. Si viniese ahora mi amigo Peyriet, le diría que yo no le conozco y que debemos empezar de nuevo. ¿Cuándo, en efecto, le he conocido a mi amigo Peyriet? Hoy sería la primera vez que nos conocemos. Le diría que se vaya y regrese y entre a verme, como si no me conociera, es decir, por la primera vez.

Ahora yo no conozco a nadie ni nada. Me advierto en un país extraño, en el que todo cobra relieve de nacimiento, luz de epifanía inmarcesible. No, señor. No hable usted a ese caballero. Usted no lo conoce y le sorprendería tan inopinada parla. No ponga usted el pie sobre esa piedrecilla: quién sabe no es piedra y vaya usted a dar en el vacío. Sea usted precavido, puesto que estamos en un mundo absolutamente inconocido.

¡Cuán poco tiempo he vivido! Mi nacimiento es tan reciente, que no hay unidad de medida para contar mi edad. ¡Si acabo de nacer! ¡Si aún no he vivido todavía! Señores: soy tan pequeñito, que el día apenas cabe en mí.

Nunca, sino ahora, oí el estruendo de los carros, que cargan piedras para una gran construcción del boulevard Haussmann. Nunca, sino ahora, avancé paralelamente a la primavera, diciéndola: "Si la muerte hubiera sido otra . . ." Nunca, sino ahora, vi la luz áurea del sol sobre las cúpulas del Sacré-Coeur. Nunca, sino ahora, se me acercó un niño y me miró hondamente con su boca. Nunca, sino ahora, supe que existía una puerta, otra puerta y el canto cordial de las distancias.

¡Dejadme! La vida me ha dado ahora en toda mi muerte.

[1926]

DISCOVERY OF LIFE

Gentlemen! Today is the first time that I become aware of the presence of life. Gentlemen! I beg you to leave me alone for a moment, so I can savor this formidable, spontaneous, and recent emotion of life, which today, for the first time, enraptures me and makes me happy to the point of tears.   *

My joy comes from the unprecedented nature of my emotion. My exultation comes from the fact that before I did not feel the presence of life. I have never felt it. If anyone says that I have felt it he is lying. He is lying and his lie hurts me to such a degree that it would make me miserable. My joy comes from my faith in this personal discovery of life, and no one can go against this faith. If anyone would try, his tongue would fall out, his bones would fall out and he would risk picking up somebody else's, not his own, to keep standing before my eyes.

Never, except now, has there been life. Never, except now, have people walked by. Never, except now, have there been houses and avenues, air and horizons. If my friend Peyriet came over right now, I would tell him that I do not know him and that we must begin anew. When, in fact, have I known my friend Peyriet? Today would be the first time that we have known each other. I would tell him to go away and come back and call on me, as if he did not know me, that is, for the first time.

Now I do not know anyone or anything. I notice I am in a strange land where everything acquires a newborn eminence, a light of unfading epiphany. No, sir. Do not speak to that gentleman. You do not know him and such unexpected chatter would surprise him. Do not put your foot on that little stone: who knows it is not a stone and you will plunge into the void. Be cautious, for we are in a totally aknown world.   *

What a short time I have lived! My birth is so recent, there is no unit of measure to count my age. I have just been born! I have not even lived yet! Gentlemen: I am so tiny, that the day hardly fits inside me.

Never, except now, did I hear the racket of the carts, that carry stones for a great construction on boulevard Haussmann. Never, except now, did I advance parallel to the spring, saying to it: "If death had been another . . ." Never, except now, did I see the golden light of the sun on the cupolas of Sacré-Coeur. Never, except now, did a child approach me and look at me deeply with his mouth. Never, except now, did I know a door existed, another door and the cordial song of the distances.

Leave me alone! Life has now struck me in all my death.   *

Una mujer de senos apacibles, ante los que la lengua de la vaca resulta una glándula violenta. Un hombre de templanza, mandibular de genio, apto para marchar de a dos con los goznes de los cofres. Un niño está al lado del hombre, llevando por el revés, el derecho animal de la pareja.

¡Oh la palabra del hombre, libre de adjetivos y de adverbios, que la mujer declina en su único caso de mujer, aun entre las mil voces de la Capilla Sixtina! ¡Oh la falda de ella, en el punto maternal donde pone el pequeño las manos y juega a los pliegues, haciendo a veces agrandar las pupilas de la madre, como en las sanciones de los confesionarios!

Yo tengo mucho gusto de ver así al Padre, al Hijo y al Espíritusanto, con todos los emblemas e insignias de sus cargos.

A woman with peaceful breasts, before which a cow's tongue becomes a violent gland. A temperate man, mandibular in character, able to march side by side with the coffer's hinges. A child is at the side of the man, carrying in reverse, the animal rights of the couple.

Oh the word of man, free from adjectives and adverbs, which woman declines in her unique female case, even among the thousand voices of the Sistine Chapel! Oh that skirt of hers, at the maternal point where the child puts his hands and plays with the pleats, sometimes making his mother's pupils dilate, as in the sanctions of the confessionals!

I derive a great pleasure from seeing the Father, the Son and the Holyghost like this, with all the emblems and insignias of their offices.

Cesa el anhelo, rabo al aire. De súbito, la vida se amputa, en seco. Mi propia sangre me salpica en líneas femeninas, y hasta la misma urbe sale a ver esto que se pára de improviso.

—Qué ocurre aquí, en este hijo del hombre?—clama la urbe, y en una sala del Louvre, un niño llora de terror a la vista del retrato de otro niño.

—Qué ocurre aquí, en este hijo de mujer?—clama la urbe, y a una estatua del siglo de los Ludovico, le nace una brizna de yerba en plena palma de la mano.

Cesa el anhelo, a la altura de la mano enarbolada. Y yo me escondo detrás de mí mismo, a aguaitarme si paso por lo bajo o merodeo en alto.

Longing ceases, tail in the air. Suddenly, life amputates itself, abruptly. My own blood splashes me in feminine lines, and even the city itself comes out to see what it is that stops unexpectedly.

—What's going on here, in this son of man?—the city shouts, and in a hall of the Louvre, a child cries in terror at the sight of the portrait of another child.

—What's going on here, in this son of woman?—the city shouts, and in a statue from the Ludwigian century, a blade of grass is born right in the palm of its hand.

Longing ceases, at the height of the raised hand. And I hide behind myself, to watch if I slip through below or maraud on high.

—No vive ya nadie en la casa—me dices—; todos se han ido. La sala, el dormitorio, el patio, yacen despoblados. Nadie ya queda, pues que todos han partido.

Y yo te digo: Cuando alguien se va, alguien queda. El punto por donde pasó un hombre, ya no está solo. Unicamente está solo, de soledad humana, el lugar por donde ningún hombre ha pasado. Las casas nuevas están más muertas que las viejas, porque sus muros son de piedra o de acero, pero no de hombres. Una casa viene al mundo, no cuando la acaban de edificar, sino cuando empiezan a habitarla. Una casa vive únicamente de hombres, como una tumba. De aquí esa irresistible semejanza que hay entre una casa y una tumba. Sólo que la casa se nutre de la vida del hombre, mientras que la tumba se nutre de la muerte del hombre. Por eso la primera está de pie, mientras que la segunda está tendida.

Todos han partido de la casa, en realidad, pero todos se han quedado en verdad. Y no es el recuerdo de ellos lo que queda, sino ellos mismos. Y no es tampoco que ellos queden en la casa, sino que continúan por la casa. Las funciones y los actos se van de la casa en tren o en avión o a caballo, a pie o arrastrándose. Lo que continúa en la casa es el órgano, el agente en gerundio y en círculo. Los pasos se han ido, los besos, los perdones, los crímenes. Lo que continúa en la casa es el pie, los labios, los ojos, el corazón. Las negaciones y las afirmaciones, el bien y el mal, se han dispersado. Lo que continúa en la casa, es el sujeto del acto.

—No one lives in the house anymore—you tell me—; all have gone. The living room, the bedroom, the patio, are deserted. No one remains any longer, since everyone has departed.

And I say to you: When someone leaves, someone remains. The point through which a man passed, is no longer empty. The only place that is empty, with human solitude, is that through which no man has passed. New houses are deader than old ones, for their walls are of stone or steel, but not of men. A house comes into the world, not when people finish building it, but when they begin to inhabit it. A house lives only off men, like a tomb. That is why there is an irresistible resemblance between a house and a tomb. Except that the house is nourished by the life of man, while the tomb is nourished by the death of man. That is why the first is standing, while the second is laid out.

Everyone has departed from the house, in reality, but all have remained in truth. And it is not their memory that remains, but they themselves. Nor is it that they remain in the house, but that they continue about the house. Functions and acts leave the house by train or by plane or on horseback, walking or crawling. What continues in the house is the organ, the agent in gerund and in circle. The steps have left, the kisses, the pardons, the crimes. What continues in the house are the foot, the lips, the eyes, the heart. Negations and affirmations, good and evil, have dispersed. What continues in the house, is the subject of the act.

Existe un mutilado, no de un combate sino de un abrazo, no de la guerra sino de la paz. Perdió el rostro en el amor y no en el odio. Lo perdió en el curso normal de la vida y no en un accidente. Lo perdió en el orden de la naturaleza y no en el desorden de los hombres. El coronel Piccot, Presidente de "Les Gueules Cassées", lleva la boca comida por la pólvora de 1914. Este mutilado que conozco, lleva el rostro comido por el aire inmortal e inmemorial.

Rostro muerto sobre el tronco vivo. Rostro yerto y pegado con clavos a la cabeza viva. Este rostro resulta ser el dorso del cráneo, el cráneo del cráneo. Vi una vez un árbol darme la espalda y vi otra vez un camino que me daba la espalda. Un árbol de espaldas sólo crece en los lugares donde nunca nació ni murió nadie. Un camino de espaldas sólo avanza por los lugares donde ha habido todas las muertes y ningún nacimiento. El mutilado de la paz y del amor, del abrazo y del orden y que lleva el rostro muerto sobre el tronco vivo, nació a la sombra de un árbol de espaldas y su existencia transcurre a lo largo de un camino de espaldas.

Como el rostro está yerto y difunto, toda la vida psíquica, toda la expresión animal de este hombre, se refugia, para traducirse al exterior, en el peludo cráneo, en el tórax y en las extremidades. Los impulsos de su ser profundo, al salir, retroceden del rostro y la respiración, el olfato, la vista, el oído, la palabra, el resplandor humano de su ser, funcionan y se expresan por el pecho, por los hombros, por el cabello, por las costillas, por los brazos y las piernas y los pies.

Mutilado del rostro, tapado del rostro, cerrado del rostro, este hombre, no obstante, está entero y nada le hace falta. No tiene ojos y ve y llora. No tiene narices y huele y respira. No tiene oídos y escucha. No tiene boca y habla y sonríe. No tiene frente y piensa y se sume en sí mismo. No tiene mentón y quiere y subsiste. Jesús conocía al mutilado de la función, que tenía ojos y no veía y tenía orejas y no oía. Yo conozco al mutilado del órgano, que ve sin ojos y oye sin orejas.

There is a man mutilated not from combat but from an embrace, not from war but from peace. He lost his face through love and not through hate. He lost it in the normal course of life and not in an accident. He lost it in the order of nature and not in the disorder of men. Colonel Piccot, President of "Les Gueules Cassées," lives with his mouth eaten away by the gunpowder of 1914. This mutilated man I know, has his face eaten away by the immortal and immemorial air.

A dead face above the living torso. A stiff face fastened with nails to the living head. This face turns out to be the backside of the skull, the skull of the skull. I once saw a tree turn its back on me and another time I saw a road that turned its back on me. A tree turned backward only grows where no one ever died or was born. A road turned backward only advances through places where there have been all deaths and no birth. The man mutilated by peace and by love, by an embrace and by order and who lives with a dead face above his living trunk, was born in the shadow of a tree turned backward and his existence takes place along a road turned backward.

As his face is stiff and dead, all the psychic life, all the animal expression of this man, takes refuge, to translate itself outwardly, in his hairy skull, in his thorax and in his extremities. Impulses from his deep being, on going out, back away from his face and breathing, his sense of smell, his sight, his hearing, his speech, the human radiance of his being, function and are expressed through his chest, through his shoulders, through his hair, through his ribs, through his arms and his legs and his feet.

Face mutilated, face covered, face closed, this man, nevertheless, is whole and lacks nothing. He has no eyes and he sees and cries. He has no nose and he smells and breathes. He has no ears and he listens. He has no mouth and he talks and smiles. No forehead and he thinks and withdraws into himself. No chin and he desires and subsists. Jesus knew the man whose mutilation left him functionless, who had eyes and could not see and had ears and could not hear. I know the man whose mutilation left him organless, who sees without eyes and hears without ears.

LA NECESIDAD DE MORIR

París, 1926.

Señores:

Tengo el gusto de deciros, por medio de estas líneas, que la muerte, más que un castigo, pena o limitación impuesta al hombre, es una necesidad, la más imperiosa e irrevocable de todas las necesidades humanas. La necesidad que tenemos de morir, sobrepuja a la necesidad de nacer y vivir. Podríamos quedarnos sin nacer pero no podríamos quedarnos sin morir. Nadie ha dicho hasta ahora: "Tengo necesidad de nacer". En cambio, sí se suele decir: "Tengo necesidad de morir". Por otro lado, nacer es, a lo que parece, muy fácil, pues nadie ha dicho nunca que le haya sido muy difícil y que le haya costado esfuerzo venir a este mundo; mientras que morir es más difícil de lo que se cree. Esto prueba que la necesidad de morir es enorme e irresistible, pues sabido es que cuanto más difícilmente se satisface una necesidad, ésta se hace más grande. Se anhela más lo que es menos accesible.

Si a una persona le escribieran diciéndole siempre que su madre sigue gozando de buena salud, acabaría al fin por sentir una misteriosa inquietud, no precisamente sospechando que se le engaña y que, posiblemente su madre debe haber muerto, sino bajo el peso de la necesidad, sutil y tácita, que le acomete, de que su madre debe morir. Esa persona hará sus cálculos respectivos y pensará para sus adentros: "No puede ser. Es imposible que mi madre no haya muerto hasta ahora". Sentirá, al fin, una necesidad angustiosa de saber que su madre ha muerto. De otra manera, acabará por darlo por hecho.

Una antigua leyenda del Islam cuenta que un hijo llegó a vivir trescientos años, en medio de una raza en que la vida acababa a lo sumo a los cincuenta años. En el decurso de un exilio, el hijo, a los doscientos años de edad, preguntó por su padre y le dijeron: "Está bueno". Pero, cuando cincuenta años más tarde, volvió a su pueblo y supo que el autor de sus días había muerto hacía doscientos años, se mostró muy tranquilo, murmurando: "Ya lo sabía yo desde hace muchos años". Naturalmente. La necesidad de la muerte de su padre, había sido en él, a su hora, irrevocable, fatal y se había cumplido fatalmente y también a su hora, en la realidad.

Rubén Darío ha dicho que la pena de los dioses es no alcanzar la muerte. En cuanto a los hombres, si éstos, desde que tienen conciencia, *estuviesen seguros* de alcanzar la muerte, serían dichosos para siempre. Pero por desgracia, los hombres *no están nunca seguros* de morir: sienten el afán obscuro y el ansia de morir, *mas dudan siempre* de que morirán. La pena de los hombres, diremos nosotros, es no estar nunca ciertos de la muerte.

THE NEED TO DIE

Gentlemen:

It pleases me to inform you, by means of these lines, that death, more than a punishment, penalty or limitation imposed on man, is a necessity, the most imperative and irrevocable of all human necessities. Our need to die surpasses our need to be born and to live. We could do without being born but we could not do without dying. Until now no one has said: "I have a need to be born." However, one frequently does say: "I have a need to die." On the other hand, to be born is, so it seems, very easy, since no one has ever said that it was very difficult for him and that he put forth a lot of effort to enter this world; whereas dying is more difficult than one thinks. This proves that the need to die is enormous and irresistible, since it is well known that the more difficult it is to satisfy a necessity the larger it looms. One yearns more for that which is less accessible.

If someone were to write to another always telling him that his mother continued to enjoy good health, the recipient would end up feeling a mysterious discomfort, not really suspecting that he was being lied to and that, most likely his mother must have died, but under the weight of the subtle and tacit need overwhelming him that his mother ought to die. This person would make the respective calculations and think to himself: "This cannot be. It is impossible that my mother is not already dead." In the end, he will feel an anguished need to know that his mother has died. Otherwise, he will end up accepting it as a fact.

An ancient Islamic legend recounts that a son reached his three-hundredth year among a people for whom life ended at the most at fifty. While in exile, the son, in his two-hundredth year, asked about his father and was told: "He's in good health." But when, fifty years later, he returned to his town and learned that the author of his days had died two hundred years ago, he seemed tranquil, murmuring: "I have known this for many years." Of course. The son's need for his father to die had been for him, in its hour, irrevocable, fatal and had been fatally fulfilled also in its hour, in reality.

Rubén Darío has said that the sorrow of the gods lies in not reaching death. As for men, if, from the moment they are conscious, *they could be sure* of reaching death, they would be happy forever. But unfortunately, *men are never sure* of dying: they feel an obscure desire and a yearning to die, *but they always doubt* that they will die. The sorrow of men, we declare, lies in never being certain of death.

ME ESTOY RIENDO

Un guijarro, uno solo, el más bajo de todos,
controla
a todo el médano aciago y faraónico.

El aire adquiere tensión de recuerdo
                                    y de anhelo,
y bajo el sol se calla
hasta exigir el cuello a las pirámides.

Sed. Hidratada melancolía de la tribu errabunda,
gota
a
gota,
del siglo al minuto.

Son tres Treses paralelos,
barbados de barba inmemorial,
en marcha   3   3   3

Es el tiempo este anuncio de gran zapatería,
es el tiempo, que marcha descalzo
de la muerte   hacia   la muerte.

    1926

I AM LAUGHING

A pebble, one only, the lowest of all,
controls
the whole ill-fated Pharaonic sandbank.

The air acquires tension of memory
                              and of yearning,
and under the sun it keeps quiet
until demanding the pyramids' necks.

Thirst. Hydrated melancholy of the wandering tribe,
drop
by
drop,
from the century to the minute.

They are three parallel Threes,
bearded with immemorial beard,
marching   3   3   3

It is time this advertisement of a great shoe store,
it is time, that marches barefoot
from death   toward   death.

He aquí que hoy saludo, me pongo el cuello y vivo,
superficial de pasos insondable de plantas.
Tal me recibo de hombre, tal más bien me despido
y de cada hora mía retoña una distanciA.

Queréis más? encantado.
Políticamente, mi palabra
emite cargos contra mi labio inferior
y económicamente,
cuando doy la espalda a Oriente,
distingo en dignidad de muerte a mis visitas.

Desde ttttales códigos regulares saludo
al soldado desconocido
al verso perseguido por la tinta fatal
y al saurio que Equidista diariamente
de su vida y su muerte,
como quien no hace la cosa.

El tiempo tiene hun miedo ciempiés a los relojes.

*

(Los lectores pueden poner el título
que quieran a este poema)

1926

Behold that today I salute, I adjust my collar and live,
superficial in steps fathomless in soles.
So do I graduate as a man, or rather so do I take leave
and from each of my hours sprouts a distAnce.   *

You want more? with pleasure.
Politically, my word
spreads charges against my lower lip
and economically,
when I turn my back to the Orient,
I distinguish my visitors with mortal dignity.

From ssssuch regular codes I salute   *
the unknown soldier
the poetic line pursued by fatal ink
and the saurian that Equidists daily
from its life and its death
as if it were something else.

Time has uh centipede fear of clocks.

                        *

(Readers can give whatever title
they like to this poem)

ALTURA Y PELOS

¿Quién no tiene su vestido azul?
¿Quién no almuerza y no toma el tranvía,
con su cigarrillo contratado y su dolor de bolsillo?
¡Yo que tan sólo he nacido!
¡Yo que tan sólo he nacido!

¿Quién no escribe una carta?
¿Quién no habla de un asunto muy importante,
muriendo de costumbre y llorando de oído?
¡Yo que solamente he nacido!
¡Yo que solamente he nacido!

¿Quién no se llama Carlos o cualquier otra cosa?
¿Quién al gato no dice gato gato?
¡Ay, yo que sólo he nacido solamente!
¡Ay! yo que sólo he nacido solamente!

1927

Who doesn't own a blue suit?
Who doesn't eat lunch and board the streetcar
with his hired cigarette and his pocket-edition pain?
I who was only born!
I who was only born!

Who doesn't write a letter?
Who doesn't talk about something very important,
dying from habit and weeping from hearing?
I who was solely born!
I who was solely born!

Who isn't called Carlos or some other thing?
Who to the kitty doesn't say kitty kitty?
Ay! I who only was solely born!
Ay! I who only was solely born!

Sin haberlo advertido jamás, exceso por turismo
y sin agencias
de pecho en pecho hacia la madre unánime.

Hasta París ahora vengo a ser hijo. Escucha,
Hombre, en verdad te digo que eres el HIJO ETERNO
pues para ser hermano tus brazos son escasamente iguales
y tu malicia para ser padre, es mucha.
La talla de mi madre moviéndome por índole
de movimiento,
y poniéndome serio, me llega exactamente al corazón:
pesando cuanto cayera de vuelo con mis tristes abuelos,
mi madre me oye en diámetro callándose en altura.

Mi metro está midiendo ya dos metros
mis huesos concuerdan en género y en número
y el verbo encarnado habita entre nosotros
y el verbo encarnado habita, al hundirme en el baño,
un alto grado de perfección.

1927

Without ever having realized it, excess through tourism
and without agencies
from chest on chest toward the unanimous mother.

As far as Paris now I come to be a son. Listen,
Man, verily I say unto thee thou art the ETERNAL SON
because to be a brother thy arms are hardly equal
and thy malice to be a father, is abundant.
My mother's stature, moving me for the sake
of movement,
and making me serious, reaches me exactly at my heart:
weighing all that has fallen at once from my sad grandparents,
my mother hears me in diameter keeping quiet on high.

My meter is now measuring two meters
my bones agree in gender and in number
and the word made flesh dwells among us
and the word made flesh dwells, as I sink into the bathtub,
in a high degree of perfection.

SOMBRERO, ABRIGO, GUANTES

Enfrente a la Comedia Francesa, está el Café
de la Regencia; en él hay una pieza
recóndita, con una butaca y una mesa.
Cuando entro, el polvo inmóvil se ha puesto ya de pie.

Entre mis labios hechos de jebe, la pavesa
de un cigarrillo humea, y en el humo se ve
dos humos intensivos, el tórax del Café,
y en el tórax, un óxido profundo de tristeza.

Importa que el otoño se injerte en los otoños,
importa que el otoño se integre de retoños,
la nube, de semestres; de pómulos, la arruga.

Importa oler a loco postulando
¡qué cálida es la nieve, qué fugaz la tortuga,
el cómo qué sencillo, qué fulminante el cuándo!

HAT, OVERCOAT, GLOVES

In front of the Comédie Française, is the Café
de la Régence; in it is a room
set apart, with an armchair and a table.
When I enter, the unmoving dust has already risen.

Between my lips made of rubber, the ember
of a cigarette smokes, and in the smoke can be seen
two intense fumes, the thorax of the Café,
and in the thorax, a profound oxide of sadness.

It is important that autumn graft itself to autumns,
important that autumn integrate itself with sprouts,
the cloud, with semesters; with cheekbones, the wrinkle.

It is important to smell like a madman postulating
how warm the snow is, how fleeting the turtle,
how simple the how, how fulminating the when!

 ¡Cuatro conciencias
simultáneas enrédanse en la mía!
¡Si vierais cómo ese movimiento
apenas cabe ahora en mi conciencia!
¡Es aplastante! Dentro de una bóveda
pueden muy bien
adosarse, ya internas o ya externas,
segundas bóvedas, mas nunca cuartas;
mejor dicho, sí,
mas siempre y, a lo sumo, cual segundas.
No puedo concebirlo; es aplastante.
Vosotros mismos a quienes inicio en la noción
de estas cuatro conciencias simultáneas,
enredadas en una sola, apenas os tenéis
de pie ante mi cuadrúpedo intensivo.
¡Y yo, que le entrevisto (Estoy seguro)!

 [1927/1928]

Four consciousnesses   *
simultaneously are entangled in my own!
If you could only see how that movement
hardly fits now in my consciousness!
It's overwhelming! Inside a vault
they can easily
double up, now internal now external
second vaults, but never fourth;
more specifically, yes,
but always and, at most, as seconds.
I cannot conceive it; it's overwhelming.
Those of you who I initiate into the notion
of these four simultaneous consciousnesses,
entangled in only one, hardly keep
upright before my intense quadruped.
And I, who interview him (I am sure)!

Entre el dolor y el placer median tres criaturas,
de las cuales una mira a un muro,
la segunda usa de ánimo triste
y la tercera avanza de puntillas;
pero, entre tú y yo,
sólo existen segundas criaturas.

Apoyándose en mi frente, el día
conviene en que, de veras,
hay mucho de exacto en el espacio;
pero, si la dicha, que, al fin, tiene un tamaño,
principia ¡ay! por mi boca,
¿quién me preguntará por mi palabra?

Al sentido instantáneo de la eternidad
corresponde
este encuentro investido de hilo negro,
pero a tu despedida temporal,
tan sólo corresponde lo inmutable,
tu criatura, el alma, mi palabra.

[1927/1928]

Between pain and pleasure there are three creatures,
among which one looks at a wall,
the second puts on a sad disposition
and the third advances on tiptoes;
but, between you and me,
only second creatures exist.

Leaning on my forehead, the day
agrees that, in truth,
much is exact in space;
but, if the happiness, that, after all, has dimension,
begins, ay! in my mouth,
who is going to ask me for my word?

To the instantaneous meaning of eternity   *
corresponds
this encounter vested with black thread,
but to your temporal farewell
corresponds solely what is immutable,
your creature, the soul, my word.

En el momento en que el tenista lanza magistralmente
su bala, le posee una inocencia totalmente animal;
en el momento
en que el filósofo sorprende una nueva verdad,
es una bestia completa.
Anatole France afirmaba
que el sentimiento religioso
es la función de un órgano especial del cuerpo humano,
hasta ahora ignorado y se podría
decir también, entonces,
que, en el momento exacto en que un tal órgano
funciona plenamente,
tan puro de malicia está el creyente,
que se diría casi un vegetal.
¡Oh alma! ¡Oh pensamiento! ¡Oh Marx! ¡Oh Feuerbach!

[1927/1928]

The moment the tennis player masterfully serves
his bullet, a totally animal innocence possesses him;
the moment
the philosopher surprises a new truth,
he is an absolute beast.
Anatole France affirmed
that religious feeling
is the function of a special organ in the human body,
until now unrecognized and one could
also say, then,
that the exact moment when such an organ
fully functions
the believer is so clear of malice,
he could almost be considered a vegetable.
Oh soul! Oh thought! Oh Marx! Oh Feuerbach!

Tendríamos ya una edad misericordiosa, cuando mi padre ordenó nuestro ingreso a la escuela. Cura de amor, una tarde lluviosa de febrero, mamá servía en la cocina el yantar de oración. En el corredor de abajo, estaban sentados a la mesa, mi padre y mis hermanos mayores. Y mi madre iba sentada al pie del mismo fuego del hogar. Tocaron a la puerta.

—Tocan a la puerta!—mi madre.

—Tocan a la puerta!—mi propia madre.

—Tocan a la puerta!—dijo toda mi madre, tocándose las entrañas a trastos infinitos, sobre toda la altura de quien viene.

—Anda, Nativa, la hija, a ver quién viene.

Y, sin esperar la venia maternal, fuera Miguel, el hijo, quien salió a ver quién venía así, oponiéndose a lo ancho de nosotros.

Un tiempo de rúa contuvo a mi familia. Mamá salió, avanzando inversamente y como si hubiera dicho: *las partes*. Se hizo patio afuera. Nativa lloraba de una tal visita, de un tal patio y de la mano de mi madre. Entonces y cuando, dolor y paladar techaron nuestras frentes.

—Porque no le dejé que saliese a la puerta,—Nativa, la hija—, me ha echado Miguel al pavo. A su paVO.

¡Qué diestra de subprefecto, la diestra del padrE, revelando, el hombre, las falanjas filiales del niño! Podía así otorgarle la ventura que el hombre deseara más tarde. Sin embargo:

—Y mañana, a la escuela,—disertó magistralmente el padre, ante el público semanal de sus hijos.

Y tal, la ley, la causa de la ley. Y tal también la vida.

Mamá debió llorar, gimiendo apenas la madre. Ya nadie quiso comer. En los labios del padre cupo, para salir rompiéndose, una fina cuchara que conozco. En las fraternas bocas, la absorta amargura del hijo, quedó atravesada.

Mas, luego, de improviso, salió de un albañal de aguas llovedizas y de aquel mismo patio de la visita mala, una gallina, no ajena ni ponedora, sino brutal y negra. Cloqueaba en mi garganta. Fue una gallina vieja, maternalmente viuda de unos pollos que no llegaron a incubarse. Origen olvidado de ese instante, la gallina era viuda de sus hijos. Fueran hallados vacíos todos los huevos. La clueca después tuvo el verbo.

Nadie la espantó. Y de espantarla, nadie dejó arrullarse por su gran calofrío maternal.

—Dónde están los hijos de la gallina vieja?

—Dónde están los pollos de la gallina vieja?

¡Pobrecitos! ¡Dónde estarían!

[1927/1928]

LANGUIDLY HER LIQUOR

We probably already were of a compassionate age, when my father commanded us to enter school. A priestess of love, one rainy February afternoon, mama served $*$ the viandry of prayer in the kitchen. In the downstairs interior corridor, my father and older brothers were seated at the table. And my mother went sitting by the very fire of the hearth. Someone knocked at the door.

—Someone's knocking at the door!—my mother.

—Someone's knocking at the door!—my own mother.

—Someone's knocking at the door!—said all of my mother, playing her entrails $*$ with infinite frets, over the whole height of whoever was coming.

—Go, Nativa, the daughter, see who's there.

And, without waiting for maternal permission, it was Miguel, the son, who went out to see who had come like this, opposing the width of all of us.

A street time held our family. Mama went out, advancing inversely and as if she might have said: *the private parts*. The outside became a patio. Nativa was crying from such a visit, from such a patio and from her mother's hand. Then and when, pain and palate roofed our foreheads.

—Because I didn't let him go to the door,—Nativa, the daughter,—Miguel has made me blush. With his bLush. $*$

What a subprefectural right hand, the right hand of the faTher, revealing, the man, the filial phalanges of the child! He could thus grant him the happiness that the man would desire later on. However:

—And tomorrow, to school,—father magisterially lectured, before the weekly public of his children.

And thus, the law, the cause of the law. And thus also life.

Mama probably wept, mother hardly moaning. Now no one wanted to eat. A delicate spoon, known to me, fit in father's lips, to emerge breaking. In the brotherly mouths, the entranced bitterness of the son, got stuck.

But, afterward, unexpectedly, neither alien nor egg-laying, but enormous and black, a hen came out of a rainwater drain and from the very same patio as the bad visitor. She clucked in my throat. She was an old hen, maternally widowed from some chicks that did not get to be incubated. The forgotten origin of that instant, the hen was the widow of her children. All the eggs were found empty. The brooder $*$ afterward had the word.

No one frightened her. And in case she was frightened, no one allowed himself to be lulled by her great maternal chill.

—Where are the old hen's children?

—Where are the old hen's chicks?

Poor little things! Where could they be?

Los trescientos estados de mujer de la Tour Eiffel, están helados. La herzciana crin de cultura de la torre, su pelusa de miras, su vivo aceraje, engrapado al sistema moral de Descartes, están helados.

Le Bois de Boulogne, verde por cláusula privada, está helado.

La Cámara de Diputados, donde Briand clama: "Hago un llamamiento a los pueblos de la tierra . . .", y a cuyas puertas el centinela acaricia, sin darse cuenta, su cápsula de humanas inquietudes, su simple bomba de hombre, su eterno principio de Pascal, está helada.

Los Campos Elíseos, grises por cláusula pública, están helados.

Las estatuas que periplan la Plaza de la Concordia y sobre cuyos gorros frigios se oye al tiempo estudiar para infinito, están heladas.

Los dados de los calvarios católicos de París, están helados hasta por la cara de los treses.

Los gallos civiles, suspensos en las agujas góticas de Notre-Dame y del Sacré-Coeur, están helados.

La doncella de las campiñas de París, cuyo pulgar no se repite nunca al medir el alcance de sus ojos, está helada.

El andante a dos rumbos de "El pájaro de fuego", de Strawinsky, está helado.

Los garabatos escritos por Einstein en la pizarra del anfiteatro Richelieu de la Sorbona, están helados.

Los billetes de avión para el viaje de París a Buenos Aires, en dos horas, 23 minutos, 8 segundos, están helados.

El sol está helado.

El fuego central de la tierra está helado.

El padre, meridiano, y el hijo, paralelo, están helados.

Las dos desviaciones de la historia están heladas.

Mi acto menor de hombre está helado.

Mi oscilación sexual está helada.

[1927/1928]

The three-hundred womanly states of the Eiffel Tower, are frozen. The Hertzian cultural mane of the tower, its downy sights, its vivid steelwork, bolted to the moral Cartesian system, are frozen.

The Bois de Boulogne, green from private clause, is frozen.

The Chamber of Deputies, where Briand cries out: "I hereby call on all the peoples of the earth . . .", and at whose doors the guard unconsciously caresses his cartridge of human uneasiness, his simple manly bomb, his eternal Pascalian principle, is frozen.

The Champs-Elysées, gray from public clause, is frozen.

The statues that periplanate the Place de la Concorde and above whose Phrygian caps time can be heard studying to be infinite, are frozen.

The dice of the Parisian Catholic Calvaries, are frozen even on the face of the threes.

Astonished on the Gothic needles of Notre-Dame and Sacré-Coeur, the civil roosters, are frozen.

The maiden from the Parisian countryside, whose thumb never repeats itself while measuring the range of her eyes, is frozen.

The bidirectional andante of Stravinsky's "The Firebird," is frozen.

On the Richelieu amphitheater blackboard of the Sorbonne Einstein's scribblings, are frozen.

The airplane tickets for the flight from Paris to Buenos Aires—two hours, 23 minutes, 8 seconds—are frozen.

The sun is frozen.

The fire at the center of the earth is frozen.

The meridian father and the parallel son, are frozen.

The two deviations of history are frozen.

My minor manly act is frozen.

My sexual oscillation is frozen.

RUIDO DE PASOS DE UN GRAN CRIMINAL

Cuando apagaron la luz, me dio ganas de reír. Las cosas reanudaron en la oscuridad sus labores, en el punto donde se habían detenido: en un rostro, los ojos bajaron a las conchas nasales y allí hicieron inventario de ciertos valores ópticos extraviados, llevándolos en seguida; a la escama de un pez llamó imperiosamente una escama naval; tres gotas de lluvia paralelas detuviéronse a la altura de un umbral, a esperar a otra que no se sabe por qué se había retardado; el guardia de la esquina se sonó ruidosamente, insistiendo en singular sobre la ventanilla izquierda de la nariz; la grada más alta y la más baja de una escalinata en caracol volvieron a hacerse señas alusivas al último transeúnte que subió por ellas. Las cosas, a la sombra, reanudaron sus labores, animadas de libre alegría y se conducían como personas en un banquete de alta etiqueta, en que de súbito se apagasen las luces y se quedase todo en tinieblas.

Cuando apagaron la luz, realizóse una mejor distribución de hitos y de marcos en el mundo. Cada ritmo fue a su música; cada fiel de balanza se movió lo menos que puede moverse un destino, esto es, hasta casi adquirir presencia absoluta. En general, se produjo un precioso juego, de liberación y de justeza entre las cosas. Yo las veía y me puse contento, puesto que en mí también corcoveaba la gracia de la sombra numeral.

No sé quién hizo de nuevo luz. El mundo volvió a agazaparse en sus raídas pieles: la amarilla del domingo, la ceniza del lunes, la húmeda del martes, la juiciosa del miércoles, la de zapa del jueves, la triste del viernes, la haraposa del sábado. El mundo volvió a aparecer así, quieto, dormido o haciéndose el dormido. Una espeluznante araña, de tres patas quebradas, salía de la manga del sábado.

[1927/1928]

When they turned off the lights, I felt like laughing. Things renewed their labors in the dark, at the point where they had been stopped; in a face, the eyes lowered to the nasal shells and took an inventory of certain missing optical powers, retrieving them one by one; a naval scale imperiously summoned the scales of a fish; three parallel raindrops halted at the height of a lintel, awaiting another drop that doesn't know why it has been delayed; the policeman on the corner blew his nose noisily, emphasizing in particular his left nostril; the highest and the lowest steps of a spiral staircase began to make signs to each other that alluded to the last passerby to climb them. Things, in the dark, renewed their labors, animated by an uninhibited happiness, conducting themselves like people at a great ceremonial banquet, where the lights went out and all remained in the dark.

When they turned off the light, a better distribution of boundaries and frames was carried out around the world. Each rhythm was its own music; each needle of a scale moved as little as a destiny could move, that is to say, until nearly acquiring an absolute presence. In general, a delightful game was created between things, one of liberation and justice. I watched them and grew content, since in myself as well the grace of the numeral dark curvetted.

I don't know who let there be light again. The world began to crouch once more in its shabby pelts: the yellow one of Sunday, the ashen one of Monday, the humid one of Tuesday, the judicious one of Wednesday, sharkskin for Thursday, a sad one for Friday, a tattered one for Saturday. Thus the world reappeared, quiet, sleeping, or pretending to sleep. A hair-raising spider, with three broken legs, emerged from Saturday's sleeve.

CONFLICTO ENTRE LOS OJOS Y LA MIRADA

Muchas veces he visto cosas que otros también han visto. Esto me inspira una cólera sutil y de puntillas, a cuya íntima presencia manan sangre mis flancos solidarios.

—Ha abierto sol, —le digo a un hombre.

Y él me ha respondido:

—Sí. Un sol flavo y dulce.

Yo he sentido que el sol está, de veras, flavo y dulce. Tengo deseo entonces de preguntar a otro hombre por lo que sabe de este sol. Aquél ha confirmado mi impresión y esta confirmación me hace daño, un vago daño que me acosa por las costillas. ¿No es, pues, cierto que al abrir el sol, estaba yo de frente? Y, siendo así, aquel hombre ha salido, como desde un espejo lateral, a mansalva, a murmurar, a mi lado: "Sí. Un sol flavo y dulce". Un adjetivo se recorta en cada una de mis sienes. No. Yo preguntaré a otro hombre por este sol. El primero se ha equivocado o hace broma, pretendiendo suplantarme.

—Ha abierto sol, —le digo a otro hombre.

—Sí, muy nublado, —me responde.

Más lejos todavía, he dicho a otro:

—Ha abierto sol.

Y éste me arguye:

—Un sol a medias.

¡Dónde podré ir que no haya un espejo lateral, cuya superficie viene a darme de frente, por mucho que yo avance de lado y mire yo de frente!

A los lados del hombre van y vienen bellos absurdos, premiosa caballería suelta, que reclama cabestro, número y jinete. Mas los hombres aman poner el freno por amor al jinete y no por amor al animal. Yo he de poner el freno, tan sólo por amor al animal. Y nadie sentirá lo que yo siento. Y nadie ha de poder ya suplantarme.

[1927/1928]

THE CONFLICT BETWEEN THE EYES AND THE GAZE

Often I have seen things that others have also seen. This inspires me with a subtle, tiptoeing anger, into whose intimate presence blood flows from my solidary flanks.

—The sun has broken through,—I say to a man.

And he's responded to me:

—Yes. A sweet, fallow sun.

I had felt that the sun truly is sweet and fallow. So I want to ask another man what he knows about this sun. He confirmed my impression and this confirmation hurts me, a vague hurt that digs in under my ribs. Is it not, then, certain that I was facing the sun as it broke through? And, this being the case, that man had emerged as from a side mirror, without risking anything, to murmur at my side: "Yes. A sweet, fallow sun." An adjective stands out on each side of my temples. No. I will ask another man about this sun. The first one had lied or joked, as if to supplant me.

—The sun has broken through,—I say to another man.

—Yes, very overcast,—he responds.

Even further away, I've said to another:

—The sun has broken through.

And this one argues:

—An incomplete sun.

Where can I go where there will be no side mirror, whose surface faces me head-on, no matter how much I advance sideways and look straight ahead!

Beautiful absurdities appear alongside a man and disappear, an urgent agile steed, requiring a halter, number, and rider. But men love to bridle for love of the rider and not for love of the animal. And no one will feel what I feel. And no one will have the power now to supplant me.

PIEDRA NEGRA SOBRE UNA PIEDRA BLANCA

Me moriré en París con aguacero,
un día del cual tengo ya el recuerdo.
Me moriré en París—y no me corro—
talvez un jueves, como es hoy, de otoño.

Jueves será, porque hoy, jueves, que proso
estos versos, los húmeros me he puesto
a la mala y, jamás como hoy, me he vuelto,
con todo mi camino, a verme solo.

César Vallejo ha muerto, le pegaban
todos sin que él les haga nada;
le daban duro con un palo y duro

también con una soga; son testigos
los días jueves y los huesos húmeros,
la soledad, la lluvia, los caminos . . .

I will die in Paris in a downpour,
a day which I can already remember.
I will die in Paris—and I don't budge—   *
maybe a Thursday, like today, in autumn.

Thursday it will be, because today, Thursday,
as I prose these lines, I have forced on   *
my humeri and, never like today, have I turned,
with all my journey, to see myself alone.

César Vallejo has died, they beat him,
all of them, without him doing anything to them;
they gave it to him hard with a stick and hard

likewise with a rope; witnesses are
the Thursdays and the humerus bones,
the loneliness, the rain, the roads . . .

SALUTACIÓN ANGÉLICA

Eslavo con respecto a la palmera,
alemán de perfil al sol, inglés sin fin,
francés en cita con los caracoles,
italiano ex profeso, escandinavo de aire,
español de pura bestia, tal el cielo
ensartado en la tierra por los vientos,
tal el beso del límite en los hombros.

Mas sólo tú demuestras, descendiendo
o subiendo del pecho, bolchevique,
tus trazos confundibles,
tu gesto marital,
tu cara de padre,
tus piernas de amado,
tu cutis por teléfono,
tu alma perpendicular
a la mía,
tus codos de justo
y un pasaporte en blanco en tu sonrisa.

Obrando por el hombre, en nuestras pausas,
matando, tú, a lo largo de tu muerte
y a lo ancho de un abrazo salubérrimo,
vi que cuando comías después, tenías gusto,
vi que en tus sustantivos creció yerba.

Yo quisiera, por eso,
tu calor doctrinal, frío y en barras,
tu añadida manera de mirarnos
y aquesos tuyos pasos metalúrgicos,
aquesos tuyos pasos de otra vida.

Y digo, bolchevique, tomando esta flaqueza
en su feroz linaje de exhalación terrestre:
hijo natural del bien y del mal
y viviendo talvez por vanidad, para que digan,
me dan tus simultáneas estaturas mucha pena,
puesto que tú no ignoras en quién se me hace tarde diariamente,
en quién estoy callado y medio tuerto.

[1931]

ANGELIC SALUTATION

Slav in regard to the palm tree,
German with profile to the sun, English with no limits,
French in a rendezvous with snails,
Italian on purpose, Scandinavian made of air,
purely brutal Spaniard, thus the sky
strung on the earth by the winds,
thus the limit's kiss on the shoulders.

But you alone, Bolshevik, demonstrate,
descending or rising from your chest,
your confusable characteristics,
your marital gesture,
your paternal face,
your lover's legs,
your complexion by telephone,
your soul perpendicular
to mine,
your elbows of a just man
and a blank passport in your smile.

Working for man, during our pauses,
killing, you, along your death
and abreast a most salubrious embrace,
I saw that when afterward you ate, you had taste,
I saw that grass grew in your nouns.

Therefore, I would like
your doctrinal warmth, cold and in rods,
your added way of looking at us
and those metallurgic steps of yours,
your steps of another life.

And I say, Bolshevik, taking this weakness
in its ferocious lineage of earthly exhalation:
the natural son of good and of evil
and living perhaps out of vanity, to have others talk,
your simultaneous statures make me very sad,
because you can't but know in whom I am late daily,
in whom I am silent and almost one-eyed.

Y no me digan nada,
que uno puede matar perfectamente,
ya que, sudando tinta,
uno hace cuanto puede, no me digan . . .

Volveremos, señores, a vernos con manzanas;
tarde la criatura pasará,
la expresión de Aristóteles armada
de grandes corazones de madera,
la de Heráclito injerta en la de Marx,
la del suave sonando rudamente . . .
Es lo que bien narraba mi garganta:
uno puede matar perfectamente.

Señores,
caballeros, volveremos a vernos sin paquetes;
hasta entonces exijo, exijiré de mi flaqueza
el acento del día, que,
según veo, estuvo ya esperándome en mi lecho.
Y exijo del sombrero la infausta analogía del recuerdo,
ya que, a veces, asumo con éxito mi inmensidad llorada,
ya que, a veces, me ahogo en la voz de mi vecino
y padezco
contando en maíces los años,
cepillando mi ropa al son de un muerto
o sentado borracho en mi ataúd . . .

[1931/1932]

And don't say another word to me,   *
since one can kill perfectly,
now that, sweating ink,
one does what one can, don't say another . . .

We will, gentlemen, see each other again with apples;
late the creature will pass,
the expression of Aristotle armed
with great hearts of wood,
that of Heraclitus grafted on that of Marx,
that of the gentle sounding coarsely . . .
This is what was well narrated by my throat:
one can kill perfectly.

Gentlemen,
sirs, we will see each other again without packages;
until then I demand, I shall demand of my frailty
the accent of the day, that,
as I see it, was already awaiting me in my bed.
And I demand of my hat the accursed analogy of memory,
since, at times, I assume successfully my wept immensity,
since, at times, I drown in my neighbor's voice
and endure
counting on kernels the years,
brushing my clothes to the tune of a corpse
or sitting up drunk in my coffin . . .

Fue domingo en las claras orejas de mi burro,
de mi burro peruano en el Perú (Perdonen la tristeza)
Mas hoy ya son las once en mi experiencia personal,
experiencia de un solo ojo, clavado en pleno pecho,
de una sola burrada, clavada en pleno pecho,
de una sola hecatombe, clavada en pleno pecho.

Tal de mi tierra veo los cerros retratados,
ricos en burros, hijos de burros, padres hoy de vista,
que tornan ya pintados de creencias,
cerros horizontales de mis penas.

En su estatua, de espada,
Voltaire cruza su capa y mira el zócalo,
pero el sol me penetra y espanta de mis dientes incisivos
un número crecido de cuerpos inorgánicos.

Y entonces sueño en una piedra
verduzca, diecisiete,
peñasco numeral que he olvidado,
sonido de años en el rumor de aguja de mi brazo,
lluvia y sol en Europa, y ¡cómo toso! ¡cómo vivo!
¡cómo me duele el pelo al columbrar los siglos semanales!
y cómo, por recodo, mi ciclo microbiano,
quiero decir mi trémulo, patriótico peinado.

[1931/1932]

It was Sunday in the clear ears of my jackass,
of my Peruvian jackass in Peru (Pardon my sadness)
But today is already eleven o'clock in my personal experience,
experience of a single eye, nailed right in the chest,
of a single asininity, nailed right in the chest,
of a single hecatomb, nailed right in the chest.

So do I see the portrayed hills of my country,
rich in jackasses, sons of jackasses, parents today in sight,
that now return painted with beliefs,
the horizontal hills of my sorrows.

In his statue, with a sword,
Voltaire pulls his cape to and looks at the square,   *
but the sun penetrates me and frightens from my incisors
an increased number of inorganic bodies.

And then I dream on a verdant
stone, seventeen,
numeral boulder that I've forgotten,
sound of years in the needle rumor of my arm,
rain and sun in Europe, and, how I cough! how I live!
how my hair aches me upon descrying the weekly centuries!
and how, with a twist, my microbial cycle,
I mean my tremulous, patriotically combed hair.

Hoy me gusta la vida mucho menos,
pero siempre me gusta vivir: ya lo decía.
Casi toqué la parte de mi todo y me contuve
con un tiro en la lengua detrás de mi palabra.

Hoy me palpo el mentón en retirada
y en estos momentáneos pantalones yo me digo:
¡Tánta vida y jamás!
¡Tántos años y siempre mis semanas! . . .
Mis padres enterrados con su piedra
y su triste estirón que no ha acabado;
de cuerpo entero hermanos, mis hermanos,
y, en fin, mi sér parado y en chaleco.

Me gusta la vida enormemente,
pero, desde luego,
con mi muerte querida y mi café
y viendo los castaños frondosos de París
y diciendo:
Es un ojo éste, aquél; una frente ésta, aquélla. . . . Y repitiendo:
¡Tánta vida y jamás me falla la tonada!
¡Tántos años y siempre, siempre, siempre!

Dije chaleco, dije
todo, parte, ansia, dije casi, por no llorar.
Que es verdad que sufrí en aquel hospital que queda al lado
y está bien y está mal haber mirado
de abajo para arriba mi organismo.

Me gustará vivir siempre, así fuese de barriga,
porque, como iba diciendo y lo repito,
¡tánta vida y jamás! ¡Y tántos años,
y siempre, mucho siempre, siempre siempre!

[1931/1932]

Today I like life much less,
but I always like to live: I've often said it.
I almost touched the part of my whole and restrained myself
with a shot in the tongue behind my word.

Today I touch my chin in retreat
and in these momentary trousers I tell myself:
So much life and never!
So many years and always my weeks! . . .
My parents buried with their stone
and their sad stiffening that has not ended;
full-length brothers, my brothers,
and, finally, my being standing and in a vest.

I like life enormously,
but, of course,   *
with my beloved death and my café
and looking at the leafy chestnut trees of Paris
and saying:
This is an eye, that one too, this a forehead, that one too . . . And repeating:
So much life and never does the tune fail me!
So many years and always, always, always!

I said vest, said
whole, part, yearning, said almost, to avoid crying.
For it is true that I suffered in that hospital close by
and it is good and it is bad to have watched
from below up my organism.

I would like to live always, even flat on my belly,
because, as I was saying and I say it again,
so much life and never! And so many years,
and always, much always, always always!   *

GLEBA

Con efecto mundial de vela que se enciende,
el prepucio directo, hombres a golpes,
funcionan los labriegos a tiro de neblina,
con alabadas barbas,
pie práctico y reginas sinceras de los valles.

Hablan como les vienen las palabras,
cambian ideas bebiendo
orden sacerdotal de una botella;
cambian también ideas tras de un árbol, parlando
de escrituras privadas, de la luna menguante
y de los ríos públicos! (Inmenso! Inmenso! Inmenso!)

Función de fuerza
sorda y de zarza ardiendo,
paso de palo,
gesto de palo,
acápites de palo,
la palabra colgando de otro palo.

De sus hombros arranca, carne a carne, la herramienta florecida,
de sus rodillas bajan ellos mismos por etapas hasta el cielo,
y, agitando
y
agitando sus faltas en forma de antiguas calaveras,
levantan sus defectos capitales con cintas,
su mansedumbre y sus
vasos sanguíneos, tristes, de jueces colorados.

Tienen su cabeza, su tronco, sus extremidades,
tienen su pantalón, sus dedos metacarpos y un palito;
para comer vistiéronse de altura
y se lavan la cara acariciándose con sólidas palomas.

Por cierto, aquestos hombres
cumplen años en los peligros,
echan toda la frente en sus salutaciones;
carecen de reloj, no se jactan jamás de respirar
y, en fin, suelen decirse: Allá, las putas, Luis Taboada, los ingleses;
allá ellos, allá ellos, allá ellos!

[1931/1932]

With the universal effect of a candle that catches fire,
foreskins direct, hacked out men,
the peasants function within fog range,   *
with extolled beards,
practical feet and the sincere "reginas of the valley."   *

   They speak as the words come,
they exchange ideas drinking
sacerdotal order from a bottle;
they also trade ideas behind a tree, chatting
about private writings, about the waning moon
and about the public rivers (Immense! Immense! Immense!)

   Function of deaf
force and of the burning bush,
step of a staff,
gesture of a staff,
paragraph of a staff,
the word hanging from another staff.

   From their shoulders the flowered tool, flesh to flesh, tears,
from their knees they descend themselves by stages unto heaven,
and, agitating
and
agitating their shortcomings in the shape of ancient skulls,
they raise their deadly flaws with ribbons,
their meekness and their
sad blood vessels of flushed judges.

   They own their heads, their trunks, their extremities,
they own their pants, their metacarpal fingers and a little staff;
to eat they dressed themselves in height
and they wash their faces caressing them with solid doves.

   Certainly, these men
put on years in risks,
they fling out all their forehead in their salutations;
they lack clocks, never do they brag about breathing
and, in short, they always say: To hell with the whores, Luis Taboada, the English;   *
t'hell with'm, t'hell with'm, t'hell with'm!

Pero antes que se acabe
toda esta dicha, piérdela atajándola,
tómale la medida, por si rebasa tu ademán; rebásala,
ve si cabe tendida en tu extensión.

Bien la sé por su llave,
aunque no sepa, a veces, si esta dicha
anda sola, apoyada en tu infortunio
o tañida, por sólo darte gusto, en tus falanjas.
Bien la sé única, sola,
de una sabiduría solitaria.

En tu oreja el cartílago está hermoso
y te escribo por eso, te medito:
No olvides en tu sueño de pensar que eres feliz,
que la dicha es un hecho profundo, cuando acaba,
pero al llegar, asume
un caótico aroma de asta muerta.

Silbando a tu muerte,
sombrero a la pedrada,
blanco, ladeas a ganar tu batalla de escaleras,
soldado del tallo, filósofo del grano, mecánico del sueño.
(¿Me percibes, animal?
¿me dejo comparar como tamaño?
No respondes y callado me miras
a través de la edad de tu palabra).

Ladeando así tu dicha, volverá
a clamarla tu lengua, a despedirla,
dicha tan desgraciada de durar.
Antes, se acabará violentamente,
dentada, pedernalina estampa,
y entonces oirás cómo medito
y entonces tocarás cómo tu sombra es ésta mía desvestida
y entonces olerás cómo he sufrido.

[1931/1932]

But before all this
happiness ends, lose it interrupting it,
take its measure, if it exceeds your gesture; exceed it,
see if it fits stretched out in your size.

Well do I know it by its key,
even if I do not know, at times, if this happiness
walks alone, leaned on your misfortune
or played, just to please you, on your phalanhes.   *
Well do I know it is unique, alone
with a solitary wisdom.

In your ear the cartilage looks beautiful
and so I write you, I meditate you:
Do not forget in your dream to think that you are happy,
that happiness is a profound fact, when it ends,
but upon arriving it takes on
the chaotic odor of a dead horn.

Whistling at your death,   *
hat rakishly tilted,   *
a target, you sway to win your battle of the stairs,   *
soldier of the stalk, philosopher of the grain, mechanic of the dream.
(Do you perceive me, animal?
do I allow myself to be compared like a measurement?
You do not respond and silent you look at me
across the age of your word).

Swaying your happiness like this, your tongue
will again cry out for it, will again dismiss it,
happiness too unfortunate to last.
Instead, it will end violently,
a dentate, flinty print,
and then you will hear how I meditate
and then you will touch how your shadow is my own undressed
and then you will smell how I have suffered.

EPÍSTOLA A LOS TRANSEÚNTES

Reanudo mi día de conejo,
mi noche de elefante en descanso.

Y, entre mí, digo:
ésta es mi inmensidad en bruto, a cántaros,
éste mi grato peso, que me buscara abajo para pájaro;
éste es mi brazo
que por su cuenta rehusó ser ala,
éstas son mis sagradas escrituras,
éstos mis alarmados compañones.

Lúgubre isla me alumbrará continental,
mientras el capitolio se apoye en mi íntimo derrumbe
y la asamblea en lanzas clausure mi desfile.

Pero cuando yo muera
de vida y no de tiempo,
cuando lleguen a dos mis dos maletas,
éste ha de ser mi estómago en que cupo mi lámpara en pedazos,
ésta aquella cabeza que expió los tormentos del círculo en mis pasos,
éstos esos gusanos que el corazón contó por unidades,
éste ha de ser mi cuerpo solidario
por el que vela el alma individual; éste ha de ser
mi hombligo en que maté mis piojos natos,
ésta mi cosa cosa, mi cosa tremebunda.

En tanto, convulsiva, ásperamente
convalece mi freno,
sufriendo como sufro del lenguaje directo del león;
y, puesto que he existido entre dos potestades de ladrillo,
convalezco yo mismo, sonriendo de mis labios.

[1932]

EPISTLE TO THE PASSERSBY

I resume my day of a rabbit,
my night of an elephant in repose.   *

And, within myself, I say:
this is my immensity in the raw, in jugfuls,
this is my grateful weight, that sought me below as a pecker;
this is my arm
that on its own refused to be a wing,
these are my sacred writings,
these my alarmed cullions.   *

A lugubrious island will illuminate me continental,
while the capitol leans on my innermost collapse
and the lance-filled assembly brings to a close my parade.

But when I die
of life and not of time,
when my two suitcases come to two,
this will be my stomach in which my lamp fit in pieces,
this that head that atoned for the circular torment in my steps,
these those worms that my heart counted one by one,
this will be my solidary body
over which the individual soul keeps watch; this will be
my navehall in which I killed my innate lice,   *
this my thing thing, my dreadful thing.

Meanwhile, convulsively, harshly,   *
my restraint convalesces,
suffering like I suffer the direct language of the lion;
and, because I have existed between two brick powers,
I myself convalesce, smiling at my lips.

PRIMAVERA TUBEROSA

Esta vez, arrastrando briosa sus pobrezas
al sesgo de mi pompa delantera,
coteja su coturno con mi traspié sin taco,
la primavera exacta de picotón de buitre.

La perdí en cuanto tela de mis despilfarros,
juguéla en cuanto pomo de mi aplauso;
el termómetro puesto, puesto el fin, puesto el gusano,
contusa mi doblez del otro día,
aguardéla al arrullo de un grillo fugitivo
y despedíla uñoso, somático, sufrido.

Veces latentes de astro,
ocasiones de ser gallina negra,
entabló la bandida primavera
con mi chusma de aprietos,
con mis apocamientos en camisa,
mi derecho soviético y mi gorra.

Veces las del bocado lauríneo,
con símbolos, tabaco, mundo y carne,
deglusión translaticia bajo palio,
al són de los testículos cantores;
talentoso torrente el de mi suave suavidad,
rebatible a pedradas, ganable con tan sólo suspirar . . .
Flora de estilo, plena,
citada en fangos de honor por rosas auditivas . . .
Respingo, coz, patada sencilla,
triquiñuela adorada . . . Cantan . . . Sudan . . .

[1932]

TUBEROUS SPRING

This time, vigorously dragging its misery
oblique to my foremost pomp,
the spring, punctual with vulture beakax,   *
compares its cothurnus to my heelless stumble.

I lost it as the fabric of my squanderings,
gambled it away as the flask of my applause;
the thermometer placed, the end placed, the worm placed,
my duplicity of the other day bruised,
I awaited it to the cooing of a fugitive cricket
and discharged it fingernaily, somatic, long-suffering.

Latent times of a heavenly body,
occasions of being a black hen,
were fastened by the bandit spring
to my rabble of hassles,
to my vacillation in shirtsleeves,
my Soviet law and my cap.

These times of the lauraceous mouthful,
with symbols, tobacco, world and flesh,
metaphorical degllusion under pallium   *
to the sound of the singing testicles;
talented torrent of my gentle gentleness,
refutable by stonings, winnable with just a sigh . . .
Flora of style, complete,
cited in swamps of honor by auditory roses . . .
Buck, hoofblow, simple kick,
adored little trick . . . They sing . . . They sweat . . .

Hasta el día en que vuelva, de esta piedra
nacerá mi talón definitivo,
con su juego de crímenes, su yedra,
su obstinación dramática, su olivo.

Hasta el día en que vuelva, prosiguiendo,
con franca rectitud de cojo amargo,
de pozo en pozo, mi periplo, entiendo
que el hombre ha de ser bueno, sin embargo.

Hasta el día en que vuelva y hasta que ande
el animal que soy, entre sus jueces,
nuestro bravo meñique será grande,
digno, infinito dedo entre los dedos.

Until the day that I return, from this stone
my definitive heel will be born,
with its game of crimes, its ivy,
its dramatic obstinacy, its olive tree.

Until the day that I return, continuing,
with the frank uprightness of a bitter cripple,
from well to well, my wandering, I understand
that man has to be good, all the same.

Until the day that I return and until
the animal that I am walks, among his judges,
our brave little finger will be big,
worthy, an infinite finger among the fingers.

Por último, sin ese buen aroma sucesivo
sin él,
sin su cuociente melancólico,
cierra su manto mi ventaja suave,
mis condiciones cierran sus cajitas.

¡Ay, cómo la sensación arruga tánto!
¡ay, cómo una idea fija me ha entrado en una uña!

Albino, áspero, abierto, con temblorosa hectárea,
mi deleite cae viernes,
mas mi triste tristumbre se compone de cólera y tristeza
y, a su borde arenoso e indoloro,
la sensación me arruga, me arrincona.

Ladrones de oro, víctimas de plata:
el oro que robara yo a mis víctimas,
            ¡rico de mí olvidándolo!
la plata que robara a mis ladrones,
            ¡pobre de mí olvidándolo!

Execrable sistema, clima en nombre del cielo, del bronquio y la quebrada,
la cantidad enorme de dinero que cuesta el ser pobre . . .

Finally, without that good continuous aroma,
without it,
without its melancholy quotient,
my soft advantage closes its cloak,
my conditions close their little boxes.

Ay, how much the sensation wrinkles!
ay, how a fixed idea has gotten in under my fingernail!

Albino, brusque, open, with a trembling hectare,
my delight falls Friday,
but my sad tombsadness is composed of anger and sadness   *
and, at its sandy and painless edge,
the sensation wrinkles me, corners me.

Thieves of gold, victims of silver:
the gold I robbed from my victims,
      rich me if I forget it!
the silver I robbed from my thieves,
      poor me if I forget it!

Abominable system, climate in the name of heaven, of the bronchus and the gorge,
the incredible amount of money that it takes to be poor . . .

LA RUEDA DEL HAMBRIENTO

Por entre mis propios dientes salgo humeando,
dando voces, pujando,
bajándome los pantalones . . .
Váca mi estómago, váca mi yeyuno,
la miseria me saca por entre mis propios dientes,
cogido con un palito por el puño de la camisa.

Una piedra en que sentarme
¿no habrá ahora para mí?
Aun aquella piedra en que tropieza la mujer que ha dado a luz,
la madre del cordero, la causa, la raíz,
¿ésa no habrá ahora para mí?
¡Siquiera aquella otra,
que ha pasado agachándose por mi alma!
Siquiera
la calcárida o la mala (humilde océano)
o la que ya no sirve ni para ser tirada contra el hombre,
¡ésa dádmela ahora para mí!

Siquiera la que hallaren atravesada y sola en un insulto,
¡ésa dádmela ahora para mí!
Siquiera la torcida y coronada, en que resuena
solamente una vez el andar de las rectas conciencias,
o, al menos, esa otra, que arrojada en digna curva,
va a caer por sí misma,
en profesión de entraña verdadera,
¡ésa dádmela ahora para mí!

Un pedazo de pan, ¿tampoco habrá ahora para mí?
Ya no más he de ser lo que siempre he de ser,
pero dadme
una piedra en que sentarme,
pero dadme,
por favor, un pedazo de pan en que sentarme,
pero dadme
en español
algo, en fin, de beber, de comer, de vivir, de reposarse,
y después me iré . . .
Hallo una extraña forma, está muy rota
y sucia mi camisa
y ya no tengo nada, esto es horrendo.

THE HUNGRY MAN'S RACK

From between my own teeth I come out smoking,
shouting, pushing,
pulling down my pants . . .
My stomach empties, my jejunum empties,
misery pulls me out between my own teeth,
caught in my shirt cuff by a little stick.

Will a stone to sit down on
now be denied me?
Even that stone on which trips the woman who has given birth,
the mother of the lamb, the cause, the root,
that one will now be denied me?
At least that other one
which has gone cowering through my soul!
At least
the calcarid or the evil one (humble ocean)   *
or the one no longer even worth throwing at man,
that one give it to me now!

At least the one they will have found lying alone across an insult,
that one give it to me now!
At least the twisted and crowned, on which resounds
only once the walk of moral rectitude,
or, at least, the other one, that flung in dignified curve,
will fall by itself,
avowing true entrails,
that one give it to me now!

A piece of bread, that too denied me?
Now I no longer have to be what I always have to be,
but give me
a stone to sit down on,
but give me,
please, a piece of bread to sit down on,
but give me
in Spanish
something, finally, to drink, to eat, to live off, to rest on,
and then I'll go away . . .
I find a strange shape, my shirt is
filthy and in shreds
and now I have nothing, this is hideous.

Considerando en frío, imparcialmente,
que el hombre es triste, tose y, sin embargo,
se complace en su pecho colorado;
que lo único que hace es componerse
de días;
que es lóbrego mamífero y se peina . . .

Considerando
que el hombre procede suavemente del trabajo
y repercute jefe, suena subordinado;
que el diagrama del tiempo
es constante diorama en sus medallas
y, a medio abrir, sus ojos estudiaron,
desde lejanos tiempos,
su fórmula famélica de masa . . .

Comprendiendo sin esfuerzo
que el hombre se queda, a veces, pensando,
como queriendo llorar,
y, sujeto a tenderse como objeto,
se hace buen carpintero, suda, mata
y luego canta, almuerza, se abotona . . .

Considerando también
que el hombre es en verdad un animal
y, no obstante, al voltear, me da con su tristeza en la cabeza . . .

Examinando, en fin,
sus encontradas piezas, su retrete,
su desesperación, al terminar su día atroz, borrándolo . . .

Comprendiendo
que él sabe que le quiero,
que le odio con afecto y me es, en suma, indiferente . . .

Considerando sus documentos generales
y mirando con lentes aquel certificado
que prueba que nació muy pequeñito . . .

le hago una seña,
viene,
y le doy un abrazo, emocionado.
¡Qué más da! Emocionado . . . Emocionado . . .

[1934/1935]

Considering coldly, impartially,
that man is sad, coughs and, nevertheless,
takes pleasure in his reddened chest;
that the only thing he does is to be made up
of days;
that he is a gloomy mammal and combs his hair . . .

Considering
that man proceeds softly from work
and reverberates boss, sounds employee;
that the diagram of time
is a constant diorama on his medals
and, half-open, his eyes have studied,
since distant times,
his famished mass formula . . .

Understanding without effort
that man pauses, occasionally, thinking,
as if wanting to cry,
and, subject to lying down like an object,
becomes a good carpenter, sweats, kills
and then sings, eats lunch, buttons himself up . . .

Considering too
that man is truly an animal
and, nevertheless, upon turning, hits my head with his sadness . . .

Examining, finally,
his discordant parts, his toilet,
his desperation, upon finishing his atrocious day, erasing it . . .

Understanding
that he knows I love him,
that I hate him with affection and, in short, am indifferent to him . . .   *

Considering his general documents
and scrutinizing with a magnifying glass that certificate
that proves he was born very tiny . . .

I make a gesture to him,
he approaches,
I hug him, and it moves me.
What's the difference! It moves me . . . moves me . . .

Parado en una piedra,
desocupado,
astroso, espeluznante,
a la orilla del Sena, va y viene.
Del río brota entonces la conciencia,
con peciolo y rasguños de árbol ávido:
del río sube y baja la ciudad, hecha de lobos abrazados.

El parado la ve yendo y viniendo,
monumental, llevando sus ayunos en la cabeza cóncava,
en el pecho sus piojos purísimos
y abajo
su pequeño sonido, el de su pelvis,
callado entre dos grandes decisiones,
y abajo,
más abajo,
un papelito, un clavo, una cerilla . . .

¡Este es, trabajadores, aquel
que en la labor sudaba para afuera,
que suda hoy para adentro su secreción de sangre rehusada!
Fundidor del cañón, que sabe cuántas zarpas son acero,
tejedor que conoce los hilos positivos de sus venas,
albañil de pirámides,
constructor de descensos por columnas
serenas, por fracasos triunfales,
parado individual entre treinta millones de parados,
andante en multitud,
¡qué salto el retratado en su talón
y qué humo el de su boca ayuna, y cómo
su talle incide, canto a canto, en su herramienta atroz, parada,
y qué idea de dolorosa válvula en su pómulo!

También parado el hierro frente al horno,
paradas las semillas con sus sumisas síntesis al aire,
parados los petróleos conexos,
parada en sus auténticos apóstrofes la luz,
parados de crecer los laureles,
paradas en un pie las aguas móviles
y hasta la tierra misma, parada de estupor ante este paro,
¡qué salto el retratado en sus tendones!

>

Idle on a stone,
unemployed,
scroungy, horrifying,
at the bank of the Seine, he comes and goes.
Conscience then sprouts from the river,
with the petiole and outlines of the greedy tree;
from the river rises and falls the city, made of embraced wolves.

The idle one sees it coming and going,
monumental, carrying his fastings on his concave head,
on his chest his purest lice
and below
his little sound, that of his pelvis,
silent between two big decisions,
and below,
further below,
a paperscrap, a nail, a match . . .   *

This is, workers, that man
who in his work sweated from inside out,
who today sweats from outside in his secretion of rejected blood!   *
Cannon caster, who knows how many claws are steel,
weaver who knows the positive threads of his veins,
mason of the pyramids,
builder of descents through serene
columns, through triumphant failures,
idle individual among thirty million idle,
wandering multitudes,
what a leap is portrayed in his heel
and what smoke from his fasting mouth, and how
his waist incises, edge to edge, his brutal tool, idle,
and what an idea of a painful valve in his cheekbone!

  Likewise idle the iron before the furnace,
idle the seeds with their submissive synthesis in the air,
idle the linked petroleums,
idle in its authentic apostrophes the light,
idle without growth the laurels,
idle on one foot the mobile waters
and even the earth itself, idle from stupor before this lockout,
what a leap is portrayed in his tendons!   >

> ¡qué transmisión entablan sus cien pasos!
¡cómo chilla el motor en su tobillo!
¡cómo gruñe el reloj, paseándose impaciente a sus espaldas!
¡cómo oye deglutir a los patrones
el trago que le falta, camaradas,
y el pan que se equivoca de saliva,
y, oyéndolo, sintiéndolo, en plural, humanamente,
¡cómo clava el relámpago
su fuerza sin cabeza en su cabeza!
y lo que hacen, abajo, entonces, ¡ay!
más abajo, camaradas,
el papelucho, el clavo, la cerilla,
el pequeño sonido, el piojo padre!

[1934/1935]

what a transmission his hundred steps start up!
how the motor in his ankle screeches!
how the clock grumbles, wandering impatiently in his back!
how he hears the owners knock back
the shot that he lacks, comrades,
and the bread getting into the wrong saliva,   *
and, hearing it, feeling it, in plural, humanly,
how lightning nails   *
its headless force into his head!
and what they do, below, then, aie!
further below, comrades,
the dirtypaperscrap, the nail, the match,
the little sound, the stallion louse!   *

La vida, esta vida
me placía, su instrumento, esas palomas . . .
Me placía escucharlas gobernarse en lontananza,
advenir naturales, determinado el número,
y ejecutar, según sus aflicciones, sus dianas de animales.

Encogido,
oí desde mis hombros
su sosegada producción,
cave los albañales sesgar sus trece huesos,
dentro viejo tornillo hincharse el plomo.
Sus paujiles picos,
pareadas palomitas,
las póbridas, hojeándose los hígados,
sobrinas de la nube . . . Vida! Vida! Esta es la vida!

Zurear su tradición rojo les era,
rojo moral, palomas vigilantes,
talvez rojo de herrumbre,
si caían entonces azulmente.

Su elemental cadena,
sus viajes de individuales pájaros viajeros,
echaron humo denso,
pena física, pórtico influyente.

Palomas saltando, indelebles
palomas olorosas,
manferidas venían, advenían
por azarosas vías digestivas,
a contarme sus cosas fosforosas,
pájaros de contar,
pájaros transitivos y orejones . . .

No escucharé ya más desde mis hombros
huesudo, enfermo, en cama,
ejecutar sus dianas de animales . . . Me doy cuenta.

[1936]

Life, this life
pleased me, its instrument, those doves . . .
It pleased me to hear them direct themselves far away,
arrive spontaneously, in fixed numbers,
and perform, according to their afflictions, their animal reveilles.

Hunched,
I heard from my shoulders
their quiet production,
their thirteen bones slant ner the sewers,   * *
the lead swell inside the old screw.
Their guan beaks,
coupled dovelings,
the poorotten, leafing their livers,   *
nieces of the cloud . . . Life! Life! This is life!

  To coo their tradition was red to them,
moral red, vigilant doves,
maybe rust red,
if they fell then bluely.   *

  Their elementary chain,
their journeys of individual traveling birds,
emitted dense smoke,   *
physical pain, influential portico.

  Doves hopping, indelible
fragrant doves,
assayably they came, arriving
through hazardous digestive tracts,
to tell me their phosphorous things,
birds of reckoning,
transitive and Incan-noble birds . . .

  No longer will I hear them from my shoulders
bony, sick, in bed,
perform their animal reveilles . . . I realize that.

PARÍS, OCTUBRE 1936

De todo esto yo soy el único que parte.
De este banco me voy, de mis calzones,
de mi gran situación, de mis acciones,
de mi número hendido parte a parte,
de todo esto yo soy el único que parte.

De los Campos Elíseos o al dar vuelta
la extraña callejuela de la Luna,
mi defunción se va, parte mi cuna,
y, rodeada de gente, sola, suelta,
mi semejanza humana dase vuelta
y despacha sus sombras una a una.

Y me alejo de todo, porque todo
se queda para hacer la coartada:
mi zapato, su ojal, también su lodo
y hasta el doblez del codo
de mi propia camisa abotonada.

PARIS, OCTOBER 1936

From all this I am the only one who parts.
From this bench I go away, from my pants,
from my great situation, from my actions,
from my number split part to part,
from all this I am the only one who parts.

From the Champs-Elysées or as the strange
backstreet of the Moon curves around,
my death goes away, my cradle parts,
and, surrounded by people, alone, estranged,
my human resemblance turns around,
dispatching its shadows one by one.

And I move away from all, since all
remain to provide my alibi:
my shoe, its eyelet, as well as its mud
and even the elbow bend
of my own shirt buttoned up.

¡Y si después de tántas palabras,
no sobrevive la palabra!
¡Si después de las alas de los pájaros,
no sobrevive el pájaro parado!
¡Más valdría, en verdad,
que se lo coman todo y acabemos!

¡Haber nacido para vivir de nuestra muerte!
¡Levantarse del cielo hacia la tierra
por sus propios desastres
y espiar el momento de apagar con su sombra su tiniebla!
¡Más valdría, francamente,
que se lo coman todo y qué más da! . . .

¡Y si después de tánta historia, sucumbimos,
no ya de eternidad,
sino de esas cosas sencillas, como estar
en la casa o ponerse a cavilar!
¡Y si luego encontramos,
de buenas a primeras, que vivimos,
a juzgar por la altura de los astros,
por el peine y las manchas del pañuelo!
¡Más valdría, en verdad,
que se lo coman todo, desde luego!

Se dirá que tenemos
en uno de los ojos mucha pena
y también en el otro, mucha pena
y en los dos, cuando miran, mucha pena . . .
Entonces . . . ¡Claro! . . . Entonces . . . ¡ni palabra!

[1936]

And if after so many words,
the word itself does not survive!
If after the wings of the birds,
the standing bird doesn't survive!
It would be much better, really,
for them to blow it all and be done with it!   *

To have been born to live off our death!
To raise ourselves from the sky toward the earth
through our own disasters
and to spy the moment to extinguish our darkness with our shadow!
It would be much better, frankly,
for them to blow it all, what's the difference! . . .

And if after so much history, we die,
no longer of eternity
but of those simple things, like being
at home or starting to ponder!
And if then we discover,
all of a sudden, that we are living,
to judge by the height of heavenly bodies,
off the comb and the stains of a handkerchief!
It would be much better, really,
for them to blow it all, yes of course!

It will be said that we have
in one eye much sorrow
and also in the other, much sorrow
and in both, when they look, much sorrow . . .
Then! . . . Of course! . . . Then . . . not a word!

¡Dulzura por dulzura corazona!
¡Dulzura a gajos, eras de vista,
esos abiertos días, cuando monté por árboles caídos!
Así por tu paloma palomita,
por tu oración pasiva,
andando entre tu sombra y el gran tezón corpóreo de tu sombra.

Debajo de ti y yo,
tú y yo, sinceramente,
tu candado ahogándose de llaves,
yo ascendiendo y sudando
y haciendo lo infinito entre tus muslos.
(El hotelero es una bestia,
sus dientes, admirables; yo controlo
el orden pálido de mi alma:
señor, allá distante . . . paso paso . . . adiós, señor . . .)

Mucho pienso en todo esto conmovido, perduroso
y pongo tu paloma a la altura de tu vuelo
y, cojeando de dicha, a veces,
repósome a la sombra de ese árbol arrastrado.

Costilla de mi cosa,
dulzura que tú tapas sonriendo con tu mano;
tu traje negro que se habrá acabado,
amada, amada en masa,
¡qué unido a tu rodilla enferma!

Simple ahora te veo, te comprendo avergonzado
en Letonia, Alemania, Rusia, Bélgica, tu ausente,
tu portátil ausente,
hombre convulso de la mujer temblando entre sus vínculos.

¡Amada en la figura de tu cola irreparable,
amada que yo amara con fósforos floridos,
quand on a la vie et la jeunesse,
c'est déjà tellement!

>

Sweetness through heartsown sweetness!   *
Sweetness in sections, eras by sight,
those open days, when I climbed over fallen trees!
Thus over your dove doveling,
over your passive sentence,
moving between your shadow and the great corporal teatnacity of your shadow.   *

Under thee and I,
you and I, in all sincerity,
your padlock choking with keys,
me climbing and sweating
and creating infinity between your thighs.
(The hotel manager is an ass,
his teeth, admirable; I control
the pallid order of my soul:
sir, you way over there . . . step step . . . good-bye, sir . . .)

I think a lot about all of this stirred, foreverish   *
and place your dove at the height of your flight
and, limping with happiness, at times,
I rest in the shadow of that dragged tree.

Rib of my thing,
sweetness that you cover smiling with your hand;
your black dress probably worn out,
beloved, beloved in mass,
how bound to your sick knee!

Simple I see you now, I understand you ashamed
in Lithuania, Germany, Russia, Belgium, your absent one,
your portable absent one,
man convulsed from the woman trembling between his ties.

Beloved in the figure of your irreparable tail,
my love who I loved with flowery matches,
quand on a la vie et la jeunesse,   *
c'est déjà tellement!   >

>   Cuando ya no haya espacio
entre tu grandeza y mi postrer proyecto,
amada,
volveré a tu media, haz de besarme,
bajando por tu media repetida,
tu portátil ausente, dile así . . .

[1931/1937]

>   When there is no longer space
between your greatness and my last project,
my love,
I'll return to your stocking, you well kiss me,   *
going down along your repeated stocking,
your portable absent one, tell him this way . . .

PIENSAN LOS VIEJOS ASNOS

Ahora vestiríame
de músico por verle,
chocaría con su alma, sobándole el destino con mi mano,
le dejaría tranquilo, ya que es un alma a pausas,
en fin, le dejaría
posiblemente muerto sobre su cuerpo muerto.

Podría hoy dilatarse en este frío,
podría toser; le vi bostezar, duplicándose en mi oído
su aciago movimiento muscular.
Tal me refiero a un hombre, a su placa positiva
y, ¿por qué nó? a su boldo ejecutante,
aquel horrible filamento lujoso;
a su bastón con puño de plata con perrito,
y a los niños
que él dijo eran sus fúnebres cuñados.

Por eso vestiríame hoy de músico,
chocaría con su alma que quedóse mirando a mi materia . . .

¡Mas ya nunca veréle afeitándose al pie de su mañana;
ya nunca, ya jamás, ya para qué!
¡Hay que ver! ¡Qué cosa cosa!
¡qué jamás de jamases su jamás!

[1931/1932, 1937]

OLD ASSES THINKING

Now I would dress up
as a musician to see him,
would collide with his soul, kneading his destiny with my hand,
I would leave him at peace, now that he is a soul at intervals,
in short, I would leave him
possibly dead on his dead body.

He could expand today in this cold,
could cough; I saw him yawn, duplicating in my ear
his ominous muscular movement.
So do I talk about a man, about his positive plate,
and, why not, about his executing boldo,
that horrible luxurious filament;
about his silver-headed cane with a little dog,
and about the children
whom he referred to as his funereal brothers-in-law.

That is why I would dress up today as a musician,
would collide with his soul that kept looking at my matter . . .

But never again will I see him shaving at the foot of his morning;
now never, now never again, what for!
It's something to see! What a thing thing!
what a never of the nevers his never!

TELÚRICA Y MAGNÉTICA

¡Mecánica sincera y peruanísima
la del cerro colorado!
¡Suelo teórico y práctico!
¡Surcos inteligentes; ejemplo: el monolito y su cortejo!
¡Papales, cebadales, alfalfares, cosa buena!
¡Cultivos que integra una asombrosa jerarquía de útiles
y que integran con viento los mujidos,
las aguas con su sorda antigüedad!

¡Cuaternarios maíces, de opuestos natalicios,
los oigo por los pies cómo se alejan,
los huelo retornar cuando la tierra
tropieza con la técnica del cielo!
¡Molécula exabrupto! ¡Atomo terso!

¡Oh campos humanos!
¡Solar y nutricia ausencia de la mar,
y sentimiento oceánico de todo!
¡Oh climas encontrados dentro del oro, listos!
¡Oh campo intelectual de cordillera,
con religión, con campo, con patitos!
¡Paquidermos en prosa cuando pasan
y en verso cuando páranse!
¡Roedores que miran con sentimiento judicial en torno!
¡Oh patrióticos asnos de mi vida!
¡Vicuña, descendiente
nacional y graciosa de mi mono!
¡Oh luz que dista apenas un espejo de la sombra,
que es vida con el punto y, con la línea, polvo
y que por eso acato, subiendo por la idea a mi osamenta!

¡Siega en época del dilatado molle,
del farol que colgaron de la sien
y del que descolgaron de la barreta espléndida!
¡Angeles de corral,
aves por un descuido de la cresta!
¡Cuya o cuy para comerlos fritos
con el bravo rocoto de los temples!
(¿Cóndores? ¡Me friegan los cóndores!)

>

TELLURIC AND MAGNETIC

                                                 *

Sincere and utterly Peruvian mechanics   *
that of the reddened hill!   *
Soil theoretical and practical!
Intelligent furrows: example; the monolith and its retinue!
Potato fields, barley fields, alfalfa fields, good things!
Cultivations which integrate an astonishing hierarchy of tools
and which integrate with wind the lowings,
the waters with their deaf antiquity!

Quaternary maize, with opposed birthdays,
I hear through my feet how they move away,
I smell them return when the earth
clashes with the sky's technique!
Abruptly molecule! Terse atom!

Oh human fields!   *
Solar and nutritious absence of the sea,
and oceanic feeling for everything!
Oh climates found within gold, ready!
Oh intellectual field of cordilleras,
with religion, with fields, with ducklings!
Pachyderms in prose when passing
and in poetry when stopping!
Rodents who peer with judicial feeling all around!
Oh my life's patriotic asses!
Vicuña, national
and graceful descendant of my ape!
Oh light hardly a mirror from shadow,
which is life with the period and, with the line, dust
and that is why I revere, climbing through the idea to my skeleton!

Harvest in the epoch of the spread pepper tree,   *
of the lantern hung from a human temple
and of the one unhung from the magnificent barret!   *
Poultry-yard angels,
birds by a slipup of the cockscomb!
Cavess or cavy to be eaten fried   *
with the hot bird pepper from the templed valleys!   *
(Condors? Screw the condors!)   >   *

> ¡Leños cristianos en gracia
al tronco feliz y al tallo competente!
¡Familia de los líquenes,
especies en formación basáltica que yo
respeto
desde este modestísimo papel!
¡Cuatro operaciones, os sustraigo
para salvar al roble y hundirlo en buena ley!
¡Cuestas en infraganti!
¡Auquénidos llorosos, almas mías!
¡Sierra de mi Perú, Perú del mundo,
y Perú al pie del orbe; yo me adhiero!
¡Estrellas matutinas si os aromo
quemando hojas de coca en este cráneo,
y cenitales, si destapo,
de un solo sombrerazo, mis diez templos!
¡Brazo de siembra, bájate, y a pie!
¡Lluvia a base del mediodía,
bajo el techo de tejas donde muerde
la infatigable altura
y la tórtola corta en tres su trino!
¡Rotación de tardes modernas
y finas madrugadas arqueológicas!
¡Indio después del hombre y antes de él!
¡Lo entiendo todo en dos flautas
y me doy a entender en una quena!
¡Y lo demás, me las pelan! . . .

[1931/1932, 1936, 1937]

> Christian logs by the grace of
a happy trunk and a competent stalk!
Family of lichens,
species in basalt formation that I
respect
from this most modest paper!
Four operations, I subtract you
to save the oak and sink it in sterling!
Slopes caught in the act!
Tearful Auchenia, my own souls!   *
Sierra of my Peru, Peru of the world,
and Peru at the foot of the globe: I adhere!
Morning stars if I aromatize you
burning coca leaves in this skull,
and zenithal ones, if I uncover,
with one hat doff, my ten temples!
Arm sowing, get down and on foot!
Rain based on noon,
under the tile roof where indefatigable
altitude gnaws
and the turtle dove cuts her trill in three!
Rotation of modern afternoons
and delicate archaeological daybreaks.
Indian after man and before him!
I understand all of it on two flutes
and I make myself understood on a quena!   *
As for the others, they can jerk me off! . . .   *

Los mineros salieron de la mina
remontando sus minas venideras,
fajaron su salud con estampidos
y, elaborando su función mental,
cerraron con sus voces
el socavón, en forma de síntoma profundo.

¡Era de ver sus polvos corrosivos!
¡Era de oír sus óxidos de altura!
Cuñas de boca, yunques de boca, aparatos de boca (¡Es formidable!)

El orden de sus túmulos,
sus inducciones plásticas, sus respuestas corales,
agolpáronse al pie de ígneos percances
y airente amarillura conocieron los trístidos y tristes,
imbuidos
del metal que se acaba, del metaloide pálido y pequeño.

Craneados de labor,
y calzados de cuero de vizcacha
calzados de senderos infinitos,
y los ojos de físico llorar,
creadores de la profundidad,
saben, a cielo intermitente de escalera,
bajar mirando para arriba,
saben subir mirando para abajo.

¡Loor al antiguo juego de su naturaleza,
a sus insomnes órganos, a su saliva rústica!
¡Temple, filo y punta, a sus pestañas!
¡Crezcan la yerba, el liquen y la rana en sus adverbios!
¡Felpa de hierro a sus nupciales sábanas!
¡Mujeres hasta abajo, sus mujeres!
¡Mucha felicidad para los suyos!
¡Son algo portentoso, los mineros
remontando sus ruinas venideras,
elaborando su función mental
y abriendo con sus voces
el socavón, en forma de síntoma profundo!
¡Loor a su naturaleza amarillenta,
a su linterna mágica,   >

The miners came out of the mine   *
climbing over their future ruins,
they girdled their health with blasts
and, elaborating their mental function,
closed with their voices
the shaft, in the shape of a profound symptom.

Just to have seen their corrosive dust!
Just to have heard their oxides of the heights!
Mouth wedges, mouth anvils, mouth apparatus (It is tremendous!)

The order of their tumuli,
their plastic inductions, their choral responses,
crowded at the foot of fiery misfortunes
and aerent yellowing known by the saddish and the sad ones,   *
imbued
with the metal that peters out, the pallid and humble metalloid.

Craniated with labor
and shod with viscacha hide
shod with infinite paths,
and eyes of physical weeping,   *
creators of the profundity,
they know, from the ladder's intermittent sky,
how to climb down looking up,
how to climb up looking down.

Praise for the ancient game of their nature,
for their sleepless organs, for their rustic saliva!
Temper, edge and point, for their eyelashes!
May grass, lichen and frogs grow in their adverbs!
Iron plush for their nuptial sheets!
Women to the depths, their women!
Much happiness for their people!
They're something prodigious, those miners
climbing over their future ruins,
elaborating their mental function
and opening with their voices
the shaft, in the shape of a profound symptom!
Praise for their yellowish nature,
for their magic lantern,   >

>   a sus cubos y rombos, a sus percances plásticos,
a sus ojazos de seis nervios ópticos
y a sus hijos que juegan en la iglesia
y a sus tácitos padres infantiles!
¡Salud, oh creadores de la profundidad! . . . (Es formidable)

[1931/1932, 1937]

for their cubes and rhombs, for their plastic misfortunes,
for their huge eyes with six optical nerves
and for their children who play in the church
and for their tacit infantile parents!
Hail, oh creators of the profundity! . . . (It is tremendous)

De disturbio en disturbio
subes a acompañarme a estar solo;
yo lo comprendo andando de puntillas,
con un pan en la mano, un camino en el pie
y haciendo, negro hasta sacar espuma,
mi perfil su papel espeluznante.

Ya habías disparado para atrás tu violencia
neumática, otra época, mas luego
me sostienes ahora en brazo de honra fúnebre
y sostienes el rumbo de las cosas en brazo de honra fúnebre,
la muerte de las cosas resumida en brazo de honra fúnebre.

Pero, realmente y puesto
que tratamos de la vida,
cuando el hecho de entonces eche crin en tu mano,
al seguir tu rumor como regando,
cuando sufras en suma de kanguro,
olvídame, sosténme todavía, compañero de cantidad pequeña,
azotado de fechas con espinas,
olvídame y sosténme por el pecho,
jumento que te paras en dos para abrazarme;
duda de tu excremento unos segundos,
observa cómo el aire empieza a ser el cielo levantándose,
hombrecillo,
hombrezuelo,
hombre con taco, quiéreme, acompáñame . . .

Ten presente que un día
ha de cantar un mirlo de sotana
sobre mi tonelada ya desnuda.
(Cantó un mirlo llevando las cintas de mi gramo entre su pico)
Ha de cantar calzado de este sollozo innato,
hombre con taco,
y, simultánea, doloridamente,
ha de cantar calzado de mi paso,
y no oírlo, hombrezuelo, será malo,
será denuesto y hoja,
pesadumbre, trenza, humo quieto.   >

From disturbance to disturbance
you rise to accompany me to be alone;
I realize this walking on tiptoes,
bread in hand, a road on foot
and, black until it foams over,
my profile playing its terrifying role.

You have already fired your pneumatic violence
backwards, another epoch, but then
you now support me on the arm of funereal honor
and support the course of things on the arm of funereal honor,
the death of things summarized on the arm of funereal honor.

But, actually, and since
we deal with life,
when the fact of then grows mane in your hand,
upon following your rustle like watering,
when you suffer in short from kangaroo,   *
forget me, support me still, companion of small amount,
whipped by dates with thorns,
forget me and support me by my chest,
donkey who stands up on two to embrace me;
doubt your excrement for a moment,
observe how the air begins to be sky rising,
dear little man,
petty little man,
man with shoe heel, love me, keep me company . . .   *

Keep in mind that one day
a blackbird in cassock will sing
over my ton finally naked.
(A blackbird did sing carrying the ribbons of my gram in its beak)
It will sing shod with this innate sob,
man with shoe heel,
and, simultaneously, grievously,
will sing shod with my step,
and not to hear it, petty little man, will be bad,
will be insult and leaf,
sorrow, braid, motionless smoke.   >

>   Perro parado al borde de una piedra
es el vuelo en su curva;
también tenlo presente, hombrón hasta arriba.
Te lo recordarán el peso bajo, de ribera adversa,
el peso temporal, de gran silencio,
más eso de los meses y aquello que regresa de los años.

[1936/1937]

A dog standing by the edge of a stone
is the flight in its curve;
keep that in mind too, lustful man until above.
The low weight, of an adverse shore,
the temporal weight, of great silence, will remind you of this,
plus that of the months and that which returns from the years.

Quisiera hoy ser feliz de buena gana,
ser feliz y portarme frondoso de preguntas,
abrir por temperamento de par en par mi cuarto, como loco,
y reclamar, en fin,
en mi confianza física acostado,
sólo por ver si quieren,
sólo por ver si quieren probar de mi espontánea posición,
reclamar, voy diciendo,
por qué me dan así tánto en el alma.

Pues quisiera en sustancia ser dichoso,
obrar sin bastón, laica humildad, ni burro negro.
Así las sensaciones de este mundo,
los cantos subjuntivos,
el lápiz que perdí en mi cavidad
y mis amados órganos de llanto.

Hermano persuasible, camarada,
padre por la grandeza, hijo mortal,
amigo y contendor, inmenso documento de Darwin:
¿a qué hora, pues, vendrán con mi retrato?
¿A los goces? ¿Acaso sobre goce amortajado?
¿Más temprano? ¿Quién sabe, a las porfías?

A las misericordias, camarada,
hombre mío en rechazo y observación, vecino
en cuyo cuello enorme sube y baja,
al natural, sin hilo, mi esperanza . . .

[1937]

Today I would like to be happy willingly,
to be happy and behave leafy with questions,
by temperament to open wide my room, like a mad man,
and to demand, in short,
reclined on my physical trust,
only to see if they would like,
only to see if they would like to try my spontaneous position,
to demand, I keep saying,
why they hit me like this so much in my soul.   *

For I would like in substance to be happy,
to proceed without cane, laic humility, or black jackass.
Thus the sensations of this world,
the subjunctive songs,
the pencil that I lost in my cavity
and my beloved organs for crying.

Persuadable brother, comrade,
father through greatness, mortal son,
friend and opponent, immense document of Darwin:
at what hour, then, will they come with my portrait?   *
At the delights? Perhaps around delight shrouded?
Earlier? Who knows, at the disputations?

At the misericordias, comrade,   *
fellow man in rejection and observation, neighbor
in whose enormous neck rises and lowers,
naked, without thread, my hope . . .

II

Calor, cansado voy con mi oro, a donde
acaba mi enemigo de quererme.
¡C'est Septembre attiédi, por ti, Febrero!
Es como si me hubieran puesto aretes.

París, y 4, y 5, y la ansiedad
colgada, en el calor, de mi hecho muerto.
¡C'est Paris, reine du monde!
Es como si se hubieran orinado.

Hojas amargas de mensual tamaño
y hojas del Luxemburgo polvorosas.
¡C'est l'été, por ti, invierno de alta pleura!
Es como si se hubieran dado vuelta.

Calor, París, Otoño, ¡cuánto estío
en medio del calor y de la urbe!
¡C'est la vie, mort de la Mort!
Es como si contaran mis pisadas.

¡Es como si me hubieran puesto aretes!
¡Es como si se hubieran orinado!
¡Es como si te hubieras dado vuelta!
¡Es como si contaran mis pisadas!

4 Set. 1937

II

Heat, tired I go with my gold, where
my enemy has just finished loving me.
C'est Septembre attiédi, for you, February!   *
It's as if they had put earrings on me.

Paris, and 4, and 5, and the anxiety   *
hanging in the heat, from my dead act.
C'est Paris, reine du monde!
It's as if they had urinated.

Bitter leaves of monthly size
and dusty leaves from the Luxembourg.
C'est l'été, for you, winter of high pleura!
It's as if they had turned around.

Heat, Paris, Autumn, so much summer
in the midst of the heat and of the city!
C'est la vie, mort de la Mort!
It's as if they had counted my steps.

It's as if they had put earrings on me!
It's as if they had urinated!
It's as if you yourself had turned around!
It's as if they had counted my steps!

Un pilar soportando consuelos,
pilar otro,
pilar en duplicado, pilaroso
y como nieto de una puerta oscura.
Ruido perdido, el uno, oyendo, al borde del cansancio;
bebiendo, el otro, dos a dos, con asas.

¿Ignoro acaso el año de este día,
el odio de este amor, las tablas de esta frente?
¿Ignoro que esta tarde cuesta días?
¿Ignoro que jamás se dice "nunca", de rodillas?

Los pilares que vi me están oyendo;
otros pilares son, doses y nietos tristes de mi pierna.
¡Lo digo en cobre americano,
que le debe a la plata tánto fuego!

Consolado en terceras nupcias,
pálido, nacido,
voy a cerrar mi pila bautismal, esta vidriera,
este susto con tetas,
este dedo en capilla,
corazónmente unido a mi esqueleto.

6 Set. 1937

One pillar supporting solace,
another pillar,
a duplicate pillar, pillarous   *
and like the grandchild of a dark door.
Lost noise, the one, listening, at the edge of fatigue;
drinking, the other, two by two, with handles.

Don't I know the year of this day,
the hatred of this love, the tablets of this forehead?
Don't I know that this afternoon costs days?
Don't I know that never does one say "never," on one's knees?

The pillars that I saw are listening to me;
there are other pillars, twos and sad grandchildren of my leg.
I say it in American copper,
which owes to silver so much fire!

Consoled by third marriages,
pallid, born,
I'm going to close my baptismal font, this showcase,   *
this fright with tits,
this finger in death row,
hearterially joined to my skeleton.   *

Al cavilar en la vida, al cavilar
despacio en el esfuerzo del torrente,
alivia, ofrece asiento el existir,
condena a muerte;
envuelto en trapos blancos cae,
cae planetariamente
el clavo hervido en pesadumbre; cae!
(Acritud oficial, la de mi izquierda;
viejo bolsillo, en sí considerada, esta derecha.)

¡Todo está alegre, menos mi alegría
y todo, largo, menos mi candor,
mi incertidumbre!
A juzgar por la forma, no obstante, voy de frente,
cojeando antiguamente,
y olvido por mis lágrimas mis ojos (Muy interesante)
y subo hasta mis pies desde mi estrella.

Tejo; de haber hilado, héme tejiendo.
Busco lo que me sigue y se me esconde entre arzobispos,
por debajo de mi alma y tras del humo de mi aliento.
Tal era la sensual desolación
de la cabra doncella que ascendía,
exhalando petróleos fatídicos,
ayer domingo en que perdí mi sábado.

Tal es la muerte, con su audaz marido.

7 Set. 1937

Upon meditating on life, upon meditating   *
slowly on the vigor of the torrent,
existence lightens, offers support,
condemns to death;
wrapped in white rags it falls,
falls planetarily,
the nail boiled in sorrow; it falls!
(Official acrimony, that of my left;
old pocket, in itself considered, this right.)

All is joyful, except my joy
and all, long, except my candor,
my incertitude!
To judge by the form, nevertheless, I go forward,
anciently limping,
and forget through my tears my eyes (Very interesting)
and climb up to my feet from my star.

I weave; from having spun, I'm weaving.
I search for what follows me and hides from me among archbishops,
under my soul and behind the smoke of my breath.
Such was the sensual desolation
of the maiden goat who ascended,
exhaling fatidic petroleums,
yesterday Sunday on which I lost my Saturday.

Such is death, with her audacious husband.

POEMA PARA SER LEÍDO Y CANTADO

Sé que hay una persona
que me busca en su mano, día y noche,
encontrándome, a cada minuto, en su calzado.
¿Ignora que la noche está enterrada
con espuelas detrás de la cocina?

Sé que hay una persona compuesta de mis partes,
a la que integro cuando va mi talle
cabalgando en su exacta piedrecilla.
¿Ignora que a su cofre
no volverá moneda que salió con su retrato?

Sé el día,
pero el sol se me ha escapado;
sé el acto universal que hizo en su cama
con ajeno valor y esa agua tibia, cuya
superficial frecuencia es una mina.
¿Tan pequeña es, acaso, esa persona,
que hasta sus propios pies así la pisan?

Un gato es el lindero entre ella y yo,
al lado mismo de su tasa de agua.
La veo en las esquinas, se abre y cierra
su veste, antes palmera interrogante . . .
¿Qué podrá hacer sino cambiar de llanto?

Pero me busca y busca. ¡Es una historia!

7 Set. 1937

POEM TO BE READ AND SUNG

I know there is a person
who looks for me in her hand, day and night,
finding me, every minute, in her shoes.
Doesn't she know that the night is buried
with spurs behind the kitchen?

I know there is a person composed of my parts,
who I make whole when my waist
gallops off on its punctual little stone.
Doesn't she know that the coin
imprinted with her effigy will not return to her coffer?

I know the day,
but the sun has escaped me;
I know the universal act she performed in her bed
with alien courage and that tepid water, whose
superficial frequency is a mine.
Is that person, perhaps, so small
that even her own feet step on her?

A cat is the boundary between her and me,
right at the edge of its measure of water.
I see her on the street corners, her robe
opening and closing, formerly an inquiring palm tree . . .
What can she do but change weeping?

But she looks and looks for me. What a story!

El acento me pende del zapato;
le oigo perfectamente
sucumbir, lucir, doblarse en forma de ámbar
y colgar, colorante, mala sombra.
Me sobra así el tamaño,
me ven jueces desde un árbol,
me ven con sus espaldas ir de frente,
entrar a mi martillo,
pararme a ver a una niña
y, al pie de un urinario, alzar los hombros.

Seguramente nadie está a mi lado,
me importa poco, no lo necesito;
seguramente han dicho que me vaya:
lo siento claramente.

¡Cruelísimo tamaño el de rezar!
¡Humillación, fulgor, profunda selva!
Me sobra ya tamaño, bruma elástica,
rapidez por encima y desde y junto.
¡Imperturbable! ¡Imperturbable! Suenan
luego, después, fatídicos teléfonos.
Es el acento; es él.

12 Set. 1937

The accent hangs from my shoe;
I hear it succumb
perfectly, shine, fold in the shape of amber
and dangle, coloring, an evil shade.
Thus my size exceeds me,
judges observe me from a tree
with their backs, observe me walk forward,
enter my hammer,
stop to look at a girl
and, at the foot of a urinal, shrug my shoulders.

For sure no one's at my side,
I could care less, don't need it;
for sure they've told me to be off:
I feel it clearly.

The cruelest size is that of prayer!
Humiliation, fulgor, deep forest!
Already size exceeds me, elastic fog,
rapidity above, since and close by.
Imperturbable! Imperturbable! Fatidic
phones ring at once, afterward.
It's the accent; it's it.

La punta del hombre,
el ludibrio pequeño de encojerse
tras de fumar su universal ceniza;
punta al darse en secretos caracoles,
punta donde se agarra uno con guantes,
punta el lunes sujeto por seis frenos,
punta saliendo de escuchar a su alma.

De otra manera,
fueran lluvia menuda los soldados
y ni cuadrada pólvora, al volver de los bravos desatinos,
y ni letales plátanos; tan sólo
un poco de patilla en la silueta.
De otra manera, caminantes suegros,
cuñados en misión sonora,
yernos por la vía ingratísima del jebe,
toda la gracia caballar andando
puede fulgir esplendorosamente!

¡Oh pensar geométrico al trasluz!
¡Oh no morir bajamente
de majestad tan rauda y tan fragante!
¡Oh no cantar; apenas
escribir y escribir con un palito
o con el filo de la oreja inquieta!

Acorde de lápiz, tímpano sordísimo,
dondoneo en mitades robustas
y comer de memoria buena carne,
jamón, si falta carne,
y un pedazo de queso con gusanos hembras,
gusanos machos y gusanos muertos.

14 Set. 1937

The tip of man,
the petty mockery of shrinking
after smoking his universal ash;
tip yielding to secret snails,
tip one grasps wearing gloves,
tip Monday restrained with six bridles,
tip emerging from listening to his soul.

Otherwise,
the soldiers could have been fine rain
and neither square gunpowder, returning from their brave follies,
nor deadly bananas; only
a bit of sideburn on the silhouette.
Otherwise, walking fathers-in-law,
brothers-in-law on a sonorous mission,
sons-in-law by the most unpleasant route of a rubber,
all the equine grace walking
can flash resplendently!

Oh to think geometrically against the light!
Oh not to die lowly
from majesty so swift and so fragrant!
Oh not to sing; barely
to write and to write with a little stick
or with the edge of a restless ear!

Pencil chord, deafest eardrum,
stirrut in robust halves   *
and to eat by heart choice meat,
ham, if there is no meat,
and a piece of cheese with female worms,
male worms and dead worms.

¡Oh botella sin vino! ¡oh vino que enviudó de esta botella!
Tarde cuando la aurora de la tarde
flameó funestamente en cinco espíritus.
Viudez sin pan ni mugre, rematando en horrendos metaloides
y en células orales acabando.

¡Oh siempre, nunca dar con el jamás de tánto siempre!
¡oh mis buenos amigos, cruel falacia,
parcial, penetrativa en nuestro trunco,
volátil, jugarino desconsuelo!

¡Sublime, baja perfección del cerdo,
palpa mi general melancolía!
¡Zuela sonante en sueños,
zuela
zafia, inferior, vendida, lícita, ladrona,
baja y palpa lo que eran mis ideas!

Tu y él y ellos y todos,
sin embargo,
entraron a la vez en mi camisa,
en los hombros madera, entre los fémures, palillos;
tú particularmente,
habiéndome influido;
él, fútil, colorado, con dinero
y ellos, zánganos de ala de otro peso.

¡Oh botella sin vino! ¡oh vino que enviudó de esta botella!

16 Set. 1937

Oh bottle without wine! oh wine the widower of this bottle!
Afternoon when the aurora of the afternoon
flamed balefully in five spirits.
Widowhood without bread or grime, finishing in hideous metalloids
and in oral cells ending.

Oh always, never to find the never of so much always!
oh my good friends, a cruel deceit,
partial, piercing our truncated
volatile, frolicful grief!   *

The sublime, low perfection of the pig,
gropes my customary melancholy!
Adz sounding in dreams,
adz
asinine, inferior, betrayed, lawful, thief,
lowering and groping what were once my ideas!

You and he and they and everyone,
nevertheless,
inserted at the same time into my shirt,
into my shoulders wood, between my femurs, little sticks;
you particularly,
having influenced me;
he, futile, reddened, with money,
and they, winged drones of another weight.

Oh bottle without wine! oh wine the widower of this bottle!

Va corriendo, andando, huyendo
de sus pies . . .
Va con dos nubes en su nube,
sentado apócrifo, en la mano insertos
sus tristes paras, sus entonces fúnebres.

Corre de todo, andando
entre protestas incoloras; huye
subiendo, huye
bajando, huye
a paso de sotana, huye
alzando al mal en brazos,
huye
directamente a sollozar a solas.

Adonde vaya,
lejos de sus fragosos, cáusticos talones,
lejos del aire, lejos de su viaje,
a fin de huir, huir y huir y huir
de sus pies—hombre en dos pies, parado
de tánto huir—habrá sed de correr.

¡Y ni el árbol, si endosa hierro de oro!
¡Y ni el hierro, si cubre su hojarasca!
Nada, sino sus pies,
nada sino su breve calofrío,
sus paras vivos, sus entonces vivos . . .

18 Set. 1937

He goes running, walking, fleeing
from his feet . . .
He goes with two clouds on his cloud,
apocryphal sitting, his sad fors,
his funereal thens, inserted in his hand.

He runs from everything, walking
between colorless protests; he flees
ascending, flees
descending, flees
at a cassock pace, flees
raising evil in his arms,
flees
directly to sob alone.

Wherever he goes,
far from his rough, caustic heels,
far from the air, far from his journey,
in order to flee, to flee and to flee and to flee
from his feet—man on both feet, checked
from so much flight—will have a thirst for running.

And neither the tree, if it endorses iron with gold!
Nor iron, if it covers up its dead leaves!
Nothing, but his feet,
nothing but his brief chill,
his fors alive, his thens alive . . .

*

Al fin, un monte
detrás de la bajura; al fin, humeante nimbo
alrededor, durante un rostro fijo.

Monte en honor del pozo,
sobre
filones de gratuita plata de oro.

Es la franja a que arrástranse,
seguras de sus tonos de verano,
las que eran largas válvulas difuntas;
el taciturno marco de este arranque
natural, de este augusto zapatazo,
de esta piel, de este intrínseco destello
digital, en que estoy entero, lúbrico.

Quehaceres en un pie, mecha de azufre,
oro de plata y plata hecha de plata
y mi muerte, mi hondura, mi colina.

¡Pasar
abrazado a mis brazos,
destaparme después o antes del corcho!
Monte que tántas veces manara
oración, prosa fluvial de llanas lágrimas;
monte bajo, compuesto de suplicantes gradas
y, más allá, de torrenciales torres;
niebla entre el día y el alcohol del día,
caro verdor de coles, tibios asnos
complementarios, palos y maderas;
filones de gratuita plata de oro.

19 Set. 1937

At last, a mountain
behind the lowness: at last, a smoking nimbus
around, during a fixed face.

Mountain in honor of the well,
over
veins of free silver of gold.

It is the border toward which drag,
sure of their summer tones,
those who were defunct long valves;
the taciturn setting of this natural
outburst, of this august shoeblow,
of this skin, of this intrinsic digital
gleam, in which I am whole, lubricious.

Chores on a foot, fuse of sulfur,
gold of silver and silver made of silver
and my death, my depth, my knoll.

To pass
clasped in my arms,
to uncork myself after or before the cork!
Mountain that so often flowed
prayer, fluvial prose of sincere tears;
brushwood, composed of supplicant grades
and, beyond, of torrential towers;
fog between the day and the alcohol of the day,
dear verdure of cabbages, lukewarm asses
that blend in, sticks and wood;
veins of free silver of gold.

Quiere y no quiere su color mi pecho,
por cuyas bruscas vías voy, lloro con palo,
trato de ser feliz, lloro en mi mano,
recuerdo, escribo
y remacho una lágrima en mi pómulo.

Quiere su rojo el mal, el bien su rojo enrojecido
por el hacha suspensa,
por el trote del ala a pie volando,
y no quiere y sensiblemente
no quiere aquesto el hombre;
no quiere estar en su alma
acostado, en la sien latidos de asta,
el bimano, el muy bruto, el muy filósofo.

Así, casi no soy, me vengo abajo
desde el arado en que socorro a mi alma
y casi, en proporción, casi enaltézcome.
Que saber por qué tiene la vida este perrazo,
por qué lloro, por qué,
cejón, inhábil, veleidoso, hube nacido
gritando;
saberlo, comprenderlo
al son de un alfabeto competente,
sería padecer por un ingrato.

¡Y no! ¡No! ¡No! ¡Qué ardid, ni paramento!
Congoja, sí, con sí firme y frenético,
coriáceo, rapaz, quiere y no quiere, cielo y pájaro;
congoja, sí, con toda la bragueta.
Contienda entre dos llantos, robo de una sola ventura,
vía indolora en que padezco en chanclos
de la velocidad de andar a ciegas

22 Set. 1937

My chest wants and does not want its color,
through whose rough paths I go, I cry with a stick,
try to be happy, cry in my hand,
remember, write
and rivet a tear into my cheekbone.

Evil wants its red, good its red reddened
by the suspended ax,
by the trot of the wing flying on foot,
and man does not want, sensitively
does not want this;
he does not want to be lying down
in his soul, horn throbs in his temples,
the bimanous, the very brutish, the very philosophical.

Thus, I am almost not, I collapse
from the plow with which I succor my soul
and almost, in proportion, almost exalt myself.
To know why this dog dogs life,
why I cry, why,
big-browed, inept, fickle, I was born   *
screaming;
to know it, to comprehend it
to the sound of a competent alphabet
would be to suffer for an ingrate.

And no! No! No! Neither scheme, nor ornament!
Anguish, yes, with a yes firm and frenetic,
coriaceous, rapacious, want and does not want, sky and pecker;
anguish, yes, with all my zipper.   *
Struggle between two sobs, theft of a sole chance,
painless path on which I endure in clogs
the velocity of walking blind.

Esto
sucedió entre dos párpados; temblé
en mi vaina, colérico, alcalino,
parado junto al lúbrico equinoccio,
al pie del frío incendio en que me acabo.

Resbalón alcalino, voy diciendo,
más acá de los ajos, sobre el sentido almíbar,
más adentro, muy más, de las herrumbres,
al ir el agua y al volver la ola.
Resbalón alcalino
también y grandemente, en el montaje colosal del cielo.

¡Qué venablos y harpones lanzaré, si muero
en mi vayna; daré en hojas de plátano sagrado
mis cinco huesecillos subalternos,
y en la mirada, la mirada misma!
(Dicen que en los suspiros se edifican
entonces acordeones óseos, táctiles;
dicen que cuando mueren así los que se acaban,
¡ay! mueren fuera del reloj, la mano
agarrada a un zapato solitario)

Comprendiéndolo y todo, coronel
y todo, en el sentido llorante de esta voz,
me hago doler yo mismo, extraigo tristemente,
por la noche, mis uñas;
luego no tengo nada y hablo solo,
reviso mis semestres
y para henchir mi vértebra, me toco.

23 Set. 1937

This   *
happened between two eyelids; I quivered
in my sheath, choleric, alkaline,
standing by the lubricious equinox,
at the foot of the cold blaze in which I perish.

Alkaline slip, I keep saying,
closer than garlic, on top of the syrup sense,
deeper in, much deeper, than rust,
on going the water and on coming the wave.
Alkaline slip
too, a big one, in the colossal staging of the sky.   *

What darts and arpoons I will hurl, if I die   *
in my sheeth; in sacred banana leaves I will offer up   *
my five subaltern little bones,   *
and in the look, the look itself!
(It is said that it is with sighs one builds   *
then bony, tactile accordions;
it is said that when those who perish die this way,
aie! they die outside the clock, the hand
clutching a solitary shoe)

Comprehending it all, cymatium
and all, in the crying sense of this voice,
I make myself suffer, I extract sadly,
at night, my fingernails;
then I have nothing and talk alone,
I revise my semesters   *
and in order to gorge my vertebra, touch myself.

Quedéme a calentar la tinta en que me ahogo
y a escuchar mi caverna alternativa,
noches de tacto, días de abstracción.

Se estremeció la incógnita en mi amígdala
y crují de una anual melancolía,
noches de sol, días de luna, ocasos de París.

Y todavía, hoy mismo, al atardecer,
digiero sacratísimas constancias,
noches de madre, días de biznieta
bicolor, voluptuosa, urgente, linda.

Y aun
alcanzo, llego hasta mí en avión de dos asientos,
bajo la mañana doméstica y la bruma
que emergió eternamente de un instante.

Y todavía,
aun ahora,
al cabo del cometa en que he ganado
mi bacilo feliz y doctoral,
he aquí que caliente, oyente, tierro, sol y luno,
incógnito atravieso el cementerio,
tomo a la izquierda, hiendo
la yerba con un par de endecasílabos,
años de tumba, litros de infinito,
tinta, pluma, ladrillos y perdones.

24 Set. 1937

I stayed on to warm up the ink in which I drown   *
and to listen to my alternative cavern,
tactile nights, abstracted days.

The unknown shuddered in my tonsil
and I creaked from an annual melancholy,
solar nights, lunar days, Parisian sunsets.

And still, this very day, at dusk   *
I digest the most sacred certainties,
maternal nights, great-granddaughter days,
bicolored, voluptuous, urgent, lovely.

And yet
I arrive, I reach myself in a two-seated plane
under the domestic morning and the mist
which emerged eternally from an instant.

And still,
even now,
at the tail of the comet in which I have earned
my happy and doctoral bacillus,   *
behold that warm, listener, male earth, sun and male moon,   *
incognito I cross the cemetery,
head off to the left, splitting
the grass with a pair of hendecasyllables,
tombal years, infinitary liters,   *
ink, pen, bricks and forgiveness.

La paz, la abispa, el taco, las vertientes,
el muerto, los decílitros, el búho,
los lugares, la tiña, los sarcófagos, el vaso, las morenas,
el desconocimiento, la olla, el monaguillo,
las gotas, el olvido,
la potestad, los primos, los arcángeles, la aguja,
los párrocos, el ébano, el desaire,
la parte, el tipo, el estupor, el alma . . .

Dúctil, azafranado, externo, nítido,
portátil, viejo, trece, ensangrentado,
fotografiadas, listas, tumefactas,
conexas, largas, encintadas, pérfidas . . .

Ardiendo, comparando,
viviendo, enfureciéndose,
golpeando, analizando, oyendo, estremeciéndose,
muriendo, sosteniéndose, situándose, llorando . . .

Después, éstos, aquí,
después, encima,
quizá, mientras, detrás, tánto, tan nunca,
debajo, acaso, lejos,
siempre, aquello, mañana, cuánto,
cuánto! . . .

Lo horrible, lo suntuario, lo lentísimo,
lo augusto, lo infructuoso,
lo aciago, lo crispante, lo mojado, lo fatal,
lo todo, lo purísimo, lo lóbrego,
lo acerbo, lo satánico, lo táctil, lo profundo . . .

25 Set. 1937

The peace, the wausp, the shoe heel, the slopes,   *
the dead one, the deciliters, the owl,
the places, the ringworm, the sarcophagi, the glass, the brunettes,
the ignorance, the kettle, the altar boy,
the drops, the oblivion,
the potentate, the cousins, the archangels, the needle,
the priests, the ebony, the rebuff,
the part, the type, the stupor, the soul . . .

Flexible, saffroned, external, neat,
portable, old, thirteen, blood-smeared,
those photographed, ready, tumescent,
those linked, long, beribboned, perfidious . . .

Burning, comparing,
living, raging,
striking, analyzing, hearing, shuddering,
dying, standing firm, succeeding, weeping . . .

After, these, here,
after, above,
perhaps, while, behind, so much, so never,
below, by chance, distant,
always, that one, tomorrow, how much,
how much! . . .

The horrible, the sumptuous, the slowest,
the august, the fruitless,
the ominous, the convulsive, the wet, the fatal,
the whole, the purest, the lugubrious,
the bitter, the satanic, the tactile, the profound . . .

Transido, salomónico, decente,
ululaba; compuesto, caviloso, cadavérico, perjuro,
iba, tornaba, respondía; osaba,
fatídico, escarlata, irresistible.

En sociedad, en vidrio, en polvo, en hulla,
marchóse; vaciló, en hablando en oro; fulguró,
volteó, en acatamiento;
en terciopelo, en llanto, replegóse.

¿Recordar? ¿Insistir? ¿Ir? ¿Perdonar?
Ceñudo, acabaría
recostado, áspero, atónito, mural;
meditaba estamparse, confundirse, fenecer.

Inatacablemente, impunemente,
negramente, husmeará, comprenderá;
vestiráse oralmente;
inciertamente irá, acobardaráse, olvidará.

26 Set. 1937

Racked, Solomonic, decent,   *
he was ululating; composed, pensive, cadaverous, perjured,
he was going, was returning, was responding; he was daring,
fatidic, scarlet, irresistible.

In society, in glass, in dust, in pit coal,
he took off; he wavered, golden-tongued; he flashed,
he rolled over, in respect;
in velvet, in tears, he fell back.

To remember? To insist? To go? To forgive?
Scowling, he will end up
stretched out, gruff, aghast, mural;
he was planning to imprint himself, to blend in, to perish.

Unattackably, impunibly,
blackly, he will sniff, will comprehend;
he will dress up orally;
uncertainly he will go, will chicken out, will forget.

¿Y bien? ¿Te sana el metaloide pálido?
¿Los metaloides incendiarios, cívicos,
inclinados al río atroz del polvo?

Esclavo, es ya la hora circular
en que en las dos aurículas se forman
anillos guturales, corredizos, cuaternarios.

Señor esclavo, en la mañana mágica
se ve, por fin,
el busto de tu trémulo ronquido,
vense tus sufrimientos a caballo,
pasa el órgano bueno, el de tres asas,
hojeo, mes por mes, tu monocorde cabellera,
tu suegra llora
haciendo huesecillos de sus dedos,
se inclina tu alma con pasión a verte
y tu sien, un momento, marca el paso.

Y la gallina pone su infinito, uno por uno;
sale la tierra hermosa de las humeantes sílabas,
te retratas de pie junto a tu hermano,
truena el color oscuro bajo el lecho
y corren y entrechócanse los pulpos.

Señor esclavo ¿y bien?
¿Los metaloides obran en tu angustia?

27 Set. 1937

Well? Does the pallid metalloid heal you?
The inflammatory, civic metalloids,
bent over the atrocious river of dust?

Slave, it's already the circular hour
in which your two auricles become
guttural, sliding, quaternary rings.

Mr. slave, on the magic morning
the bust of your tremulous snore
is seen, at last,
your sufferings on horseback are seen,
the good organ goes by, the one with three handles,
I leaf, month after month, your monochord head of hair,
your mother-in-law cries
making little bones out of her fingers,
your soul bends passionately to see you   *
and your temple, momentarily, marks time.

And the hen lays her infinite, one by one;
the beautiful earth emerges from smoking syllables,
your picture is taken standing next to your brother,
obscure color thunders under the bed
and the octopi run and collide.

And now, Mr. slave?
Do the metalloids work on your anguish?

¡De puro calor tengo frío,
hermana Envidia!
Lamen mi sombra leones
y el ratón me muerde el nombre,
¡madre alma mía!

¡Al borde del fondo voy,
cuñado Vicio!
La oruga tañe su voz,
y la voz tañe su oruga,
¡padre cuerpo mío!

¡Está de frente mi amor,
nieta Paloma!
De rodillas, mi terror
y de cabeza, mi angustia,
¡madre alma mía!

Hasta que un día sin dos,
esposa Tumba,
mi último hierro dé el son
de una víbora que duerme,
¡padre cuerpo mío! . . .

29 Set. 1937

From sheer heat I am cold,
sister Envy!
Lions lick my shadow
and the mouse nibbles at my name,
mother my soul!

To the pit's edge I go,
brother-in-law Vice!
The caterpillar plays its voice,
and the voice plays its caterpillar,   *
father my body!

My love is facing me,
granddaughter Dove!
My terror on its knees
and my anguish on its head,
mother my soul!

Until a day without two,
wife Tomb,
my final iron makes the sound
of a sleeping viper,
father my body! . . .

Confianza en el anteojo, nó en el ojo;
en la escalera, nunca en el peldaño;
en el ala, nó en el ave
y en ti sólo, en ti sólo, en ti sólo.

Confianza en la maldad, nó en el malvado;
en el vaso, mas nunca en el licor;
en el cadáver, no en el hombre
y en ti sólo, en ti sólo, en ti sólo.

Confianza en muchos, pero ya no en uno;
en el cauce, jamás en la corriente;
en los calzones, no en las piernas
y en ti sólo, en ti sólo, en ti sólo.

Confianza en la ventana, no en la puerta;
en la madre, mas no en los nueve meses;
en el destino, no en el dado de oro,
y en ti sólo, en ti sólo, en ti sólo.

5 Oct. 1937

Confidence in glasses, *not* in the eye;   *
in the staircase, never in the step;
in the wing, *not* in the bird
and in yourself alone, in yourself alone, in yourself alone.

Confidence in wickedness, *not* in the wicked;
in the glass, but never in the liquor;
in the corpse, not in the man
and in yourself alone, in yourself alone, in yourself alone.

Confidence in many, but no longer in one;
in the riverbed, never in the current;
in pants, not in legs
and in yourself alone, in yourself alone, in yourself alone.

Confidence in the window, not in the door;
in the mother, but not in the nine months;
in destiny, not in the gold die,
and in yourself alone, in yourself alone, in yourself alone.

¿Hablando de la leña, callo el fuego?
¿Barriendo el suelo, olvido el fósil?
Razonando,
¿mi trenza, mi corona de carne?
(¡Contesta, amado Hermeregildo, el brusco;
pregunta, Luis, el lento!)

¡Encima, abajo, con tamaña altura!
¡Madera, tras el reino de las fibras!
¡Isabel, con horizonte de entrada!
¡Lejos, al lado, astutos Atanacios!

¡Todo, la parte!
Unto a ciegas en luz mis calcetines,
en riesgo, la gran paz de este peligro,
y mis cometas, en la miel pensada,
el cuerpo, en miel llorada.

¡Pregunta, Luis; responde, Hermeregildo!
¡Abajo, arriba, al lado, lejos!
¡Isabel, fuego, diplomas de los muertos!
¡Horizonte, Atanacio, parte, todo!
¡Miel de miel, llanto de frente!
¡Reino de la madera,
corte oblicuo a la línea del camello,
fibra de mi corona de carne!

TERREMOTO

6 Oct. 1937

Speaking of kindling, do I silence fire?   *
Sweeping the ground, I overlook the fossil?
Reasoning,
my braid, my crown of flesh?
(Answer, beloved Hermeregildo, the brusque;   *
ask, Luis, the slow!)

   Above, below, about this high!
Wood, beyond the kingdom of fibers!
Isabel, with the horizon as entrance!
Distant, close by, astute Atanacios!

   The whole, the part!
Blindly I anoint my socks with light,
with risk, the great peace of this danger,
and my comets, with thought honey,
the body, with wept honey.

   Ask, Luis; respond, Hermeregildo!
Below, above, close by, distant!
Isabel, the fire, the diplomas of the dead!
The horizon, Atanacio, the part, the whole!
Honey of honey, forward weep!
The kingdom of wood,
cut oblique to the camel line,
fiber of my crown of flesh!

EARTHQUAKE

Escarnecido, aclimatado al bien, mórbido, hurente,
doblo el cabo carnal y juego a copas,
donde acaban en moscas los destinos,
donde comí y bebí de lo que me hunde.

Monumental adarme,
féretro numeral, los de mi deuda,
los de mi deuda, cuando caigo altamente,
ruidosamente, amoratadamente.

Al fondo, es hora,
entonces, de gemir con toda el hacha
y es entonces el año del sollozo,
el día del tobillo,
la noche del costado, el siglo del resuello.
Cualidades estériles, monótonos satanes,
del flanco brincan,
del ijar de mi yegua suplente;
pero, donde comí, cuánto pensé!
pero cuánto bebí donde lloré!

Así es la vida, tal
como es la vida, allá, detrás
del infinito; así, espontáneamente,
delante de la sien legislativa.

Yace la cuerda así al pie del violín,
cuando hablaron del aire, a voces, cuando
hablaron muy despacio del relámpago.
Se dobla así la mala causa, vamos
de tres en tres a la unidad; así
se juega a copas
y salen a mi encuentro los que aléjanse,
acaban los destinos en bacterias
y se debe todo a todos.

7 Oct. 1937

Mocked, acclimated to goodness, morbid, hurent,
I round the carnal cape and bet on hearts,
where destinies end up in flies,
where I ate and drank what is dragging me under.

Monumental dram,
numeral casket, those of my debt,
those of my debt, when I fall highly,
loudly, beatblackandbluely.

At bottom, it's time,
then, to groan with the whole ax,
and it's then the year of the sob,
the day of the ankle,
the night of the side, the century of hard breathing.
Sterile qualities, monotonous satans,
leap from the flank,
from the loin of my substitute mare;
but, where I ate, how much I thought!
but how much I drank where I cried!

That's life, as
life is, over there, behind
the infinite; thus, spontaneously,
before one's legislative temple.

Thus the string lies at the base of the violin,
when they spoke about air, shouting, when
they spoke very slowly about lightning.
Thus the wrong cause doubles, we go
three by three to unity; thus
one bets on hearts
and those moving away come to meet me,
destinies end up in bacteria
and everything is owed to everyone.

*

*

*

Alfonso: estás mirándome, lo veo,
desde el plano implacable donde moran
lineales los siempres, lineales los jamases
(Esa noche, dormiste, entre tu sueño
y mi sueño, en la rue de Riboutté)
Palpablemente,
tu inolvidable cholo te oye andar
en París, te siente en el teléfono callar
y toca en el alambre a tu último acto
tomar peso, brindar
por la profundidad, por mí, por ti.

Yo todavía
compro "du vin, du lait, comptant les sous"
bajo mi abrigo, para que no me vea mi alma,
bajo mi abrigo aquel, querido Alfonso,
y bajo el rayo simple de la sien compuesta;
yo todavía sufro, y tú, ya no, jamás, hermano!
(Me han dicho que en tus siglos de dolor,
amado sér,
amado estar,
hacías ceros de madera. ¿Es cierto?)

En la "boîte de nuit", donde tocabas tangos,
tocando tu indignada criatura su corazón,
escoltado de ti mismo, llorando
por ti mismo y por tu enorme parecido con tu sombra,
monsieur Fourgat, el patrón, ha envejecido.
¿Decírselo? ¿Contárselo? No más,
Alfonso; eso, ya nó!

El hôtel des Ecoles funciona siempre
y todavía compran mandarinas;
pero yo sufro, como te digo,
dulcemente, recordando
lo que hubimos sufrido ambos, a la muerte de ambos,
en la apertura de la doble tumba,
de esa otra tumba con tu sér,
y de ésta de caoba con tu estar;
sufro, bebiendo un vaso de ti, Silva,
un vaso para ponerse bien, como decíamos,
y después, ya veremos lo que pasa . . .

>

Alfonso: you are looking at me, I see,
from the implacable plane where
the lineal always, the lineal nevers, dwell
(That night, you slept, between your dream
and my dream, on rue de Riboutté)
Palpably,
your unforgettable cholo hears you walk
in Paris, he feels you go silent on the phone
and it is your last act's turn on the wire   *
to test its weight, to drink
to the depths, to me, to you.

    I still
buy "du vin, du lait, comptant les sous"   *
under my overcoat, so that my soul will not see me,
under my overcoat that one, dear Alfonso,   *
and under the simple ray of my compound temple;
I still suffer, and you, not now, never again, brother!
(I have been told that in your centuries of pain,
beloved being,   *
beloved to be,
you made zeros of wood. Is that true?)

    In the "boîte de nuit," where you played tangos,   *
your indignant child playing out his heart,
escorting yourself, crying
for yourself and for your enormous resemblance to your shadow,
Monsieur Fourgat, the owner, has aged.
To let him know? To tell him about it? No more,
Alfonso; that's it, not now!

    Hôtel des Écoles is open as always
and they still buy tangerines;
but I suffer, like I say,
sweetly, remembering
what we both suffered, in both of our deaths,
in the opening of the double tomb,   *
of that other tomb with your being,
and of this mahogany one with your to be;
I suffer, drinking a glass of you, Silva,
a glass to straighten me out, as we used to say,
and afterward, we'll see what happens . . .   >

>   Es éste el otro brindis, entre tres,
taciturno, diverso
en vino, en mundo, en vidrio, al que brindábamos
más de una vez al cuerpo
y, menos de una vez, al pensamiento.
Hoy es más diferente todavía;
hoy sufro dulce, amargamente,
bebo tu sangre en cuanto a Cristo el duro,
como tu hueso en cuanto a Cristo el suave,
porque te quiero, dos a dos, Alfonso,
y casi lo podría decir, eternamente.

9 Oct. 1937

This is the other toast, among three,
solemn, diverse
in wine, in world, in glass, the one that we raised
more than once to the body
and, less than once, to the mind.
Today is even more different;
today I suffer bitterly sweet,
I drink your blood as to Christ the hard,
I eat your bone as to Christ the soft,
because I love you, two by two, Alfonso,
and could almost say so, eternally.

¡Hay gentes tan desgraciadas, que ni siquiera
tienen cuerpo; cuantitativo el pelo,
baja, en pulgadas, la genial pesadumbre;
el modo, arriba;
no me busques, la muela del olvido,
parecen salir del aire, sumar suspiros mentalmente, oír
claros azotes en sus paladares!

Vanse de su piel, rascándose el sarcófago en que nacen
y suben por su muerte de hora en hora
y caen, a lo largo de su alfabeto gélido, hasta el suelo.

¡Ay de tánto! ¡ay de tan poco! ¡ay de ellas!
¡Ay en mi cuarto, oyéndolas con lentes!
¡Ay en mi tórax, cuando compran trajes!
¡Ay de mi mugre blanca, en su hez mancomunada!

¡Amadas sean las orejas sánchez,
amadas las personas que se sientan,
amado el desconocido y su señora,
el prójimo con mangas, cuello y ojos!

¡Amado sea aquel que tiene chinches,
el que lleva zapato roto bajo la lluvia,
el que vela el cadáver de un pan con dos cerillas,
el que se coje un dedo en una puerta,
el que no tiene cumpleaños,
el que perdió su sombra en un incendio,
el animal, el que parece un loro,
el que parece un hombre, el pobre rico,
el puro miserable, el pobre pobre!

¡Amado sea
el que tiene hambre o sed, pero no tiene
hambre con qué saciar toda su sed,
ni sed con qué saciar todas sus hambres!

¡Amado sea el que trabaja al día, al mes, a la hora,
el que suda de pena o de vergüenza,
aquel que va, por orden de sus manos, al cinema,
el que paga con lo que le falta,

>

There are people so wretched, they don't even
have a body; quantitative the hair,
lowers, in inches, the affable grief;
the mode, above;
don't look for me, the molar of oblivion,
they appear to come out of the air, to add up sighs mentally, to hear
sharp lashes on their palates!

They leave their skin, scratching at the sarcophagus in which they are born
and rise through their death hour after hour
and fall, along their frozen alphabet, to the ground.

Pity for *so much!* pity for so little! pity for those women!
The pity in my room, hearing them wear glasses!
The pity in my thorax, when they buy dresses!
Pity for my white grime, in their combined scum!

Beloved be the Sanchez ears,
beloved the people who sit down,
beloved the unknown man and his wife,
the neighbor with sleeves, neck and eyes!

Beloved be that one with bedbugs,
the one who wears a torn shoe in the rain,
the one waking the corpse of a loaf with two matches,
the one who clothes a door on a finger,
the one who has no birthdays,
the one who lost his shadow in a fire,
the beast, the one who looks like a parrot,
the one who looks like a man, the rich poor man,
the complete skinflint, the poor poor man!

Beloved be
the one who is hungry or thirsty, but has no
hunger with which to satiate all his thirst,
nor thirst with which to satiate all his hungers!

Beloved be the one who works by the day, by the month, by the hour,
the one who sweats from pain or from shame,
that one who goes, by order of his hands, to the movies,
the one who pays with what he lacks,

*

>

> el que duerme de espaldas,
el que ya no recuerda su niñez; amado sea
el calvo sin sombrero,
el justo sin espinas,
el ladrón sin rosas,
el que lleva reloj y ha visto a Dios,
el que tiene un honor y no fallece!

¡Amado sea el niño, que cae y aún llora
y el hombre que ha caído y ya no llora!

¡Ay de tánto! ¡Ay de tan poco! ¡Ay de ellos!

11 Oct. 1937

> the one who sleeps on his back,
the one who no longer remembers his childhood; beloved be
the bald man without a hat,
the just man without thorns,
the thief without roses,
the one who wears a watch and has seen God,
the one who has an honor and does not die!

Beloved be the child, who falls and still cries
and the man who has fallen and no longer cries!

Pity for *so much!* Pity for so little! Pity for them!

DESPEDIDA RECORDANDO UN ADIÓS

Al cabo, al fin, por último,
torno, volví y acábome y os gimo, dándoos
la llave, mi sombrero, esta cartita para todos.
Al cabo de la llave está el metal en que aprendiéramos
a desdorar el oro, y está, al fin
de mi sombrero, este pobre cerebro mal peinado,
y, último vaso de humo, en su papel dramático,
yace este sueño práctico del alma.

¡Adiós, hermanos san pedros,
heráclitos, erasmos, espinozas!
¡Adiós, tristes obispos bolcheviques!
¡Adiós, gobernadores en desorden!
¡Adiós, vino que está en el agua como vino!
¡Adiós, alcohol que está en la lluvia!

¡Adiós también, me digo a mí mismo,
adiós, vuelo formal de los milígramos!
¡También adiós, de modo idéntico,
frío del frío y frío del calor!
Al cabo, al fin, por último, la lógica,
los linderos del fuego,
la despedida recordando aquel adiós.

12 Oct. 1937

FAREWELL REMEMBERING A GOOD-BYE

At the end, in the end, at last,
I turn, I've returned and I'm finished and moan to you, giving you
the key, my hat, this brief letter for everyone.
At the end of the key is the metal where we learned
to ungild the gold, and there is, in the end
of my hat, this poor brain badly combed,
and, a last glass of smoke, on its dramatic role,
this practical dream of the soul rests.

Good-bye, brother Saint Peters,
Heraclituses, Erasmuses, Spinozas!
Good-bye, sad Bolshevik bishops!
Good-bye, governers in turmoil!
Good-bye, wine that's in water like wine!
Good-bye, alcohol that's in the rain!

Good-bye, likewise, I say to myself,
good-bye, formal flight of milligrams!
Likewise good-bye, in an identical way,
cold of the cold and the cold of warmth!
At the end, in the end, at last, logic,
the boundaries of fire,
the farewell remembering that good-bye.

*

A lo mejor, soy otro; andando, al alba, otro que marcha
en torno a un disco largo, a un disco elástico:
mortal, figurativo, audaz diafragma.
A lo mejor, recuerdo al esperar, anoto mármoles
donde índice escarlata, y donde catre de bronce,
un zorro ausente, espúreo, enojadísimo.
A lo mejor, hombre al fin,
las espaldas ungidas de añil misericordia,
a lo mejor, me digo, más allá no hay nada.

Me da la mar el disco, refiriéndolo,
con cierto margen seco, a mi garganta;
¡nada, en verdad, más ácido, más dulce, más kanteano!
Pero sudor ajeno, pero suero
o tempestad de mansedumbre,
decayendo o subiendo, ¡eso, jamás!

Echado, fino, exhúmome,
tumefacta la mezcla en que entro a golpes,
sin piernas, sin adulto barro, ni armas,
una aguja prendida en el gran átomo . . .
¡No! ¡Nunca! ¡Nunca ayer! ¡Nunca después!

Y de ahí este tubérculo satánico,
esta muela moral de plesiosaurio
y estas sospechas póstumas,
este índice, esta cama, estos boletos.

21 Oct. 1937

Chances are, I'm another; walking, at dawn, another who proceeds
around a long disk, an elastic disk:
a mortal, figurative, audacious diaphragm.
Chances are, I remember while waiting, I annotate marble
where scarlet index, and where bronze cot,
an absent, spurious, enraged fox.
Chances are, a man after all,
my shoulders anointed with indigo misericordia,
chances are, I say to myself, beyond there is nothing.

The sea gives me the disk, referring it,
with a certain dry margin, to my throat;
nothing, truly, more acidic, sweeter, more Kantian!
But somebody else's sweat, but a serum   *
or tempest of meekness,
decaying or rising—that, never!

Lying down, slender, I exhume myself,
smashing my way into the tumefied mixture,
without legs, without adult clay, nor weapons,
a needle stuck in the great atom . . .
No! Never! Never yesterday! Never later!

Hence this satanic tuber,
this moral plesiosaurian molar
and these posthumous suspicions,
this index, this bed, these tickets.

Profesor de sollozo—he dicho a un árbol—
palo de azogue, tilo
rumoreante, a la orilla del Marne, un buen alumno
leyendo va en tu naipe, en tu hojarasca,
entre el agua evidente y el sol falso,
su tres de copas, su caballo de oros.

Rector de los capítulos del cielo,
de la mosca ardiente, de la calma manual que hay en los asnos;
rector de honda ignorancia, un mal alumno
leyendo va en tu naipe, en tu hojarasca,
el hambre de razón que le enloquece
y la sed de demencia que le aloca.

Técnico en gritos, árbol consciente, fuerte,
fluvial, doble, solar, doble, fanático,
conocedor de rosas cardinales, totalmente
metido, hasta hacer sangre, en aguijones, un alumno
leyendo va en tu naipe, en tu hojarasca,
su rey precoz, telúrico, volcánico, de espadas.

¡Oh profesor, de haber tánto ignorado!
¡oh rector, de temblar tánto en el aire!
¡oh técnico, de tánto que te inclinas!
¡Oh tilo! ¡oh palo rumoroso junto al Marne!

21 Oct. 1937

THE BOOK OF NATURE

Professor of sobbing—I said to a tree—
staff of quicksilver, rumorous
linden, at the bank of the Marne, a good student
is reading in your deck of cards, in your dead foliage,
between the evident water and the false sun,
his three of hearts, his queen of diamonds.

Rector of the chapters of heaven,
of the burning fly, of the manual calm there is in asses;
rector of deep ignorance, a bad student
is reading in your deck of cards, in your dead foliage,
the hunger for reason that maddens him
and the thirst for dementia that drives him mad.

Technician of shouts, conscious tree, strong,
fluvial, double, solar, double, fanatic,
connoisseur of cardinal roses, totally
embedded, until drawing blood, in stingers, a student
is reading in your deck of cards, in your dead foliage,
his precocious, telluric, volcanic, king of spades.

Oh professor, from having been so ignorant!
oh rector, from trembling so much in the air!
oh technician, from so much bending over!
Oh linden, oh murmurous staff by the Marne!

MARCHA NUPCIAL

A la cabeza de mis propios actos,
corona en mano, batallón de dioses,
el signo negativo al cuello, atroces
el fósforo y la prisa, estupefactos
el alma y el valor, con dos impactos

al pie de la mirada; dando voces;
los límites, dinámicos, feroces;
tragándome los lloros inexactos,

me encenderé, se encenderá mi hormiga,
se encenderán mi llave, la querella
en que perdí la causa de mi huella.

Luego, haciendo del átomo una espiga,
encenderé mis hoces al pie de ella
y la espiga será por fin espiga.

22 Oct. 1937

At the head of my own acts,
crown in hand, battalion in apotheosis,
the negative sign on my neck, atrocious
the match and the haste, flabbergasted
the soul and the courage, with double impact

at the foot of the gaze; vociferous;
the limits, dynamic, ferocious;
swallowing my inexact lachrymation,

I will ignite, my ant will ignite, *
my key will ignite, the scrape
in which I lost the cause of my trace.

Then, making from the atom a wheat spike,
I will ignite my sickles at her base
and the spike will be finally a spike.

Tengo un miedo terrible de ser un animal
de blanca nieve, que sostuvo padre
y madre, con su sola circulación venosa,
y que, este día espléndido, solar y arzobispal,
día que representa así a la noche,
linealmente
elude este animal estar contento, respirar
y transformarse y tener plata.

Sería pena grande
que fuera yo tan hombre hasta ese punto.
Un disparate, una premisa ubérrima
a cuyo yugo ocasional sucumbe
el gonce espiritual de mi cintura.
Un disparate . . . En tanto,
es así, más acá de la cabeza de Dios,
en la tabla de Locke, de Bacon, en el lívido pescuezo
de la bestia, en el hocico del alma.

Y, en lógica aromática,
tengo ese miedo práctico, este día
espléndido, lunar, de ser aquél, éste talvez,
a cuyo olfato huele a muerto el suelo,
el disparate vivo y el disparate muerto.

¡Oh revolcarse, estar, toser, fajarse,
fajarse la doctrina, la sien, de un hombro al otro,
alejarse, llorar, darlo por ocho
o por siete o por seis, por cinco o darlo
por la vida que tiene tres potencias.

22 Oct. 1937

I have a terrible fear of being an animal
of white snow, who supported father
and mother, with only his veiny circulation,
and that, this splendid day, solar and archiepiscopal,
day that thus represents the night,
it lineally
eludes this animal to be happy, to breathe
and to transform himself and to have money.

It would be a great pity
if I were a real man to that degree.
A folly, a most fruitful premise
to whose occasional yoke the spiritual
hinge of my waist succumbs.
A folly . . . Meanwhile,
it's like that, this side of the head of God,
in the *tabula* of Locke, of Bacon, in the livid neck
of the beast, in the snout of the soul.

And, in aromatic logic,
I have this practical fear, this splendid
lunar day, of being that one, this one perhaps,
to whose nose the ground, the alive folly
and the dead folly smell of death.

Oh to wallow, to exist, to cough, to bind,
to bind the doctrine, one's temple, from shoulder to shoulder,
to move away, to weep, to let it go for eight
or for seven or for six, for five, or to let it go
for the life that holds three powers.

La cólera que quiebra al hombre en niños,
que quiebra al niño en pájaros iguales,
y al pájaro, después, en huevecillos;
la cólera del pobre
tiene un aceite contra dos vinagres.

La cólera que al árbol quiebra en hojas,
a la hoja en botones desiguales
y al botón, en ranuras telescópicas;
la cólera del pobre
tiene dos ríos contra muchos mares.

La cólera que quiebra al bien en dudas,
a la duda, en tres arcos semejantes
y al arco, luego, en tumbas imprevistas;
la cólera del pobre
tiene un acero contra dos puñales.

La cólera que quiebra al alma en cuerpos,
al cuerpo en órganos desemejantes
y al órgano, en octavos pensamientos;
la cólera del pobre
tiene un fuego central contra dos cráteres.

26 Oct. 1937

The anger that breaks the man into children,
that breaks the child into equal birds,
and the bird, afterward, into little eggs;
the anger of the poor
has one oil against two vinegars.

The anger that breaks the tree into leaves,
the leaf into unequal buds
and the bud, into telescopic grooves;
the anger of the poor
has two rivers against many seas.

The anger that breaks goodness into doubts,
doubt, into three similar arcs
and the arc, then, into unforeseeable tombs;
the anger of the poor
has one sword against two daggers.

The anger that breaks the soul into bodies,
the body into dissimilar organs
and the organ, into octave thoughts;
the anger of the poor
has one central fire against two craters.

INTENSIDAD Y ALTURA

Quiero escribir, pero me sale espuma,
quiero decir muchísimo y me atollo;
no hay cifra hablada que no sea suma,
no hay pirámide escrita, sin cogollo.

Quiero escribir, pero me siento puma;
quiero laurearme, pero me encebollo.
No hay toz hablada, que no llegue a bruma,
no hay dios ni hijo de dios, sin desarrollo.

Vámonos, pues, por eso, a comer yerba,
carne de llanto, fruta de gemido,
nuestra alma melancólica en conserva.

Vámonos! Vámonos! Estoy herido;
Vámonos a beber lo ya bebido,
vámonos, cuervo, a fecundar tu cuerva.

27 Oct. 1937

INTENSITY AND HEIGHT

I want to write, but out comes foam,
I want to say so much and I mire;
there is no spoken cipher which is not a sum,
there is no written pyramid, without a core.

I want to write, but I feel like a puma;
I want to laurel myself, but I stew in onions.
There is no spoken coughv, which doesn't come to brume,   *
there is no god nor son of god, without progression.

For that, then, let's go eat grass,
the flesh of sobs, the fruit of wails,
our melancholy soul canned.

Let's go! Let's go! I'm struck;
let's go drink that already drunk,
raven, let's go fecundate your mate.

GUITARRA

El placer de sufrir, de odiar, me tiñe
la garganta con plásticos venenos,
mas la cerda que implanta su orden mágico,
su grandeza taurina, entre la prima
y la sexta
y la octava mendaz, las sufre todas.

El placer de sufrir . . . ¿Quién? ¿a quién?
¿quién, las muelas? ¿a quién la sociedad,
los carburos de rabia de la encía?
¿Cómo ser
y estar, sin darle cólera al vecino?

Vales más que mi número, hombre solo,
y valen más que todo el diccionario,
con su prosa en verso,
con su verso en prosa,
tu función águila,
tu mecanismo tigre, blando prójimo.

El placer de sufrir,
de esperar esperanzas en la mesa,
el domingo con todos los idiomas,
el sábado con horas chinas, belgas,
la semana, con dos escupitajos.

El placer de esperar en zapatillas,
de esperar encogido tras de un verso,
de esperar con pujanza y mala poña;
el placer de sufrir: zurdazo de hembra
muerta con una piedra en la cintura
y muerta entre la cuerda y la guitarra,
llorando días y cantando meses.

28 Oct. 1937

GUITAR

The pleasure of suffering, of hating, dyes
my throat with plastic venoms,
but the bristle that implants its magic order,
its taurine grandeur, between the first string
and the sixth
and the mendacious eighth, suffers them all.   *

The pleasure of suffering . . . Who? whom?
who, the molars? whom society,
the carbides of rage in the gums?
How to be
and to be here, without angering one's neighbor?   *

You are worthier than my number, man alone,
and worthier than all the dictionary,
with its prose in poetry,
its poetry in prose,
are your eagle display,
your tiger machinery, bland fellow man.

The pleasure of suffering,
of hoping for hope at the table,
Sunday with all its languages,
Saturday with Chinese, Belgian hours,
the week, with two hockers.

The pleasure of waiting in slippers,
of waiting cringing behind a line,
of waiting empowered with a sick pintle;   *
the pleasure of suffering: hard left by a female
dead with a stone on her waist
and dead between the string and the guitar,
crying the days and singing the months.   *

Oye a tu masa, a tu cometa, escúchalos; no gimas
de memoria, gravísimo cetáceo;
oye a la túnica en que estás dormido,
oye a tu desnudez, dueña del sueño.

Relátate agarrándote
de la cola del fuego y a los cuernos
en que acaba la crin su atroz carrera;
rómpete, pero en círculos;
fórmate, pero en columnas combas;
descríbete atmosférico, sér de humo,
a paso redoblado de esqueleto.

¿La muerte? ¡Opónle todo tu vestido!
¿La vida? ¡Opónle parte de tu muerte!
Bestia dichosa, piensa;
dios desgraciado, quítate la frente.
Luego, hablaremos.

29 Oct. 1937

Hear your mass, your comet, listen to them; don't moan   *
by heart, most ponderous cetacean;
hear the tunic in which you are asleep,
hear your nakedness, the mistress of the dream.

    Relate to yourself grasping
the tail of the fire and the horns
in which the mane ends its atrocious race;
break yourself, but in circles;
shape yourself, but in curved columns;
describe yourself atmospheric, being of smoke,
in the double-quick step of a skeleton.   *

    Death? Oppose it with all your clothes!
Life? Oppose it with part of your death!
Fortunate beast, think;
unfortunate god, take off your forehead.
Then, we will talk.

¿Qué me da, que me azoto con la línea
y creo que me sigue, al trote, el punto?

¿Qué me da, que me he puesto
en los hombros un huevo en vez de un manto?

¿Qué me ha dado, que vivo?
¿Qué me ha dado, que muero?

¿Qué me da, que tengo ojos?
¿Qué me da, que tengo alma?

¿Qué me da, que se acaba en mí mi prójimo
y empieza en mi carrillo el rol del viento?

¿Qué me ha dado, que cuento mis dos lágrimas,
sollozo tierra y cuelgo el horizonte?

¿Qué me ha dado, que lloro de no poder llorar
y río de lo poco que he reído?

¿Qué me da, que ni vivo ni muero?

30 Oct. 1937

What's got into me, that I whip myself with the line
and believe that I'm followed, at a trot, by the period?

What's got into me, that I have placed
an egg on my shoulders instead of a mantle?

What's gotten into me, that I'm alive?
What's gotten into me, that I'm dying?

What's got into me, that I have eyes?
What's got into me, that I have a soul?

What's got into me, that my fellow man ends in me
and the roll of the wind starts up in my cheek?

What's gotten into me, that I count my two tears,
sob earth and hang the horizon?   *

What's gotten into me, that I cry from not being able to cry
and laugh at the little I've laughed?

What's got into me, that I'm neither alive nor dead?

ANIVERSARIO

¡Cuánto catorce ha habido en la existencia!
¡Qué créditos con bruma, en una esquina!
¡Qué diamante sintético, el del casco!
¡Cuánta más dulcedumbre
a lo largo, más honda superficie:
¡cuánto catorce ha habido en tan poco uno!

¡Qué deber,
qué cortar y qué tajo,
de memoria a memoria, en la pestaña!
¡Cuanto más amarillo, más granate!
¡Cuánto catorce en un solo catorce!

Acordeón de la tarde, en esa esquina,
piano de la mañana, aquella tarde;
clarín de carne,
tambor de un solo palo,
guitarra sin cuarta ¡cuánta quinta,
y cuánta reunión de amigos tontos
y qué nido de tigres el tabaco!
¡Cuánto catorce ha habido en la existencia!

¿Qué te diré ahora,
quince feliz, ajeno, quince de otros?
Nada más que no crece ya el cabello,
que han venido por las cartas,
que me brillan los seres que he parido,
que no hay nadie en mi tumba
y que me han confundido con mi llanto.

¡Cuánto catorce ha habido en la existencia!

31 Oct. 1937

ANNIVERSARY

How much fourteen there's been in existence!
What credits with fog, on a corner!
What a synthetic diamond the skull is!
The lengthier the sweetness,
the deeper the surface:
how much fourteen there's been in so little one!   *

What a debt,
what to cut and what a slash,
from memory to memory, in the eyelash!
The more yellow, the more garnet!
How much fourteen in a single fourteen!

Accordion of the evening, on that corner,
piano of the morning, that evening;
bugle of flesh,
drum of a single stick,
guitar with no fourth string, how much fifth,
and what a gathering of silly friends   *
and what a nest of tigers the tobacco!
How much fourteen there's been in existence!

What will I say to you now,
happy fifteen, strange, fifteen of others?
Just that my hair no longer grows,
that they've come for the letters,
that the beings I've given birth to bedazzle me,
that there's no one in my tomb
and that they've confused me with my weeping!

How much fourteen there's been in existence!

PANTEÓN

He visto ayer sonidos generales,
    mortuoriamente,
    puntualmente alejarse,
cuando oí desprenderse del ocaso
    tristemente,
    exactamente un arco, un arcoíris.

Vi el tiempo generoso del minuto,
    infinitamente
atado locamente al tiempo grande,
pues que estaba la hora
    suavemente,
premiosamente henchida de dos horas.

Dejóse comprender, llamar, la tierra
    terrenalmente;
negóse brutalmente así a mi historia,
y si vi, que me escuchen, pues, en bloque,
si toqué esta mecánica, que vean
    lentamente,
despacio, vorazmente, mis tinieblas.

Y si vi en la lesión de la respuesta,
    claramente,
la lesión mentalmente de la incógnita,
si escuché, si pensé en mis ventanillas
nasales, funerales, temporales,
    fraternalmente,
piadosamente echadme a los filósofos.

Mas no más inflexión precipitada
en canto llano, y no más
el hueso colorado, el son del alma
    tristemente
erguida ecuestremente en mi espinazo,
ya que, en suma, la vida es
    implacablemente,
imparcialmente horrible, estoy seguro.

31 Oct. 1937

PANTHEON

Yesterday I saw general sounds,
      mortuarily,
      punctually recede,
when I heard detach from the sunset
      sadly,
      exactly a bow, a rainbow.

I saw the generous time of the minute,
      infinitely
tied insanely to great time,
for the hour was
      softly,
tightly swollen with two hours.

The earth let itself be comprehended, named,
      terrenely;
it thus brutally denied my history,
and if I saw, let them hear me, then, in bloc,
if I touched this mechanism, let them see
      slowly,
little by little, voraciously, my darknesses.

And if I saw in the lesion of the response,
      clearly,
mentally the lesion of the unknown,
if I heard, if I thought about my nasal,
funereal, temporal, nostrils,
      fraternally,
piously throw me to the philosophers.

But no more impetuous inflection
in plain song, and no more
reddened bone, the sound of the soul
      sadly
straightened equestrianly in my spine,
now that, in short, life is
      implacably,
impartially horrible, I am sure.

Un hombre está mirando a una mujer,
está mirándola inmediatamente,
con su mal de tierra suntuosa
y la mira a dos manos
y la tumba a dos pechos
y la mueve a dos hombres.

Pregúntome entonces, oprimiéndome
la enorme, blanca, acérrima costilla:
Y este hombre
¿no tuvo a un niño por creciente padre?
¿Y esta mujer, a un niño
por constructor de su evidente sexo?

Puesto que un niño veo ahora,
niño ciempiés, apasionado, enérgico;
veo que no le ven
sonarse entre los dos, colear, vestirse;
puesto que los acepto,
a ella en condición aumentativa,
a él en la flexión del heno rubio.

Y exclamo entonces, sin cesar ni uno
de vivir, sin volver ni uno
a temblar en la justa que venero:
¡Felicidad seguida
tardíamente del Padre,
del Hijo y de la Madre!
¡Instante redondo,
familiar, que ya nadie siente ni ama!
¡De qué deslumbramiento áfono, tinto,
se ejecuta el cantar de los cantares!
¡De qué tronco, el florido carpintero!
¡De qué perfecta axila, el frágil remo!
¡De qué casco, ambos cascos delanteros!

2 Nov. 1937

A man is looking at a woman,
is looking at her immediately,
with his sumptuous homesickness
and he looks at her two-handedly
and he knocks her down two-chestedly
and he moves her two-shoulderedly.

I ask myself then, overpowering
my enormous, white, zealous rib:
And this man
hasn't he had a child as a growing father?
And this woman, a child
as the builder of her evident sex?

Because I see a child now,
a centipede child, impassioned, energetic:
I see that they do not see him
blow his nose between them, wag his tail, get dressed;
because I accept them,
her in the augmentative condition,
him in the flexion of golden hay.

And I exclaim then, without ceasing even once
to live, without turning even once
to tremble in the joust I venerate:
Happiness followed
belatedly of the Father,
of the Son and of the Mother!
Round, familiar
instant, that no one any longer feels or loves!
From what an aphonic, dark-red dazzle
the Song of Songs is performed!
From what a trunk, the florid carpenter!
From what a perfect armpit, the fragile oar!
From what a hoof, both forehoofs!

DOS NIÑOS ANHELANTES

No. No tienen tamaño sus tobillos; no es su espuela
suavísima, que da en las dos mejillas.
Es la vida no más, de bata y yugo.

No. No tiene plural su carcajada,
ni por haber salido de un molusco perpetuo, aglutinante,
ni por haber entrado al mar descalza,
es la que piensa y marcha, es la finita.
Es la vida no más; sólo la vida.

Lo sé, lo intuyo cartesiano, autómata,
moribundo, cordial, en fin, espléndido.
Nada hay
sobre la ceja cruel del esqueleto;
nada, entre lo que dio y tomó con guante
la paloma, y con guante,
la eminente lombriz aristotélica;
nada delante ni detrás del yugo;
nada de mar en el océano
y nada
en el orgullo grave de la célula.
Sólo la vida; así: cosa bravísima.

Plenitud inextensa,
alcance abstracto, venturoso, de hecho,
glacial y arrebatado, de la llama;
freno del fondo, rabo de la forma.
Pero aquello
para lo cual nací ventilándome
y crecí con afecto y drama propios,
mi trabajo rehúsalo,
mi sensación y mi arma lo involucran.
Es la vida y no más, fundada, escénica.   >

TWO YEARNING CHILDREN

No. Their ankles have no size; it's not their softest   *
spur, that jabs their two cheeks.
It's just life, with robe and yoke.

No. Their guffaw has no plural,   *
not even for having emerged from a perpetual, agglutinating mollusk,
not even for having entered the sea barefoot,
it's what thinks and walks, it's the finite.
It's just life; only life.

I know it, I intuit it a Cartesian, an automaton,   *
moribund, cordial, in short, magnificent.
Nothing is
over the cruel brow of its skeleton;
nothing, between what the dove gave and took back
with a glove, and with a glove,
the eminent Aristotelian earthworm;
nothing before or behind the yoke;
nothing of the sea in the ocean
and nothing
in the grave pride of the cell.
Only life; that is: a hell of a tough thing.   *

Limited plenitude,
abstract reach, fortunate, in fact,   *
glacial and snatched away, from the flame;
restrainer of depth, tail of form.
But that
for which I was born ventilating myself
and grew up with my own tenderness and drama,
is rejected by my work,
is implicated by my feelings and my weapon.
It's life and that's all, grounded, scenic.   >

>   Y por este rumbo,
su serie de órganos extingue mi alma
y por este indecible, endemoniado cielo,
mi maquinaria da silbidos técnicos,
paso la tarde en la mañana triste
y me esfuerzo, palpito, tengo frío.

2 Nov. 1937

And in this way,
my soul extinguishes its series of organs
and in this inexpressible, hellish sky,
my machinery emits technical hisses,
I pass the afternoon in the sad morning
and I struggle, I throb, I am cold.

LOS NUEVE MONSTRUOS

I, desgraciadamente,
el dolor crece en el mundo a cada rato,
crece a treinta minutos por segundo, paso a paso,
y la naturaleza del dolor, es el dolor dos veces
y la condición del martirio, carnívora, voraz,
es el dolor dos veces
y la función de la yerba purísima, el dolor
dos veces
y el bien de sér, dolernos doblemente.

Jamás, hombres humanos,
hubo tánto dolor en el pecho, en la solapa, en la cartera,
en el vaso, en la carnicería, en la aritmética!
Jamás tánto cariño doloroso,
jamás tan cerca arremetió lo lejos,
jamás el fuego nunca
jugó mejor su rol de frío muerto!
Jamás, señor ministro de salud, fue la salud
más mortal
y la migraña extrajo tánta frente de la frente!
Y el mueble tuvo en su cajón, dolor,
el corazón, en su cajón, dolor,
la lagartija, en su cajón, dolor.

Crece la desdicha, hermanos hombres,
más pronto que la máquina, a diez máquinas, y crece
con la res de Rousseau, con nuestras barbas;
crece el mal por razones que ignoramos
y es una inundación con propios líquidos,
con propio barro y propia nube sólida!
Invierte el sufrimiento posiciones, da función
en que el humor acuoso es vertical
al pavimento,
el ojo es visto y esta oreja oída,
y esta oreja da nueve campanadas a la hora
del rayo, y nueve carcajadas
a la hora del trigo, y nueve sones hembras
a la hora del llanto, y nueve cánticos
a la hora del hambre y nueve truenos
y nueve látigos, menos un grito.

>

THE NINE MONSTERS

AND, unfortunately,   *
pain grows in the world all the time,
grows thirty minutes a second, step by step,
and the nature of the pain, is twice the pain
and the condition of the martyrdom, carnivorous, voracious,
is twice the pain
and the function of the purest grass, twice
the pain
and the good of being, our dolor doubled.

Never, human men,
was there so much pain in the chest, in the lapel, in the wallet,
in the glass, in the butcher's shop, in arithmetic!
Never so much painful affection,
never did the distance charge so close,
never did the fire ever
play better its role of dead cold!
Never, Mr. Minister of Health, was health
more mortal,
did the migraine extract so much forehead from the forehead!
Did the cabinet have in its drawer, pain,
the heart, in its drawer, pain,
the lizard, in its drawer, pain.

Misfortune grows, brother men,
faster than the machine, at ten machines, and grows
with Rousseau's livestock, with our beards;
evil grows for reasons we know not
and is a flood with its own liquids,
its own mud and its own solid cloud!   *
Suffering inverts positions, it acts
in that the aqueous humor is vertical
to the pavement,
the eye is seen and this ear heard,
and this ear sounds nine strokes at the hour   *
of lightning, and nine guffaws
at the hour of wheat, and nine female sounds
at the hour of weeping, and nine canticles
at the hour of hunger, and nine thunderclaps
and nine lashes, minus a scream.   >

>   El dolor nos agarra, hermanos hombres,
por detrás, de perfil,
y nos aloca en los cinemas,
nos clava en los gramófonos,
nos desclava en los lechos, cae perpendicularmente
a nuestros boletos, a nuestras cartas;
y es muy grave sufrir, puede uno orar . . .
Pues de resultas
del dolor, hay algunos
que nacen, otros crecen, otros mueren,
y otros que nacen y no mueren, otros
que sin haber nacido, mueren, y otros
que no nacen ni mueren (son los más)
Y también de resultas
del sufrimiento, estoy triste
hasta la cabeza, y más triste hasta el tobillo,
de ver al pan, crucificado, al nabo,
ensangrentado,
llorando, a la cebolla,
al cereal, en general, harina,
a la sal, hecha polvo, al agua, huyendo,
al vino, un ecce-homo,
tan pálida a la nieve, al sol tan ardio!
¡Cómo, hermanos humanos,
no deciros que ya no puedo y
ya no puedo con tánto cajón,
tánto minuto, tánta
lagartija y tánta
inversión, tánto lejos y tánta sed de sed!
Señor Ministro de Salud: ¿qué hacer?
¡Ah! desgraciadamente, hombres humanos,
hay, hermanos, muchísimo que hacer

3 Nov. 1937 .

>   The pain grabs us, brother men,
from behind, in profile,
and drives us wild in the movies,
nails us to the gramophones,
unnails us in bed, falls perpendicularly
onto our tickets, our letters,
and it is very serious to suffer, one might pray . . .
For as a result
of the pain, there are some
who are born, others grow, others die,
and others who are born and do not die, others
who die, without having been born, and others
who neither are born nor die (the majority)
And likewise as a result
of suffering, I am sad
up to my head, and sadder down to my ankle,
from seeing bread, crucified, the turnip,
bloodied,
the onion, crying,
cereal, in general, flour,
salt, made dust, water, fleeing,
wine, an ecce-homo,
such pallid snow, such an arduent sun!   *
How, human brothers,
not to tell you that I can no longer stand it and
can no longer stand so much drawer,
so much minute, so much
lizard and so much
inversion, so much distance and so much thirst for thirst!
Mr. Minister of Health: what to do?
Ah! unfortunately, human men,
there is, brothers, much too much to do.

Un hombre pasa con un pan al hombro
¿Voy a escribir, después, sobre mi doble?

Otro se sienta, ráscase, extrae un piojo de su axila, mátalo
¿Con qué valor hablar del psicoanálisis?

Otro ha entrado a mi pecho con un palo en la mano
¿Hablar luego de Sócrates al médico?

Un cojo pasa dando el brazo a un niño
¿Voy, después, a leer a André Breton?

Otro tiembla de frío, tose, escupe sangre
¿Cabrá aludir jamás al Yo profundo?

Otro busca en el fango huesos, cáscaras
¿Cómo escribir, después, del infinito?

Un albañil cae de un techo, muere y ya no almuerza
¿Innovar, luego, el tropo, la metáfora?

Un comerciante roba un gramo en el peso a un cliente
¿Hablar, después, de cuarta dimensión?

Un banquero falsea su balance
¿Con qué cara llorar en el teatro?

Un paria duerme con el pie a la espalda
¿Hablar, después, a nadie de Picasso?

Alguien va en un entierro sollozando
¿Cómo luego ingresar a la Academia?

Alguien limpia un fusil en su cocina
¿Con qué valor hablar del más allá?

Alguien pasa contando con sus dedos
¿Cómo hablar del no-yó sin dar un grito?

5 Nov. 1937

A man walks by with a baguette on his shoulder
Am I going to write, after that, about my double?   *

Another sits, scratches, extracts a louse from his armpit, kills it
How dare one speak about psychoanalysis?

Another has entered my chest with a stick in hand
To talk then about Socrates with the doctor?

A cripple passes by holding a child's hand
After that I'm going to read André Breton?

Another trembles from cold, coughs, spits blood
Will it ever be possible to allude to the deep Self?   *

Another searches in the muck for bones, rinds
How to write, after that, about the infinite?

A bricklayer falls from a roof, dies and no longer eats lunch
To innovate, then, the trope, the metaphor?

A merchant cheats a customer out of a gram
To speak, after that, about the fourth dimension?

A banker falsifies his balance sheet
With what face to cry in the theater?

An outcast sleeps with his foot behind his back
To speak, after that, to anyone about Picasso?

Someone goes to a burial sobbing
How then become a member of the Academy?

Someone cleans a rifle in his kitchen
How dare one speak about the beyond?

Someone passes by counting with his fingers
How speak of the non-self without screaming?   *

Hoy le ha entrado una astilla.
Hoy le ha entrado una astilla cerca, dándole
cerca, fuerte, en su modo
de ser y en su centavo ya famoso.
Le ha dolido la suerte mucho,
todo;
le ha dolido la puerta,
le ha dolido la faja, dándole
sed, aflixión
y sed del vaso pero no del vino.
Hoy le salió a la pobre vecina del aire,
a escondidas, humareda de su dogma;
hoy le ha entrado una astilla.

La inmensidad persíguela
a distancia superficial, a un vasto eslabonazo.
Hoy le salió a la pobre vecina del viento,
en la mejilla, norte, y en la mejilla, oriente;
hoy le ha entrado una astilla.

¿Quién comprará, en los días perecederos, ásperos,
un pedacito de café con leche,
y quién, sin ella, bajará a su rastro hasta dar luz?
¿Quién será, luego, sábado, a las siete?
¡Tristes son las astillas que le entran
a uno,
exactamente ahí precisamente!
Hoy le entró a la pobre vecina de viaje,
una llama apagada en el oráculo;
hoy le ha entrado una astilla.

Le ha dolido el dolor, el dolor joven,
el dolor niño, el dolorazo, dándole
en las manos
y dándole sed, aflixión
y sed del vaso, pero no del vino.
¡La pobre pobrecita!

6 Nov. 1937

Today a splinter has gotten into her.
Today a splinter has gotten into her close, striking her
close, hard, in her mode
of being and in her now famous centavo.
Fate has pained her terribly,
all over;
the door has pained her,
the girdle has pained her, giving her
thirst, afflixion   *
and thirst for the glass but not for the wine.
Today, secretly, the smoke of her dogma   *
poured out of the poor neighbor of the air;
today a splinter has gotten into her.

Immensity pursues her   *
at a superficial distance, at a vast linkage.
Today on one cheek, north, and on one cheek, east
came out of the poor neighbor of the wind;
today a splinter has gotten into her.

Who will buy, in these harsh, perishable days,
a smidgen of café con leche,
and who, without her, will descend her trace until giving birth?
Who will it be, then, Saturday, at seven?
Sad are the splinters that get into her
one,
exactly there precisely!
Today a flame quenched in the oracle got into
the poor neighbor of the voyage;
today a splinter has gotten into her.

The pain has pained her, the young pain,
the child pain, excruciating pain, striking her
in her hands
and giving her thirst, afflixion
and thirst for the glass but not for the wine.
The poor, poor little thing!

Me viene, hay días, una gana ubérrima, política,
de querer, de besar al cariño en sus dos rostros,
y me viene de lejos un querer
demostrativo, otro querer amar, de grado o fuerza,
al que me odia, al que rasga su papel, al muchachito,
a la que llora por el que lloraba,
al rey del vino, al esclavo del agua,
al que ocultóse en su ira,
al que suda, al que pasa, al que sacude su persona en mi alma.
Y quiero, por lo tanto, acomodarle
al que me habla, su trenza; sus cabellos, al soldado;
su luz, al grande; su grandeza, al chico.
Quiero planchar directamente
un pañuelo al que no puede llorar
y, cuando estoy triste o me duele la dicha,
remendar a los niños y a los genios.

Quiero ayudar al bueno a ser su poquillo de malo
y me urge estar sentado
a la diestra del zurdo, y responder al mudo,
tratando de serle útil en
lo que puedo, y también quiero muchísimo
lavarle al cojo el pie,
y ayudarle a dormir al tuerto próximo.

¡Ah querer, éste, el mío, éste, el mundial,
interhumano y parroquial, provecto!
Me viene a pelo,
desde el cimiento, desde la ingle pública,
y, viniendo de lejos, da ganas de besarle
la bufanda al cantor,
y al que sufre, besarle en su sartén,
al sordo, en su rumor craneano, impávido;
al que me da lo que olvidé en mi seno,
en su Dante, en su Chaplin, en sus hombros.

Quiero, para terminar,
cuando estoy al borde célebre de la violencia
o lleno de pecho el corazón, querría
ayudar a reír al que sonríe,
ponerle un pajarillo al malvado en plena nuca,

>

There are days, there comes to me an exuberant, political hunger
to desire, to kiss tenderness on both cheeks,
and there comes to me from afar a demonstrative
desire, another desire to love, willingly or by force,
whoever hates me, whoever tears up his paper, the little boy,
the woman who weeps for the man who was weeping,
the king of wine, the slave of water,
whoever hid in his wrath,
whoever sweats, whoever passes by, whoever shakes his person in my soul.
And I desire, therefore, to adjust
the braid of whoever talks to me; the soldier's hair;
the light of the great; the greatness of the child.
I desire to iron directly
a handkerchief for whoever is unable to cry
and, when I am sad or happiness aches me,
to mend the children and the geniuses.

I desire to help the good one become a little bad
and I have an urge to be seated
to the right of the left-handed, and to respond to the mute,
trying to be useful to him
as I can, and likewise I desire very much
to wash the cripple's foot,   *
and to help my one-eyed neighbor sleep.

Ah to desire, this one, mine, this one, the world's,
interhuman and parochial, mature!
It comes perfectly timed,
from the foundation, from the public groin,
and, coming from afar, makes me hunger to kiss
the singer's muffler,
and whoever suffers, to kiss him on his frying pan,
the deaf man, fearlessly, on his cranial murmur;
whoever gives me what I forgot in my breast,
on his Dante, on his Chaplin, on his shoulders.

I desire, finally,
when I'm at the celebrated edge of violence
or my heart full of chest, I would desire
to help whoever smiles laugh,   *
to put a little bird right on the evildoer's nape,   >

>   cuidar a los enfermos enfadándolos,
comprarle al vendedor,
ayudarle a matar al matador—cosa terrible—
y quisiera yo ser bueno conmigo
en todo.

    6 Nov. 1937

>   to take care of the sick annoying them,
to buy from the vendor,
to help the killer kill—a terrible thing—
and I would desire to be good to myself
in everything.

PALMAS Y GUITARRA

Ahora, entre nosotros, aquí,
ven conmigo, trae por la mano a tu cuerpo
y cenemos juntos y pasemos un instante la vida
a dos vidas y dando una parte a nuestra muerte.
Ahora, ven contigo, hazme el favor
de quejarte en mi nombre y a la luz de la noche teneblosa
en que traes a tu alma de la mano
y huímos en puntillas de nosotros.

Ven a mí, sí, y a ti, sí,
con paso par, a vernos a los dos con paso impar,
marcar el paso de la despedida.
¡Hasta cuando volvamos! ¡Hasta la vuelta!
¡Hasta cuando leamos, ignorantes!
¡Hasta cuando volvamos, despidámonos!

¿Qué me importan los fusiles?,
escúchame;
escúchame, ¿qué impórtanme,
si la bala circula ya en el rango de mi firma?
¿Qué te importan a ti las balas,
si el fusil está humeando ya en tu olor?
Hoy mismo pesaremos
en los brazos de un ciego nuestra estrella
y, una vez que me cantes, lloraremos.
Hoy mismo, hermosa, con tu paso par
y tu confianza a que llegó mi alarma,
saldremos de nosotros, dos a dos.
¡Hasta cuando seamos ciegos!
¡Hasta
que lloremos de tánto volver!

Ahora,
entre nosotros, trae
por la mano a tu dulce personaje
y cenemos juntos y pasemos un instante la vida
a dos vidas y dando una parte a nuestra muerte.   >

CLAPPING AND GUITAR

Now, between ourselves, here,
come with me, bring your body by the hand,
let's dine together and spend a moment life
as two lives, giving a share to our death.
Now, come with yourself, do me the favor
of complaining in my name and in the light of the teneblearic night   *
in which you bring your soul by the hand
and we flee on tiptoes from ourselves.

Come to me, yes, and to you, yes,
in even step, to see the two of us out of step,
stepping in place to farewell.
Until we return! Until the return!
Until we read, uncultured!
Until we return, let's say good-bye!

What are the rifles to me?,
listen to me;
listen to me, what are they to me
if the bullet is already circulating in my signature's rank?
What are bullets to you,
if the rifle is already smoking in your odor?
This very day we'll weigh
in the arms of a blindman our star
and, once you sing to me, we'll weep.
This very day, my lovely, with your even step
and your confidence met by my alarm,
we'll come out of ourselves, two by two.
Until we go blind!
Until
we weep from so much returning!

Now,
between ourselves, bring
your sweet persona by the hand
and let's dine together and spend a moment life
as two lives, giving a share to our death.   >

> Ahora, ven contigo, hazme el favor
de cantar algo
y de tocar en tu alma, haciendo palmas.
¡Hasta cuando volvamos! ¡Hasta entonces!
¡Hasta cuando partamos, despidámonos!

8 Nov. 1937

> Now, come with yourself, do me the favor
of singing something
and playing on your soul, clapping hands.
Until we return! Till then!
Until we part, let's say good-bye!

EL ALMA QUE SUFRIÓ DE SER SU CUERPO

Tú sufres de una glándula endocrínica, se ve,
o, quizá,
sufres de mí, de mi sagacidad escueta, tácita.
Tú padeces del diáfano antropoide, allá, cerca,
donde está la tiniebla tenebrosa.
Tú das vuelta al sol, agarrándote el alma,
extendiendo tus juanes corporales
y ajustándote el cuello; eso se ve.
Tú sabes lo que te duele,
lo que te salta al anca,
lo que baja por ti con soga al suelo.
Tú, pobre hombre, vives; no lo niegues,
si mueres; no lo niegues,
si mueres de tu edad ¡ay! y de tu época.
Y, aunque llores, bebes,
y, aunque sangres, alimentas a tu híbrido colmillo,
a tu vela tristona y a tus partes.
Tú sufres, tú padeces y tú vuelves a sufrir horriblemente,
desgraciado mono,
jovencito de Darwin,
alguacil que me atisbas, atrocísimo microbio.
Y tú lo sabes a tal punto,
que lo ignoras, soltándote a llorar.
Tú, luego, has nacido; eso
también se ve de lejos, infeliz y cállate,
y soportas la calle que te dio la suerte
y a tu ombligo interrogas: ¿dónde? ¿cómo?

Amigo mío, estás completamente,
hasta el pelo, en el año treinta y ocho,
nicolás o santiago, tal o cual,
estés contigo o con tu aborto o con-
migo
y cautivo en tu enorme libertad,
arrastrado por tu hércules autónomo . . .

>

THE SOUL THAT SUFFERED FROM BEING ITS BODY

You suffer from an endocrine gland, it's obvious,
or, perhaps,
suffer from me, from my tacit, stark sagacity.
You endure the diaphanous anthropoid, over there, nearby,   *
where the tenebrous darkness is.
You revolve around the sun, grabbing on to your soul,
extending your corporal Juans
and adjusting your collar; that's obvious.
You know what aches you,
what leaps on your rump,
what descends through you by rope to the ground.
You, poor man, you live; don't deny it,
if you die; don't deny it,
if you die from your age, ay, and from your epoch.
And, even if you cry, you drink,
and, even if you bleed, you nourish your hybrid eyetooth,
your wistful candle and your private parts.
You suffer, you endure and again you suffer horribly,
miserable ape,   *
Darwin's lad,
bailiff spying on me, most atrocious microbe.
And you know this so well,
that you ignore it, bursting into tears.
You, then, were born; that
too is obvious at a distance, poor devil and shut up,
and you put up with the street fate gave you
and you question your navel: where? how?   *

My friend, you are completely,
up to your hair, in the year thirty-eight,
Nicolas or Santiago, someone or other,
either with yourself or with your abortion or with
me
and captive in your enormous freedom,
dragged on by your autonomous Hercules . . .   >

> Pero si tú calculas en tus dedos hasta dos,
es peor; no lo niegues, hermanito.

¿Que nó? ¿Que sí, pero que nó?
¡Pobre mono! . . . ¡Dame la pata! . . . No. La mano, he dicho.
¡Salud! ¡Y sufre!

9 Nov. 1937

But if you calculate on your fingers up to two,
it's worse; don't deny it, little brother.

    You say no? You say yes, but no?
Poor ape! . . . Gimme your paw! . . . No. Your hand, I meant.
To your health! Keep suffering!

YUNTAS

Completamente. Además, ¡vida!
Completamente. Además, ¡muerte!

Completamente. Además, ¡todo!
Completamente. Además, ¡nada!

Completamente. Además, ¡mundo!
Completamente. Además, ¡polvo!

Completamente. Además, ¡Dios!
Completamente. Además, ¡nadie!

Completamente. Además, ¡nunca!
Completamente. Además, ¡siempre!

Completamente. Además, ¡oro!
Completamente. Además, ¡humo!

Completamente. Además, ¡lágrimas!
Completamente. Además, ¡risas! . . .

¡Completamente!

9 Nov. 1937

Completely. Furthermore, life!
Completely. Furthermore, death!

Completely. Furthermore, everything!
Completely. Furthermore, nothing!

Completely. Furthermore, world!
Completely. Furthermore, dust!

Completely. Furthermore, God!
Completely. Furthermore, no one!

Completely. Furthermore, never!
Completely. Furthermore, always!

Completely. Furthermore, gold!
Completely. Furthermore, smoke!

Completely. Furthermore, tears!
Completely. Furthermore, laughs! . . .

Completely!

Acaba de pasar el que vendrá
proscrito, a sentarse en mi triple desarrollo;
acaba de pasar criminalmente.

Acaba de sentarse más acá,
a un cuerpo de distancia de mi alma,
el que vino en un asno a enflaquecerme;
acaba de sentarse de pie, lívido.

Acaba de darme lo que está acabado,
el calor del fuego y el pronombre inmenso
que el animal crió bajo su cola.

Acaba
de expresarme su duda sobre hipótesis lejanas
que él aleja, aún más, con la mirada.

Acaba de hacer al bien los honores que le tocan
en virtud del infame paquidermo,
por lo soñado en mí y en él matado.

Acaba de ponerme (no hay primera)
su segunda aflixión en plenos lomos
y su tercer sudor en plena lágrima.

Acaba de pasar sin haber venido.

12 Nov. 1937

He who will come has just passed
banished, to sit down on my triple unfolding;
has just passed criminally.

Has just sat down closer,
a body away from my soul,
he who came on an ass to debilitate me;
has just sat down standing, livid.

Has just given me that which is finished,
the heat of the fire and the immense pronoun
that the animal suckled under its tail.

Has just
expressed to me his doubts about remote hypotheses
which he distances, even further, with his look.

Has just bestowed on the good its rightful honors
by virtue of the infamous pachyderm,
through what is dreamed in me and in him killed.

Has just fixed (there is no first)
his second afflixion smack in my loins   *
and his third sweat smack in my tear.

Has just passed without having come.   *

Viniere el malo, con un trono al hombro,
y el bueno, a acompañar al malo a andar;
dijeren "sí" el sermón, "no" la plegaria
y cortare el camino en dos la roca . . .

Comenzare por monte la montaña,
por remo el tallo, por timón el cedro
y esperaren doscientos a sesenta
y volviere la carne a sus tres títulos . . .

Sobrare nieve en la noción del fuego,
se acostare el cadáver a mirarnos,
la centella a ser trueno corpulento
y se arquearen los saurios a ser aves . . .

Faltare excavación junto al estiércol,
naufragio al río para resbalar,
cárcel al hombre libre, para serlo,
y una atmósfera al cielo, y hierro al oro . . .

Mostraren disciplina, olor, las fieras,
se pintare el enojo de soldado,
me dolieren el junco que aprendí,
la mentira que inféctame y socórreme . . .

Sucediere ello así y así poniéndolo,
¿con qué mano despertar?
¿con qué pie morir?
¿con qué ser pobre?
¿con qué voz callar
¿con cuánto comprender, y, luego, a quién?

No olvidar ni recordar
que por mucho cerrarla, robáronse la puerta,
y de sufrir tan poco estoy muy resentido,
y de tánto pensar, no tengo boca.

19 Nov. 1937

Were the evil one to come, shouldering a throne,
and the good one, to accompany him on his way;
were the sermon to say "yes," the prayer "no"
and the road to cut the rock in two . . .

Were the mountain to begin as a mount,
the stalk as an oar, the cedar as a tiller
and two hundred to wait for sixty
and the flesh to recapture its three titles . . .

Were snow to be in excess in the notion of fire,   *
were the corpse to lie down to watch us,
the flash to be corpulent thunder
and the saurians arch to be birds . . .

Were dung to lack an excavation nearby,   *
the river a shipwreck so as to slide,
the free man jail, so as to be free
and the sky an atmosphere, and gold iron . . .   *

Were wild beasts to show discipline, odor,
were anger to paint itself up as a soldier,
were the reed that I learned to pain me,
the lie that infects and sustains me . . .

Were it to happen this way and putting it this way,
with what hand to awake?
with what foot to die?
with what to be poor?   *
with what voice to grow silent?
with how much to understand, and then, whom?

Not to forget nor to remember
that from closing it too often, they stole the door,
and that from suffering so little I am very resentful,
and that from so *much* thinking, I have no mouth.   *

¡Ande desnudo, en pelo, el millonario!
¡Desgracia al que edifica con tesoros su lecho de muerte!
¡Un mundo al que saluda;
un sillón al que siembra en el cielo;
llanto al que da término a lo que hace, guardando los comienzos;
ande el de las espuelas;
poco dure muralla en que no crezca otra muralla;
dése al mísero toda su miseria,
pan, al que ríe;
hagan perder los triunfos y morir los médicos;
haya leche en la sangre;
añádase una vela al sol,
ochocientos al veinte;
pase la eternidad bajo los puentes!
¡Desdén al que viste,
corónense los pies de manos, quepan en su tamaño;
siéntese mi persona junto a mí!
¡Llorar al haber cabido en aquel vientre,
bendición al que mira aire en el aire,
muchos años de clavo al martillazo;
desnúdese el desnudo,
vístase de pantalón la capa,
fulja el cobre a expensas de sus láminas,
majestad al que cae de la arcilla al universo,
lloren las bocas, giman las miradas,
impídase al acero perdurar,
hilo a los horizontes portátiles,
doce ciudades al sendero de piedra,
una esfera al que juega con su sombra;
un día hecho de una hora, a los esposos;
una madre al arado en loor al suelo,
séllense con dos sellos a los líquidos,
pase lista el bocado,
sean los descendientes,
sea la codorniz,
sea la carrera del álamo y del árbol;
venzan, al contrario del círculo, el mar a su hijo
y a la cana el lloro;
dejad los áspides, señores hombres,
surcad la llama con los siete leños,

>

Let the millionaire walk naked, stark naked!   *
Disgrace for whoever builds his deathbed with treasures!
A world for whoever greets;
an armchair for whoever sows in the sky;
weeping for whoever finishes what he makes, keeping the beginnings;
let the spur-wearer walk;
no duration for that wall on which another wall is not growing;
give to the wretched all his wretchedness,
bread, to whoever laughs;
let the triumphs lose, the doctors die;
let there be milk in blood;
let a candle be added to the sun,
eight hundred to twenty;
let eternity pass under the bridges!
Scorn whoever gets dressed,
crown feet with hands, fit them in their size;
let my self sit next to me!
To weep having fit in that womb,
blessed be whoever observes air in the air,
many years of nail for the hammer stroke;
strip the naked,
make the cape put on pants,
let copper gleam at the expense of its plates,
majesty for whoever falls from the clay into the universe,
let the mouths weep, the looks moan,
prevent steel from enduring,
thread for the portable horizons,
twelve cities for the stone path,
a sphere for whoever plays with his shadow;
a day made of one hour, for the husband and wife;
a mother for the plow in praise of soil,
seal liquids with two seals,
let the mouthful call roll,
let the descendents be,
let the quail be,
let the race of the poplar and the tree be;
contrary to circular expectations, let the sea defeat his son
and weeping the gray hair;
leave the asps alone, fellow men,
furrow the flame with seven logs,   >

> vivid,
elévese la altura,
baje el hondor más hondo,
conduzca la onda su impulsión andando,
tenga éxito la tregua de la bóveda!
¡Muramos;
lavad vuestro esqueleto cada día;
no me hagáis caso,
una ave coja al déspota y a su alma;
una mancha espantosa, al que va solo;
gorriones al astrónomo, al gorrión, al aviador!
¡Lloved, solead,
vigilad a Júpiter, al ladrón de ídolos de oro,
copiad vuestra letra en tres cuadernos,
aprended de los cónyuges cuando hablan, y
de los solitarios, cuando callan;
dad de comer a los novios,
dad de beber al diablo en vuestras manos,
luchad por la justicia con la nuca,
igualaos,
cúmplase el roble,
cúmplase el leopardo entre dos robles,
seamos,
estemos,
sentid cómo navega el agua en los océanos,
alimentaos,
concíbase el error, puesto que lloro,
acéptese, en tanto suban por el risco, las cabras y sus crías;
desacostumbrad a Dios a ser un hombre,
creced . . . !
Me llaman. Vuelvo.

19 Nov. 1937

live,
raise the height,
lower the deepage deeper,   *
let the wave accompany its impulse walking,
the crypt's truce succeed!
May we die;
wash your skeleton daily;
pay no attention to me,
a lame bird for the despot and his soul;
a dreadful stain, for whoever goes it alone;
sparrows for the astronomer, for the sparrow, for the aviator!
Give off rain, beam sun,
keep an eye on Jupiter, on the thief of your gold idols,
copy your writing in three notebooks,
learn from the married when they speak, and
from the solitary, when they are silent;
give the sweethearts something to eat,
the devil in your hands something to drink,
fight for justice with your nape,
make yourselves equal,
let the oak be fulfilled,
let the leopard between two oaks be fulfilled,
let us be,
let us be here,
feel how water navigates the oceans,
nourish yourselves,
let the error be conceived, since I am weeping,
accept, while goats and their young climb the crags;
make God break the habit of being a man,
grow . . . !
They are calling me. I'll be back.

Al revés de las aves del monte,
que viven del valle,
aquí, una tarde,
aquí, presa, metaloso, terminante,
vino el Sincero con sus nietos pérfidos,
y nosotros quedámonos, que no hay
más madera en la cruz de la derecha,
ni más hierro en el clavo de la izquierda,
que un apretón de manos entre zurdos.

Vino el Sincero, ciego, con sus lámparas.
Se vio al Pálido, aquí, bastar
al Encarnado;
nació de puro humilde el Grande;
la guerra,
esta tórtola mía, nunca nuestra,
diseñóse, borróse, ovó, matáronla.

Llevóse el Ebrio al labio un roble, porque
amaba, y una astilla
de roble, porque odiaba;
trenzáronse las trenzas de los potros
y la crin de las potencias;
cantaron los obreros; fui dichoso.

El Pálido abrazóse al Encarnado
y el Ebrio, saludónos, escondiéndose.
Como era aquí y al terminar el día,
¡qué más tiempo que aquella plazoleta!
¡qué año mejor que esa gente!
¡qué momento más fuerte que ese siglo!

Pues de lo que hablo no es
sino de lo que pasa en esta época, y
de lo que ocurre en China y en España, y en el mundo.
(Walt Whitman tenía un pecho suavísimo y res-
piraba y nadie sabe lo que él hacía cuando lloraba en su comedor)

Pero, volviendo a lo nuestro,
y al verso que decía, fuera entonces
que vi que el hombre es malnacido,
mal vivo, mal muerto, mal moribundo,
y, naturalmente,

>

Contrary to the mountain birds,
that live off the valley,
here, one afternoon,
here, prey, metalous, conclusive,   *
the Sincere came with his treacherous grandchildren,
and we remained, because there is no
more wood in the cross of the right,
nor more iron in the nail of the left,
than a warm handshake between the left-handed.

The Sincere came, blind, with his lamps.
The Pallid was seen, here, to be enough
for the Incarnated;
by sheer humbleness the Great was born;   *
the war,
this turtledove of mine, never ours,
sketched itself, erased itself, laid eggs, they killed it.

The Inebriated raised an oak to his lip, because
he loved, and a splinter
of oak, because he hated;
the braids of the colts and the mane
of the powers braided themselves;
the workers sang; I was happy.

The Pallid embraced the Incarnated
and the Inebriated, greeted us, hiding himself.
Since it took place here and when the day ended,
what longer time than that little plaza!
what year better than those people!
what moment stronger than that century!

For what I'm talking about is
nothing other than what is taking place in our epoch, and   *
what is occurring in China and in Spain, and in the world.
(Walt Whitman had the softest of chests and brea-
thed and nobody knows what he was up to when he was sobbing in his dining room)

But, returning to our affairs,
and to the poetry that I was reciting, it was then
that I saw that man is lowborn,
base alive, base dead, base dying,
and, naturally,   >

>   el tartufo sincero desespérase,
el pálido (es el pálido de siempre)
será pálido por algo,
y el ebrio, entre la sangre humana y la leche animal,
abátese, da, y opta por marcharse.

   Todo esto
agítase, ahora mismo,
en mi vientre de macho extrañamente.

20 Nov. 1937

the sincere hypocrite despairs,
the pallid (the one who is always pallid)
will be for some reason pallid,
and the inebriated, between human blood and animal milk,
slumps, gives up, and decides to take off.

All this
stirs, right now,
in my male belly strangely.   *

Ello es que el lugar donde me pongo
el pantalón, es una casa donde
me quito la camisa en alta voz
y donde tengo un suelo, un alma, un mapa de mi España.
Ahora mismo hablaba
de mí conmigo, y ponía
sobre un pequeño libro un pan tremendo
y he, luego, hecho el traslado, he trasladado,
queriendo canturrear un poco, el lado
derecho de la vida al lado izquierdo;
más tarde, me he lavado todo, el vientre,
briosa, dignamente;
he dado vuelta a ver lo que se ensucia,
he raspado lo que me lleva tan cerca
y he ordenado bien el mapa que
cabeceaba o lloraba, no lo sé.

Mi casa, por desgracia, es una casa,
un suelo por ventura, donde vive
con su inscripción mi cucharita amada,
mi querido esqueleto ya sin letras,
la navaja, un cigarro permanente.
De veras, cuando pienso
en lo que es la vida,
no puedo evitar de decírselo a Georgette,
a fin de comer algo agradable y salir,
por la tarde, comprar un buen periódico,
guardar un día para cuando no haya,
una noche también, para cuando haya
(así se dice en el Perú—me excuso);
del mismo modo, sufro con gran cuidado,
a fin de no gritar o de llorar, ya que los ojos
poseen, independientemente de uno, sus pobrezas,
quiero decir, su oficio, algo
que resbala del alma y cae al alma.

Habiendo atravesado
quince años; después, quince, y, antes, quince,
uno se siente, en realidad, tontillo,
es natural, por lo demás ¡qué hacer!
¿Y qué dejar de hacer, que es lo peor?   >

    The fact is the place where I put on
my pants, is a house where
I take off my shirt out loud
and where I have a floor, a soul, a map of my Spain.
Just now I was speaking
about me with myself, and placing
on top of a little book a huge loaf
and I have, then, made the transfer, I've transferred,
desiring to hum a little, the right
side of life to the left side;
later, I've washed all of me, my belly,
vigorously, with dignity;
I've turned around to see what soils itself,
I've scraped what takes me so near
and have neatly arranged the map that
was nodding or weeping, I don't know.

    My house, unfortunately, is a house,
a floor fortunately, where with its
inscription my beloved little spoon lives,
my dear now unlettered skeleton,
the razor, a permanent cigar.
Truthfully, when I think
about what life is,
I can't help expressing it to Georgette,
to be able to eat something agreeable and go out,
for the afternoon, to buy a good newspaper,
to save a day for when there isn't one,
a night too, for when there is
(as one says in Peru—my apologies);
in the same way, I suffer with great care,
in order to not shout or weep, now that our eyes
have, independently of one, their poverties,
I mean, their occupation, something
that slips from the soul and falls to the soul.

    Having crossed
fifteen years; after, fifteen, and, before, fifteen,
one feels, really, a little stupid,
it's natural, on the other hand, what can one do!
And what to stop doing, that's even worse?   >

> Sino vivir, sino llegar
a ser lo que es uno entre millones
de panes, entre miles de vinos, entre cientos de bocas,
entre el sol y su rayo que es de luna
y entre la misa, el pan, el vino y mi alma.

Hoy es domingo y, por eso,
me viene a la cabeza la idea, al pecho el llanto
y a la garganta, así como un gran bulto.
Hoy es domingo, y esto
tiene muchos siglos; de otra manera,
sería, quizá, lunes, y vendríame al corazón la idea,
al seso, el llanto
y a la garganta, una gana espantosa de ahogar
lo que ahora siento,
como un hombre que soy y que he sufrido.

21 Nov. 1937

Only to live, only to become
what one is among millions
of loaves, among thousands of wines, among hundreds of mouths,
between the sun and its beam, a moonbeam
and among the Mass, the bread, the wine and my soul.

Today is Sunday and, for this reason,
the idea comes to my head, the weeping to my chest
and to my throat, like a big lump.
Today is Sunday, and this fact
is many centuries old; otherwise,
it would be, perhaps, Monday, and the idea would come to my heart,
the weeping, to my brain
and to my throat, a dreadful urge to drown
what I now feel,
like a man that I am and who has suffered.

Algo te identifica con el que se aleja de ti, y es la facultad común de volver: de ahí tu más grande pesadumbre.

Algo te separa del que se queda contigo, y es la esclavitud común de partir: de ahí tus más nimios regocijos.

Me dirijo, en esta forma, a las individualidades colectivas, tanto como a las colectividades individuales y a los que, entre unas y otras, yacen marchando al son de las fronteras o, simplemente, marcan el paso inmóvil en el borde del mundo.

Algo típicamente neutro, de inexorablemente neutro, interpónese entre el ladrón y su víctima. Esto, asimismo, puede discernirse tratándose del cirujano y del paciente. Horrible medialuna, convexa y solar, cobija a unos y otros. Porque el objeto hurtado tiene también su peso indiferente, y el órgano intervenido, también su grasa triste.

¿Qué hay de más desesperante en la tierra, que la imposibilidad en que se halla el hombre feliz de ser infortunado y el hombre bueno, de ser malvado?

¡Alejarse! ¡Quedarse! ¡Volver! ¡Partir! Toda la mecánica social cabe en estas palabras.

[24 Nov. 1937]

Something identifies you with the one who leaves you, and it is the common power to return: thus your greatest sorrow.

Something separates you from the one who remains with you, and it is the common slavery of departing: thus your meagerest rejoicing.

I address myself, in this way, to collective individualities, as well as to individual collectivities and to those who, between the two, lie marching to the sound of the frontiers or, simply, mark time without moving at the edge of the world.

Something typically neuter, inexorably neuter, comes between the thief and his victim. This, likewise, can be noticed in the relationship between the surgeon and the patient. A horrible half-moon, convex and solar, covers both of them. For the stolen object has also its indifferent weight, and the operated on organ, also its sad fat.

What on earth is more exasperating, than the impossibility for the happy man to be unlucky and the good man, to be wicked?

To leave! To remain! To return! To depart! The whole social mechanism fits in these words.   *

En suma, no poseo para expresar mi vida, sino mi muerte.

Y, después de todo, al cabo de la escalonada naturaleza y del gorrión en bloque, me duermo, mano a mano con mi sombra.

Y, al descender del acto venerable y del otro gemido, me reposo pensando en la marcha impertérrita del tiempo.

¿Por qué la cuerda, entonces, si el aire es tan sencillo? ¿Para qué la cadena, si existe el hierro por sí solo?

César Vallejo, el acento con que amas, el verbo con que escribes, el vientecillo con que oyes, sólo saben de ti por tu garganta.

César Vallejo, póstrate, por eso, con indistinto orgullo, con tálamo de ornamentales áspides y exagonales ecos.

Restitúyete al corpóreo panal, a la beldad; aroma los florecidos corchos, cierra ambas grutas al sañudo antropoide; repara, en fin, tu antipático venado; tente pena.

¡Que no hay cosa más densa que el odio en voz pasiva, ni más mísera ubre que el amor!

¡Que ya no puedo andar, sino en dos harpas!

¡Que ya no me conoces, sino porque te sigo instrumental, prolijamente!

¡Que ya no doy gusanos, sino breves!

¡Que ya te implico tánto, que medio que te afilas!

¡Que ya llevo unas tímidas legumbres y otras bravas!

Pues el afecto que quiébrase de noche en mis bronquios, lo trajeron de día ocultos deanes y, si amanezco pálido, es por mi obra: y, si anochezco rojo, por mi obrero. Ello explica, igualmente, estos cansancios míos y estos despojos, mis famosos tíos. Ello explica, en fin, esta lágrima que brindo por la dicha de los hombres.

¡César Vallejo, parece
mentira que así tarden tus parientes,
sabiendo que ando cautivo,
sabiendo que yaces libre!
¡Vistosa y perra suerte!
¡César Vallejo, te odio con ternura!

25 Nov. 1937

In short, I have nothing with which to express my life, except my death.   *

And, after everything, at the end of graded nature and of the sparrow in bloc, I sleep, hand in hand with my shadow.

And, upon descending from the venerable act and from the other moan, I repose thinking about the inexorable march of time.

Why the rope, then, if air is so simple? What is the chain for, if iron exists on its own?

César Vallejo, the accent with which you love, the language with which you write, the light wind with which you hear, only know of you through your throat.

César Vallejo, prostrate yourself, therefore, with vague pride, with a nuptial bed of ornamental asps and hexagonal echoes.

Return to the corporeal honeycomb, to beauty; aromatize the blossomed corks, close both grottoes to the enraged anthropoid; mend, finally, your unpleasant stag; feel sorry for yourself.

For there is nothing denser than the hate in a passive voice, no stingier udder than love!

For I'm no longer able to walk, except on two harps!

For you no longer know me, unless instrumentally, longwindedly, I follow you!

For I no longer issue worms, but briefs!

For I now implicate you so much, you almost become sharp!

For I now carry some timid vegetables and others that are fierce!

So the affection that ruptures at night in my bronchia, was brought during the day by occult deans and, if I wake up pale, it's because of my work: and, if I go to sleep red, because of my worker. This explains, equally, this weariness of mine and these spoils, my famous uncles. This explains, finally, this tear that I toast to the happiness of men.

César Vallejo, it's hard
to believe that your relatives are so late,
knowing that I walk a captive,
knowing that you lie free!
Flashy and rotten luck!
César Vallejo, I hate you with tenderness!

Otro poco de calma, camarada;
un mucho inmenso, septentrional, completo,
feroz, de calma chica,
al servicio menor de cada triunfo
y en la audaz servidumbre del fracaso.

Embriaguez te sobra, y no hay
tanta locura en la razón, como este
tu raciocinio muscular, y no hay
más racional error que tu experiencia.

Pero, hablando más claro
y pensándolo en oro, eres de acero,
a condición que no seas
tonto y rehuses
entusiasmarte por la muerte tánto
y por la vida, con tu sola tumba.

Necesario es que sepas
contener tu volumen sin correr, sin afligirte,
tu realidad molecular entera
y más allá, la marcha de tus vivas
y más acá, tus mueras legendarios.

Eres de acero, como dicen,
con tal que no tiembles y no vayas
a reventar, compadre
de mi cálculo, enfático ahijado
de mis sales luminosas!

Anda, no más; resuelve,
considera tu crisis, suma, sigue,
tájala, bájala, ájala;
el destino, las energías íntimas, los catorce
versículos del pan: ¡cuántos diplomas
y poderes, al borde fehaciente de tu arranque!
¡Cuánto detalle en síntesis, contigo!
¡Cuánta presión idéntica, a tus pies!
¡Cuánto rigor y cuánto patrocinio!

Es idiota
ese método de padecimiento,
esa luz modulada y virulenta,

>

A little more calm, comrade;
an immense much, northern, complete,
ferocious, of small calm,
in the minor service of each triumph
and in the audacious servitude of defeat.

You have intoxication to spare, and there's not
so much craziness in reason, as in this
your muscular reasoning, and there's no
more rational error than your experience.

But, speaking more clearly
and pondering it in gold, you are of steel,
on condition that you are not
dumb and refuse
to become so enthusiastic about death
and about life, with your only tomb.

It's necessary for you to learn
how to contain your volume without running, without distress,   *
your entire molecular reality
and beyond, the march of your cheers
and closer, your legendary condemnations.

You are of steel, as they say,
providing you do not quaver and do not start
exploding, godfather
of my calculation, emphatic godson
of my luminous salts!

Go right ahead; decide,
ponder your crisis, add, carry,
hack it up, humble it, crumble it;
destiny, the intimate energies, the fourteen
versicles of bread; how many diplomas
and powers, at the authentic edge of your start!
How much synthesized detail, with you!
How much identical pressure, at your feet!
How much rigor and how much patronage!

It's idiotic
that method of suffering,
that modified and virulent light,   >

> si con sólo la calma haces señales
serias, características, fatales.

Vamos a ver, hombre;
cuéntame lo que me pasa,
que yo, aunque grite, estoy siempre a tus órdenes.

28 Nov. 1937

if with only the calm you flash serious,
characteristic, fatal signals.

    Let's see, man;
tell me what's happening to me,
for, even when shouting, I'm always at your command.

LOS DESGRACIADOS

Ya va a venir el día; da
cuerda a tu brazo, búscate debajo
del colchón, vuelve a pararte
en tu cabeza, para andar derecho.
Ya va a venir el día, ponte el saco.

Ya va a venir el día; ten
fuerte en la mano a tu intestino grande, reflexiona,
antes de meditar, pues es horrible
cuando le cae a uno la desgracia
y se le cae a uno a fondo el diente.

Necesitas comer, pero, me digo,
no tengas pena, que no es de pobres
la pena, el sollozar junto a su tumba;
remiéndate, recuerda,
confía en tu hilo blanco, fuma, pasa lista
a tu cadena y guárdala detrás de tu retrato.
Ya va a venir el día, ponte el alma.

Ya va a venir el día; pasan,
han abierto en el hotel un ojo,
azotándolo, dándole con un espejo tuyo . . .
¿Tiemblas? Es el estado remoto de la frente
y la nación reciente del estómago.
Roncan aún . . . ¡Qué universo se lleva este ronquido!
¡Cómo quedan tus poros, enjuiciándolo!
¡Con cuántos doses ¡ay! estás tan solo!
Ya va a venir el día, ponte el sueño.

Ya va a venir el día, repito
por el órgano oral de tu silencio
y urge tomar la izquierda con el hambre
y tomar la derecha con la sed; de todos modos,
abstente de ser pobre con los ricos,
atiza
tu frío, porque en él se integra mi calor, amada víctima.
Ya va a venir el día, ponte el cuerpo.

>

THE WRETCHED

The day is about to come; wind
up your arm, look for yourself under
the mattress, stand once more
on your head, so as to walk straight.
The day is about to come, put on your coat.

The day is about to come; grip
your large intestine tightly in your hand, reflect,
before meditating, for it is horrible
when misfortune befalls one
and one's tooth falls out completely.

You have to eat, but, I tell myself,
do not grieve, for grief and graveside
sobbing do not belong to the poor;
patch yourself, remember,
trust in your white thread, smoke, call roll
on your chain and keep it behind your portrait.
The day is about to come, put on your soul.

The day is about to come; they go by,
they've opened up an eye in the hotel,
lashing it, beating it with one of your mirrors . . .
You're trembling? It is the remote state of the forehead
and the recent nation of the stomach.
They're still snoring . . . What a universe is stolen by this snore!
What state your pores are in, on judging it!
With so many twos, ay! how alone you are!
The day is about to come, put on your dream.

The day is about to come, I repeat
through the oral organ of your silence
and it is urgent to take the left with hunger
and to take the right with thirst; in any case,
abstain from being poor among the rich,
poke
your cold, for my warmth is one with it, beloved victim.
The day is about to come, put on your body.   >

>   Ya va a venir el día;
la mañana, la mar, el meteoro, van
en pos de tu cansancio, con banderas,
y, por tu orgullo clásico, las hienas
cuentan sus pasos al compás del asno,
la panadera piensa en ti,
el carnicero piensa en ti, palpando
el hacha en que están presos
el acero y el hierro y el metal; jamás olvides
que durante la misa no hay amigos.
Ya va a venir el día, ponte el sol.

    Ya viene el día; dobla
el aliento, triplica
tu bondad rencorosa
y da codos al miedo, nexo y énfasis,
pues tú, como se observa en tu entrepierna y siendo
el malo ¡ay! inmortal,
has soñado esta noche que vivías
de nada y morías de todo . . .

[Fin de Noviembre–Primera semana de Diciembre 1937]

The day is about to come;
the morning, the sea, the meteor, go
in pursuit of your weariness, with banners,
and, because of your classic pride, the hyenas
count their steps in time with the ass,
the female baker thinks about you,
the butcher thinks about you, palpating
the cleaver in which the steel
and the iron and the metal are prisoners; never forget
that during Mass there are no friends.
The day is about to come, put on your sun.

The day is coming; double
your breath, triple
your rancorous goodness
and scorn fear, connections and affectation,
for you, as one can observe in your crotch, the evil one
being aie! immortal,
have dreamed tonight that you were living
on nothing and dying from everything . . .

Y, en fin, pasando luego al dominio de la muerte,
que actúa en escuadrón, previo corchete,
párrafo y llave, mano grande y diéresis,
¿a qué el pupitre asirio? ¿a qué el cristiano púlpito,
el intenso jalón del mueble vándalo
o, todavía menos, este esdrújulo retiro?

¿Es para terminar,
mañana, en prototipo del alarde fálico,
en diabetis y en blanca vacinica,
en rostro geométrico, en difunto,
que se hacen menester sermón y almendras,
que sobran literalmente patatas
y este espectro fluvial en que arde el oro
y en que se quema el precio de la nieve?
¿Es para eso, que morimos tánto?
¿Para sólo morir,
tenemos que morir a cada instante?
¿Y el párrafo que escribo?
¿Y el corchete deísta que enarbolo?
¿Y el escuadrón en que falló mi casco?
¿Y la llave que va a todas las puertas?
¿Y la forense diéresis, la mano,
mi patata y mi carne y mi contradicción bajo la sábana?

¡Loco de mí, lovo de mí, cordero
de mí, sensato, caballísimo de mí!
¡Pupitre, sí, toda la vida; púlpito,
también, toda la muerte!
Sermón de la barbarie: estos papeles;
esdrújulo retiro: este pellejo.

De esta suerte, cogitabundo, aurífero, brazudo,
defenderé mi presa en dos momentos,
con la voz y también con la laringe,
y del olfato físico con que oro   >

SERMON ON DEATH

And, finally, passing now into the domain of death,
which acts as squadron, former bracket,
paragraph and key, huge hand and dieresis,
for what the Assyrian desk? for what the Christian pulpit,
the intense tug of Vandal furniture
or, even less, this proparoxytonic retreat?

Is it in order to end,
tomorrow, as a prototype of phallic display,
as diabetes and in a white chamber pot,
as a geometric face, as a dead man,
that sermon and almonds become necessary,
that there are literally too many potatoes
and this watery specter in which gold blazes
and in which the price of snow burns?
Is it for this, that we die so much?
Only to die,
must we die each instant?
And the paragraph that I write?
And the deistic bracket that I raise on high?
And the squadron in which my helmet failed?
And the key which fits all doors?
And the forensic dieresis, the hand,
my potato and my flesh and my contradiction under the bedsheet?   *

Out of my mind, out of my wolvum, out of   *
my lamb, out of my sensible horsessence!
Desk, yes, my whole life long; pulpit,
likewise, my whole death long!
Sermon on barbarism: these papers;
proparoxytonic retreat: this skin.

In this way, cognitive, auriferous, thick-armed,   *
I will defend my catch in two moments,
with my voice and also with my larynx,
and of the physical smell with which I pray   >

> y del instinto de inmovilidad con que ando,
me honraré mientras viva—hay que decirlo;
se enorgullecerán mis moscardones,
porque, al centro, estoy yo, y a la derecha,
también, y, a la izquierda, de igual modo.

8 Dic. 1937

and of the instinct for immobility with which I walk,
I will be proud while I'm alive—it must be said;
my horseflies will swell with pride,
because, at the center, I am, and to the right,
likewise, and, to the left, equally.

ESPAÑA, APARTA DE MÍ ESTE CÁLIZ (1939)

SPAIN, TAKE THIS CUP FROM ME

I

HIMNO A LOS VOLUNTARIOS DE LA REPÚBLICA

Voluntario de España, miliciano
de huesos fidedignos, cuando marcha a morir tu corazón,
cuando marcha a matar con su agonía
mundial, no sé verdaderamente
qué hacer, dónde ponerme; corro, escribo, aplaudo,
lloro, atisbo, destrozo, apagan, digo
a mi pecho que acabe, al bien, que venga,
y quiero desgraciarme;
descúbrome la frente impersonal hasta tocar
el vaso de la sangre, me detengo,
detienen mi tamaño esas famosas caídas de arquitecto
con las que se honra el animal que me honra;
refluyen mis instintos a sus sogas,
humea ante mi tumba la alegría
y, otra vez, sin saber qué hacer, sin nada, déjame,
desde mi piedra en blanco, déjame,
solo,
cuadrumano, más acá, mucho más lejos,
al no caber entre mis manos tu largo rato extático,
quiebro contra tu rapidez de doble filo
mi pequeñez en traje de grandeza!

Un día diurno, claro, atento, fértil
¡oh bienio, el de los lóbregos semestres suplicantes,
por el que iba la pólvora mordiéndose los codos!
¡oh dura pena y más duros pedernales!
¡oh frenos los tascados por el pueblo!
Un día prendió el pueblo su fósforo cautivo, oró de cólera
y soberanamente pleno, circular,
cerró su natalicio con manos electivas;
arrastraban candado ya los déspotas
y en el candado, sus bacterias muertas . . .

¿Batallas? ¡No! Pasiones. Y pasiones precedidas
de dolores con rejas de esperanzas,
de dolores de pueblos con esperanzas de hombres!
¡Muerte y pasión de paz, las populares!
¡Muerte y pasión guerreras entre olivos, entendámonos!
Tal en tu aliento cambian de agujas atmosféricas los vientos

>

I
HYMN TO THE VOLUNTEERS FOR THE REPUBLIC

Spanish volunteer, civilian-fighter   *
of veritable bones, when your heart marches to die,
when it marches to kill with its worldwide
agony, I don't know truly
what to do, where to place myself; I run, write, applaud,
weep, glimpse, destroy, they extinguish, I say
to my chest that it should end, to the good, that it should come,
and I want to ruin myself;
I bare my impersonal forehead until touching
the vessel of blood, I stop,
my size is checked by those famous architectural falls
with which the animal that honors me honors itself;
my instincts flow back to their ropes,
joy smokes before my tomb
and, again, without knowing what to do, without anything, leave me,
from my blank stone, leave me,
alone,
quadrumane, closer, much more distant,
since your long ecstatic moment won't fit between my hands,   *
I swirl my tininess costumed in greatness
against your double-edged speed!

One fertile, attentive, clear, diurnal day
—oh biennial, those lugubrious semesters of begging,   *
through which the gunpowder went biting its elbows!
oh hard sorrow and harder flints!
oh bits champed by the people!
One day the people struck their captive match, prayed with anger
and supremely full, circular,
closed their birthday with elective hands;
the despots were already dragging padlock
and in the padlock, their dead bacteria . . .

Battles? No! Passions. And passions preceded
by aches with bars of hopes,
by aches of the people with hopes of men!
Death and passion for peace, of common people!
Death and passion for war among olive trees, let's get it straight!
Thus in your breath the winds change atmospheric needles   >

>	y de llave las tumbas en tu pecho,
tu frontal elevándose a primera potencia de martirio.

El mundo exclama: "¡Cosas de españoles!" Y es verdad. Consideremos,
durante una balanza, a quema ropa,
a Calderón, dormido sobre la cola de un anfibio muerto
o a Cervantes, diciendo: "Mi reino es de este mundo, pero
también del otro": ¡punta y filo en dos papeles!
Contemplemos a Goya, de hinojos y rezando ante un espejo,
a Coll, el paladín en cuyo asalto cartesiano
tuvo un sudor de nube el paso llano
o a Quevedo, ese abuelo instantáneo de los dinamiteros
o a Cajal, devorado por su pequeño infinito, o todavía
a Teresa, mujer, que muere porque no muere
o a Lina Odena, en pugna en más de un punto con Teresa . . .
(Todo acto o voz genial viene del pueblo
y va hacia él, de frente o transmitidos
por incesantes briznas, por el humo rosado
de amargas contraseñas sin fortuna)
Así tu criatura, miliciano, así tu exangüe criatura,
agitada por una piedra inmóvil,
se sacrifica, apártase,
decae para arriba y por su llama incombustible sube,
sube hasta los débiles,
distribuyendo españas a los toros,
toros a las palomas . . .

Proletario que mueres de universo, ¡en qué frenética armonía
acabará tu grandeza, tu miseria, tu vorágine impelente,
tu violencia metódica, tu caos teórico y práctico, tu gana
dantesca, españolísima, de amar, aunque sea a traición, a tu enemigo!
¡Liberador ceñido de grilletes,
sin cuyo esfuerzo hasta hoy continuaría sin asas la extensión,
vagarían acéfalos los clavos,
antiguo, lento, colorado, el día,
nuestros amados cascos, insepultos!
¡Campesino caído con tu verde follaje por el hombre,
con la inflexión social de tu meñique,
con tu buey que se queda, con tu física,
también con tu palabra atada a un palo
y tu cielo arrendado

and in your chest the tombs change key,
your frontal rising to the first power of martyrdom.

The world exclaims: "Merely Spanish matters!" And it's true. Consider,
on balance, point-blank,
Calderón, asleep on the tail of a dead amphibian,   *
or Cervantes, saying: "My kingdom is of this world, but
also of the next one": point and edge in two roles!
Contemplate Goya, on his knees and praying before a mirror,
Coll, the paladin in whose Cartesian assault   *
a simple walk had the sweat of a cloud,
or Quevedo, that instantaneous grandfather of the dynamiters,   *
or Cajal, devoured by his tiny infinite, or even   *
Teresa, a woman, dying because she was not dying,   *
or Lina Odena, in conflict with Teresa on more than one point . . .   *
(Every act or brilliant voice comes from the people
and goes toward them, directly or conveyed
by incessant filaments, by the rosy smoke
of bitter watchwords which failed)
Thus your child, civilian-fighter, thus your anemic child,
stirred by a motionless stone,
sacrifices herself, wanders off,
decays upward and through her incombustible flame rises,
rises to the weak,
distributing spains to the bulls,
bulls to the doves . . .

Proletarian who dies of universe, in what frantic harmony
your grandeur will end, your extreme poverty, your propelling whirlpool,
your methodical violence, your theoretical and practical chaos, your Dantesque
hunger, so very Spanish, to love, even treacherously, your enemy!
Liberator wrapped in shackles,
without whose effort extension would still be today without handles,
nails would wander headless,
the day, ancient, slow, reddened,
our beloved skulls, unburied!
Peasant fallen with your green foliage for man,
with the social inflection of your little finger,
with your ox that remains, with your physics,
likewise with your word tied to a stick
and your rented sky   >

> y con la arcilla inserta en tu cansancio
y la que estaba en tu uña, caminando!
¡Constructores
agrícolas, civiles y guerreros,
de la activa, hormigueante eternidad: estaba escrito
que vosotros haríais la luz, entornando
con la muerte vuestros ojos;
que, a la caída cruel de vuestras bocas,
vendrá en siete bandejas la abundancia, todo
en el mundo será de oro súbito
y el oro,
fabulosos mendigos de vuestra propia secreción de sangre,
y el oro mismo será entonces de oro!

¡Se amarán todos los hombres
y comerán tomados de las puntas de vuestros pañuelos tristes
y beberán en nombre
de vuestras gargantas infaustas!
Descansarán andando al pie de esta carrera,
sollozarán pensando en vuestras órbitas, venturosos
serán y al son
de vuestro atroz retorno, florecido, innato,
ajustarán mañana sus quehaceres, sus figuras soñadas y cantadas!

¡Unos mismos zapatos irán bien al que asciende
sin vías a su cuerpo
y al que baja hasta la forma de su alma!
¡Entrelazándose hablarán los mudos, los tullidos andarán!
¡Verán, ya de regreso, los ciegos
y palpitando escucharán los sordos!
¡Sabrán los ignorantes, ignorarán los sabios!
¡Serán dados los besos que no pudisteis dar!
¡Sólo la muerte morirá! ¡La hormiga
traerá pedacitos de pan al elefante encadenado
a su brutal delicadeza; volverán
los niños abortados a nacer perfectos, espaciales
y trabajarán todos los hombres,
engendrarán todos los hombres,
comprenderán todos los hombres!   >

and with clay inserted into your fatigue
and with that under your fingernail, walking!
Agricultural
builders, civilian and military,
of a busy, swarming eternity: it was written
that you would create the light, half-closing
your eyes in death;
that, at the cruel fall of your mouths,
abundance will come on seven platters, everything
in the world will be suddenly gold
and the gold,
fabulous beggars for your own secretion of blood,
and the gold itself will then be of gold!

    All men will love each other
and will eat holding the corners of your sad handkerchiefs
and will drink in the name
of your ill-fated throats!
They will rest walking at the edge of this course,
they will sob thinking of your orbits, fortunate
they will be and to the sound
of your atrocious, burgeoned, inborn return,
they will adjust their chores tomorrow, the figures they've dreamt and sung!

    The same shoes will fit whoever climbs
without trails to his body
and whoever descends to the form of his soul!
Entwining each other the mutes will speak, the paralyzed will walk!
The blind, now returning, will see
and throbbing the deaf will hear!
The ignorant will know, the wise will not!
Kisses will be given that you could not give!
Only death will die! The ant
will bring morsels of bread to the elephant chained
to his brutal gentleness; aborted children
will be born again perfect, spatial
and all men will work,
all men will beget,
all men will understand!   >

¡Obrero, salvador, redentor nuestro,
perdónanos, hermano, nuestras deudas!
Como dice un tambor al redoblar, en sus adagios:
qué jamás tan efímero, tu espalda!
qué siempre tan cambiante, tu perfil!

  ¡Voluntario italiano, entre cuyos animales de batalla
un león abisinio va cojeando!
¡Voluntario soviético, marchando a la cabeza de tu pecho universal!
¡Voluntarios del sur, del norte, del oriente
y tú, el occidental, cerrando el canto fúnebre del alba!
¡Soldado conocido, cuyo nombre
desfila en el sonido de un abrazo!
¡Combatiente que la tierra criara, armándote
de polvo,
calzándote de imanes positivos,
vigentes tus creencias personales,
distinto de carácter, íntima tu férula,
el cutis inmediato,
andándote tu idioma por los hombros
y el alma coronada de guijarros!
¡Voluntario fajado de tu zona fría,
templada o tórrida,
héroes a la redonda,
víctima en columna de vencedores:
en España, en Madrid, están llamando
a matar, voluntarios de la vida!

  ¡Porque en España matan, otros matan
al niño, a su juguete que se pára,
a la madre Rosenda esplendorosa,
al viejo Adán que hablaba en alta voz con su caballo
y al perro que dormía en la escalera.
Matan al libro, tiran a sus verbos auxiliares,
a su indefensa página primera!
Matan el caso exacto de la estatua,
al sabio, a su bastón, a su colega,
al barbero de al lado—me cortó posiblemente,
pero buen hombre y, luego, infortunado;
al mendigo que ayer cantaba enfrente,

Worker, our savior and redeemer,
forgive us, brother, our debts!
As a drum says in its roll, in its adagios:
what an ephemeral never, your back!
what a changing always, your profile!

Italian volunteer, among whose animals of battle
an Abyssinian lion is limping!   *
Soviet volunteer, marching at the head of your universal chest!
Volunteers from the south, from the north, from the east
and you, the westerner, closing the funereal song of the dawn!
Known soldier, whose name
files by in the sound of an embrace!
Fighter who the earth raised, arming you
with dust,
shoeing you with positive magnets,
your personal beliefs in force,
distinct in character, your ferule intimate,   *
complexion immediate,
your language moving about your shoulders
and your soul crowned with cobblestones!
Volunteer bound by your cold,
temperate or torrid zone,
heroes in the round,
victim in a column of conquerors:
in Spain, in Madrid, the command is
to kill, volunteers who fight for life!

Because in Spain they kill, others kill
the child, his toy that stops working,
radiant mother Rosenda,
old Adam who talked out loud with his horse
and the dog that slept on the stairs.
They kill the book, they fire at its auxiliary verbs,
at its defenseless first page!
They kill the exact case of the statue,
the sage, his cane, his colleague,
the neighborhood barber next door—maybe he cut me,
but a good man and, then, unlucky;
the beggar who yesterday was singing out in front,   >

> a la enfermera que hoy pasó llorando,
al sacerdote a cuestas con la altura tenaz de sus rodillas . . .

¡Voluntarios,
por la vida, por los buenos, matad
a la muerte, matad a los malos!
¡Hacedlo por la libertad de todos,
del explotado y del explotador,
por la paz indolora—la sospecho
cuando duermo al pie de mi frente
y más cuando circulo dando voces—
y hacedlo, voy diciendo,
por el analfabeto a quien escribo,
por el genio descalzo y su cordero,
por los camaradas caídos,
sus cenizas abrazadas al cadáver de un camino!

Para que vosotros,
voluntarios de España y del mundo, vinierais,
soñé que era yo bueno, y era para ver
vuestra sangre, voluntarios . . .
De esto hace mucho pecho, muchas ansias,
muchos camellos en edad de orar.
Marcha hoy de vuestra parte el bien ardiendo,
os siguen con cariño los reptiles de pestaña inmanente
y, a dos pasos, a uno,
la dirección del agua que corre a ver su límite antes que arda.

the nurse who today passed by crying,
the priest burdened with the stubborn height of his knees . . .

    Volunteers,
for life, for the good ones, kill
death, kill the evil ones!
Do it for the freedom of all,
of the exploited and the exploiter,
for a painless peace—I glimpse it
when I sleep at the foot of my forehead
and even more when I go around shouting—
and do it, I keep saying,
for the illiterate to whom I write,
for the barefoot genius and his lamb,
for the fallen comrades,
their ashes clasped to the corpse of a road!

    So that you,
volunteers for Spain and for the world, would come,
I dreamt that I was good, and it was to see
your blood, volunteers . . .
Since then there's been much chest, much anxiety,
many camels old enough to pray.
Today good on your behalf marches in flames,
reptiles with immanent eyelashes follow you affectionately
and, at two steps, one step,
the direction of the water coursing to see its limit before it burns.

II

BATALLAS

Hombre de Estremadura,
oigo bajo tu pie el humo del lobo,
el humo de la especie,
el humo del niño,
el humo solitario de dos trigos,
el humo de Ginebra, el humo de Roma, el humo de Berlín
y el de París y el humo de tu apéndice penoso
y el humo que, al fin, sale del futuro.
¡Oh vida! ¡oh tierra! ¡oh España!
¡Onzas de sangre,
metros de sangre, líquidos de sangre,
sangre a caballo, a pie, mural, sin diámetro,
sangre de cuatro en cuatro, sangre de agua
y sangre muerta de la sangre viva!

Estremeño, ¡oh, no ser aún ese hombre
por el que te mató la vida y te parió la muerte
y quedarse tan solo a verte así, desde este lobo,
cómo sigues arando en nuestros pechos!
Estremeño, conoces
el secreto en dos voces, popular y táctil,
del cereal: ¡que nada vale tánto
como una gran raíz en trance de otra!
¡Estremeño acodado, representando al alma en su retiro,
acodado a mirar
el caber de una vida en una muerte!

¡Estremeño, y no haber tierra que hubiere
el peso de tu arado, ni más mundo
que el color de tu yugo entre dos épocas; no haber
el orden de tus póstumos ganados!
¡Estremeño, dejásteme
verte desde este lobo, padecer,
pelear por todos y pelear
para que el individuo sea un hombre,
para que los señores sean hombres,
para que todo el mundo sea un hombre, y para
que hasta los animales sean hombres,

>

II
BATTLES   *

   Man from Estremadura,   *
under your foot I hear the smoke of the wolf,   *
the smoke of the species,   *
the smoke of the child,
the solitary smoke of two wheats,
the smoke of Geneva, the smoke of Rome, the smoke of Berlin
and that of Paris and the smoke of your painful appendix
and the smoke that, finally, comes out of the future.
Oh life! oh earth! oh Spain!
Ounces of blood,
meters of blood, liquids of blood,
blood on horseback, on foot, mural, without diameter,
blood four by four, blood of water
and dead blood from living blood!   *

   Estremanian, oh not yet to be that man
for whom life killed you and death gave birth to you   *
and to stay on only to see you like this, from this wolf,
how you keep plowing our chests!   *
Estremanian, you know
the secret in both voices, popular and tactile,
of the cereal: that nothing is as valuable
as a big root on the verge of another!
Estremanian bent on elbow, picturing the soul in its retreat,   *
bent on elbow to observe
the fitting of a life in a death!

   Estremanian, and not to have land that would have
the weight of your plow, nor other world
than the color of your yoke between two epochs; not to have
the order of your posthumous herds!
Estremanian, you allowed me
to see you from this wolf, to endure,
to fight for everyone and to fight
so that the individual can become a man,
so that misters can become men,
so that the whole world can become a man, and so
that even animals can become men,   >

> el caballo, un hombre,
el reptil, un hombre,
el buitre, un hombre honesto,
la mosca, un hombre, y el olivo, un hombre
y hasta el ribazo, un hombre
y el mismo cielo, todo un hombrecito!

    Luego, retrocediendo desde Talavera,
en grupos de a uno, armados de hambre, en masas de a uno,
armados de pecho hasta la frente,
sin aviones, sin guerra, sin rencor,
el perder a la espalda
y el ganar
más abajo del plomo, heridos mortalmente de honor,
locos de polvo, el brazo a pie,
amando por las malas,
ganando en español toda la tierra,
retroceder aún, ¡y no saber
dónde poner su España,
dónde ocultar su beso de orbe,
dónde plantar su olivo de bolsillo!

    Mas desde aquí, más tarde,
desde el punto de vista de esta tierra,
desde el duelo al que fluye el bien satánico,
se ve la gran batalla de Guernica.
¡Lid a priori, fuera de la cuenta,
lid en paz, lid de las almas débiles
contra los cuerpos débiles, lid en que el niño pega,
sin que le diga nadie que pegara,
bajo su atroz diptongo
y bajo su habilísimo pañal,
y en que la madre pega con su grito, con el dorso de una lágrima
y en que el enfermo pega con su mal, con su pastilla y su hijo
y en que el anciano pega
con sus canas, sus siglos y su palo
y en que pega el presbítero con dios!
¡Tácitos defensores de Guernica!
¡oh débiles! ¡oh suaves ofendidos,
que os eleváis, crecéis,
y llenáis de poderosos débiles el mundo! >

the horse, a man,
the reptile, a man,
the vulture, an honest man,
the fly, a man, and the olive tree, a man
and even the riverbank, a man
and the very sky itself, a whole little man!   *

   Then, retreating from Talavera,   *
in groups of one, armed with hunger, in masses of one,
armed with chest up to the forehead,
without airplanes, without war, without rancor,
their loss in their backs   *
and the gain
lower than lead, mortally wounded by honor,
crazed by dust, their arm on foot,
loving unwillingly,   *
conquering the whole earth in a Spanish way,   *
to retreat still, and not to know
where to put their Spain,
where to hide their global kiss
where to plant their pocket-size olive tree!   *

   But from here, later,   *
from the viewpoint of this land,
from the sorrow to which the satanic good flows,
the great battle of Guernica can be seen.   *
An a priori combat, unreckoned,
combat in peace, combat of weak souls
against weak bodies, combat in which the child strikes,
without anyone telling him to strike,
below his atrocious diphthong
and beneath his most adequate diaper,
and in which a mother strikes with her scream, with the backside of a tear
and in which the sick one strikes with his disease, with his pill and his son
and in which the old man strikes
with his white hair, his centuries and his staff
and in which the priest strikes with God!
Tacit defenders of Guernica,   *
oh weak ones! oh offended gentle ones,
who rise up, grow,
and fill the world with powerful weak ones!   >

>   En Madrid, en Bilbao, en Santander,
los cementerios fueron bombardeados,
y los muertos inmortales,
de vigilantes huesos y hombro eterno, de las tumbas,
los muertos inmortales, de sentir, de ver, de oír
tan bajo el mal, tan muertos a los viles agresores,
reanudaron entonces sus penas inconclusas,
acabaron de llorar, acabaron
de esperar, acabaron
de sufrir, acabaron de vivir,
acabaron, en fin, de ser mortales!

   ¡Y la pólvora fue, de pronto, nada,
cruzándose los signos y los sellos,
y a la explosión salióle al paso un paso,
y al vuelo a cuatro patas, otro paso
y al cielo apocalíptico, otro paso
y a los siete metales, la unidad,
sencilla, justa, colectiva, eterna!

   ¡Málaga sin padre ni madre,
ni piedrecilla, ni horno, ni perro blanco!
¡Málaga sin defensa, donde nació mi muerte dando pasos
y murió de pasión mi nacimiento!
¡Málaga caminando tras de tus pies, en éxodo,
bajo el mal, bajo la cobardía, bajo la historia cóncava, indecible,
con la yema en tu mano: tierra orgánica!
y la clara en la punta del cabello: todo el caos!
¡Málaga huyendo
de padre a padre, familiar, de tu hijo a tu hijo,
a lo largo del mar que huye del mar,
a través del metal que huye del plomo,
al ras del suelo que huye de la tierra
y a las órdenes ¡ay!
de la profundidad que te quería!
¡Málaga a golpes, a fatídico coágulo, a bandidos, a infiernazos,
a cielazos,
andando sobre duro vino, en multitud,
sobre la espuma lila, de uno en uno,
sobre huracán estático y más lila,
y al compás de las cuatro órbitas que aman

In Madrid, in Bilbao, in Santander,
the cemeteries were bombed,   *
and the immortal dead,
with vigilant bones and eternal shoulder, from their tombs,
the immortal dead, upon feeling, upon seeing, upon hearing
how low the evil, how dead the vile aggressors,
resumed then their unconcluded anguish,
they finished weeping, finished
hoping, finished
aching, finished living,
finished, finally, being mortal!

And the gunpowder was, suddenly, nothing,
signs and seals crossing each other,
and before the explosion a step intervened,
and before the flight on all fours, another step
and before the apocalyptic sky, another step
and before the seven metals, unity,
simple, just, collective, eternal.   *

Málaga without father or mother,   *
nor pebble, nor oven, nor white dog!
Málaga defenseless, where my death was born taking steps
and my birth died of passion!
Málaga walking behind your feet, in exodus,
under evil, under cowardice, under the concave, inexpressible history,
with the yolk in your hand: organic earth!
and the white in your hair tips: the whole chaos!
Málaga fleeing
from father to father, familiar, from your son to your son,
along the sea which flees from the sea,
through the metal which flees from the lead,
grazing the ground which flees from the earth
and to the orders aie!
of the profundity that loved you!
Málaga beaten up, fatidically clotted, bandit-infested, hellstruck,
heavenslashed,
walking over the hard wine, in multitudes,
over lilac scum, one by one,
over a more lilac and static hurricane,
and to the rhythm of the four orbits that love   >

> y de las dos costillas que se matan!
¡Málaga de mi sangre diminuta
y mi coloración a gran distancia,
la vida sigue con tambor a tus honores alazanes,
con cohetes, a tus niños eternos
y con silencio a tu último tambor,
con nada, a tu alma,
y con más nada, a tu esternón genial!
¡Málaga, no te vayas con tu nombre!
¡Que si te vas,
te vas
toda, hacia ti, infinitamente toda en son total,
concorde con tu tamaño fijo en que me aloco,
con tu suela feraz y su agujero
y tu navaja antigua atada a tu hoz enferma
y tu madero atado a un martillo!
¡Málaga literal y malagueña,
huyendo a Egipto, puesto que estás clavada,
alargando en sufrimiento idéntico tu danza,
resolviéndose en ti el volumen de la esfera,
perdiendo tu botijo, tus cánticos, huyendo
con tu España exterior y tu orbe innato!
¡Málaga por derecho propio
y en el jardín biológico, más Málaga!
¡Málaga en virtud
del camino, en atención al lobo que te sigue
y en razón del lobezno que te espera!
¡Málaga, que estoy llorando!
¡Málaga, que lloro y lloro!

> and of the two ribs that kill each other!
Málaga of my diminutive blood
and my coloration at a great distance,
life follows with a drum your sorrel-draped honors,
with rockets, your eternal children,
and with silence your last drum,
with nothing, your soul,
and with more nothing, your genial breastbone!
Málaga, don't go away with your name!
For if you go,
you go
wholly, toward yourself, infinitely whole in its whole,
in agreement with your fixed size in which I go mad,
with your fertile shoe sole and its hole
and your old jackknife tied to your sick sickle
and your log tied to a hammer!
Literal and malagueñan Málaga,   *
fleeing to Egypt, because you are nailed,
prolonging in identical suffering your dance,
reducing to yourself the volume of the sphere,
losing your water-jug, your canticles, fleeing
with your exterior Spain and your inborn world!
Málaga by its own right
and in the biological garden, more Málaga!
Málaga by virtue
of the road, in view of the wolf that follows you
and because of the wolf-cub that awaits you!
Málaga how I am weeping!
Málaga, how I weep and weep!

III

Solía escribir con su dedo grande en el aire:
"¡Viban los compañeros! Pedro Rojas",
de Miranda de Ebro, padre y hombre,
marido y hombre, ferroviario y hombre,
padre y más hombre, Pedro y sus dos muertes.

Papel de viento, lo han matado: ¡pasa!
Pluma de carne, lo han matado: ¡pasa!
¡Abisa a todos compañeros pronto!

Palo en el que han colgado su madero,
lo han matado;
¡lo han matado al pie de su dedo grande!
¡Han matado, a la vez, a Pedro, a Rojas!

¡Viban los compañeros
a la cabecera de su aire escrito!
¡Viban con esta b del buitre en las entrañas
de Pedro
y de Rojas, del héroe y del mártir!

Registrándole, muerto, sorprendiéronle
en su cuerpo un gran cuerpo, para
el alma del mundo,
y en la chaqueta una cuchara muerta.

Pedro también solía comer
entre las criaturas de su carne, asear, pintar
la mesa y vivir dulcemente
en representación de todo el mundo.
Y esta cuchara anduvo en su chaqueta,
despierto o bien cuando dormía, siempre,
cuchara muerta viva, ella y sus símbolos.
¡Abisa a todos compañeros pronto!
¡Viban los compañeros al pie de esta cuchara para siempre!

Lo han matado, obligándole a morir
a Pedro, a Rojas, al obrero, al hombre, a aquél
que nació muy niñín, mirando al cielo,
y que luego creció, se puso rojo
y luchó con sus células, sus nos, sus todavías, sus hambres, sus pedazos.   >

He used to write with his big finger in the air:
"Long live all combanions! Pedro Rojas,"   *
from Miranda de Ebro, father and man,
husband and man, railroad-worker and man,
father and more man, Pedro and his two deaths.

Wind paper, he was killed: pass on!
Flesh pen, he was killed: pass on!
Advise all combanions quick!

Stick on which they have hanged his log,
he was killed;
he was killed at the base of his big finger!   *
They have killed, in one blow, Pedro, Rojas!

Long live all combanions
written at the head of his air!
Let them live with this buzzard b in Pedro's
and in Rojas's
and in the hero's and in the martyr's guts!

Searching him, dead, they surprised
in his body a great body, for
the soul of the world,
and in his jacket a dead spoon.

Pedro too used to eat
among the creatures of his flesh, to clean up, to paint
the table and to live sweetly
as a representative of everyone.
And this spoon was in his jacket,
awake or else when he slept, always,
dead alive spoon, this one and its symbols.
Advise all combanions quick!
Long live all combanions at the base of this spoon forever!

He was killed, they forced him to die,
Pedro, Rojas, the worker, the man, the one
who was born a wee baby, looking at the sky,
and who afterward grew up, blushed
and fought with his cells, his nos, his yets, his hungers, his pieces.   >   *

> Lo han matado suavemente
entre el cabello de su mujer, la Juana Vásquez,
a la hora del fuego, al año del balazo
y cuando andaba cerca ya de todo.

Pedro Rojas, así, después de muerto,
se levantó, besó su catafalco ensangrentado,
lloró por España
y volvió a escribir con el dedo en el aire:
"¡Viban los compañeros! Pedro Rojas".
Su cadáver estaba lleno de mundo.

7 Nov. 1937

He was killed softly
in his wife's hair, Juana Vásquez by name,
at the hour of fire, in the year of the gunshot,
and when he was already close to everything.   *

 Pedro Rojas, thus, after being dead,
got up, kissed his blood-smeared casket,
wept for Spain
and again wrote with his finger in the air:
"Long live all combanions! Pedro Rojas."
His corpse was full of world.

IV

Los mendigos pelean por España
mendigando en París, en Roma, en Praga
y refrendando así, con mano gótica, rogante,
los pies de los Apóstoles, en Londres, en New York, en Méjico.
Los pordioseros luchan suplicando infernalmente
a Dios por Santander,
la lid en que ya nadie es derrotado.
Al sufrimiento antiguo
danse, encarnízanse en llorar plomo social
al pie del individuo,
y atacan a gemidos, los mendigos,
matando con tan solo ser mendigos.

Ruegos de infantería,
en que el arma ruega del metal para arriba,
y ruega la ira, más acá de la pólvora iracunda.
Tácitos escuadrones que disparan,
con cadencia mortal, su mansedumbre,
desde un umbral, desde sí mismos, ¡ay! desde sí mismos.
Potenciales guerreros
sin calcetines al calzar el trueno,
satánicos, numéricos,
arrastrando sus títulos de fuerza,
migaja al cinto,
fusil doble calibre: sangre y sangre.
¡El poeta saluda al sufrimiento armado!

23 Oct. 1937

IV

The beggars fight for Spain,
begging in Paris, in Rome, in Prague
thus authenticating, with an imploring, Gothic hand,
the Apostles' feet, in London, in New York, in Mexico City.
The mendicants fight satanically begging   *
God for Santander,
the combat in which no longer is anyone defeated.
They deliver themselves to
the old suffering, they glut their fury at the foot of the individual,   *
by weeping social lead,
and they attack with moans, these beggars,
killing by merely being beggars.   *

Pleas of the infantry,   *
in which the weapon pleads from the metal up,
and wrath pleads, this side of the wrathful gunpowder.
Tacit squadrons which fire
their meekness, with mortal cadence,
from a doorway, from themselves, ay, from themselves.
Potential fighters
without socks when shoeing thunder,
satanic, numerical,
dragging their titles of strength,
crumb under belt,   *
double-caliber rifle: blood and blood.
The poet hails armed suffering!

V

¡Ahí pasa! ¡Llamadla! ¡Es su costado!
¡Ahí pasa la muerte por Irún:
sus pasos de acordeón, su palabrota,
su metro del tejido que te dije,
su gramo de aquel peso que he callado . . . ¡si son ellos!

¡Llamadla! ¡Daos prisa! Va buscándome en los rifles,
como que sabe bien dónde la venzo,
cuál es mi maña grande, mis leyes especiosas, mis códigos terribles.
¡Llamadla! Ella camina exactamente como un hombre, entre las fieras,
se apoya de aquel brazo que se enlaza a nuestros pies
cuando dormimos en los parapetos
y se pára a las puertas elásticas del sueño.

¡Gritó! ¡Gritó! ¡Gritó su grito nato, sensorial!
Gritara de vergüenza, de ver cómo ha caído entre las plantas,
de ver cómo se aleja de las bestias,
de oír cómo decimos: ¡Es la muerte!
¡De herir nuestros más grandes intereses!

(Porque elabora su hígado la gota que te dije, camarada;
porque se come el alma del vecino)

¡Llamadla! Hay que seguirla
hasta el pie de los tanques enemigos,
que la muerte es un ser sido a la fuerza,
cuyo principio y fin llevo grabados
a la cabeza de mis ilusiones,
por mucho que ella corra el peligro corriente
que tú sabes
y que haga como que hace que me ignora.

¡Llamadla! No es un ser, muerte violenta,
sino, apenas, lacónico suceso;
más bien su modo tira, cuando ataca,
tira a tumulto simple, sin órbitas ni cánticos de dicha;
más bien tira su tiempo audaz, a céntimo impreciso
y sus sordos quilates, a déspotas aplausos.
Llamadla, que en llamándola con saña, con figuras,
se la ayuda a arrastrar sus tres rodillas,
como, a veces,

>

There she goes! Call her! It's her side!
There goes Death through Irún:
her accordion steps, her curse word,
her meter of cloth that I've mentioned to you,
her gram of that weight I've kept to myself . . . they're the ones!

Call her! Hurry! She's searching for me among the rifles,
since she well knows where I defeat her,
what my great cunning is, my deceptive laws, my terrible codes.
Call her! She walks exactly like a man, among wild beasts,
she leans on that arm which entwines our feet
when we sleep on the parapets
and she stops at the elastic gates of dream.

She shouted! She shouted! Shouted her born, sensorial shout!
Would that she shouted from shame, from seeing how she's fallen among the plants,
from seeing how she withdraws from the beasts,
from hearing how we say: It's Death!
From wounding our greatest interests!

(Because her liver produces the drop that I told you about, comrade;
because she eats the soul of our neighbor)

Call her! We must follow her
to the foot of the enemy tanks,
for Death is a being been by force,
whose beginning and end I carry engraved
at the head of my illusions,
however much she would run the normal risk
that you know
and though she would pretend to pretend to ignore me.

Call her! Violent Death is not a being,
but, barely, a laconic event;
instead her way aims, when she attacks,
aims at a simple tumult, without orbits or joyous canticles;
instead her audacious moment aims, at an imprecise centime
and her deaf carats, at despotic applause.
Call her, for by calling her with fury, with figures,
you help her drag her three knees,
as, at times,   >

> a veces duelen, punzan fracciones enigmáticas, globales,
como, a veces, me palpo y no me siento.

¡Llamadla! ¡Daos prisa! Va buscándome,
con su coñac, su pómulo moral,
sus pasos de acordeón, su palabrota.
¡Llamadla! No hay que perderle el hilo en que la lloro.
De su olor para arriba, ¡ay de mi polvo, camarada!
De su pus para arriba, ¡ay de mi férula, teniente!
De su imán para abajo, ¡ay de mi tumba!

IMAGEN ESPAÑOLA DE LA MUERTE

at times global, enigmatic fractions hurt, pierce,
as, at times, I touch myself and don't feel myself.

    Call her! Hurry! She is searching for me,
with her cognac, her moral cheekbone,
her accordion steps, her curse word.
Call her! The thread of my tears for her must not be lost.
From her smell up, woe is my dust, comrade!
From her pus up, woe is my ferule, lieutenant!
From her magnet down, woe is my tomb!

SPANISH IMAGE OF DEATH

VI
CORTEJO TRAS LA TOMA DE BILBAO

Herido y muerto, hermano,
criatura veraz, republicana, están andando en tu trono,
desde que tu espinazo cayó famosamente;
están andando, pálido, en tu edad flaca y anual,
laboriosamente absorta ante los vientos.

Guerrero en ambos dolores,
siéntate a oír, acuéstate al pie del palo súbito,
inmediato de tu trono;
voltea;
están las nuevas sábanas, extrañas;
están andando, hermano, están andando.

Han dicho: "Cómo! Dónde!...", expresándose
en trozos de paloma,
y los niños suben sin llorar a tu polvo.
Ernesto Zúñiga, duerme con la mano puesta,
con el concepto puesto,
en descanso tu paz, en paz tu guerra.

Herido mortalmente de vida, camarada,
camarada jinete,
camarada caballo entre hombre y fiera,
tus huesecillos de alto y melancólico dibujo
forman pompa española, pompa
laureada de finísimos andrajos!

Siéntate, pues, Ernesto,
oye que están andando, aquí, en tu trono,
desde que tu tobillo tiene canas.
¿Qué trono?
¡Tu zapato derecho! ¡Tu zapato!

13 Set. 1937

VI

CORTEGE AFTER THE CAPTURE OF BILBAO   *

Wounded and dead, brother,
truthful creature, Loyalist, they are walking on your throne,   *
ever since your backbone fell famously;
they are walking, pale, on your lean and yearly age,
laboriously entranced before the winds.

Warrior in both sorrows,
sit down and listen, lie down at the foot of the sudden stick,
next to your throne;
turn around;
the new bedsheets are strange;
they are walking, brother, they are walking.

They've said: "How! Where! . . ." expressing it
in shreds of dove,
and the children go up to your dust without crying.
Ernesto Zúñiga, sleep with your hand placed,
with your concept placed,
your peace at rest, your war at peace.

Mortally wounded by life, comrade,
comrade rider,
comrade horse between man and wild beast,
your delicate bones of high and melancholy design
form Spanish pomp, pomp
laurelled with the finest rags!

Sit up, then, Ernesto,
listen how they are walking, here, on your throne,
ever since your ankle grew gray hair.
What throne?
Your right shoe! Your shoe!

VII

Varios días el aire, compañeros,
muchos días el viento cambia de aire,
el terreno, de filo,
de nivel el fusil republicano.
Varios días España está española.

Varios días el mal
mobiliza sus órbitas, se abstiene,
paraliza sus ojos escuchándolos.
Varios días orando con sudor desnudo,
los milicianos cuélganse del hombre.
Varios días, el mundo, camaradas,
el mundo está español hasta la muerte.

Varios días ha muerto aquí el disparo
y ha muerto el cuerpo en su papel de espíritu
y el alma es ya nuestra alma, compañeros.
Varios días el cielo,
éste, el del día, el de la pata enorme.

Varios días, Gijón;
muchos días, Gijón;
mucho tiempo,Gijón;
mucha tierra, Gijón;
mucho hombre, Gijón;
y mucho dios, Gijón,
muchísimas Españas ¡ay! Gijón.

Camaradas,
varios días el viento cambia de aire.

5 Nov. 1937

VII

For several days the air, companions,
for many days the wind changes air,
the terrain, its edge,
its level the Loyalist rifle.
For several days Spain looks Spanish.

For several days evil
mobilizes its orbits, abstains,
paralyzes its eyes listening to them.
For several days praying with naked sweat,
the civilian-fighters hang from man.
For several days, the world, comrades,
the world looks Spanish unto death.

For several days here the firing has died
and the body has died in its spiritual role
and the soul, companions, has become our soul.
For several days the sky,
this one, the one with a day, the one with an enormous paw.

For several days, Gijón;   *
for many days, Gijón;
for much time, Gijón;
for much land, Gijón;
for much man, Gijón;
and for much god, Gijón,
for very many Spains ay! Gijón.   *

Comrades,
for several days the wind changes air.

VIII

Aquí,
Ramón Collar,
prosigue tu familia soga a soga,
se sucede,
en tanto que visitas, tú, allá, a las siete espadas, en Madrid,
en el frente de Madrid.

¡Ramón Collar, yuntero
y soldado hasta yerno de tu suegro,
marido, hijo limítrofe del viejo Hijo del Hombre!
Ramón de pena, tú, Collar valiente,
paladín de Madrid y por cojones; Ramonete,
aquí,
los tuyos piensan mucho en tu peinado!

¡Ansiosos, ágiles de llorar, cuando la lágrima!
¡Y cuando los tambores, andan; hablan
delante de tu buey, cuando la tierra!

¡Ramón! ¡Collar! ¡A ti! Si eres herido,
no seas malo en sucumbir; ¡refrénate!
Aquí,
tu cruel capacidad está en cajitas;
aquí,
tu pantalón oscuro, andando el tiempo,
sabe ya andar solísimo, acabarse;
aquí,
Ramón, tu suegro, el viejo,
te pierde a cada encuentro con su hija!

¡Te diré que han comido aquí tu carne,
sin saberlo,
tu pecho, sin saberlo,
tu pie;
pero cavilan todos en tus pasos coronados de polvo!

¡Han rezado a Dios,
aquí;
se han sentado en tu cama, hablando a voces   >

VIII

Back here,   *
Ramón Collar,   *
your family carries on from rope to rope,
one after another,
while you visit, you, out there, at the hour of seven swords, in Madrid,
at the Madrid front.

Ramón Collar, ox-driver
and soldier even son-in-law of his father-in-law,
husband, son bordering the old Son of Man!
Ramón of sorrow, you, brave Collar,   *
paladin of Madrid and by sheer balls; Ramonete,
back here,
your folks think a lot about your combed hair!

Anxious, quick to cry, during the tear!
And during the drums, they walk; they speak
before your ox, during the earth!

Ramón! Collar! To you! If you are wounded,
don't act up when you succumb; restrain yourself!
Back here,
your capacity for cruelty is in little boxes;
back here,
your dark trousers, after a while,
finally know how to walk in utter solitude, how to wear out;
back here,
Ramón, your father-in-law, the old man,
loses you each time he encounters his daughter!

I tell you that back here they've eaten your flesh,
without realizing it,
your chest, without realizing it,
your foot;
but they all brood over your steps crowned with dust!

They've prayed to God,
back here;
they've sat on your bed, talking loudly   >

> entre tu soledad y tus cositas;
no sé quién ha tomado tu arado, no sé quién
fue a ti, ni quién volvió de tu caballo!

¡Aquí, Ramón Collar, en fin, tu amigo!
¡Salud, hombre de Dios, mata y escribe!

10 Set. 1937

between your solitude and your little things;
I don't know who has taken over your plow, don't know who
went after you, nor who returned from your horse!

Back here, Ramón Collar, at last, your friend!   *
Greetings, man of God, kill and write!

IX
PEQUEÑO RESPONSO A UN HÉROE DE LA REPÚBLICA

Un libro quedó al borde de su cintura muerta,
un libro retoñaba de su cadáver muerto.
Se llevaron al héroe,
y corpórea y aciaga entró su boca en nuestro aliento;
sudamos todos, el hombligo a cuestas;
caminantes las lunas nos seguían;
también sudaba de tristeza el muerto.

Y un libro, en la batalla de Toledo,
un libro, atrás un libro, arriba un libro, retoñaba del cadáver.

Poesía del pómulo morado, entre el decirlo
y el callarlo,
poesía en la carta moral que acompañara
a su corazón.
Quedóse el libro y nada más, que no hay
insectos en la tumba,
y quedó al borde de su manga el aire remojándose
y haciéndose gaseoso, infinito.

Todos sudamos, el hombligo a cuestas,
también sudaba de tristeza el muerto
y un libro, yo lo vi sentidamente,
un libro, atrás un libro, arriba un libro
retoñó del cadáver ex abrupto.

10 Set. 1937

IX
SHORT PRAYER FOR A LOYALIST HERO

A book remained edging his dead waist,
a book was sprouting from his dead corpse.   *
The hero was carried off,   *
and corporeal and ominous his mouth entered our breath;
we all sweated, under the load of our navehalls;   *
moons were following us on foot;
the dead man was also sweating from sadness.

And a book, during the battle for Toledo,
a book, behind a book, above a book, was sprouting from the corpse.

Poetry of the royal purple cheekbone, between saying it   *
and keeping quiet about it,
poetry in the moral map that had accompanied
his heart.
The book remained and nothing else, for there are no
insects in the tomb,
and at the edge of his sleeve the air remained soaking,
becoming gaseous, infinite.

All of us sweated, under the load of our navehalls,
the dead man was also sweating from sadness
and a book, I saw it feelingly,
a book, behind a book, above a book
sprouted from the corpse abruptly.

INVIERNO EN LA BATALLA DE TERUEL

¡Cae agua de revólveres lavados!
Precisamente,
es la gracia metálica del agua,
en la tarde nocturna en Aragón,
no obstante las construídas yerbas,
las legumbres ardientes, las plantas industriales.

Precisamente,
es la rama serena de la química,
la rama de explosivos en un pelo,
la rama de automóviles en frecuencia y adioses.

Así responde el hombre, así, a la muerte,
así mira de frente y escucha de costado,
así el agua, al contrario de la sangre, es de agua,
así el fuego, al revés de la ceniza, alisa sus rumiantes ateridos.

¿Quién va, bajo la nieve? ¡Están matando? No.
Precisamente,
va la vida coleando, con su segunda soga.

¡Y horrísima es la guerra, solivianta,
lo pone a uno largo, ojoso;
da tumba la guerra, da caer,
da dar un salto extraño de antropoide!
Tú lo hueles, compañero, perfectamente,
al pisar
por distracción tu brazo entre cadáveres;
tú lo ves, pues, tocaste tus testículos, poniéndote rojísimo;
tú lo oyes en tu boca de soldado natural.

Vamos, pues, compañero;
nos espera tu sombra apercibida,
nos espera tu sombra acuartelada,
mediodía capitán, noche soldado raso . . .
Por eso, al referirme a esta agonía,
aléjome de mí gritando fuerte:
¡Abajo mi cadáver! . . . Y sollozo.

X
WINTER DURING THE BATTLE FOR TERUEL   *

Water falls from washed revolvers!
Precisely
it is the metallic grace of the water,
in the nocturnal afternoon in Aragón,
in spite of the constructed grass,
the burning vegetables, the industrial plants.

Precisely
it is the serene branch of Chemistry,   *
the branch of explosives in one hair,
the branch of automobiles in frequencies and good-byes.

This is how man responds, as well, to death,
this is how he looks forward and listens sideways,
this is how water, contrary to blood, is made of water,
this is how fire, the opposite of ash, smooths its frozen ruminants.

Who goes there, under the snow? Are they killing? No.
Precisely
it is life wagging along, with its second rope.

And war is utter horror, it incites,
it makes one long, eye-filled;
war entombs, fells,
makes one make an odd anthropoid leap!
You smell it, companion, perfectly,
upon stepping
distractedly on your arm among the corpses;
you see it, for you touched your testicles, blushing intensely;   *
you hear it in your natural soldier's mouth.

Let's go, then, companion;
your alerted shadow awaits us,
your quartered shadow awaits us,
noon captain, night common soldier . . .
That is why, on referring to this agony,
I withdraw from myself shouting wildly:
Down with my corpse! . . . And sob.

XI

Miré el cadáver, su raudo orden visible
y el desorden lentísimo de su alma;
le vi sobrevivir; hubo en su boca
la edad entrecortada de dos bocas.
Le gritaron su número: pedazos.
Le gritaron su amor: ¡más le valiera!
Le gritaron su bala: ¡también muerta!

Y su orden digestivo sosteníase
y el desorden de su alma, atrás, en balde.
Le dejaron y oyeron, y es entonces
que el cadáver
casi vivió en secreto, en un instante;
mas le auscultaron mentalmente, ¡y fechas!
lloráronle al oído, ¡y también fechas!

3 Set. 1937

I looked at the corpse, his swift visible order
and at the sluggish disorder of his soul;
I saw him survive; in his mouth there was
the interrupted age of two mouths.
They shouted his number at him: bits and pieces.
They shouted his love at him: all the better for him!
They shouted his bullet at him: likewise dead!

And his digestive order held up
and the turmoil of his soul, behind, in vain.
They left him and listened, and it is then
that the corpse
almost lived secretly, for an instant;
but they auscultated him mentally—and dates!
they wept in his ear—more dates!

XII

MASA

Al fin de la batalla,
y muerto el combatiente, vino hacia él un hombre
y le dijo: "No mueras, te amo tánto!"
Pero el cadáver ¡ay! siguió muriendo.

Se le acercaron dos y repitiéronle:
"No nos dejes! ¡Valor! ¡Vuelve a la vida!"
Pero el cadáver ¡ay! siguió muriendo.

Acudieron a él veinte, cien, mil, quinientos mil,
clamando: "Tánto amor, y no poder nada contra la muerte!"
Pero el cadáver ¡ay! siguió muriendo.

Le rodearon millones de individuos,
con un ruego común: "¡Quédate, hermano!"
Pero el cadáver ¡ay! siguió muriendo.

Entonces, todos los hombres de la tierra
le rodearon; les vio el cadáver triste, emocionado;
incorporóse lentamente,
abrazó al primer hombre; echóse a andar . . .

10 Nov. 1937

XII
MASS

At the end of the battle,
the combatant dead, a man approached him
and said to him: "Don't die; I love you so much!"
But the corpse, alas! kept on dying.

Two more came up to him and repeated:
"Don't leave us! Be brave! Come back to life!"
But the corpse, alas! kept on dying.   *

Twenty, a hundred, a thousand, five hundred thousand appeared,
crying out: "So much love, and no power against death!"
But the corpse, alas! kept on dying.

Millions of individuals surrounded him,
with a common plea: "Don't leave us, brother!"
But the corpse, alas! kept on dying.

Then, all the inhabitants of the earth
surrounded him; the corpse looked at them sadly, deeply moved;
he got up slowly,
embraced the first man; started to walk . . .

XIII
REDOBLE FÚNEBRE A LOS ESCOMBROS DE DURANGO

Padre polvo que subes de España,
Dios te salve, libere y corone,
padre polvo que asciendes del alma.

Padre polvo que subes del fuego,
Dios te salve, te calce y dé un trono,
padre polvo que estás en los cielos.

Padre polvo, biznieto del humo,
Dios te salve y ascienda a infinito,
padre polvo, biznieto del humo.

Padre polvo en que acaban los justos,
Dios te salve y devuelva a la tierra,
padre polvo en que acaban los justos.

Padre polvo que creces en palmas,
Dios te salve y revista de pecho,
padre polvo, terror de la nada.

Padre polvo, compuesto de hierro,
Dios te salve y te dé forma de hombre,
padre polvo que marchas ardiendo.

Padre polvo, sandalia del paria,
Dios te salve y jamás te desate,
padre polvo, sandalia del paria.

Padre polvo que avientan los bárbaros,
Dios te salve y te ciña de dioses,
padre polvo que escoltan los átomos.

Padre polvo, sudario del pueblo;
Dios te salve del mal para siempre,
padre polvo español, padre nuestro.

Padre polvo que vas al futuro,
Dios te salve, te guíe y te dé alas,
padre polvo que vas al futuro.

22 Oct. 1937

XIII

FUNEREAL DRUMROLL FOR THE RUINS OF DURANGO ✳

Father dust who rises from Spain,
God save, liberate and crown you,
father dust who ascends from the soul.

Father dust who rises from the fire,
God save you, shoe you and offer a throne,
father dust who art in heaven.

Father dust, great-grandson of the smoke,
God save and raise you to infinity,
father dust, great-grandson of the smoke.

Father dust in whom the just end,
God save and return you to earth,
father dust in whom the just end.

Father dust who grows into palms,
God save and invest you with chest,
father dust, terror of the void.

Father dust, made up of iron,
God save you and give you human form,
father dust who marches burning.

Father dust, sandal of the pariah,
God save you and never unbind you,
father dust, sandal of the pariah.

Father dust whom the barbarians winnow,
God save you and encircle you with gods,
father dust whom atoms escort.

Father dust, shroud of the people,
God save you from evil forever,
Spanish father dust, our father!

Father dust who goes into the future,
God save you, guide you and give you wings,
father dust who goes into the future.

XIV

¡Cúidate, España, de tu propia España!
¡Cúidate de la hoz sin el martillo,
cúidate del martillo sin la hoz!
¡Cúidate de la víctima apesar suyo,
del verdugo apesar suyo
y del indiferente apesar suyo!
¡Cúidate del que, antes de que cante el gallo,
negárate tres veces,
y del que te negó, después, tres veces!
¡Cúidate de las calaveras sin las tibias,
y de las tibias sin las calaveras!
¡Cúidate de los nuevos poderosos!
¡Cúidate del que come tus cadáveres,
del que devora muertos a tus vivos!
¡Cúidate del leal ciento por ciento!
¡Cúidate del cielo más acá del aire
y cúidate del aire más allá del cielo!
¡Cúidate de los que te aman!
¡Cúidate de tus héroes!
¡Cúidate de tus muertos!
¡Cúidate de la República!
¡Cúidate del futuro! . . .

10 Oct. 1937

Beware, Spain, of your own Spain!
Beware of the sickle without the hammer,
beware of the hammer without the sickle!
Beware of the victim in spite of himself,
of the hangman in spite of himself
and of the uncommitted in spite of himself!
Beware of the one who, before the cock crows,
will have denied you three times,
and of the one who denied you, afterward, three times!
Beware of skulls without tibias
and of tibias without skulls!
Beware of the new powerful ones!
Beware of the one who eats your corpses,
of the one who devours your living dead!
Beware of the one hundred percent loyal!
Beware of the sky this side of the air
and beware of the air beyond the sky!
Beware of those who love you!
Beware of your heroes!
Beware of your dead!
Beware of the Republic!
Beware of the future! . . .

XV
ESPAÑA, APARTA DE MÍ ESTE CÁLIZ

Niños del mundo,
si cae España—digo, es un decir—
si cae
del cielo abajo su antebrazo que asen,
en cabestro, dos láminas terrestres;
niños, ¡qué edad la de las sienes cóncavas!
¡qué temprano en el sol lo que os decía!
¡qué pronto en vuestro pecho el ruido anciano!
¡qué viejo vuestro 2 en el cuaderno!

¡Niños del mundo, está
la madre España con su vientre a cuestas;
está nuestra maestra con sus férulas,
está madre y maestra,
cruz y madera, porque os dio la altura,
vértigo y división y suma, niños;
está con ella, padres procesales!

Si cae—digo, es un decir—si cae
España, de la tierra para abajo,
niños, ¡cómo vais a cesar de crecer!
¡cómo va a castigar el año al mes!
¡cómo van a quedarse en diez los dientes,
en palote el diptongo, la medalla en llanto!
¡Cómo va el corderillo a continuar
atado por la pata al gran tintero!
¡Cómo vais a bajar las gradas del alfabeto
hasta la letra en que nació la pena!

Niños,
hijos de los guerreros, entre tanto,
bajad la voz, que España está ahora mismo repartiendo
la energía entre el reino animal,
las florecillas, los cometas y los hombres.
¡Bajad la voz, que está
con su rigor, que es grande, sin saber
qué hacer, y está en su mano
la calavera hablando y habla y habla,
la calavera, aquélla de la trenza,
la calavera, aquélla de la vida!

>

XV
SPAIN, TAKE THIS CUP FROM ME   *

   Children of the world,
if Spain falls—I mean, it's just a thought—
if her forearm
falls downward from the sky seized,
in a halter, by two terrestrial plates;
children, what an age of concave temples!   *
how early in the sun what I was telling you!
how quickly in your chest the ancient noise!
how old your 2 in the notebook!

   Children of the world, mother
Spain is with her belly on her back;
our teacher is with her ferules,
she appears as mother and teacher,
cross and wood, because she gave you height,
vertigo and division and addition, children;
she is with herself, legal parents!

      If she falls—I mean, it's just a thought—if Spain
falls, from the earth downward,
children, how you will stop growing!
how the year will punish the month!
how you will never have more than ten teeth,
how the diphthong will remain in downstroke, the gold star in tears!
How the little lamb will stay
tied by its leg to the great inkwell!
How you'll descend the steps of the alphabet
to the letter in which pain was born!

   Children,
sons of fighters, meanwhile,
lower your voice, for right at this moment Spain is distributing
her energy among the animal kingdom,
little flowers, comets, and men.
Lower your voice, for she
sudders convulsively, not knowing
what to do, and she has in her hand
the talking skull, chattering away,
the skull, the one with a braid,
the skull, the one with life!   >

> ¡Bajad la voz, os digo;
bajad la voz, el canto de las sílabas, el llanto
de la materia y el rumor menor de las pirámides, y aún
el de las sienes que andan con dos piedras!
¡Bajad el aliento, y si
el antebrazo baja,
si las férulas suenan, si es la noche,
si el cielo cabe en dos limbos terrestres,
si hay ruido en el sonido de las puertas,
si tardo,
si no veis a nadie, si os asustan
los lápices sin punta, si la madre
España cae—digo, es un decir—
salid, niños del mundo; id a buscarla!...

> Lower your voice, I tell you;
lower your voice, the song of the syllables, the wail
of matter and the faint murmur of the pyramids, and even
that of your temples which walk with two stones!
Lower your breathing, and if
the forearm comes down,
if the ferules sound, if it is night,
if the sky fits between two terrestrial limbos,   *
if there is noise in the creaking of doors,
if I am late,
if you do not see anyone, if the blunt pencils
frighten you, if mother
Spain falls—I mean, it's just a thought—
go out, children of the world, go look for her! . . .

NOTES TO THE POEMS

The Spanish text used here is that to be found in César Vallejo, Obras completas, vol. 1, Obra poética, edited and annotated by Ricardo González Vigil (Lima: Banco de Crédito del Perú, 1991), henceforth identified in this book as the RGV edition. Of the numerous single-volume editions of Vallejo's poetry, the RGV is the most recent and is authoritative.

Uncommon words in the translations are defined in these notes only if they are not listed in the second or third edition of Webster's New International Dictionary. The translations generally follow Vallejo's punctuation, even when it is irregular (and a bit out of sync with what might be the English equivalent), because it is often intrinsic to the way a phrase or line should be voiced.

THE BLACK HERALDS

The poems in César Vallejo's first book, Los heraldos negros, were written between 1915 and 1918. While the book was published in 1918, it was not distributed until July 1919. It appears that the distribution delay came about because Vallejo was waiting for Abraham Valdelomar, a well-known Lima intellectual, to write a foreword, which Valdelomar never delivered. Vallejo paid for the edition himself. It received several long, favorable reviews in Lima and in Trujillo.

EPIGRAPH   The gospel verse, quoted in Latin, is Matthew 19:12.

Sacred Defoliacity   (page 27)
TITLE   The word deshojación in the title appears to be a coined word based on deshojadura, or deshojamiento, meaning "defoliation."

Nervestorm of Anguish   (page 31)
TITLE   Nervazón appears to be a coined word based on nevazón (snowstorm, blizzard) and nervios (nerves).

. . . . ?   (page 57)
all rituary   The Spanish rituario (rituary) appears to have been coined from the word rito (rite).

Imperial Nostalgias, III   (page 79)
corequenque   A fabulous bird, which according to the Incans was discovered on a small lake at the foot of snow-covered Vilcanota. The Incans carefully extracted two feathers from its wings, which their sovereign then displayed as his insignia of supreme authority. The word is probably based on curiquingue (caracara).

Imperial Nostalgias, IV   (page 79)

La Grama . . . La Ramada   La Grama is a rural horse track outside Trujillo, and La Ramada its sole grandstand. Apparently it had ceased to be active in Vallejo's time, becoming a sad, dilapidated place.

Ebony Leaves   (page 81)

tahuashando   A neologism based on the Quechuan word *tahua* (four). José Cerna-Bazán, author of *Sujeto a cambio: De las relaciones del texto y la sociedad en la escritura de César Vallejo*, has often wondered about this word, so he asked his father, José Diego Cerna López (who, as part of his work, was often in the La Libertad area of the Peruvian sierra in the 1930s). His father told him: "Ah, yes, that word was used, or is still used, I should say, when we would arrive at an observation point, especially at a crossroads, with our mules, and we would look around to see if anyone else was coming down the road."

Cerna-Bazán mentions that when he read to his father Vallejo's line using the word, the latter said, "Sure, that's it—Vallejo is saying that this person is *tahuashando*."

Autochthonous Tercet, I   (page 85)

yaraví   A song in which indigenous and Spanish melodic elements have been fused. The word is a hybrid in tonality as well as spirit and appears to derive from the Incan *harawi*, which was adapted for religious hymns from the time of the conquest until the eighteenth century.

Quenaing   A neologism based on *quena*, the term for a five-holed Quechuan flute (which once accompanied the *yaravís*).

the Pallas   Beautifully adorned young women who perform group dances that were originally part of the religious festivals in Cuzco.

Autochthonous Tercet, III   (page 87)

caja from Tayanga   The *caja* is a musical instrument combining a kind of drum with a ditch reed (from which *quenas* can be made). Tayanga is a northern Peruvian town specializing in the fabrication of *cajas*.

huaino   The most well-known and representative indigenous dance of Peru, with happy, flirtatious movements (and sometimes words).

Huaco   (page 91)

coricanchas   The Coricancha was the great Temple of the Sun in Cuzco; using the Incan walls as a base, the Spanish conquistadors built the cathedral of Santo Domingo. In the poem's fourth stanza, Vallejo suggests that the Coricancha of the Sun rises up against the cathedral.

Village Scene   (page 97)

dronedongs   This obscure Spanish neologism, *dondonea*, appears twice in Vallejo's poetry (the second time "The tip of man" in *Human Poems*). In his 1988 edition of Vallejo's *Obra poética*, Américo Ferrari associates the neologism with the word *doneo* (which he defines as "flirtation" or "flattery"), but that meaning does not seem appropriate here. González Vigil does not comment. Given the context, in which an Indian voice is compared to a cemetery bell, the word seems to refer to the bell clanging—or to be an attempt to fuse the sound of the Indian's voice with the sound of the bell. It is with this in mind that I have come up with *dronedongs*.

The Voice in the Mirror (page 105)

Brahacmanic Vallejo has placed an "ac" in the middle of the Spanish *brahmanico* (Brahmanic) to form the word *brahacmanicos*. Ferrari conjectures that the poet may have confused the spelling of the word with *dracma* (drachma). González Vigil does not comment.

The Miserable Supper (page 123)

kick our poor sponge *Estiraremos la rodilla* (literally, will we stretch our knees) is a play on *estirar la pata* (literally, "to stretch the foot" but in slang meaning "to kick the bucket," die). I have adjusted the English accordingly.

Muleteers (page 149)

"paca-paca" A species of *lechuza* (screech owl).

oxidental The Spanish *oxidentales* is a neologism that appears to be a fusion of *occidentales* (occidental) and *óxido* (oxide). Vallejo repeats it in *Trilce* LXIII.

Januneid (page 157)

TITLE The Spanish "Enereida" is a neologism fusing *enero* (January) with *Eneida* (Aeneid). The English version matches it.

Epexegesis (page 161)

TITLE Thought by some scholars to be a neologism, the word *espergesia* actually exists in Spanish. It is a rhetorical term that means "using a surplus of words for a fuller and more embellished declaration." This definition is to be found in the *Diccionario de autoridades de la Real Academia Española,* in the first edition, 1732. The word I have chosen in an attempt to match it in English is defined as follows (in *Webster's New International Dictionary*): "Provision of additional explanation or definition; that which is added for elucidation."

TRILCE

The earliest poems in *Trilce* were probably written before Vallejo's first book, *Los heraldos negros*, appeared. The only source for the dates of individual poems (the book is not organized chronologically, and Vallejo himself offers no information in this regard) is Juan Espejo Asturrizaga's memoir of Vallejo's Peruvian years, *César Vallejo: Itinerario del hombre*. Américo Ferrari, Juan Larrea, and André Coyné have all disputed some of them, but in spite of some guesswork and certain questionable date-event associations, Espejo's dates are valuable. He was in close association with Vallejo during the years of *Trilce*'s composition; he occasionally heard a poem read shortly after it was written, and in one case he actually watched Vallejo write a first draft. *Trilce* was published in Lima in 1922, with a solid introduction by Antenor Orrego. As Vallejo later commented, the book immediately fell into a void—there was no public response. It is worth noting that 1922 also saw the publication of *The Wasteland* and *Ulysses,* as well as the completion of *The Duino Elegies*—in short, it was a banner year for a modernism, which in the works by Eliot, Joyce, and Vallejo was already on the cusp of postmodernism.

According to Espejo (112–14), forty-eight of the seventy-seven poems were written in 1919. Twenty-one were written in the following years:

> 1918: LX, LXV, LXVI
> 1920: XIX, XXII, XXIV, XXVIII, LII, LXIII, LXVII, LXX, LXXV
> 1921: VII, XIV, XXIX, XXX, XXXII, XXXVI, XLVIII
> 1922: XXVI, LIX

The remaining eight poems (I, II, XVIII, XX, XLI, L, LVIII, LXI) were supposedly written during Vallejo's incarceration in the Central Trujillo Jail, between November 7, 1920, and February 26, 1921. Espejo also mentions that while in jail, Vallejo rewrote and radically transformed poems previously written between March 1919 and April 1920 (99). Thus it may be that Vallejo worked out the poetics of *Trilce* during his imprisonment.

I have not annotated all irregular or "difficult words." While I have commented on words I consider neologisms, I have not noted all words in which one letter is replaced with another in such a way that only the appearance (and not the sound) is slightly changed. I have simply made a corresponding change in the English word to alter its appearance but not change its sound. When the misspelling in Spanish evokes a second word, I have commented. While for the most part I have stayed clear of interpretations, preferring to let the reader deal with *Trilce*'s complexities, when it seemed appropriate, I have attempted to let the reader in on the thought process that led to certain translational decisions. For more extensive commentary, the reader is referred to the RGV edition (or the Ferrari *Colección archivos* edition, which has a useful glossary to all of Vallejo's poetry).

For biographical tie-ins, I refer the reader to Espejo—with the warning that in spite of his clearly comradely intentions, Espejo often uses fairly simple biographical information to explain poems that to varying degrees have consumed their referentiality in their writing.

TITLE   *Trilce*'s title is a neologism and the gate guardian of the book. This masterpiece of international modernism has its perilous, heroic predicament embedded in its title, and sewn, like filaments, into the work itself.

The story goes that Vallejo had originally called the book "Cráneos de bronce" (Bronze Skulls—possibly with indigenous skin coloring in mind), and had planned to sign it with the pseudonym "César Perú" (perhaps in the spirit of Anatole France). At the last minute, friends convinced him that the pseudonym was a mistake; however, the first pages had already been printed, and the author was told that the cost to reprint them would come to three libras, a small amount, but money he really didn't have. His friend Espejo Asturrizaga recalls: "[Vallejo] repeated 'tres, tres, tres,' several times, with that insistence he had for repeating and deforming words, 'tressss, trissss, trieesss, tril, trilssss.' He got tongue-tied, and in the process 'trilsssce' came out . . . 'trilce? trilce?' He paused for a moment and then exclaimed: 'OK, it will carry my own name, but the book itself will be called *Trilce*'" (109).

Other commentators have conjectured that the word was formed by fusing *triste* (sad) and *dulce* (sweet). While there is no reason to think that Espejo made up this story, I believe that the poems contain internal evidence attesting to the neologism's conceptual status, which involves the meaning of the book as a whole and goes considerably beyond an impulsive deformation of words. In his memoir, Espejo constantly offers anecdotes and recollections as explanations for the meaning of poems that remain utterly enigmatic, in spite of his commentary. His anecdote explaining the origin of the word *trilce* is an example.

A more thoughtful response to the formation of the word was made by Henry Gifford, who, with Charles Tomlinson, translated a dozen or so poems from *Trilce* in the early 1970s. Gifford writes: "For 'trilce,' Vallejo compounded two numerals, *trillon* and *trece*, a trillion and thirteen. A truncated trillion is held prisoner by the ill-chanced and broken thirteen. Or, perhaps, like the arm of the Venus de Milo in another *Trilce* poem, it should be seen rather as uncreated, subject to the 'perennial imperfection' of life" (*Ten Versions from* Trilce *by César Vallejo*, trans. Charles Tomlinson and Henry Gifford [Cerrillos, NM: San Marcos Press, 1970], introduction).

Although Gifford does not support his numerical observation with evidence from *Trilce*, the confirmation is there. In an early version of XXXII, which appeared in a Lima newspaper in 1921, the last line read:

Tres trillones y trece calories! . . .

It is possible that at some stage of revising/completing the book, Vallejo spotted the potentially new word in this line, and, pulling the *tril* from the left side of *trillones*, and the *ce* from the right side of *trece*, coined *trilce*. And while the *tri-* and the *tre-* of the two key words signify "three," it is fascinating to notice what happens to that "three," and to the zeros, when *lones* and *tre* are shed: *tril* signifies a one, followed by an ambiguous number of zeros (since before it can complete the eighteen zeros found in the Spanish *trillon*—which in American English means "quintillion," not "trillion"—it is truncated and hooked onto *ce*). And by eliminating the *tre* from *trece*, Vallejo has made use of only the latter part of the word, which signifies "ten" (like the English "teen" in "thirteen"). Thus written out as a number, *trilce* looks something like this:

1,0000000000000000 . . . 10

While the word *evokes* threeness, there is no actual three in it. Instead, we have a ghost of threeness, and a mass of indefinite zeros, with the one of trillion bounding the left, and the one of ten nearly bounding the right—a word, in effect, without interior determination.

So how might we contextualize *trilce*? In XVI, we find that the poet seeks to "galloon [himself] with zeros on the left" (see the note on this line for an alternative reading). Since the greatest part of the zero mass is on the "tril" (left) side of *trilce*, such a line suggests that Vallejo may have been aware of the title idea—if he had not already coined the word itself—when XVI was written (Espejo claims that this poem was written in 1919).

In XXXVIII we are informed that a mysterious crystal "has passed from animal,/and now goes off to form lefts,/the new Minuses." Again, "the new Minuses," especially of or on the "left," could very well refer to the nebulous zero mass of *trilce*.

The word *left* first appears in the book at the end of the very cryptic poem IV: "Heat. Ovary. Almost transparency. / All has been cried out.   Has been completely waked / in deep left." While *en plena izquierda* can be translated a number of ways (in full left, in the heart of left, right in the left, at the height of left, etc.), contextual considerations back up this translation of the phrase. This is not a high or a full left, but a deep one, with an indefinite extension that is negative, of the underworld, as opposed to positive, of height or heaven.

At the end of XXXVI—Vallejo's *ars poética*—readers are commanded to "Make way for the new odd number / potent with orphanhood!" Surely this new odd number is *trilce* itself, word and title, Vallejo's own Via Negativa, with orphanhood (suggested by the ones) stranded in a Milky Way of zeros, or, to turn the phrase slightly, *trilce* as an orphan is potent because it is self-conceived, belonging to the world of poetry, not to the world of numbers that we use to block out time.

I   (page 167)

Who's making all that racket   Espejo writes that while Vallejo was in the Trujillo jail, inmates were taken outside to use the latrines four times a day. There the guards would coarsely urge them to hurry up (123). The first two stanzas of poem L indicate that this is not gratuitous but quite pertinent information. Looking at the first stanza of this opening poem, it would seem that the racket-makers are the wardens and guards, and that the "islands" are the inmates' turds. For a study of the construction of this poem, see "A Translational Understanding of *Trilce #I*" in my collection of essays *Companion Spider* (Wesleyan University Press, 2002).

guano   The dried excrement of seabirds, found mixed with bones and feathers on certain Peruvian coastal islands, was widely used as fertilizer. Guano workers visited the mainland ports and cities on their days off, and Vallejo would have been able to observe them not just in Trujillo but also in the vicinity of the jail.

fecapital   Based on *tesoro* (treasure), the word *tesórea* has provoked differing interpretations. Giovanni Meo Zilio identifies it as a neologism incorporating the latter part of *estercórea* (excrement), influenced by the guano references in the stanza (as well as by the "islands" in the first).

ponk   The Spanish *calabrina*, meaning "an intolerable, intense stench," is archaic. If I had used the word *stench*, the translation would reflect the common Spanish word *hedor*—thus the necessity, in such cases, of finding archaic English words (or expressions) for their Spanish equivalents.

muzziled   The Spanish *abozaleada* is based on *abozalada* (muzzled), with an *-ear* infinitive ending substituted for the standard *-ar* ending. Meo Zilio considers the word to be a neologism.

II   (page 169)

song on   With *cancionan*, the noun *canción* (song) is forced to function as the verb *cantar* (to sing).

What call all that stands our end on hAIR?   In the phrase *Qué se llama cuanto heriza nos? heriza* appears to be a fusion of two verbs: *eriza* (bristles) and *hiere* (wounds). Larrea proposes that this neologism is based on *horripilar* (to horripilate, to make one's hair bristle or stand on end). Since there is no way to fuse *bristles* and *wounds*, and since the rare Latinate *horripilate* misses the idiomatic playfulness of the Spanish, I have taken a slightly different route by playing with the notion of hair standing on end. By reversing the verb and its object, Vallejo redirects the emphasis, which my inversion attempts to pick up, as it also redirects the meaning of *end*. At the same time, spotting the *air* in *hair*, I lift it up, as Vallejo might have, had he seen its equivalent in Spanish. This sense of seizing words by their hair, as it were, and pulling them this way and that, is endemic to *Trilce*. At the beginning of the line, the replacement of *Cómo se llama* with *Qué se llama* is regional and idiomatic.

III   (page 171)
Santiago   The old, blind bell ringer of Santiago de Chuco, Vallejo's birthplace and hometown.
Aguedita, Nativa, Miguel   Vallejo's two youngest sisters and his youngest brother.
souls in torment   The word *penas* used in this way is a Peruvianism.

IV   (page 173)
trifurca   The Spanish *trifurcas* is a neologism based on *trifurcado* (trifurcate).
embitternessed   The Spanish *amargurada* is a neologism derived from *amargura* (bitterness) and *amargar* (to embitter).
aljid   Vallejo has substituted a "j" for the "g" in *álgidas* (algid), changing the appearance of the word but not its sound. This sort of substitution occurs regularly throughout *Trilce*.
spiritive   The word *espirativa* is derived from adding the suffix -*iva* (-ive) to *espíritu* (spirit).
nuthin to ddo about it   The phrase *qué la bamos a hhazer* is a sound and syntactic distortion of *qué vamos a hacer con ella* (nothing to do about it).

V   (page 175)
rhinestoned   A neologism, the Spanish *avaloriados* is probably based on *avalorar* (to value) and *abalorio* (glass beads, or any showy article of little value).
glise   Probably based on the French *glisser* (to glide). An evocation of *glissé* (in ballet, a glissade, or glide).

VI   (page 177)
Otilian   The Spanish *otilinas* is based on the first name of Vallejo's lover in Lima (1918–1919), Otilia Villanueva. When she became pregnant and Vallejo refused to marry her, Otilia was sent away by her family to San Mateo de Surco in the sierra, and the poet lost his position as director of the Instituto Nacional, a private school with which Otilia's family was involved.
lustred   An old Spanish word, *fratesadas* means "to give a luster to hose after washing them," using a glass or wooden trowel-shaped object.
tawny berry of handiwork   According to the 1884 *Diccionario de peruanismos* by Juan de Arona (republished in Biblioteca de cultura peruana, no. 10 [Paris: Desclée, de Brouwer, 1938]), the *capulí (Prunus capulí)* is a bush that yields a flower and a dark-yellow berry, much appreciated throughout the Peruvian sierra for its delicate, ornamental beauty. Américo Ferrari comments that *color capuli* is similar to *moreno* (dark complexioned, swarthy) and *trigueño* (olive skinned: see line 14 in the same poem). *Capulin* appears to be the English equivalent; *Webster's*, however, defines it as a Mexican tree with a *red* berry. In regard to the word *obrería*, Vallejo's usage appears to be idiomatic and to refer solely to Otilia as an *obrera* (worker) that is, a laundress. He implies in this line that Otilia is the fruit of her own labor.

VII   (page 179)

barret   The *barreta* is probably a miners' tool, a small straight bar with one sharpened end, used like a crowbar. Larrea wrote to Barcia that he was under the impression that the word was also Santiago de Chuco slang for "penis." González Vigil writes that it evokes the legendary "golden staff" of Manco Capac that, on disappearing into the earth, led him to found at that very spot the city of Cuzco. The word reoccurs in "Telluric and Magnetic" in *Human Poems*.

VIII   (page 181)

saltatory   From the Greek *hyphállomai*, *hifalto* is a rare, ornithological word for birds that walk by hopping. Dr. Carlos Senar of the Zoological Museum of Barcelona, who researched this word for me, writes that "it has a taxonomic meaning and so can be used to refer to all birds of the Order Passeriformes" (personal correspondence, March 1990). The largest order of birds, Passeriformes includes over seven thousand species and subspecies. Ferrari wrote to me that he understands *el hifalto poder* as "the power that moves via hops," stressing the idea of discontinuity or leaps. I disagree with several critics and translators who believe that the word is a neologism based on *hijo* (son) and *falto* (lack). *Saltatory*, from the Latin *saltare*, "to leap," is defined in *Webster's Second New International Dictionary* as "proceeding or taking place by a leap or leaps, rather than by gradual, orderly, continuous steps or transitions." On one level, the word sounds the discontinuous, dissonant poetics of *Trilce*.

IX   (page 183)

Espejo offers an anecdote that he considers pertinent to this poem (85). In late 1919, in Lima, Vallejo was summoned to a darkened room where a mysterious young woman passionately offered herself to him. He had no idea who she was. The two met again over the course of several days, and although they conversed and shared confidences, she never revealed her identity. Espejo also explains that according to Vallejo, the substitution of "v" for "b" in several words, as well as its repetition, graphically emphasizes the word *vulva*. As in the case of the *heriza* problem in II, it was not possible to find a direct match for this variation, so I have attempted to register the sound and wordplay in a slightly different way.

all readies truth   The first two words in the Spanish, *todo avía verdad*, play off *todavía* (yet, still, nevertheless), while the second word sounds like a past tense of *haber* (to have).

I transasfixiate   *Envetarse* is a rare verb that has at least two meanings, both of which may be operative here with *enveto*. In Ecuador, it means "to dominate"; according to Eduardo Neale-Silva, Vallejo uses it in this sense in a 1927 article, "El arco del triunfo" (The arch of triumph), in speaking of *un fornido mozo en actitud de envetar un toro* (a husky youth getting ready to subdue a bull). The use of *toroso* (torose, taurine) in the third stanza supports this meaning. However, in Peru the word also means "to become asphyxiated by the poisonous emanations from the veins of a mine," and given the context of "Bolivarian asperities" (rugged landscapes in which mines might very well exist), this meaning also seems pertinent (though I notice that by using the verb actively, Vallejo reverses its passive usage as a mining term).

X   (page 185)

we saddleframe   The noun *arzón* (saddle frame) forced to function as a verb in *arzonamos*.

and seated enpeacocks tranquil nosegays *(y sentado empavona tranquilas misturas)*   According to the *Diccionario de peruanismos*, a *mistura* is a small bouquet of local, fragrant flowers, such as frangipani, jasmine, passion flower, gillyflower, including for additional ornamentation such berries as *capulí*—see note on VI. In this setting, the standard meaning of *empavonar* ("to blue steel," or, in Latin America, "to grease") seems most inappropriate. In Central America, *empavonar* can mean the same as *emperifollarse* (to doll oneself up), a meaning that draws on *pavón* (peacock) and *pavonear* (to strut). I interpret the line to mean that the patient is arranging nosegays in a vain way that evokes a peacock display.

XI   (page 187)
bitewashed sepulchers   In *rebocados sepulcros,* by misspelling *revocados* (whitewashed, resurfaced), Vallejo has brought *bocados* (mouthful, snack, or bite) into the word. The translational challenge in such a situation is not only to misspell the appropriate word in English but also to pick up some of the secondary meaning in Spanish.

teneblearic   Here, with the Spanish *tenebloso,* the misspelling of *tenebroso* (tenebrous, tenebrific) suggests a coinage of the English *tenebrific* and *bleary.*

XII   (page 189)
Tramontation   The Spanish *Tramonto* appears to be a nounlike neologism based on the verb *tramontar,* which can mean "to cross the mountains," "to sink behind the mountains" (as the sun), or, reflexively, "to help someone escape." It is clearly linked to *tramontana,* which in English is *tramontane* (on the other side of the mountain, or, a cold, violent northerly wind). In an early version of XV (dated by Espejo to 1919), we find the word used in the last two lines: *Son dos puertas abriéndose, cerrándose, al huir / Sombra a sombra en mitad de este tramonto!* Here it is clear that Vallejo is using *tramonto* as a noun (probably eliminating the possibility that it could be a first-person singular of the verb *tramontar*), and, given the context of doors blowing open, that he probably has the violent wind meaning in mind. However, in an early version of XII (dated 1921, and reproduced in the RGV edition on p. 257), *Ocaso* (occident, or the setting of the sun) took the place of *Tramonto* in the second line. Given the uncertainty of any choice here, I have opted for *tramontation,* the setting of the sun behind a mountain.

factures   The word *fabrida* is old Spanish for *fabricar* (to fabricate, manufacture).

XIII   (page 191)
daughterloin   By adding a silent "h" to *ijar* (loin, or flank), Vallejo strongly evokes *hija* (daughter, or child).

XIV   (page 193)
rubber   Alberto Escobar reads *azogue* (quicksilver) in this line as a metaphor for semen. This reading is made plausible by line 6 and stimulated by the louts in line 4 (because of their association with the sexually driven beast in line 12 of the preceding XIII). I therefore translate *goma* not as "glue" but as "rubber." For another erotic use of quicksilver, see XXVII, line 12.

a wage of five soles *(un sueldo de cinco soles)*   The sol is Peru's monetary unit. Such a wage would have amounted to virtually nothing.

XV (page 195)

bed The word *cuja* in this usage is a Latin-Americanism.

Daudet Alphonse Daudet (1840–1897), a French writer, is known for, among other books, *Lettres de mon moulin* (1869), a collection of Provence-inspired short stories. This poem was originally written as a sonnet called "Sombras" (Shadows) and is reproduced on p. 264 of the RGV edition.

XVI (page 197)

zeros on the left Also an idiomatic expression meaning "mere ciphers" or "nobodies." I translate *ceros a la izquierda* literally here, since part of what I feel is Vallejo's preoccupation with the left and with negative numbers (e.g., the book's title, and poems IV, XXV, and XXXVIII).

XVII (page 199)

ovulatable That which can be ovulated. According to Ferrari, the word *ovulandas* is based on the verb *ovular* (to ovulate), using "the adjectival ending of a passive Latin conjugation." The same formation is found in *callandas* (silence-deserving) in XXV.

XIX (page 203)

To rummage, sweet Hélpide Jean Franco writes, in regard to the first line, "By giving Hope a Greek name (Hélpide) and capitalizing the initial letter, Vallejo is creating his own deity." However, Meo Zilio points out that Vallejo has added an "H" to the Greek *elpis, -idos,* and by doing so has evoked the *Helpis,* or *Helpido,* a genus of spiders (which elsewhere make two appearances in *Trilce* with the adjective *arachnoid* in XL and LXVII).

XX (page 205)

gullery In Spanish *chirota* is an old word for mischief or trickery. There is a remote possibility that it could be a distortion of *chirote* (a kind of linnet), or that it could play off *chirona* (slang for jail, or the clink).

XXI (page 207)

arteried The Spanish *arteriado* is a neologism based on *arteria* (artery). In LVII Vallejo does the same thing with *crater* (crater), turning it into *craterizados* (craterized).

We had to splendor *Hubimos de splendor* is apparently a mix of *tuvimos splendor* (we had splendor) and *hubimos de esplender* (we had to shine). While *splendor* does exist as a verb in English, it is rare enough to warrant picking up at least some of the deft oddness of the Spanish phrase.

tenderlovin' Based on *ternurosa,* a Spanish neologism fusing *ternura* (tenderness) and *amorosa* (loving).

XXII (page 209)

M. Jean Jacques is in the black books Vallejo is undoubtedly referring to Jean-Jacques Rousseau; *en hacerio* is an archaic phrase meaning "in utter disgrace or misfortune." Like *calabrina* in the first poem, it is appropriately rendered by a word/phrase that is archaic in English.

rainshines In northern Peruvian Spanish, *chirapar* means "to rain while the sun is shining" (based on the Quechuan word *chirapani*).

sumpage   *Posillos* is a modification of *pocillos* (sumps), which according to González Vigil evokes *poso* (sediment, residue). Unable to find an appropriate misspelling of the word in English, with my word choice I focused on the residue to be found in a sump.

XXV   (page 215)

Thrips uprear   The common meaning for *alfil* is "chess bishop" (based on the Arabic *al-fil*, or elephant, the original form of the bishop). A much less common meaning is *agüero* (omen, augury). The verb *alfar* appears to refer to the action of a horse that raises its head too high while galloping (I have not been able to track down the context for this denotation; i.e., does it relate to dressage? Arabic horsemanship?). As for its meaning, a good case can be made for "chess bishop," since in chess the bishop is next to the knight, which has a horse's head, the juxtaposition might possibly have triggered *alfan alfiles*. However, the magic of the line is in the sound connection (with the first two words followed by *a adherirse*—to adhere), so I have rejected a literal meaning-oriented translation of the line that might go: "Chess bishops hold their (horse) heads too high to adhere . . ." Because the *alfiles* seem to function as destructive agents that attach themselves to a number of unrelated and related things (which subsequently unravel, give way, hobble, and wheeze), I have decided to work with a reading of *alfiles* that I acknowledge is questionable. I propose, with the marriage of sounds also in mind, to read it as a variant of *alfilerillos*, which can denote a destructive insect (a kind of flea beetle that leaps up—or slightly stretched, a thrip). To some extent, in a poem as multidirectional as XXV, certain word choices become compromises relative to other words. For example, in line 4, *cadillos* can be translated as "cockleburs" or as "thrums" (warp ends, which can be associated with "unraveled" in line 5), and by selecting *thrips* for line 1, I thus get, in line 4, "thrips and thrums"—a sound play that may be as unusual as the sound play between the first two words in Spanish in line 1. While my translation of *Trilce* is primarily meaning oriented, there are occasions when the sound play is so paramount that it must be given equal priority with meaning (other examples: IX, lines 7–13; XX, line 1; XXXVI, lines 7–19; LII, line 30–34). It is also important in a poem like this not to select a "program" at the beginning and then steer as many meanings as possible into its stream.

  In an essay on Hart Crane in *At Their Word* (Black Sparrow Press, 1978), Cid Corman perceptively writes:

> Typical of what we think *is* Crane would be the piled-up shifting, metaphorical language, verbal gorgeousness outrunning sense, of:

> > (Let sphinxes from the ripe
> > Borage of death have cleared my tongue
> > Once and again; vermin and rod
> > No longer bind. Some sentient cloud
> > Of tears flocks through the tendoned loam:
> > Betrayed stones slowly speak.)

> Vallejo seems incipient. And Rimbaud's love of shock of language, of mere verbality. And Thomas in his even tighter conjunctions. The impulse toward mobbing sense is of our time. (55)

While I would tend to disagree with Corman's *critical* stance here, his association of these lines from Crane's magnificent "Lachrymae Christi" with Vallejo (in general, I gather) makes a lot of sense, especially with such poems as *Trilce* XXV.

ennazals   The Spanish *ennazala* is a neologism based on *nasal*, adding a prefix and turning the adjective into a verb.

innanimous   The Spanish *innánima* is a neologism based on *inánime* (lifeless, inanimate). This word is paired with *grifalda* (gerfalcon, or gyrfalcon), old Spanish for the falcon of that name. A gerfalcon is also a small culverin (in Spanish, a *grifalto*); this meaning also appears to be involved.

XXVI   (page 217)

chariot   *Aurigan* is the noun *auriga* (chariot) turned into a verb.

sinamayera   A female vendor of Philippine *sinamay*, a textile woven of abaca fiber.

sures   Southerly winds on the coasts of Chile and Peru.

XXVIII   (page 223)

Viandry   An archaic word that refers to food. It is also a medieval term for the tax or provisions given to a monarch by a town, as he and his entourage pass through. I emphasize this second (or perhaps initially primary) meaning in LXX: *Los soles andan sin yantar?* (Do suns move without purveyance?), since in this case the sun in its daily course seems to be compared to a monarch in pilgrimage. As a verb, *yantar* used to be a common word meaning "to eat." While it would be out of common usage for most Spanish speakers today, it may still be in use in remote sierra areas of Peru.

degllusion   Vallejo alters *deglución* (deglutition, swallowing), evoking *ilusión* (illusion) to form *deglusión*.

XXX   (page 227)

vagurant   The Spanish *vagoroso* is a neologism fusing *vago* (vague) with *vagaroso* (vagurant).

ensweetened   Vallejo has added his own suffix to *dulzor* (sweetness) to form *dulzorada*. While *ensweetened* does exist in English, it is obsolete. Although *sweetnessed* would also be possible, in this line it sounds awkward to me.

XXXI   (page 229)

cotton coddled   Literally, *entre algodones* means "between cottons" or "cotton pads/wads." The phrase appears, however, to make use of the expression *criado entre algodones* (molly-coddled, or pampered).

XXXII   (page 231)

Roombbb . . . Hulllablll llust . . . ster   While the sounds (Rumbbb . . . Trrraprrrr rrach . . . chaz) may be read as street noise, the fact that the words *trapa*, *racha*, and *cachaza* (which appears as such in line 9) seem to be involved invites me to reconstruct the line making use of English equivalents. With poetry, the challenge is always to translate everything.

Serpenteenic e of the sweet roll vendor   The "u" (in boldface) of the *bizcochero's* cry— "*biscochouus*"—unwinds in the air like a serpentin (a roll of color paper that is cast forth so as to unroll, as at a carnival). I change the "u" to an "e" to pick up the sound of "ee" in "serpenteenic," as well as the "ee" in "sweet" (which is echoed in line 13, along with the long "o" in "rolls"—Weeeeeetrozzz).

engyrafted   The Spanish *engirafada* is a neologism fusing *jirafa* (giraffe) with *girar* (gyrate), and the prefix *en*.

XXXIII   (page 233)
incordant   The Spanish *incordes* is a neologism based on *discorde* (discordant, dissonant).

XXXVI   (page 239)
hell-bent on winning   A *las ganadas* is a northern Peruvianism.
ammoniafies   The Spanish *amoniácase* is *amoníaco* (ammoniac, ammonia) turned into a verb. While we have a verb in English (ammonify), I do not use it, since none exists in Spanish.
neverthelessez   The Spanish *todaviiza* is the adverb *todavía* (yet, still, nevertheless,—and, in old Spanish, always) extended/warped into a verb. A few lines later, another adverb, *aunes* (evens), is treated as a plural noun.

XXXVII   (page 241)
marinera   A gallant coastal Peruvian folk dance.

XXXIX   (page 245)
I rock   The verb *mesarse* is conventionally accompanied by an object, e.g., *mesarse el pelo* (to tear out one's hair). Here the verb also appears to evoke *mecer* (to swing or rock), since *a columpio* (on a swing) appears in the next line.
transcendentary   Vallejo alters *trascendente* (transcendental) to evoke *diente* (tooth) in the neologism *trascendiente*. Since the word *dental* is part of the standard *transcendental* in English, I have coined *transcendentary*, since *dentary* means "pertaining to or bearing teeth."

XL   (page 247)
Mondayescent   The Spanish *lunesentes* is a neologism that appears to juxtapose *lunes* (Monday) with the suffix *-escentes* (-escent, denoting beginning, or beginning to be). While *lunescentes* also evokes *luna* (moon, from which Monday derives), given the stanza's context of "Sunday" and "six elbows" (the other days of the week?), Monday appears to be the neologism's primary significance.

XLI   (page 249)
slap for swap   A *tas* is a small anvil used by silversmiths, called a "stake" in English. Given the context of beating/striking (and the evocation of masturbating in jail in the first stanza), this meaning of *tas* appears to be involved. However, *taz a taz* (tit for tat) and *taz con taz* (even, equal, as in a score tied 7 to 7), are perhaps equally strong candidates for the phrase on which Vallejo's variation is based. And since we know that he often slightly deformed words, changing visual appearance with the sound more or less intact, *tas con tas* could be a visual modification of *taz con taz*. While it is always possible in such a situation to pick the most likely meaning and to translate it literally, it is more adventuresome (and more in keeping with the maverick spirit of *Trilce*) to create a phrase in English that while involving the implications of the original is as unusual as Vallejo's variation.

XLVI (page 259)

An earlier version of this poem (a sonnet called "La tarde"—"The Evening," to be found on pp. 344–45 in the RGV edition) contains Otilia's name. Espejo recalls:

> One evening, when all of us were wandering around the city [Lima], we found ourselves overlooking the Balta Bridge. It was getting dark, and at the end of the bridge we paused, taking in the tree-lined Cantagallo Avenue, where a woman street vendor's table was spread with anticuchos, Huancaina-style potatoes, cau-cau, glasses brimming with corn chicha, gorgeous ears of corn, and other things to eat. César had been here once with Otilia. He was profoundly moved, and against a ledge of the bridge, on the back of a racing form, he wrote [the sonnet "La tarde"]. (77)

For a reference to a racing form, see XXXV.

XLVII (page 261)

you deisland The word *isla* (island) is turned into a "negative" verb with the addition of the prefix *des-* (de-), forming *te desislas*. Possibly based on such standard verbs in Spanish as *desterrar* (to banish, or exile; literally "to de-earth") and *desaislarse* (to come out of seclusion or isolation; to de-isolate). The sense here is that the archipelago disintegrates into the depths of the sea.

mice The word *pericotes* is a Peruvianism.

XLIX (page 265)

irisizes The Spanish *iridice* is a neologism fusing *iride* (the stinking iris, or gladdon) with *iridiscente* (iridescent) to form a verb.

mashed causes The word *causas* means "causes" in English, too, but *la causa* is a purée of boiled potatoes mashed with oil and lemon. Given the food associations in the last three lines of this poem, the compound phrase in English seems appropriate.

L (page 267)

This corvine one Julio Ortega believes that *corvino* here is the masculine for *corvine*, a common Peruvian fish (known in English, too, as corvine and related to the weakfish or grouper) used in such dishes as ceviche. He bases his opinion on another conjecture, that in the second stanza *mojarilla* also refers to a fish (the *mojarra*, the same as in English). In Peru, he comments, street-smart boys are sometimes referred to as *corvinos* or *mojarillas*. The other possibilities: all dictionaries offer "crowlike, corvine" as definitions of *corvine*, and I suspect that the Cerberean warden in the poem is more crowlike than fishlike, and that he may evoke for the jailed Vallejo Poe's raven, as a figure of "nevermore." Also, all dictionaries list *mojarilla* as "a gay or jolly person," with no mention of the fish (it being listed solely as *mojarra*). Since we have just been told (in line 8) that the warden "jokes with the prisoners," it is possible that Vallejo intends to deepen his cynicism in the following line by referring to him as "jolly." Given the lack of definite evidence for either position, I have gone with the reading that the poem itself seems to back up most cogently.

LV (page 277)

Espejo was hospitalized in early 1920. He writes that when Vallejo composed this poem he was inspired by his daily visits to his friend in the hospital (87).

Samain would say   Vallejo quotes from the first two lines of "L'automne," by Albert Samain (1856–1900), which, translated by Juan Ramón Jiménez, was included in *La poesía francesa moderna* (1913), edited by Díez-Canedo and Fortún. This is the book that introduced Vallejo to French Symbolist poetry. Among the poets included were Nerval, Baudelaire, Gautier, Corbière, Laforgue, Rimbaud, Verlaine, Mallarmé, Jammes, Maeterlinck, and Claudel. Samain's poetry, written in a Symbolist vein, was distinguished by its melancholy tone and musical qualities. Jean Franco calls the quoted poem "a nostalgic evocation of human alienation healed by the essential harmony of nature" (109). *Trilce* explicitly demonstrates a rupture with this kind of Symbolism. Here is the Samain poem:

> Comme dans un préau d'hospice ou de prison,
> L'air est calme et d'une tristesse contenue;
> Et chaque feuille d'or tombe, l'heure venue,
> Ainsi qu'un souvenir, lente, sur le gazon.
>
> Le Silence entre nous marche . . . Coeurs de mensonge.
> Chacun, las du voyage, et mûr pour d'autres songes,
> Rêve égoïstement de retourner au port.
>
> Mais les bois ont, ce soir, tant de mélancolie,
> Que notre Coeur s'émeut à son tour et s'oublie
> A parler du passé, sous le ciel qui s'endort,
>
> Doucement, à mi-voix, comme d'un enfant mort.

At one point Espejo dates LV in 1919, but after mentioning his hospitalization in 1920, he changes the date to that year. It occurs to me that after 105 days in jail, Vallejo would have been extremely sensitive to a description of the air in a prison yard as "calm," especially if he associated this place with being shouted at while using outdoor latrines (see commentary on the first poem in *Trilce*). Thus a case might be made for LV having been composed in 1921, after Vallejo's release from jail.

La Prensa   Daily Lima newspaper (1903–1984).

empatrolled   The Spanish *empatrullado* is a neologism based on *patrullado* (patrolled).

LVIII (page 283)

stripshredding   The Spanish *se harapan* is a neologism based on *harapo* (rag) and possibly *arroparse* (to clothe oneself, wrap up). Since the *desnudos* (nudes) in the line above are probably pinups the prisoners have tacked to the wall, I attempt to create a word that inverts *arroparse* so as to evoke "stripping" by turning one's clothes into rags.

LIX (page 287)

"tender trap"   Literally a small pen or poultry yard, but, in context, *corralito* is the "tender trap" of marriage.

LX   (page 289)

vegetold   The word *vejetal* is Vallejo's misspelling of *vegetal* (vegetal), suggesting a play on *vejez* (old age).

LXI   (page 291)

Espejo writes that this poem was inspired by a journey back to Santiago de Chuco made by Vallejo and some friends after the poet had been away for several years. He recalls:

> We made an arduous journey by mule from Menocucho [the nearest train connection to Trujillo at the time]. César's brother Néstor was with us. We arrived after a three-day ride . . . at two in the morning. The town was sleeping peacefully, in a delicious silence. At Vallejo's house, we knocked on the door, with César anxious to embrace his family. We knocked and knocked, and still no one came. After a long wait, they let us in. (88)

bubblish   The Spanish *bullosas* is a neologism, possibly based on *bullir* (to boil, bubble) and/or *bullicioso* (bustling, boisterous).

LXIII   (page 295)

oxident   The Spanish *oxidente* is a neologism, first used in *Los heraldos negros*, fusing *occidente* (Occident) and *óxido* (oxide).

LXV   (page 299)

tori   Round moldings (torus, in the singular), not to be confused with Shinto temple gateways! In the same line as *tondos*, *repulgos* could be translated as architectural "borders" or as "pie edgings." I opted for the latter.

axling   *Ejando* is *eje* (axle) turned into a verb.

reveilles champing   This mysterious phrase, *tascar dianas*, might also be translated as "dianas scotching" or even more dramatically, "bull's-eyes crunching." It appears, however, to play off *tocar dianas* (to sound reveille), which would eliminate the other two denotations of "Diana." *Tascar* means "to scotch or swingle flax," as well as "to nibble, browse, or champ" (as in "to champ against the bit")—see IV, where it is also rendered as *champ*. Perhaps the sensation here is that of trumpet blasts trying to break the constraints of reveille and reach the dead mother (to awake the dead).

humblest   According to Meo Zilio (and to Anterior Orrego before him), with *humildóse* Vallejo has taken an archaic verb, *humildarse*, and substituted it for the current *humillarse*. Meo Zilio quotes Orrego: "When he says *humildarse* instead of *humillarse* reviving an archaism in the language, the habitual semantic cap has been broken and the word has been transformed, now signifying tenderness and loving reverence. The father does not lower and humiliate himself before his wife [see stanza 4], he exalts his love and gives it a tender reverence *humbling himself* 'until less than half a man,/until being the youngest child that you had.'" I am not aware of such a distinction in English, though the difference between *to humble* and *to humiliate* may be close (the former implying self-abasement without the loss of respect, the latter always implying ignominy). The translation problem is that to render *humildóse* as *humble* does not, as such, sound a difference with *humiliate*.

LXVI   (page 301)
Neale-Silva (whose interpretations sometimes strike me as far-fetched) suggests that behind this poem commemorating All Souls Day are the deaths of Vallejo's first sweetheart in Trujillo, María Rosa Sandoval (February 10, 1918), and of his mother, María de los Santos Gurrionero (August 8, 1918). Since Vallejo unconventionally capitalizes *Noviembre* and *Julio*, in LXVIII, I capitalize the full dates, as in Fourteenth of July, and so on.

LXVIII   (page 305)
atfulmasT   The horizontal part of the last stanza looks like a flag flying from the pole made by the vertical formation *atodastA*, a compression of *a toda asta* (based on the expression *a media asta*, "at half-mast").

LXX   (page 309)
Barrancos   Barranco is a Lima beach resort (now a part of the city) that Vallejo used to frequent. Between pages 368 and 369, González Vigil reproduces a photo of Vallejo at Barranco in 1919, in profile, standing in front of the surf, pants rolled up to his knees.
horizonifying   Vallejo coined *horizontizante* by fusing *horizonte* (horizon) with *izante* (as in *electrizante*, electrifying). Note that in Spanish, the *izon* and *izant* sounds play against *escaleras* and *escaladas* in the same sentence.

LXXI   (page 311)
fitted out with demilune / spurs   The Spanish *ennavajados* is a neologism based on *navaja* (razor), to which a prefix and past-participle suffix have been added. Larrea comments that the phrase refers to the attaching of demilune razors to the spurs of the gamecocks. Literally, "enrazored with cupolas."

LXXIV   (page 317)
we hardly let / fly   The Spanish *enflechamos* is a neologism based on *flecha* (arrow) and *enflechado* (loaded, with arrow ready, said of a bow).
the hanky-panky hinges   The Spanish *gozna* is a neologism, based on *gozne* (hinge) and *engoznar* (to hinge). By dropping the prefix, Vallejo evokes *goznar* (to enjoy oneself, even in a sexual way), suggesting that the *travesura* (mischief) involved sexual games. Unable to pick up this aspect of the phrase in the verb, I attempt to suggest it in my choice of noun.

LXXV   (page 319)
Espejo writes that

> on the 27th of April [1920], we left the port of Callao, on the steamer *Aysen*, for Salaverry, arriving on the 30th. At this time, Vallejo had with him in a binder most of the poems that would make up *Trilce*. His friends met us at the Trujillo station. Having just arrived from Lima, where he had been embroiled in quarrels and agitation, and in a constant flurry of activity, Vallejo was floored by the placid ambience, and immediately seemed to lose once and for all his interest in Trujillo. At the same time, he discovered his old friends asleep on their feet, going through life as if in "slow motion". . . . The following day he came to my house and read me the poem beginning "You're all dead." (87)

As Ferrari points out, the poem clearly transcends such an incident—yet at the same time, it is interesting to know its setting. In *César Vallejo: The Dialectics of Poetry and Silence,* Jean Franco quotes a convincing paragraph by the painter Macedonio de la Torre on the early-twentieth-century tedium of Trujillo (7).

Trilce was published in October 1922, and the following June Vallejo sailed from Peru for Europe, never to return to Peru. In the fall of 1923, a poem called "Trilce" appeared in the Spanish magazine *Alfar* (the name curiously evokes the opening line of XXV). This poem is now part of the various editions of Vallejo's *Obra poética completa;* however, it is impossible to link it directly to *Trilce* or to the post-Peruvian prose poems or poetry. Espejo reports that this poem was written in Peru when the *Trilce* manuscript was complete but was still being called "Cráneos de bronce." Clearly this story conflicts with the one about discovering the book's title at the last minute via wordplay. The fact that this poem was not included in the second Madrid edition of *Trilce* (1930) indicates that Vallejo did not want it to be part of the book. The poem treats "Trilce" as an ineffable location in the mind that is right here *and* unreachable. It seems to me now to be the kind of piece Vallejo might have written after *Trilce* was titled and complete, an attempt to make locational sense out of a title that he knew would appear abstract to nearly all readers. I think that the poem was definitely written and sent out before he left Peru, given the fact that he left in June and the poem appeared in a Spanish magazine less than six months later. Perhaps it is the last poem he wrote before leaving, and if so, then it is especially appropriate to present a translation of it here, at the end of this commentary on *Trilce.*

TRILCE

There is a place that I myself know
in this world, nothing less,
that we will never reach.

Where, even if our foot
were to reach it for an instant
it will be, in truth, as if we were not there.

It is that spot which is seen
every moment in this life,
walking, walking in single file.

This side of myself and of
my pair of yolks, I have glimpsed it
always distant from destinations.

Now, you can depart on foot
or out of sheer sentiment bareback,
since not even stamps could reach it.

The tea-color horizon
is dying to colonize it
as its great Whateverpart.

But the place that I myself know,
in this world, nothing less,
sought pace with its opposites.

—Close that door that
is ajar in the entrails
of that mirror. —This one?—No; its sister.

—It cannot be closed. It is not
possible to ever reach that spot
—where the bolts act up unbound.

Such is the place that I myself know.

HUMAN POEMS

The poems in *Human Poems* were written in Europe, for the most part in Paris, between 1923 and 1938. They were first published by Vallejo's widow, Georgette de Vallejo, in 1939 as *Poemas humanos*. The 1939 edition contained eighty-nine poems. Since then, ten more have been added, six by Georgette, two by Ricardo González Vigil, and two by the editor of a Cuban edition, bringing the book now to ninety-nine poems.

The title of these poems, at least in terms of the author's intentions, has never been definitively determined. For years, it was thought that Georgette either had invented the title herself or had played a variation on the title of a Gerardo Diego book, *Versos humanos*. In the 1970s, Vallejo's old friend the poet Juan Larrea, who for decades had been deeply involved in Vallejo research, established a rational ordering of the undated European poems (which had appeared in various arbitrary orders over the years in editions of *Poemas humanos*), by coordinating them with dated letters from the six typewriters Vallejo had used while in Europe. While *Poemas humanos* does appear to fall into two basic groupings of undated poems (written for the most part between 1924 and the early to mid-1930s) and dated ones (September 4–December 8, 1937), Larrea took what could be two sections of the same collection as two separate books, proposing that in 1936 Vallejo took all the poetry and prose poetry he had written since coming to Europe and called it *Nómina de huesos* (Roster of Bones), based on the title of what Larrea considered to be the first poem in the manuscript. Larrea's conjecture here was based on the fact that the title poem of Vallejo's first book, *Los heraldos negros,* is the first in that book.

As for the dated poems, since no title could be found, Larrea made a plausible, if not convincing, case for *Sermón de la barbarie* (Sermon on Barbarism), arguing that it is the key phrase in the last dated poem, "Sermón sobre la muerte," and suggests that "la barbarie" was a metaphor for "Babel," the Word *(bab-ilu)*, the "Gate of God," which Vallejo engaged in the central book of his career. My co-translator at the time, José Rubia Barcia, was himself an old friend of Larrea, and based on the latter's impressive credentials, he proposed that we accept Larrea's findings and retitle *Human Poems* as *The Complete Posthumous Poetry,* including under this general title the two books making up the old *Human Poems* along with the short collection of Spanish Civil War poems, *Spain, Take This Cup from Me.*

In the 1991 RGV edition of Vallejo's complete poetry, the editor notes that in 1929 it appears that the poet did conceive of, along with other potential books, "a Book of human poems." He reproduces the contents from one of Vallejo's notebook pages dated September 20, 1929 (made available by Georgette in 1978). While there is still no evidence that Vallejo directly linked his European poetry with such a title, which can be thought of as descriptive of poems, as well as a title per se, the only possible candidate for such a title at this point is all the European poetry, aside from the Spanish Civil War poems (the title of which has never been disputed).

Human Poems is also a title that for over sixty years has often been attached to, and associated with, this period of Vallejo's poetry. The word *humanos* occurs six times, in crucial placements, in this writing. Vallejo's poetry from 1923 to 1938 is a magisterial meditation on the sympathies, passions, compassions, and failings of humankind. It "humanizes" a common nonracial trunk in which the animal is not separated out of the human, and in this way reengages an extremely ancient matrix underlying the divisions that have resulted in body and soul, culture and wilderness.

For all these reasons I have restored *Human Poems* as the title of these now ninety-nine poems, including four new prose poems that Barcia and I were not aware of when we worked together in the 1970s.

Besides Larrea's scholarship, our work was also greatly facilitated by the Francisco Moncloa *Obra poética completa* (1968), with its facsimile reproductions of the hand-corrected typescripts for all but a few of the posthumously published European poems. Not only did such reproductions enable us to avoid the error-riddled (often pirated) editions that I had worked from in the 1960s, but they also offered us the thousands of handwritten changes that Vallejo made on the typescript. We therefore constructed a section of notes in which we translated what in our opinion was the most interesting of the legible crossed-out material. I have included most of this information in what follows here, as well as making a few additions, and I have continued to present it as work by us both, to honor Barcia's role in its essential formation.

The RGV edition lists, as part of the annotations to the undated poems, Georgette de Vallejo's conjectures about dates and in a few cases, dates of publication (that is, while such manuscripts do not bear a completion date stated by Vallejo himself, they were published in magazines in a particular year). I have chronologically ordered these poems according to conjectures and publication dates, putting the conjectural dates in brackets, while leaving brackets off the publication dates. In regard to the poems dated by Vallejo himself, I have included such dates also without brackets. As mentioned before, the fact that the dated poems appear to have been completed in a short, intense work period of several months sets them apart from the others, which may have been written over some eleven or twelve years. To respect this chronology, I have divided the current *Human Poems* into parts 1 and 2.

Good Sense   (page 327)

through consummated pacts   At the beginning of the paragraph following this line, Vallejo had originally written:

My mother is successive of beings and an alternative of hours.

she would become sad   Following this line, there is a crossed-out paragraph:

> What is there, then, about me, that my father lacks and since my returning home, leaves my mother so pensive? My father is now losing his authority and home oscillates around me, with sleeves, fillet, galloon, and lapels.

There resides the candor   There are a number of corrections from this point on, so we have translated Vallejo's original version:

> There resides her woman's illusion and the most sacred candor that becomes a brilliant melancholy in the depth of her face. In order to support her illusion and her candor, I say to her filially:
>   —There is, mother, in the world a place called Paris. A very big place and very far off, where there are more men than women, more grown-ups than children. Thick beam! Cilicious stone!
>   My mother, on hearing me, eats her lunch and shows in her mortal eyes the order in my personal life.

Violence of the Hours   (page 331)

TITLE   According to Larrea, this poem was written before Vallejo's father's death on March 24, 1924. Larrea assumes that the father would have been mentioned in the poem had it been written after his death.

interior corridors   In response to our query, Larrea wrote Barcia that Vallejo's home in Santiago de Chuco had two floors, with interior corridors encircling a small inner patio. We have thus translated *corredores* in this poem as "interior corridors," or in "Languidly Her Liquor" as "interior corridor."

there is no one in my experience   After this line, a five-line paragraph has been crossed out:

> My horse Macachón died, no longer with us but with others. My father was informed of his death, one night, a long time ago, by the alfalfa farmer Manuel Benites, the peasant who shook the hair from his shoulders with the bristles of his climates.

"The windows shuddered . . ."   (page 333)

TITLE   The following title has been crossed out: "Complement of Time in the Boyer Hospital" ("Complemento de tiempo del Hospital de Boyer"). Vallejo wrote to the poet Pablo Abril that he was in the Boyer Hospital in October 1924, to be operated on for an intestinal hemorrhage, with twenty horrible days of physical pain and incredible spiritual depression. He tells Abril that an infantile ability to cry has left him saturated with an immense piety for all things.

After this crossed-out title, the following lines are also crossed out:

> The bedsheets still stink of expedience because of the death of a man. The mattress has been turned, according to regulations. Thus the stench of the last agony will not hit you in the face. As for the one now arriving, it would be better if they looked at him, if they put him to bed, if they asked him lots of questions, for if they leave him alert, he will handle the perilous density of his importance by himself. But he understands very well that there are other men crying here and that no one will know how to answer them, if his mouth looks at the mouth of the others, of us, the sick ones.

Ay   The word *ay* often appears in Vallejo's poetry, and I have usually resisted converting it literally into *alas*, which for me has a different tenor and a less poignant edge. I have tried to pick up the emotional sense of the word in each context in which I encountered it, at times spelling it differently or putting an exclamation mark after it to render it more acutely.

forgive us our chests   Larrea suggests that *nos perdonan pecho* might mean "they forgive us the sin of having chests (and allow us, as a consequence, to breathe)." The word *pecho*, depending on the context, can mean "chest," "breast," "heart," or even "courage." Larrea's interpretation is strengthened by the probability that the *mosca* (fly) in the following line seems to be a religious person, e.g., a nun. Since Vallejo uses *pecho* often (especially in *Spain, Take This Cup from Me*), and gives it a feeling of his own, we have decided to stick with its literal meaning in English.

Blood runs wild   This single line was originally the following three-line paragraph:

> Blood runs wild in the thermometers . . . The order of numbers reared up on 11,
> and the following numbers exclaim: head office! head office! head office!

The Low Point in Life   (page 339)

TITLE   The original title was "Concerning the Correctness of Actions" ("Acerca de la correción de los actos").

Roster of Bones   (page 341)

TITLE   "List of Bones" ("Lista de huesos") was crossed out in favor of the final title.

I Am Going to Speak of Hope   (page 343)

After the second paragraph, the following paragraph has been crossed out:

> It is necessary to differentiate my present pain, from that pain which derives from not having a cause to feel pain. Today I suffer a pain that did not have a cause nor did it lack one. There are pains like this in the bottomless kingdom, without history or future, of the heart of man. I suffer, then, without conditions or consequences. Suspended in the air, I do not know if fragile or resistant, my pain has now such sufficiency and a courage so much its own, that before it men feel a respect almost religious and almost joyous. Because oh miracle of the maximum circles! this pain is not conditioned to come or to leave.

After the last paragraph, the following paragraph was crossed out:

> And in this heart, which has neither had a cause nor the lack of one; in this heart, without back or chest, without state or name, without source or use, there is no room for hope or for memory and what is even sadder ah tremendous fall upward! how I now make my pain feel pain.

Discovery of Life   (page 345)

Before the first paragraph, the following paragraph has been crossed out:

> When was it that I savored for the first time the taste of life? When was it that I tested this impression of nature, that makes me ecstatic at this moment? Have I savored on another occasion the taste of life? Have I already tested at another time my impression of nature? I am completely convinced of not having tested it, of

never having savored it, except now. This is extraordinary! Today is the first time that I savor the taste of life; today is the first time that the effect of nature has made me ecstatic. This is extraordinary! This astonishes me and makes me brim with tears and with happiness.

aknown   The word *inconocido* appears to be a play on *desconocido* (unknown), and I have translated it accordingly.

After the fourth paragraph, the following paragraph has been crossed out:

I am possessed by the emotion of this discovery. A discovery of the unexpected and a discovery of goodness. How much has this happiness cost me? How long have I awaited it? NEITHER expectation nor price. Do you know the unexpected happiness? Do you know the unpaid happiness? This is my happiness today. That which makes me ecstatic and clothes me with an air so unused, that people will take me for a foreigner on earth. Yes. I neither know anyone nor does anyone know me.

After the last line, the following two sentences have been crossed out:

And I am now at the point of dying, before being at the point of growing old. I will die of life and not of time.

"Behold that today I salute . . ."   (page 359)

sprouts a distAnce   It appears that Vallejo put the capital "A" in the word *distanciA* to make fun of the rhyme and musicality of the whole quatrain up to that point. By capitalizing the single "a" in *distance*, I intend to throw the accent onto that syllable, creating a similar effect.

ssssuch regular codes   An attempt to pick up the *ttttales códigos regulates* of the original. A few lines later, the Spanish *un* (a) is written as *hun*. Since the "h" is not pronounced, the distortion cannot be sounded but only viewed. This sort of visual distortion occasionally occurs throughout all Vallejo's books.

Height and Hair   (page 361)

An earlier version of this poem, entitled "Lofty Attitude" ("Actitud de excelencia") exists and might be translated as follows:

Who doesn't own a blue suit
and eat lunch and board the streetcar
with his smoked cigarette and his pocket-edition pain?
ay I was only born.

Who doesn't write a letter
and talk about something very important?
ay I was only born.

Who isn't called Carlos or any other thing
and doesn't at least say kitty, kitty, kitty, kitty?
ay I was only born.

ay how I was only born.
ay how I was only born.

"Four consciousnesses . . ."   (page 367)

This poem and the following six are from the book *Contra el secreto profesional*, which according to Georgette was written for the most part between 1927 and 1928 (but not published until 1973, edited by Georgette, in Lima, by Mosca Azul Editores). This poem and the following two were apparently written out as prose poems and then rewritten by Vallejo as poems.

"Between pain and pleasure . . ."   (page 369)

To the instantaneous meaning of eternity   The third stanza of this poem, as originally written out in prose, appears to have read:

> To the instantaneous meaning of eternity corresponds this absurdity that identifies us today. But to your volume of temporal good-bye, solely corresponds the inexorable arrival.

Languidly Her Liquor   (page 373)

a priestess of love   The Spanish *cura de amor*, on which our English phrase is based, could also be translated "as a cure for love," modifying *el yantar de oración* instead of *mama*. A few lines later, *mi madre iba sentada* (my mother went sitting) is another typical construction in this piece, coherent and at the same time irrationally dense. We translate literally when a phrase is not idiomatic and appears to have been invented, as a neologism, by Vallejo.

playing her entrails with infinite frets   In Spanish *tocar* means "to knock," "to touch," and "to play" and when connected to *trastos* (originally written as *trastes*), suggests the playing of a stringed instrument, with *entrails* taking the place of *heart* or *feeling*. By altering one letter, Vallejo changed *trastes* (stops, frets) to *trastos* (junk, implements), and we have had to translate the word as if it were *trastes*, since to render the latter word would eliminate the musical image.

Miguel has made me blush. With his bLush *(me ha echado Miguel al pavo. A su paVO)*   A Peruvian idiomatic expression the meaning of which is not clear, although we feel it is probably connected with *subírsele a uno el pavo* (to blush). A literal translation would be: "Miguel has thrown me to the turkey. To his turKEY."

the hen was the widow of her children   From this line on, the original version varies considerably from the final one:

> the hen was the widow of her children, the hen is the eternal bride of the mammalian. All the eggs were found empty. The brooder afterward had the word and, in an elegant construction, past, present and chirping.
>
> One story, two stories, three stories.
>
> No one frightened her. And in case she was frightened, no one allowed himself to be lulled by her clucking nor by her viviparous chill.
>
> —Where are the old hen's children?
> —Where are the old hen's chicks?
>
> Afterward botanical works were scarce in the hamlet.
>
> One little eye, two little eyes, three little eyes.
>
> One story, two stories, three stories.

The Footfalls of a Great Criminal   (page 377)

This prose poem, along with the next, are not to be found in the RGV edition. González Vigil considers them lyric-narratives, closer to stories than to poems. I disagree and so have included them. They come from César Vallejo, *Poesía completa*, edited by Raúl Hernández Novás (Havana: Editorial Arte y Literatura, 1988).

Black Stone on a White Stone   (page 381)

TITLE   According to Carlos del Río León (in *Caretas* [April 1966]), the title of this poem is based on the fact that one day in Paris, Vallejo was very depressed and, while wearing a black overcoat, sat down on a white stone. The stone evoked a white sepulcher and his own appearance a black stone. Antenor Orrego recounts another more compelling version of the source of this poem, which is summarized by Stephen M. Hart on p. 692 below.

and I don't budge   The Spanish verb *correr* (to run) acquires a different meaning when used reflexively, mainly "to move" (forward to the left or right). The implication here appears to be that he will remain in Paris, in spite of his intuition that death awaits him there.

forced on   The Spanish *a la mala* could also be translated here as "unwillingly" (the phrase occurs in line 51 of "Battles" in *Spain, Take This Cup from Me*, and there I have translated it as "unwillingly"). In this sonnet, Vallejo uses the phrase idiomatically *and* idiosyncratically, and its specific meaning remains mysterious.

"And don't say another word to me ..."   (page 385)

The following title, "The Greatness of Common Works" ("Grandeza de los trabojos vulgares"), has been crossed out.

"It was Sunday in the clear ears of my jackass ..."   (page 387)

Voltaire pulls his cape to and looks at the square   In 1974 I discovered a postcard in Paris with exactly this scene on it. Voltaire is on a high pedestal, with his hands crossed before him, looking off to the right across the square.

"Today I like life much less ..."   (page 389)

but, of course   Before being partially crossed out, this line was corrected by hand to read:
> but entering five abreast, of course,

and always, much always, always always!   This line originally read:
> and always, much always, always in line under bastinados.

and then was changed to the following line before it was corrected to the final version:
> and always, much always, always lying down outside my body.

Glebe   (page 391)

TITLE   Originally the Spanish word *gleba* meant "clod" (in modern Spanish, *terrón*) or "soil" (in modern Spanish, *suelo* or *tierra*), but today the word persists only in the old expression *siervos de la gleba* (serfs, or slaves, of the soil) and is always associated with the idea of the worst kind of serfdom or human slavery.

within fog range   In Spanish the phrase *a tiro de neblina* is unusual and appears to derive from such common expressions as *a tiro de escopeta* (within shotgun range), or *a tiro de canon* (within cannon range).

"reginas of the valley"   According to Larrea, these "reginas" are a kind of snake. *Regina* is the Latin word for "queen."

Luis Taboada   The name of a famous Spanish humorist (1848–1906). It is not entirely certain whether Vallejo had him in mind when he used the name.

"But before all this . . ."   (page 393)

phalanhes   The Spanish *falanjas* appears to be a neologism based on *falanges* (phalanges).

Whistling at your death   The first four lines of the fourth stanza were originally five and read:

> Torso over the hill that you encircled,
> whistling at your death,
> hat rakishly tilted,
> feet over your shoulders,
> a target, rower swaying to win your battle among the fish.

hat rakishly tilted   In Spanish *pedrada* means "a blow with a stone," but in this case *sombrero a la pedrada* is a Peruvian idiom and refers to a hat either adorned with a ribbon or tilted at a rakish slant. In his book *Vallejo y su tierra*, Francisco Izquierdo Ríos wrote about Vallejo's home town, Santiago de Chuco: "The horse-breakers with fine ponchos and 'sombreros a la pedrada' made the horses caracole."

target   In Spanish *blanco* can mean "white," target," and "blank," and Vallejo may very well have had all three meanings in mind when he used the word here. In the 1967 Seghers edition of Vallejo's poetry translated by Georgette de Vallejo, and supervised by Américo Ferrari, the French word chosen here is *cible* (target).

Epistle to the Passersby   (page 395)

my night of an elephant in repose   After this line, Vallejo had originally written the following three lines:

> just in case my brute calls out in great fables
> and the sky becomes a sky of humanized earth,
> a sky at full speed, mounted slowly on a sword.

cullions   In Spanish *compañones* is an archaic word meaning "testicles." I attempt to match it in English with an obsolete word for testicles.

navehall   Vallejo misspells *ombligo* (navel) as *hombligo* (playing off *hombre*—man). There is a temptation to mistranslate the English as "humbilicus cord," but I have resisted this, since the speaker would have lost his umbilicus cord long ago.

Meanwhile, convulsively, harshly   The last stanza originally read:

> Meanwhile, convulsively, continued,
> my soft quality convalesces,
> suffering like I suffer the direct language of the lion:
> and because I have existed between two powers with moribund candles,
> I convalesce, I feel better, smiling lewdly at my lips,
> when my penis is sad in its stick
> and my destruction is good enough.

Tuberous Spring   (page 397)

vulture beakax   Here *picotón de buitre* appears to involve an unusual augmentative of *pico* (beak, pick) and in Vallejo's mind may have been connected with *azadón* (mattock). However, it is actually a Peruvian expression meaning "to strike hard," and in this context suggests that the vulture is using its beak as an ax while eating.

degllusion   Vallejo has again misspelled *deglución* as *deglusión*, this time with the "s" underlined and a question mark penciled in the left margin of the facsimile.

"Finally, without that good continuous aroma . . ."   (page 401)

tombsadness   The neologism *tristumbre* appears to contain *triste* (sad) and possibly the latter part of *pesadumbre* (sorrow). It also contains the *tumb* of *tumba* (tomb). I have attempted to approximate this neologism with one of my own.

The Hungry Man's Rack   (page 403)

calcarid   The Spanish *calcárida* appears to be a neologism based on *calcáreo* (calcareous) and *árida* (arid).

"Considering coldly . . ."   (page 405)

that I hate him with affection   This entire line originally read:

> and he knows how to mend himself with tears and songs . . .

"Idle on a stone . . ."   (page 407)

a paperscrap   This entire line originally ended with:

> his betrayed dice . . .

who today sweats from outside in his secretion of rejected blood   After this line, the following two were crossed out:

> This is the one who bled through his side,
> who today drowns in his rejected blood!

and the bread getting into the wrong saliva   This entire line originally read:

> and the nourishing bread that they don't need

how lightning nails   This and the following line originally read as one line:

> how it nails its headless nail into your clavicles!

stallion louse   As an adjective *padre* (father) is a common augmentative for almost everything, e.g., *una vida padre* (a great life), *un automóvil padre* (a great car). Here we have tried to translate the act of the lowest parasite being ironically elevated to a role of seminal importance.

"Life, this life . . ."   (page 411)

their thirteen bones . . . the old screw   These two lines, before corrections, read:

> their sacred bones slant ner the sewers,
> over an old screw, proclivitous, misfortunate.

ner   Vallejo misspelled *cabe* (near) as *cave*, and we attempt to match the slight sound change with *ner* in English.

the poorotten   The Spanish *póbridas* is a neologism derived from *pobres* (poor ones) and perhaps *podrida* (rotten).

if they fell then bluely   This phrase originally read:

> if their magnets then fell.

emitted dense smoke   This line and the three following it originally read:

> emitted dense smoke of thoughtful madmen, attacked
> by physics, and from a half-deaf pain.
> Doves hopping up from the depths,
> doves fragrant to the insult of that day.

"And if after so many words . . ."   (page 415)

for them to blow it all   The phrase *que se lo coman todo* literally means "for them to eat all of it," but we feel that Vallejo used it in its common idiomatic meaning of "to blow something," e.g., to blow a fortune.

"Sweetness through heartsown sweetness . . ."   (page 417)

heartsown   The Spanish *corazona* is an arbitrary feminine, probably of the masculine noun *corazón* (heart), although it could also be the third-person singular of a made-up verb based on *corazón,* such as *corazonar.* On the basis of the second possibility, the line could be rendered: "Sweetness through sweetness heartens!" However, since *hearten* is an accepted English word, such a rendering does not translate the uniqueness of *corazona.* So I have translated it as a noun, hoping to expose "heart's own," "heart sown," and "heart zone" in my rendering.

teatnacity   The Spanish *tezón* appears to be a neologism, linking *tesón* (tenacity) with *pezón* (nipple, teat). See line 10 of "The Narrow Theater Box" in *The Black Heralds.*

foreverish   The Spanish *perduroso* appears to be a neologism based on *perdurar* (to last long), with a suffix such as one finds in *presuroso* (hasty), for which the verb would be *apresurar* (to hasten).

quand on a la vie . . . déjà tellement!   The two lines of French read "When one has life and youth / that's already so much!"

you well kiss me   Here *haz* is an intentional misspelling of *has* (second-person singular, present tense, of *haber*—to have—used as an auxiliary verb). If Vallejo had written *has de besarme,* we would have translated it as "you will kiss me." *Haz* by itself could also mean "bundle" or "face."

Old Asses Thinking   (page 421)

TITLE   There is some evidence that this poem was inspired by the death of Vallejo's close friend from his first days in Paris, Alfonso Silva (1903–1937), a Peruvian composer and writer who returned to Peru and died in Lima on May 7, 1937. Vallejo wrote another poem, "Alfonso: you keep looking at me, I see," which was a clear and direct response to Silva's death.

boldo   A genus of Chilean evergreen shrubs, with a sweet, edible fruit; the dried-out leaves are a hypnotic and a diuretic.

now never   After this line the one following is crossed out:

> I will call him at the margin of his incased river's name!

(After completing work on *The Complete Posthumous Poetry,* in 1977, I took this erased line, re-translating part of it as "The Name Encanyoned River," as the title for a poem celebrating the dimension of my relationship with Vallejo; this title subsequently was used as the title for *The Name Encanyoned River: Selected Poems 1960–1985,* published by Black Sparrow Press in 1978.)

what a never of the nevers his never   In Spanish, the word *jamases* (the plural of an adverb meaning "never") is grammatically impossible—but it does exist in popular speech.

Telluric and Magnetic   (page 423)

TITLE   The original title, "Agricultural Meditation" ("Meditación agrícola") was crossed out. The poem was originally much more modest in scope, with the typescript ending with line 27. The rest of the poem was written out by hand.

Sincere and utterly Peruvian mechanics   The first four lines were originally three and read:

> Ascended and sincere mechanics!
> Theoretical and practical soil!
> Intelligent furrows, and with pyramid examples!

reddened hill   In the book on Vallejo by Izquierdo Ríos noted above, one reads: "In Santiago de Chuco there exists a Reddened Hill."

Oh human fields   The poem originally ended with a shortened version of this stanza and read:

> Oh human fields!
> Oh climates found within iron, ready!
> Oh intellectual field,
> with religion, and with peasant fields!
> Pachyderms in prose when passing!
> Rodents who peer with judicial feeling all around!
> Oh my life's patriotic asses!
> Oh light hardly a mirror from shadow,
> which is life with the period and, with the line, dust
> and that is why I revere, climbing through the idea to my skeleton!

(From this point on the poem is handwritten.)

pepper tree   A *molle* is a genus of tropical American trees of the sumac family, known as the pepper tree. It was the sacred tree of the Incas, and the fruit is used to make an alcoholic beverage similar to chicha.

barret   See note on *Trilce* VIII.

cavy   The *cuy* is a short-tailed, rough-haired South American rodent (guinea pigs are from the same species). A *cuya* (cavess, in our approximation) would be a female cuy.

bird pepper   A *rocoto* is a pepper, known as "bird pepper." The red fruit are small, oblong, and very pungent. The Spanish word probably derives from the Quechuan *rucuta*. In the same line, *temples* refers to valleys with temples in the Peruvian sierra.

Screw the condors!   *Me friegan los cóndores!* could also be rendered as "Those condors make me sick!" It is true that the verb *fregar* is softer in Peru than in Mexico, where it is a strong vulgar word; however, we feel that the fact that Vallejo used the word in the 1930s, when it was much more objectionable than it is today, justifies our translation. See also the note on the last line of this poem: the same Mexican friend who apparently stimulated Vallejo to use *me las pelan,* may also have inspired his use of *friegan.*

Auchenia   The Spanish *auquénidos* is derived from *auchenia,* the Latin for certain South American animals of the Camelidae family, such as llamas, vicuñas, alpacas, and guanacos— all of which have big, sad eyes.

quena See note on "Autochthonous Tercet, I" in *The Black Heralds*.

they can jerk me off! In answer to our query about *me las pelan!* Larrea wrote to Barcia: "In our Hispanomerican group in Montparnasse in 1926, we often sang a kind of ballad, thanks to a good Mexican friend, which had a refrain which went: 'Pelame la pinga' (peel my foreskin down). I would say that this is the origin of that line of Vallejo's. That he puts it in the plural surprises me—perhaps he does that out of modesty! It would translate something like 'me la menean' (they jack me off)."

"The miners came out of the mine . . ." (page 427)
The first three stanzas of the poem originally read:

> The miners came out
> climbing over their future forms,
> they greeted their health with pavilions
> and, elaborating their mental function,
> closed with their good and with their voice
> the shaft, in the shape of a profound symptom.
>
> Ah, what dust their reclined dust!
> Ah, what oxide their oxides of the heights!
> Mouth wedges, mouth anvils, mouth apparatus (It is Tremendous!)
> Great joy following, head to head, their feelings.
>
> They imagine, writings on a femur,
> their plastic inductions, their choral responses,
> crowded at the foot of fiery misfortunes
> and aerant yellowing known by the saddened,
> the sad ones, imbued
> with the metal that peters out, the pallid and humble metalloid.

(In the tenth line of the above stanzas, "head to head" was crossed out and "from saliva to saliva" penciled in, which was then rejected too.)

aerent The Spanish *airente* appears to be a neologism based on *aire* (air), to which an *-ente* suffix has been attached, a common suffix but not one normally attached to the word *aire*. In the same line, *amarillura* derives from *amarillo* (yellow) but is not of normal or frequent usage. Near the end of the same line, *trístidos,* based on *triste* (sad), appears to be a neologism; *-idos* is normally not attached to that word. Last, *tristes* could either be a plural noun of the adjective *triste* or the word for a sad song (which would have no translation). We interpret it as the former.

eyes of physical weeping After this line the following one was crossed out:

> miners of the timbre of the voice of man;

"From disturbance to disturbance . . ." (page 431)
when you suffer in short from kangaroo The line is odd without a comma, but since there is none in the Spanish—*cuando sufras en suma de kanguro*—we leave it out in the translation too.

man with shoe heel *Taco* is a South American word for *tacón* (shoe heel). From this line on the poem is handwritten, suggesting, as in the case of "Telluric and Magnetic," a later addition.

"Today I would like to be happy willingly . . ."   (page 435)

why they hit me like this so much in my soul   This line was originally different, and was then followed by two lines that were crossed out after some rewriting. The original reads:

> the wait for that which will never arrive
> and the termination of the refused waiting.
> I see everything this way, without adherence or bond.

at what hour, then, will they come with my portrait?   This line originally read:

> at what hour, then, would I desire that they love me?

At the misericordias, comrade   The final stanza originally read:

> Now I notice that I cross through my temples as a traveler:
> at the misericordias, comrade,
> fellowman in rejection and observation, more mine,
> father through the friend,
> brother through the son, in whose neck rises and lowers,
> inactive, naked, my hope . . .

"Heat, tired I go with my gold . . ."   (page 437)

C'est Septembre attiédi   The four lines of French in the poem (the third line of each of the first four stanzas) reads as follows:

> It's cooled off September.
> It's Paris, queen of the world!
> It's spring,
> It's life, death of the Death!

Paris, and 4, and 5   The poem was written on September 4, 1937. Vallejo was forty-five years old at the time. Lines 5 and 6 originally read:

> Paris, and 4, and 5, of dried anxiety,
> hanging, in the heat, from cloud and cloud.

"One pillar supporting solace . . ."   (page 439)

pillarous   The Spanish *pilaroso* appears to be a neologism, based on *pilar* (pillar), to which an *-oso* suffix has been added. It acts as an intensifier, leading us to my *pillarous*.
I'm going to close my baptismal font   This line and the following three originally read:

> I'm going to close my baptismal font, this edge,
> this fright with a sash, in the form of wrath,
> this finger without a hand,
> directly joined to my skeleton.

hearterially   The Spanish *corazónmente* is a neologism based on *corazón* (heart), with a *-mente* suffix, generally translated as "-ly" in English. The richness of the neologism (including *mente*—mind—next to *heart*) calls for an approximate equivalent in English.

"Upon meditating on life . . ."   (page 441)

The first version of this poem, significantly different than the final version, reads:

Upon meditating,
slowly on the vigor of the torrent,
existence lightens, offers support,
condemns to death;
and, wrapped in white rags, it falls,
falls with a planetary step,
the nail boiled in sorrow.
Official acrimony, that of my left;
without situation, without number, this sword.

All is joyful, except my joy
and all, long, except my furor,
my incertitude!
Through form, nevertheless, I go forward,
limping,
up to my encounter,
and forget through my tears my eyes
and climb up to my feet from my star.

I weave. From having spun, I'm weaving . . .
I search for what follows me and hides from me among archbishops,
under my soul and behind the smoke that I've smoked.
Such is death
that grew up by crushings, by gunshots,
exhaling fatidic petroleums,
yesterday, only, a Sunday of faces . . .

Such is death, with ram and all.

"The tip of man . . ."   (page 447)

stirrut   In "Village Scene" (in *The Black Heralds*), the bell and voice context led me to a translation of *dondoneo* as "dronedongs." Here in a situation that is both abstract and erotic, a different version seems called for. The neologism here strongly evokes a play on *contoneo* (strut); so by adding an "ir" to *strut*, (drawing forth *stir* and *rut*), I hope to match the strangeness of the original.

"Oh bottle without wine! . . ."   (page 449)

frolicful   The Spanish *jugarino* appears to be an adjectival neologism based on *jugar* (to play), with the suffix *-ino*. The normal Spanish adjective would have been *juguetón* (frolicsome). The *ino* gives the word an Italian flavor and also a kind of playfulness.

"He goes running, walking . . ."   (page 451)

at a cassock pace   The line originally read:

at an inkwell pace, flees

"My chest wants and does not want . . ."   (page 455)

big-browed   The Spanish *cejón* appears to be a neologism based on *ceja* (eyebrow). Vallejo uses this term in somewhat the same way that *cabezón* (headstrong) augments *cabeza* (head).

with all my zipper   This line originally read

> anguish, yes, with all the nipple

(nipple here being *tetilla*, a male nipple).

"*This* . . ."   (page 457)

This   The poem originally began without this one-word line, and its first two lines read:

> It happened between two flowers or two eyelids; I trembled
> in my sheath, with alkali, with anger,

of the sky   Originally this phrase began a new line that, along with another one, completed the stanza:

> of the sky. (I would have dealt with other themes, but
> I write them unsung, without my mouth)

arpoons   Vallejo has added an "h" to *arpons*, leading us to eliminate it from the English word.

in my sheeth   This line originally began with "from fear of death." *Vaina* (sheath) appears to be intentionally misspelled as *vayna*.

with sighs one builds   This line and the one following it read:

> (It is said that sighs hold
> then regressions that do not want to go away;

I revise my semesters   The line originally read:

> the semesters revise me in their album

"*I stayed on to warm up the ink in which I drown* . . ."   (page 459)

I stayed on to warm up   This line originally read:

> I stayed on to listen to my elbow,

And still, this very day, at dusk   This line and the next one originally read:

> And yet, this very day
> I digest extremely sacred tenths,

my happy and doctoral bacillus   This line was originally:

> my Gregorian bugles,

male earth, sun and male moon   Vallejo changes the normal endings of the words *tierra* (earth) and *luna* (moon) to make them unusual masculine nouns. The word *sol* is already a masculine noun in Spanish.

tombal years, infinitary liters   The last two lines went through several changes. Vallejo at first wrote:

> port years, infinitary liters,
> ink, pen, and pens

He then crossed out "pens," and wrote "adobes"; then he crossed out "adobes," and wrote "bricks and spectacles," to finally cross out "spectacles" and write "forgiveness."

"*The peace, the wausp, the shoe heel, the slopes* . . ."   (page 461)

wausp   The Spanish word *avispa* (wasp) appears to have been intentionally misspelled as *abispa,* once again a distortion that registers visually but not as sound. The point of this may be, in Vallejo's mind, to point up the arbitrariness of spelling in writing what is heard—and too, perhaps, to reinforce a feeling that language itself is highly unstable, especially in charged meditation, and may, like Dalí's melting watches, give way at any moment.

"Racked, Solomonic, decent . . ." (page 463)

decent   Instead of *decente*, Vallejo originally wrote *impelente* (impelling).

"Well? Does the pallid metalloid heal you?" (page 465)

your soul bends passionately to see you   This line and the following one were originally:

> your soul bends passionately to the bone
> of iron on which your temple marks time.

"From sheer heat I am cold . . ." (page 467)

and the voice plays its caterpillar   This line originally read:

> inexistent, with its soul,

"Confidence in glasses, not in the eye . . ." (page 469)

not   Vallejo puts an accent mark over the "o" in *no* in lines 1, 3, and 5. We have italicized the corresponding words in English.

"Speaking of kindling . . ." (page 471)

TITLE   In many editions of Vallejo's poetry, this poem is entitled "Terremoto" (Earthquake). On the facsimile page of the Moncloa edition, however, "Terremoto" is handwritten a couple of lines below the poem and underlined. The RGV edition reproduces this presentation.

Hermeregildo   Hermeregildo might be a misspelling of the Visigoth Saint Hermenegildo (A.D. 564–586), and Atanacios a misspelling of the Father of the Church Saint Atanasio (A.D. 295–373). Given the presence of the words *crown* and *kingdom* in the poem, Luis and Isabel may be monarchs. There is more conjecture about these figures in the RGV edition, pp. 621–22.

"Mocked, acclimated to goodness . . ." (page 473)

hurent   the Spanish *urente* appears to be intentionally misspelled as *hurente*. Vallejo used the word, spelled conventionally, in *Trilce* XVII.

to groan with the whole ax   This phrase originally read:

> or to delouse oneself

leap from the flank   This line and the following one originally read:

> leap from the margin,
> from the daily margin of my mule that walks;

"Alfonso: you are looking at me . . ." (page 475)

your last act's turn on the wire   The entire line originally read:

> and on the wire your last act to dawn,

du vin, du lait, comptant les sous   "wine, milk, counting the pennies."

Alfonso   Alfonso de Silva was a Peruvian musician whom Vallejo met in Paris in 1923. Along with this extraordinary elegy, Vallejo appears to have written a second poem referring to the death of Silva, "Piensan los viejos asnos" (Old Asses Thinking).

beloved being   The Spanish *amado sér* (beloved being) and *amado estar* (beloved to be) cannot be fully translated (without interpretation, which would distort the meaning of the original), since *ser* ("to be," as a verb) is not the same thing as *estar* ("to be," as a verb). If the two verbs are matched, the meaning distinction in English is more or less "to be" versus "to exist," since *ser* is less time-bound and temporary than *estar*. However, Vallejo has turned *ser* into a noun by placing an accent over the "e," and in doing so seems to be stressing that which is or is idealized to always be, versus that which has potential to be. To translate *estar* here as "existence" would be to lose the noun-verb relationship clearly established in Vallejo's handling of the Spanish. Notice that the "double tomb" referred to in line 34 is merely a "tomb" with Silva's "being," but a "mahogany one" with his "to be," which emphasizes the abstractness associated with *sér* and the materiality associated with *estar*.

boîte de nuit   French for "cabaret" here.

in the opening of the double tomb   This line originally read:

> in the opening of that horrible tomb without a corpse,

Stumble between Two Stars   (page 479)

the one who clothes a door   Vallejo apparently intentionally misspelled *coge* (closes) as *coje*.

Farewell Remembering a Good-bye   (page 483)

and, a last glass of smoke   This line and the following one originally read:

> and, a last glass of blood, on its dramatic role,
> there is, and until the end, the practical dream of the soul

"Chances are, I'm another . . ."   (page 485)

But somebody else's sweat   This line originally read:

> But somebody else's sweat, but my metaphysical serum

Wedding March   (page 489)

TITLE   This sonnet was originally called "Batallón de dioses" (Battalion of Gods). A second title, handwritten, was also rejected: "Séquito y epitalamio" (Retinue and Epithalamion).

I will ignite, my ant will ignite   The last two tercets originally read:

> I will ignite, my ant will ignite,
> my key will ignite, my scrape
> in which the uneven cry won its cause.
>
> Then, making from the atom a wheat spike,
> I will ignite my sickles at her base
> and the battalion will say: Go on! Let him go on!

Intensity and Height   (page 495)

coughv   The Spanish *toz* appears to be a neologism, combining *tos* (cough) with *voz* (voice).

Guitar   (page 497)

and the mendacious eighth   This line and the one following it (crossed out and not reworked) originally read:

> and the mendacious eighth, suffers from an algebra
> more mendacious, more base, more metal.

Added by hand to this crossed-out seventh line (and then also crossed out) was:

> rope, cobra and boa.

and to be here   This entire line originally read:

> and to be here, between two treacherous days?

pintle   We have been unable to find the word *poña* in any Spanish dictionary. According to Barcia, the word exists in the Spanish Galician language and was perhaps used as a euphemism by Vallejo's grandfathers. Its equivalence in Spanish is *porra*, which literally means a "strong stick" but figuratively, and when spoken as an exclamation, is a polite euphemism for *polla* (cock, slang for penis). *Mala poña* also suggests a parallelism with common Spanish expressions like *mala roña* (awful mange) and *mala saña* (terrible hatred). For the 1978 edition of *The Complete Posthumous Poetry*, Barcia and I decided on "boner" as a translation, but today this strikes me as too direct and not obscure enough. So I have chosen *pintle*, literally, a "pivot pin," which is also obsolete and vulgar slang for *penis*. The speaker in this stanza seems to have been responding to sexual frustration with considerable ambivalence, so I hope that the play on "hard left" *(zurdazo)*—to be left with an erection as well as to be hit with a left-handed blow—in the following line will help reinforce Vallejo's meaning in English.

crying the days and singing the months   after this line, the last one in the poem, Vallejo originally wrote:

> and added to the females of the dead.

"Hear your mass, your comet . . ."   (page 499)

Hear your mass   The first two lines originally read:

> Hear your finger, listen to it: don't moan
> through your hand;

in the double-quick step of a skeleton   This line originally read:

> carmine being, a being in the double-quick step of a skeleton.

"What's got into me . . ."   (page 501)

sob earth and hang the horizon   This line and the rest of the poem originally read:

> sob earth and excel in Physics?
>
> What's gotten into me, that I cry and do not cry,
> that I laugh and do not laugh?
>
> Pity for me! pity for you! pity for him!

Anniversary   (page 503)

one   Refers to the number here, not a person.

and what a gathering of silly friends This line and the following one originally read:

> and what a Great Charmer
> and what a nest of tigers in the lamp!

Two Yearning Children (page 509)

No. Their ankles have no size Vallejo's original first stanza read:

> No. The cock's aggressive jaw
> has no size
> nor is it sharpened on its ankle; it is not its toothed
> spur, that jabs their two cheeks.
> It's just life, with robe and yoke.

No. Their guffaw has no plural This line originally read:

> No. Their erectile exodus has no plural,

I know it, I intuit it This entire line and the two following it originally read:

> I know it, I intuit it a Cartesian,
> moribund, alive, in short, magnificent.
> Nothing is over the capote of the inkwell,

a hell of a tough thing A Peruvianism, based on *cosa bravísima* (literally, "a very wild thing").

abstract reach, fortunate, in fact This entire line and the two following it originally read:

> abstract reach, fortunate and anatomical, nevertheless,
> glacial and snatched away, from the flame;
> motor of the depth, restrainer of form.

The Nine Monsters (page 513)

AND The Spanish *I* with which the poem opens, appears to be an intentional misspelling of *Y* (And). The two letters are pronounced the same way in Spanish. After this line, Vallejo originally wrote the following line, then crossed it out:

> I have already said this to Doña Genoveva,

its own mud and its own solid cloud The typewritten version ends here and is dated "3 Nov. 1937." The rest of the poem is handwritten and was added after this date (which was then crossed out).

and this ear sounds nine strokes Beginning with this line, the number *nine* is repeated six times in this and the next five lines. Originally, Vallejo used *seven* in each place.

arduent The Spanish *ardio* appears to be a metaplasm derived from *ardiente* (ardent) and *arduo* (arduous). It is possible that the word *ardido* (intrepid, angry) also figures into the construction. It is also possible that Vallejo meant *arido* (arid).

"A man walks by with a baguette . . ." (page 517)

Am I going to write, after that, about my double? This line originally read:

> Am I going to write, after that, of the deep Self?

Will it ever be possible to allude to the deep Self? This line originally read:

> Will it ever be possible to allude to the durable Self?

the non-self   It would be possible to translate Vallejo's *Yo* (line 10) and *yó* (in this line) as "Ego" and "ego." Since Vallejo criticizes psychoanalysis in line 4, I have not chosen to use these terms.

"Today a splinter has gotten into her . . ."   (page 519)

afflixion   An intentional misspelling of *aflicción* (affliction), possibly to evoke *crucifixion*. This misspelling is repeated in line 32.

the smoke of her dogma   Instead of *humareda* (a great deal of smoke), Vallejo wrote *humillo* (a thin smoke or vapor) in the original version. To avoid having to write "a great deal of smoke" in English, we have translated *humareda* as "smoke" and *salió* (came out) as "poured out."

Immensity pursues her   This line originally read:

> Immensity pillages her

"There are days, there comes to me . . ."   (page 521)

to wash the cripple's foot   After this line, the following one has been crossed out:

> the foot that he lacks,

to help whoever smiles laugh   After this line, the following one has been crossed out:

> to help the elderly ones chew,

Clapping and Guitar   (page 525)

teneblearic   See note on *Trilce* XI.

The Soul That Suffered from Being Its Body   (page 529)

diaphanous   The word *diáfano* replaced *carbon* in the line.

miserable ape   After this line, the following two originally read:

> barefoot, ashen cock; Darwin's little man,
> bailiff who urinates on me, most atrocious microbe.

you question your navel   This line was originally a little different from the final version and was followed by two lines later crossed out:

> and you question your navel valiantly:
> where? how?
> and your penis; with impetuosity: for how long?

"He who will come has just passed . . ."   (page 535)

afflixion   The Spanish *aflixión* is an intentional misspelling of *aflicción* (affliction), possibly to evoke the word *crucifixion*.

Has just passed without having come   After this last line in the final version, Vallejo had originally written two more lines, which were crossed out:

> he will not forget me, in the past, when he returns,
> to remember me, in the future, when he parts.

"Were the evil one to come . . ."   (page 537)

Were snow to be in excess   This line originally read:

> Were the notion of fire to lack snow,

Were dung to lack an excavation nearby This line originally read:

> Were two to lack eleven for thirteen,

and the sky an atmosphere This line originally read:

> and the difficult an easy, and iron gold . . .

with what to be poor The original version of this line was corrected and the one following it crossed out:

> with what to be poor, if I have nothing?
> and furthermore, with whom?

I have no mouth After this line, the last one in the final version, the poem originally ended with:

> I'm not exaggerating.

"Let the millionaire walk naked . . ." (page 539)

stark naked In Spanish *en pelo* (bareback) is normally used to describe riding a horse bareback. In Peru, when used in reference to a person, it suggests stark nakedness.

deepage The Spanish *hondor* is a neologism, based on *hondo* (deep) or *hondura* (depth). The "r" appears to have been added in the same spirit that *negro* (black) has been transformed into *negror* (blackness). Since the addition of *-ness* to *deep* would not result in a neologism, I have taken a different route.

"Contrary to the mountain birds . . ." (page 543)

metalous The Spanish *metaloso* appears to be a neologism, constructed in the same way that *pilar/pilaroso* is.

by sheer humbleness the Great was born This line originally read:

> half humble all of the Great was born;

what is taking place in our epoch After this line to the end of the stanza, the original typewritten version reads:

> in the world; Walt Whitman was almost completely right.
> Walt Whitman had the softest of chests and used
> to breathe and no one knows what he was up to when he was sobbing in his
>   dining room;
> in my opinion, he could not count beyond one hundred and thirty,
> when trying to reach five hundred; it is probable.

in my male belly strangely After this line, the following one was crossed out:

> Sad is the cause; the end, even happier.

"Something identifies you with the one . . ." (page 551)

The whole social mechanism After this sentence, the following one was crossed out:

> That is why I lock myself, at times, in my hotel, to kill my corpse and to hold a
> wake over it.

The date of this poem is in brackets, since no date is typed on the worksheet. On the basis of typewriter comparisons, Larrea dates it in the later part of 1937. The November 24, 1937, date appeared in the first edition of *Poemas humanos*.

"In short, I have nothing with which to express . . ."   (page 553)

my life, except my death   After this line, the following second line was crossed out:

In short, I cure death with the sores of life.

"A little more calm . . ."   (page 555)

González Vigil conjectures that this poem is addressed to militant communists.

how to contain your volume without running   This line originally read:

how to contain your mental volume without grieving.

Sermon on Death   (page 563)

my potato and my flesh   This line originally read:

And my potato and my flesh and my contradiction worthy of opprobrium?

wolvum   The Spanish *lovo* (which plays off *loco*, "crazy") appears to be an intentional misspelling of *lobo* (wolf), a usage that González Vigil understands as a way to link the word to *ovo* (egg, or ovum). I agree and have tried to approximate this construction in English.

cognitive, auriferous   In place of *aurífero* (auriferous) Vallejo had originally written *elíptico* (elliptical). In the same line, *brazudo* (thick-armed), deriving from *brazo* (arm), is given an *-udo* suffix, an augmentative, suggesting big or strong arms.

SPAIN, TAKE THIS CUP FROM ME

The first edition of *Poemas humanos* (privately published by Georgette de Vallejo and coedited with her friend the historian Raúl Porras Barrenechea in 1939, in Paris) seemed to be without any conscious order except for the last fifteen poems entitled *España, aparta de mí este cáliz*. It is now known that although Vallejo worked feverishly on his poetry during the last months of his life, the only final draft he was able to complete was the full text of *España, aparta de mí este cáliz*, a copy of which was sent to Spain for publication. The edition was to be under the care of the Spanish poet Emilio Prados and published by a cultural unit attached to the Loyalist army at the Aragon front. The book was printed in September 1938 but could not be bound and distributed, and only a single copy survived the defeat of the Spanish Republic a few months later. On February 9, 1940, *España, aparta de mí este cáliz* was published in Mexico, by Editorial Séneca, under the care of the same Emilio Prados, with some preliminary words by Juan Larrea entitled "Profecía de América" and a portrait in ink of Vallejo by Picasso.

As with *Human Poems*, the translation of *Spain, Take This Cup from Me* is a significantly revised version of what José Rubia Barcia and I presented in the 1978 *Complete Posthumous Poetry*.

In *España*, two poems seemed more impressive before Vallejo's handwritten corrections were made; I present these pieces in a translation based on the uncorrected typescript in the notes that follow. Also in regard to *España*, I have translated, as an appendix to these notes, one sequence of eight Roman-numeraled poems (I–VIII) that were finally distributed throughout the manuscript in a different order, with some of the best writing eliminated (section II was completely suppressed, as was nearly half of III, and a half-dozen lines of IV, V, and VII). I feel that the essence of this book is in these eight sections.

I / Hymn to the Volunteers for the Republic   (page 569)

civilian-fighter   The Spanish *miliciano* literally means "militiaman." Because of current American connotations of this word, we have decided that "civilian-fighter" conveys more accurately the meaning that *miliciano* acquired during the Spanish Civil War.

since your long ecstatic moment . . . double-edged speed   Here Vallejo fully opens himself to the conflict, and thus to death, envisioning this act as a torero working against a bull's "double-edged speed." His "costumed in greatness" evokes the bullfighter's garb, the *traje de luces*. The last of these three lines originally read:

> my tininess in the form of smoke from a fire.

biennial   The biennial referred to here is the period 1934–1936, called *el bienio negro* (the black biennial), that preceded the war.

Calderón   Pedro Calderón de la Barca (1600–1681), famous Spanish playwright, author of *La vida es sueño (Life Is a Dream)*. Lines 42 through 52 are an extraordinary weave of great Spanish figures of the past and contemporary war heroes and heroines.

Coll   Antonio Coll, a popular hero during the war. He appears to have been the first, on foot, to knock out Italian tanks with homemade hand grenades.

Quevedo   Francisco de Quevedo (1580–1645), famous satirist, perhaps the Spanish poet most admired by Vallejo.

Cajal   Santiago Ramón y Cajal (1852–1934), famous histologist who shared the Nobel Prize for medicine in 1906. He specialized in the microscopic study of cells in the nervous system.

Teresa   Teresa de Jesús (1515–1582), famous writer and mystic, to whom is attributed the sonnet that begins: "I die because I am not dying."

Lina Odena   Popular heroine who died fighting Fascism on the southern front.

Abyssinian lion   An allusion to the Abyssinian "negus," or "Lion of Judea," exiled by Mussolini's invading forces. The Italians fought on both sides during the Spanish Civil War.

ferule   The word *férula*, like *pecho*, seems to have had a special significance for Vallejo. Unlike *rod*, it is not commonly used, so once again we have not interpreted it. The word comes from the giant fennel stalks traditionally used for punishing schoolboys. Vallejo uses the word several times in *Spain, Take This Cup from Me*.

II / Battles   (page 579)

TITLE   The original title was "Batallas de España" ("Battles in Spain"), followed by the Roman numeral I. Later sections of this poem have additional crossed-out Roman numerals, and several later poems in the final *Spain* sequence also have crossed-out Roman numerals, which have been changed by hand. It appears that Vallejo originally intended an eight-section poem called "Battles in Spain," some of which was crossed out and all of which was reorganized in the construction of the final version. The original "Battles in Spain" can be reconstructed from the facsimile, and since it is an excellent poem in itself, and contains considerable first-rate crossed-out material, we have translated it and, as mentioned above, will present it at the end of these notes.

Estremadura   The names Extremadura and Extremeño are misspelled in Spanish throughout the poem, written as Estremadura and Estremeño. Extremadura, the western region of Spain, is known for its poverty and absentee landowners. The first important battle of the war took place there. The region was finally overrun by colonial Moorish troops brought to Spain to fight with the Fascist rebels.

under your foot I hear the smoke of the wolf   The line originally read:

> I hear under your foot the smoke of the human wolf,

the smoke of the species   The line originally read:

> the smoke of the evolution of the species,

and dead blood from living blood   The line originally read:

> and living blood from dead blood!

This line was followed by two later omitted lines, which read:

> The blood has left me; the smoke
> has left me listening to my jaws.

for whom life killed you and death gave birth to you   The line originally read:

> for whom death killed you and life gave birth to you

how you keep plowing our chests!   The line originally read:

> how you keep plowing with your cross in our chests!

Estremanian bent on elbow   After this line, the following one was crossed out:

> to listen to the dying die

and the very sky itself   After this line, the following three lines were crossed out:

> That is why, Estremanian man, you have fallen,
> you have cleaned yourself up
> and you have ended up dying from hope!

The part of the poem originally under Roman numeral I ended here. The following thirty-two lines made up what was originally Section II of "Battles in Spain":

> The bony darkness presses on, sketches moral cheekbones,
> the gas of the armored train, the gas of the last ankle,
> the cure of evil, the narrow excavation of the soul.
> A yellow tinkling, blow of a usual finger in full tiger,
> those of Irún, when two steps from death,
> the testicle dies, behind, on its pale ground!
> A yellow tinkling, under the smell of a human
> tooth, when metal ends up being metal!
>
> Wave of the Bidasoa,
> river to river with the sky, at the height of the dust,
> and river to river with the earth, at the height of the inferno!
> A toil that they had tackled on crutches,
> falling down, falling;

narrow Irún behind an emaciated immensity,
when the imagined bone is made of bone!

A battle in which all had died
and all had fought
and in which all the sorrows leave wedges,
all the sorrows, handles,
all the sorrows, always wedge and handle!
A battle in which all had triumphed
and all had fought,
and in which all the trees left one leaf,
and man, not a single flower, and one root!

Cheekbones! And they are moral cheekbones,
those of Irún, where the forehead went to sleep
and dreamt that it was a forehead in both faculties . . .
And the blow of a usual finger in full tiger,
the one at Irún, where the sense of smell sketched a noise of eyes
and where the tooth had slept
its tranquil geological dream . . .

Terrestrial and oceanic, infinite Irún!

The part of the poem originally under Roman numeral II ended here. Irún, a Basque town
very close to the French-Spanish border, was occupied by Fascist troops on September 5,
1936, after being ferociously attacked by land, sea, and air. The Bidasoa is a river in Basque
country, a part of the French-Spanish border. The following six lines made up what was orig-
inally the beginning of Section III of "Battles in Spain":

Loss of Toledo
due to rifles loaded with affectionate bullets!
Loss of the cause of death!
Loss in the Castilian language: or bullfighting!
And a triumphal loss, drum and a half, delirious!
Loss of the Spanish loss!

Retreating from Talavera

This last line, with the addition of an initial "Then," became the first line of what is now the
fourth stanza of "Battles," or line 43.

Talavera   Talavera de la Reina, a town in the province of Toledo, taken by Fascist troops on
their way to Madrid on September 5, 1936.

their loss in their backs   This line originally read:

dying, their kneecaps on their shoulders and their loss in their backs

loving unwillingly   This line originally read:

loving unwillingly, they forced Toledo to commit suicide,

in a Spanish way   Originally, this line ended with a period and the next two lines, later
crossed out, followed:

And on the succeeding day, the third day,
as the African hoofs resounded in the sad narrow alleys,

where to plant their pocket-size olive tree   After this line, the following ten lines were crossed out:

> What noon that noon between two afternoons! Something to be seen! . . .
> Say it, Alcántara bridge,
> you say it better,
> better than the water
> which flows sobbing on its way back!
> Sun and shadow of Spain over the world!
> It hurts, truly, that noon,
> the exact size of a suicide; and remembering it,
> no one any longer,
> no one lies down outside his body . . .

(In the sixth line of this deleted material, "Toledo" was substituted for "Spain" at one point.)

But from here   This line and the two following it originally read:

> From here, from this point,
> from the point of this rectilinear line,
> from the good to which the satanic good flows,

Guernica   Immortalized by Picasso's famous painting, the town of Guernica was sacred to the Basque people. German bombers, authorized by Franco, destroyed it completely on April 26, 1937, even though it had no military value.

Tacit defenders of Guernica   In place of this line and the three following it, the end of this stanza originally read:

> Combat of Guernica in honor
> of the bull and his pale animal: man!
>
> From here, as I repeat,
> from this viewpoint,
> the defenders of Guernica can be perfectly seen!
> weak ones, offended ones,
> rising up, growing up, filling up the world with powerful weak ones!

the cemeteries were bombed   This line and the six following it originally were eight and read:

> The cemeteries were bombed, and another combat
> took place with cadavers against cadavers:
> combat of the dead dead who attacked
> the immortal dead
> with vigilant bones and eternal shoulder, with their tombs.
> The immortal dead, upon feeling, upon seeing
> how low the evil, then, aie!
> completed their unconcluded anguish,

simple, just, collective   This line was originally different and was followed by five lines later crossed out:

> simple and one, collective and one!
>
> Composition and strength of the fistful of nothingness, as they say,
> the whole living death defended life,

fighting for the whole, which is dialectical
and for the butterfly, that seeks us,
for the free sky and the free chain! . . .

Málaga without father or mother   This long stanza, a poem in its own right, was originally not part of "Battles in Spain"; it appears to have been added later when Vallejo was organizing *Spain, Take This Cup from Me*. Málaga was taken by the Italian General Roatta's troops on February 8, 1937. Thousands of the city's inhabitants fled along the coast toward Almería and were slaughtered in great numbers by German naval fire and German and Italian bombers.

Literal and malagueñan Málaga   This line originally read:

Literal Málaga, separation of posthumous grains of sand,

Given Málaga's proximity to the shore (and the references to sea and foam in the poem), there is probably, in the word *literal*, a pun on *litoral* (littoral).

III / "He used to write with his big finger . . ."   (page 587)
This poem was originally VI in "Battles in Spain." It was later taken out of that sequence and turned into III in *Spain, Take This Cup from Me*.

Pedro Rojas   Appears to be a fictitious character, a symbol of the humblest and most oppressed human beings. He has just learned to write a little, and hearing *vivan* as *viban* and *avisa* as *abisa*, misspells the words. We pick up the misspellings by using "combanions" in place of "companions."

he was killed at the base of his big finger!   This line originally was two lines:

he was killed; grow hearing his look; pass on!
stop, looking at his ears; pass on!

and fought with his cells   Originally this and the next line read:

and fought against so many sad people as they were
his cells, his nos, his yets, his hungers, his pieces.

and when he was already close to everything   After this line, the three following it were crossed out:

Pedro also used
to die at the foot of time and without lying down, a slave;
his corpse was full of world.

(This third line was later added at the end of the final version.)

IV / "The beggars fight for Spain . . ."   (page 591)
This poem was originally section VII of "Battles in Spain."

The mendicants fight satanically   This line and the two following it were originally four lines:

The mendicants fight satanically begging
God, so that the poor win the battle
of Santander, the combat in which no longer is anyone defeated,
the campaign of the wheat and its symbols.

at the foot of the individual   This line originally read:

at the foot of the individual, on the mountain at the heart's peak

killing by merely being beggars This line was originally followed by a crossed-out line that read:

> The beggars fight for the poor!

Pleas of the infantry This line originally read:

> Troops of pleas on foot,

crumb under belt This line was originally followed by a crossed-out line that read:

> functional attack behind their chests

V / *"There she goes! . . ."* (page 593)

At the end of this poem, a few spaces below it, *Imagen española de la muerte* (Spanish image of death) is written in by hand. Because of specific revisions and additions to it, we suspect that this poem was written earlier than most of the Spanish Civil War poems and/or at one point intended for inclusion in *Poemas humanos*. In its original typed version, the poem is not connected to the war itself and, in our opinion, is a stronger piece than it finally became as Vallejo worked it into the fabric of the present book. Instead of indicating changes line by line, in this case we would like to present a translation of the poem based on the original version:

> There she goes! Call her! It's her side!
> There goes Death with her carbonic acid declivity,
> her accordion steps, her curse word,
> her meter of cloth that I've mentioned to you,
> her gram of that weight I've kept to myself . . . they're the ones!
>
> Call her! Hurry! She is searching for me,
> since she well knows where I defeat her,
> what my great cunning is, my deceptive laws, my terrible codes.
> Call her! For Death walks exactly like a man,
> she leans on that arm which entwines our feet
> when we sleep
> and she stops at the elastic gates of dream.
>
> She shouted! She shouted! She shouted her born, sensorial shout!
> Would that she shouted from shame, from seeing how she's fallen among the plants,
> from seeing how she withdraws from the beasts,
> from hearing how we say: "It's Death!"
> From wounding our greatest interests!
>
> (Because her liver produces the drop that I've mentioned,
> because she eats the soul of our neighbor)
>
> Call her! We must follow her
> to her matriarchy and to her windows,
> for Death is a being been by force,
> whose beginning and end I carry feverishly engraved in my meatus, the glans penis,
> however much she would run the normal risk
> that you know
> and though she would pretend to pretend to ignore me.
>
> Call her! She is not a being,
> but, barely, a laconic event;

instead her way aims,
aims at simple tumult, without orbits or joyous canticles;
instead her audacious time aims at an imprecise centime
and her deaf carats, at despotic applause.
Call her, for by calling her with fury, with figures,
you help her drag her rapid sketch,
as, at times,
at times global, enigmatic fractions hurt,
as, at times, I touch myself and don't feel myself.

Call her! Hurry! She is searching for me,
with her side of road acid,
her accordion steps, her curse word.
Call her! The thread and the fin in which I cry for her must not be lost.
From her smell up, woe is my dust!
From her pus up, woe is my ferule!
From her magnet down, woe is my chemistry!

In the above version, there are a few textual variations:

with her carbonic acid declivity   this phrase was crossed out in favor of "with her ink and inkwell," which was crossed out in favor of "through Teruel," which led to the final "through Irún."

the glans penis   The way in which this phrase was added, by hand, to the line indicates that perhaps it was originally not a correction for "my meatus," but rather an extension of it.

VI / *Cortege after the Capture of Bilbao*   (page 597)

TITLE   Bilbao, the greatest industrial city in northern Basque Spain, fell into Fascist hands on June 18, 1937.

Loyalist   To translate *republicana* here as "Republican" would be misleading. "Loyalist" conveys the idea of one loyal to the existing government, the Spanish Republic.

VII / *"For several days the air, companions . . ."*   (page 599)

Gijón   An industrial town in the northern province of Asturias, which withstood Fascist attack for a long time before being evacuated on October 21, 1937.

for very many Spains ay! Gijón   This line was originally followed by two lines, which were later crossed out:

> For several days Spain
> ay! Spain looks like Spain forever.

VIII / *"Back here . . ."*   (page 601)

Back here   The first stanza originally read:

> Back here,
> Ramón Collar,
> your capacity tinged with foolishness
> continues, from rope to rope,
> while you visit, out there, your seven swords,
> standing, on the funereal glass of January.

Ramón Collar   Pronounced Co-yár, probably a fictitious name, symbolizing a peasant-soldier in the defense of Madrid.

Ramón of sorrow   This line originally read:

> Ramón of sorrow and with a Collar of abuses

Back here, Ramón Collar   Originally this line and the last one were three and read:

> Back here, Ramón Collar,
> your work has only produced shadow!
> Greetings, Ramón Collar, and write to us!

IX / *Short Prayer for a Loyalist Hero*   (page 605)

a book was sprouting   This line was originally followed by a line that was later crossed out:

> a book with the quality of deep fiber or filament.

The hero was carried off   This line originally read:

> The hero was carried off, knees extended over his name

navehalls   As it did in "Epistle to the Passersby," *hombligo* appears to be an intentional misspelling of *ombligo* (navel).

Poetry of the royal purple cheekbone   This third stanza originally read:

> Poetry of the royal purple cheekbone, between saying it
> and not saying it, poetry in the moral map that had accompanied
> his heart; light membranes of the human stone:
> the Christianity, the works, the great theme.
> The book remained and that is all;
> there are no insects in the tomb
> and at the edge of his sleeve the air remained soaking
> and becoming gigantic, infinite.

X / *Winter during the Battle for Teruel*   (page 607)

TITLE   The original title, "After the Battle" ("Después de la batalla"), was changed by hand to its final state. Previous to the addition of "Teruel," "Madrid" was written in and then crossed out in favor of "Teruel." The battle for Teruel took place in terrible weather (the temperature dropped below minus-20 degrees at times) from December 15, 1937, to February 22, 1938. It was perhaps the most ferocious battle of the war.

the serene branch of Chemistry   Following this line, there appears, crossed out:

> with the swift precision of a verdict

you see it, for you touched your testicles   Originally this line ended with a comma and was followed by:

> while eating a moaning oyster.

XII / *Mass*   (page 611)

After the second repetition of the refrain line ("But the corpse, alas! kept on dying"), at the end of the second stanza, the following three lines were crossed out:

> Four moved near the dead one:
> "To no longer be at your side, so you won't leave!"
> But the corpse, alas! kept on dying.

XIII / *Funereal Drumroll for the Ruins of Durango*   (page 613)

TITLE   Durango, a town in the Basque province of Viscaya, was destroyed by repeated German air raids, at almost the same time that Guernica was, on April 26, 1937. In the title, the word *drumroll* was originally *hymn*. Since the original version of this poem is quite different from the final one (and in our opinion is a stronger poem), we have decided to print the original in its entirety:

> Father dust who rises from Spain,
> God save, liberate and crown you,
> father dust who rises from the serf.
>
> Father dust who art in heaven,
> God save you, shoe and offer you a throne,
> father dust who art in the soul.
>
> Father dust who lives off the furrow,
> God save you, clothe and undress you,
> father dust who lives off men.
>
> Father dust who dresses the pariah,
> God save you, escort and shelter you,
> father dust who art in jail.
>
> Father dust in whom the hungry man ends,
> God save and return you to earth,
> father dust who haloes the poor.
>
> Father dust who flies on lances,
> God save you, hurt you and bury you,
> father dust who descends from the soul.
>
> Father dust who has so much gold,
> God save you, scatter you and give you form,
> father dust who has so much soul.
>
> Father dust who art in human temples,
> God save you and decorate your atoms,
> father dust who art in our steps.
>
> Father dust who marches in smoke,
> God save you and encircle you with gods,
> father dust who marches burning.
>
> Father dust who goes into the future,
> God save you, guide you and give you wings,
> father dust that blood has made you.
>
> Father dust who art on earth,
> God save you and nourish you with heaven,
> father dust who art in the wheat spike.
>
> Father dust who suffers from dust,
> God save you, nail and unnail you,
> father dust who was a hammer.

(In revising this poem, Vallejo crossed out stanzas three and eight and completely altered the lines and order of the others.)

XIV / *"Beware, Spain, of your own Spain . . ."*   (page 615)

In the facsimiles, this poem appears to have originally been section VIII, the final section of "Battles in Spain." The number VIII was then crossed out and XIV written in by hand.

XV / *Spain, Take This Cup from Me*   (page 617)

TITLE   Taken from the words spoken by Jesus at Gethsemane: "My Father, if it be possible, let this cup pass away from me: nevertheless, not as I will, but as thou wilt" (Matthew 26: 39). We have not felt bound to copy the bibilical version of the phrase but have rendered it more actively. In the facsimile, a handwritten XIII is crossed out in favor of a handwritten XV.

children, what an age of concave temples   As in line 41, *seines* (temples) refers only to the human head. After this line, the following one was crossed out:

> what a wheat spike on the agricultural thumb!

if the sky fits between two terrestrial limbos   this line originally read:

> if the sky fits between terrestrial plates,

Appendix: BATTLES IN SPAIN

I

> Under your foot I hear the smoke of the human wolf,
> the smoke of the evolution of the species,
> the smoke of the child,
> the solidary smoke of two wheats,
> the smoke of Geneva, the smoke of Rome, the smoke of Berlin
> and that of Paris, and the smoke of your appendix
> and the smoke that comes out, finally, from the soul.
> Oh life! oh earth! oh Spain!
> Ounces of blood,
> meters of blood, liquids of blood,
> blood on horseback, on foot, mural, without diameter,
> blood four by four, blood of water
> and living blood from dead blood.
> The blood has left me: the smoke
> has left me listening to my jaws.
>
> Estremañian, oh to still be that man
> for whom death killed you and life gave birth to you
> and to stay on only to see you like this, from this wolf,
> how you keep plowing with your cross in our chests!
> Estremañian, you know
> the secret in both voices, the popular and the tactile,

of the cereal: that nothing is as valuable as two wheats together!
Estremañian bent on elbow, picturing the soul in its retreat,
listening to the dying die
and bent on elbow to observe
the fitting of a life in a death!

Estremañian, and not to have land that would have
the weight of your plow, nor other world
than the color of your yoke between two epochs; not to have
the order of your posthumous herds!
Estremañian, you allowed me
to see you from my wolf, to endure,
to fight for everyone and to fight
so that man can become a man,
so that misters themselves can become men,
so that everyone can become a man, and so
that even animals can become men,
the horse, a man,
the reptile, a man,
the vulture, an honest man,
the fly, a man, and the olive tree, a man
and even the riverbank, a man
and the very sky itself, a whole little man!

That is why, Estremañian man, you have fallen,
you have cleaned yourself up
and you have ended up dying from hope!

II

The bony darkness presses on, sketches moral cheekbones,
the gas of the armored train, the gas of the last ankle,
the cure of evil, the narrow excavation of the soul.
A yellow tinkling, blow of a usual finger in full tiger,
those of Irún, when two steps from death,
the testicle dies, behind, on its pale ground!
A yellow tinkling, under the smell of a human
tooth, when metal ends up being metal!

Wave of the Bidasoa,
river to river with the sky, at the height of the dust,
and river to river with the earth, at the height of the inferno!
A toil that they had tackled on crutches,
falling down, falling;
narrow Irún behind an emaciated immensity,
when the imagined bone is made of bone!

A battle in which all had died
and all had fought
and in which all the sorrows leave wedges,
all the sorrows, handles,
all the sorrows, always wedge and handle!
A battle in which all had triumphed
and all had fought,
and in which all the trees left one leaf,
and man, not a single flower, and one root!

Cheekbones! And they are moral cheekbones
those of Irún, where the forehead went to sleep
and dreamt that it was a forehead in both faculties!
And the blow of a usual finger in full tiger,
the one at Irún, where the sense of smell sketched a noise of eyes
and where the tooth had slept
its tranquil geological dream . . .

Terrestrial and oceanic, infinite Irún!

III

Loss of Toledo
due to rifles loaded with affectionate bullets!
Loss of the cause of death!
Loss in the Castilian language: or bullfighting!
And a triumphal loss, drum and a half, delirious!
Loss of the Spanish loss!

Retreating from Talavera,
in groups of one, armed with hunger, in masses of one,
armed with chest up to the forehead,
without airplanes, without war, without rancor,
dying, their kneecaps on their shoulders and their loss in their backs
and the gain
lower than lead, mortally wounded by honor,
crazed by dust, their arm on foot,
loving unwillingly, they forced Toledo to commit suicide,
conquering the whole earth in a Spanish way!

And on the succeeding day, the third day,
as the African hoofs resounded in the sad narrow alleys,
to retreat still, and not to know
where to put their Spain,
where to hide their global kiss,
where to plant their pocket-size olive tree!

What noon that noon between two afternoons! Something to be seen! . . .
Say it, Alcántara bridge,
you say it better,
better than the water
which flows sobbing on its way back!
Sun and shadow of Spain over the world!
It hurts, truly, that noon,
the exact size of a suicide; and remembering it,
no one any longer,
no one lies down outside his body . . .

IV

From here, from this point,
from the point of this rectilinear line,
from the good to which the satanic good flows,
the great battle of Guernica can be seen.
An a priori combat, unreckoned,
combat in peace, combat of weak souls
against weak bodies, combat in which the child strikes,
without anyone telling him to, below his atrocious diphthong
and beneath his most adequate diaper,
and in which a mother strikes with her scream, with the backside of a tear,
and in which the sick one strikes with his disease, with his pill and his son
and in which the old man strikes hard
with his white hair, his centuries and his staff
and in which the priest strikes with God!
Combat at Guernica in honor
of the bull and his pale animal: man!

From here, as I repeat,
from this viewpoint,
the defenders of Guernica can be perfectly seen,
weak ones, offended ones,
rising up, growing up, filling up the world with powerful weak ones!

V

The cemeteries were bombed, and another combat
took place with cadavers against cadavers:
combat of the dead dead who attacked
the immortal dead,
with vigilant bones and eternal shoulder, from their tombs.
The immortal dead, upon feeling, upon seeing
how low the evil, then, aie!

completed their unconcluded anguish,
they finished crying, finished
hoping, finished
aching, finished living,
finished, finally, being mortal!

And the gunpowder was, suddenly, gunpowder,
signs and seals crossing each other,
and before the explosion a step intervened,
and before the flight on all fours, another step
and before the apocalyptic sky, another step
and before the seven metals, unity,
simple and one, collective and one!

Composition and strength of the fistful of nothingness, as they say,
the whole living death defended life,
fighting for the whole, which is dialectical
and for the butterfly, that seeks us,
for the free sky and the free chain! . . .

VI

He used to write with his big finger in the air:
"Long live all combanions! Pedro Rojas,"
from Miranda de Ebro, father and man,
husband and man, railroad-worker and man,
father and more man, Pedro and his two deaths.

Wind paper, he was killed: pass on!
Flesh pen, he was killed: pass on!
Advise all combanions quick!

Stick on which they have hanged his log,
he was killed; grow hearing his look: pass on!
stop, looking at his ears; pass on!
He was killed at the base of his big finger!
They've killed in one blow, Pedro, Rojas!

Long live all combanions
written at the head of his air!
Let them live with this buzzard b in Pedro's
and in Rojas'
and in the hero's and in the martyr's guts!

Searching him, dead, they surprised
in his body a great body, for
the soul of the world,
and in his jacket a dead spoon.

Pedro too used to eat
among the creatures of his flesh, and used to clean off
the table and used to live, at times,
as a representative of everyone together,
and this spoon was in his jacket, all his life,
awake or else when he slept, always,
dead alive spoon, this one and its symbols.
Advise all combanions quick!
Long live all combanions at the base of this spoon forever!

He was killed, they forced him to die,
Pedro, Rojas, the worker, the man, the one
who was born such a wee baby, looking at the sky
and who afterwards grew up, blushed
and fought against so many sad people as they were
his cells, his nos, his yets, his hungers, his pieces.
He was killed softly
in his wife's hair, Juana Vásquez by name,
at the hour of fire, in the year of the gunshot
and when the poor man was in pursuit of himself.

Pedro also used
to die at the foot of time and without lying down, a slave;
his corpse was full of world.
Pedro Rojas, thus, after being dead,
got up, kissed his casket,
and cried for Spain
and again wrote with his finger in the air:
"Long live all combanions! Pedro Rojas."

VII
The beggars fight for Spain oh Marx! oh Hegel!
begging in Paris, in Rome, in Prague
and thus authenticating, with an imploring, Gothic hand,
the Apostles' feet, in London, in New York, in Mexico City.
The mendicants fight satanically begging
God, so that the poor win the battle
of Santander, the combat in which no longer is anyone defeated,
the campaign of the wheat, and its symbols.
They deliver themselves to
the old suffering, they glut their fury weeping social lead
at the foot of the individual, on the mountain at the heart's peak
and they attack with moans, because the beggars
kill at a distance merely from being.
The beggars fight for the poor!

Troops of pleas on foot,
in which the weapon pleads from the metal up,
and the wrath pleads, this side of the wrathful gunpowder.
Tacit squadrons which fire,
with mortal cadence, their gentleness,
from a doorway, from themselves, ay, from themselves.
Potential fighters
without socks when shoeing thunder,
satanic, numerical,
or on horseback on their titles of strength,
crumb under belt,
functional attack behind their chests,
double-caliber rifle: blood and blood.
The poet hails armed suffering!

VIII

Beware, Spain, of your own Spain!
Beware of the sickle without the hammer,
beware of the hammer without the sickle!
Beware of the victim in spite of himself,
of the hangman in spite of himself
and of the uncommitted in spite of himself!
Beware of the one who, before the cock crows,
will have denied you three times,
and the one who denied you, afterward, three times!
Beware of the skulls without tibias
and of the tibias without skulls!
Beware of the new powerful ones!
Beware of the one who eats your corpses,
of the one who devours your living dead!
Beware of the one hundred percent loyal!
Beware of the sky this side of the air
and beware of the air beyond the sky!
Beware of those who love you!
Beware of your heroes!
Beware of your dead!
Beware of the Republic!
Beware of the future! . . .

AFTERWORD: A TRANSLATION MEMOIR

For nearly fifty years, I have been translating the poetry of César Vallejo. His writing has become the keelson in the ship of poetry I have attempted to construct. Here I would like to offer an overview of my lifelong evolving relationship with Vallejo and with translation, and to evoke some of the experiences that have come out of it. Finally, I would like to say what this companionship has meant to me, as a poet and as a human being.

While I was a student at Indiana University in 1957, a painter friend, Bill Paden, gave me a copy of the New Directions 1944 *Latin American Poetry* anthology. I was particularly impressed with the poetry of Pablo Neruda and César Vallejo. While I was able to make sense of Neruda's Latin American Surrealism by comparing it to its French prototypes, Vallejo was something else: he had a unique imagination and a highly complicated style, and his images seemed to work on several levels. He wrote bitterly about Peruvian provincial life and passionately about the Spanish Civil War. I decided at that time to read Neruda first and, other than a few poems from his first book, hold off on Vallejo until later.

I then discovered that Ángel Flores had translated all of Neruda's *Residencia en la tierra,* and on comparing his versions with those of H. R. Hays and Dudley Fitts in the anthology, I was intrigued by the differences. Without knowing any Spanish, I began to tinker with the versions. Doing so got me to thinking about going to Mexico City, which was then featured in the literary news as a mecca for the Beats and their followers. At the beginning of the summer of 1959, with a pocket Spanish-English dictionary and two hundred dollars, I hitchhiked to Mexico. The following summer, in order to improve my Spanish, I returned to Mexico, rented a room in the back of a butcher's home in Chapala, and spent the summer reading Neruda's poetry, as well as writing most of the poems that were to appear in my first book, *Mexico & North,* in 1962.

In 1960 I edited three issues of the English Department–sponsored literary triquarterly, *Folio,* where I printed some Neruda translations I had done with friends in Mexico City, and four Vallejo versions, co-translated with another graduate student, Maureen Lahey. Discovering the poetry of Neruda and Vallejo made me realize that poetry was an international phenomenon and that North American poetry was but one part of it. As a young aspiring poet, I had a hunch that I would learn something about poetry by translating it that I would not learn solely from reading poetry written in English.

I finished a master's degree in 1961 and took a job with the University of

Maryland's Far Eastern Division, teaching literature to military personnel stationed in Japan, Taiwan, and Korea. Before leaving, almost as an afterthought, I packed the copy of *Poesía de America #5, Homenaje a César Vallejo* that I had found in a Mexico City bookstore.

The following year, my first wife, Barbara, and I moved to Kyoto on the advice of the poet Gary Snyder, who was studying Zen Buddhism there. For the next two years I studied and wrote, making a living by teaching English as a second language at various Japanese companies. In 1962, having completed a small collection of Neruda translations (published in San Francisco by George Hitchcock's Amber House Press as *Residence on Earth*), I decided to investigate the Vallejo poems in the Mexican journal.

The first poem I tried to read, from *Poemas humanos,* was "Me viene, hay días, una gana ubérrima, política . . ." It was as if a hand of wet sand had come out of the original and "quicked" me in—I was quicksanded, in over my head. Or was it a spar Vallejo threw me? In this poem, Vallejo was claiming that he desired to love, and that his desire for desire led him to imagine all sorts of "interhuman" acts, like kissing a singer's muffler, or kissing a deaf man on his cranial murmur. He wanted to help everyone achieve his goal, no matter what it was, even to help the killer kill— and he wanted to be good to himself in everything. These were thoughts that, had I had them myself, I would either have dismissed or so immediately repressed that they would have evaporated. But now I realized that there was a whole wailing cathedral of desires, half-desires, mad-desires, antidesires, all of which, in the Vallejo poem, seemed caught on the edge of no-desire. And if so, what brought about these bizarre desires? The need to flee his body? His inability to act on desire? A terrible need to intercede in everyone's acts? I did not know, but trying to read him made me feel that I was in the presence of a mile-thick spirit. So I kept at it.

Soon I decided that I should not just read the eighty-nine poems in *Poemas humanos,* but I should also try to translate them. To do that meant an awesome commitment of psyche as well as time. In committing myself to such a project, was I evading the hard work of trying to find my way in poetry of my own? Or could I think of working on Vallejo as a way of working on myself? Possibly. But much of what he wrote seemed obscure to me. Did that mean my Spanish was so inadequate that I simply could not make sense of Vallejo's language? Or was it a combination of those things, plus my having tapped into something that was coherent, and instructive, but at a level I had yet to plumb?

In the afternoon I would ride my motorcycle downtown and work on translations in the Yorunomado coffeeshop. I would always sit by the carp pond on the patio. There I discovered the following words of Vallejo: "And where is the other flank of this cry of pain if, to estimate it as a whole, it breaks now from the bed of a man?" In that line I saw Vallejo in a birth bed, not knowing how to give birth, an impression that led me to a whole other realization: that artistic bearing and fruition were physical as well as mental, a matter of one's total energy. Both in translating and in working on my own poems, I felt a terrific resistance, as if every attempt I made to advance was met by a force that pushed me back. It was as if through Vallejo I had made contact with a negative impaction in my being, a nebulous depth charge that I had been carrying around with me for many years. For most of 1963 and the first half of 1964, everything I saw and felt clustered around this feeling; it seemed to dwell in a phrase from the I Ching, "the darkening of the light," as well as in the Kyoto sky, gray and overcast, yet mysteriously luminous.

I also began to have violent and morbid fantasies that seemed provoked by the combination of translating and writing. More and more I felt that I was struggling with a man as well as a text, and that this struggle was a matter of my becoming or failing to become a poet. The man I was struggling with did not want his words changed from one language to another. I also realized that in working on Vallejo's *Poemas humanos* I had ceased to be what I was before coming to Kyoto, that I now had a glimpse of another life, a life I was to create for myself, and that this other man I was struggling with was also the old Clayton who was resisting change. The old Clayton wanted to continue living in his white Presbyterian world of "light" — where man is associated with day/clarity/good and woman with night/opaqueness/bad. The darkness that was beginning to spread through my sensibility could be viewed as the breaking up of the belief in male supremacy that had generated much of that "light."

In the last half of "The Book of Yorunomado," the only poem of my own I completed to any satisfaction while living in Japan, I envisioned myself as a kind of angel-less Jacob wrestling with a figure who possessed a language the meaning of which I was attempting to wrest away. I lose the struggle and find myself on a seppuku platform in medieval Japan, being condemned by Vallejo (now playing the role of a *karo*, or overlord) to disembowel myself. I do so, cutting my ties to the "given life" and releasing a visionary figure of the imagination, named Yorunomado (in honor of my working place), who had till that point been chained to an altar in my solar plexus. In early 1964, the fruit of my struggle with Vallejo was not a successful linguistic translation but an imaginative advance in which a third figure had emerged from my intercourse with the text. Yorunomado then became another guide in the ten-year process of developing a "creative life," recorded in my book-length poem, *Coils* (1973).

I was close to completing a first draft of *Human Poems* in March 1963 when I had a very strange experience. After translating all afternoon in the Yorunomado coffeeshop, I motorcycled over to the pottery manufacturer where I taught English conversation once a week. Whenever I had things to carry on the cycle, I would strap them with a bungee cord to the platform behind the seat. That evening when I left the company, I strapped on the poem-filled notebook, my dictionary, and a copy of the Spanish book. It was now dark, and the alley was poorly lit. I had gone a half-block when I heard a voice cry in Japanese: "Hey, you dropped something!" I stopped and swerved around to find the platform empty—even the bungee cord was gone! I retraced my path on foot—nothing. I looked for the person who had called out. No one was there. While I was walking around in the dark, a large skinny dog began to follow me. I was reminded of the Mexican pariah dogs, and that association gave an eerie identity to this dog. Was it Peruvian? Was it— Vallejo? I went back the next morning to search in daylight, and of course there was no trace of the notebook. So I had to start all over again.

If I had turned Vallejo into a challenging mentor from the past, I had also found a living mentor, as complicated in his own way as Vallejo himself: he was Cid Corman, a poet, editor (of *origin* magazine and books), and translator who had taken up residence in Kyoto. I began to visit him weekly, in the evening, at the Muse coffeeshop downtown. Corman, who was eleven years my senior, seemed to like me, but he did not like the kind of self-involved poetry that I was trying to write. Since, especially in *origin,* he presented an impressive vision of what poetry could be on an international scale, I found myself in the impossible situation of wanting to address the forces erupting in me and also wanting to write poems that might make their way into his magazine. Thus while testing myself against Vallejo's Spanish, I was also working with a Corman raven on my shoulder staring critically at what I was struggling to articulate. At times the tension between Vallejo and Corman was almost unbearable. These figures who were offering me their vision of the creative also seemed to be dragging me under. I was hearing things, having terrifying nightmares, and suffering unexplainable headaches.

In the following year I completed three more drafts of *Human Poems.* Cid went over the second and third drafts, and to him I owe a special debt, not only for the time he put in on the manuscript but for what I learned from him about the art of translation.

Before talking with Cid about translation, I had thought that the goal of a translating project was to take a literal draft and *interpret* everything that was not acceptable English. By interpret I mean: to monkey with words, phrases, punctuation, line breaks, even stanza breaks, turning the literal into something that was not an original poem in English but—and here is the rub—something that because of the liberties taken was also not faithful to the original itself. Ben Belitt's Neruda translations or Robert Lowell's *Imitations* come to mind as interpretative translations. Corman taught me to respect the original at every point, to check everything (including words I thought I knew), to research arcane and archaic words, and to invent English words for coined words—in other words, to aim for a translation that was absolutely accurate *and* up to the performance level of the original (at times, quite incompatible goals). I learned to keep a notebook of my thoughts and variations on what I was translating so that I could keep this material separate, for every translator has impulses to fill in, pad out, and make something "strong" that in a more literal mode would fall flat—in short, to *pump up* or *explain* a word instead of *translating* it. By reinterpreting, the translator implies that he knows more than the original text does, that, in effect, his mind is superior to its mind. The "native text" becomes raw material for the colonizer-translator to educate and reform.

During these years of undergoing a double apprenticeship—to poetry and to translation—I was so psychically opened up by Vallejo that I had to find ways to keep my fantasies out of the translation. One way was to redirect them into my poetry, as I did with "The Book of Yorunomado." While in Paris in 1973, I visited Vallejo's tomb in the Montparnasse cemetery and imagined my relationship to him and to his work in a poem, "At the Tomb of Vallejo." And on completing the revision of a translation of *Poemas humanos* in 1977, I developed a culminative fantasia on my years with this poet called "The Name Encanyoned River," a title based on a line that Vallejo had crossed out in one of these poems. Finally, beginning with the 1977 revision, I added detailed notes to my Vallejo collections, commenting on crossed-out material as well as arcane and coined words. Thus, I was able to excavate and employ the psychic turmoil of my Kyoto life, all the while keeping the translation of a body of work contoured with its own unadulterated chasms.

Poemas humanos is made up of poems left by Vallejo at the time of his death, in April 1938, in a heavily hand-corrected typescript. When his widow, Georgette, published them in 1939 there were many errors, and the poems were presented out of chronological order. These errors were repeated and amplified in subsequent editions, many of which were pirated because Georgette would not cooperate with publishers. By the spring of 1965, now back in Bloomington, I was working from four textually differing editions of *Poemas humanos*, having seen neither the first edition nor the worksheets.

Instead of shaping up as I worked along, the whole project was becoming a nightmare. Now I was having dreams in which Vallejo's corpse, wearing muddy shoes, was laid out in bed between Barbara and me. By this time I had gotten in touch with Georgette Vallejo and explained that I did not see how I could complete the translation effectively unless I came to Peru and examined the worksheets. I hired a lawyer to draw up a contract and mailed it to her, along with samples from my fourth draft. I received one reply from her in which she did not respond to any of my requests. But I was determined to go, and with Barbara several months pregnant, we left in August 1965, with just a few hundred dollars.

Once in Lima, we moved into a small apartment next to a grade school playground on Domingo Orue in Miraflores, the district where Georgette Vallejo also lived. Georgette was a small, wiry, middle-class French woman in her late fifties. Supported by the Peruvian government, she lived rather spartanly, yet not uncomfortably, in an apartment appointed with pre-Incan pottery and weavings. I was in a very delicate position with her, because I not only needed to see the first edition and the worksheets, but I also needed her permission before I could get a publishing contract. I had not been in her apartment for fifteen minutes when she told me that my translations were full of "howlers," that Vallejo was untranslatable (she was at that time working on a French translation of his poetry), and that neither the first edition nor the worksheets were available to be studied.

The months that followed were stressful and cheerless. I had been hired as editor of a new bilingual literary magazine, to be called *Quena*, at the Peruvian North American Cultural Institute. Because I was working for the Institute (which turned out to be an annex of the American Embassy in Lima), most of the Peruvian writers and critics I met thought I was an American spy. Only when I turned in the three-hundred-page manuscript for the first issue of *Quena* did I realize what the Institute represented. My boss told me that the translations I had included of Javier Heraud could not be published in the magazine because, although the poems themselves were not political, their author, after visiting Cuba, had joined a guerrilla movement in the Peruvian jungle and had been killed by the army. Since his name was linked with Cuba and revolution, my boss told me, the Institute did not want to be involved. I refused to take the translations out of the manuscript and was fired.

At the end of 1965 I met Maureen Ahern, an American with a PhD from San Marcos University, who was then married and living with her family on a chicken farm in Cieneguilla, about twenty miles outside Lima. Maureen agreed to read through the sixth and seventh drafts of my Vallejo manuscript with me (and she would later facilitate the manuscript's first publication after I had left Peru). Her husband, Johnny, worked in Lima, and once a week he would give me a ride to their place as he drove home from work. Maureen and I would work together all of the following day, and I would ride back to Lima with Johnny the next morning. This arrangement was ideal, but it remains indissociable in my mind from a near tragedy that marked my year in Peru. On one of the evenings that I would normally have gone to Maureen's, her husband was unavailable and I stayed home. That night—it was the week after my son, Matthew, was born—Barbara began to hemorrhage. After attempting to staunch the flow I realized that if I did not get her to a hospital immediately she was going to bleed to death. I raced out of our apartment and ran through the halls of the building across the street, screaming for help. A door opened, a doctor came out, we bundled her into the back of his Volkswagen and sped to the nearest clinic. We saved her life, barely—but I shudder to think what might have happened had I gone to Cieneguilla as planned.

One afternoon someone knocked on our door, and I opened it to be told by a stranger that Georgette Vallejo wanted to see me in her apartment that evening. When I arrived, I found there a small group of Peruvian writers and intellectuals, such as Javier Sologuren, Carlos Germán Belli, and Emilio Adolfo Westphalen.

Georgette explained that she had assembled everyone to try to determine what poems I could be given permission to translate. This turned out to be a ridiculous and impossible task, with these luminaries arguing for hours over why X poem could be translated and Y poem could not. At one point, when they all agreed that a particular poem could absolutely not be translated, Georgette cried out, "But I just translated that poem into French!" Nothing was resolved, and after the writers left, I found myself despondently sitting with Georgette. She asked me if I would like a *pisco* and brought out a bottle. We began drinking, and I recalled that the editor of *Perú Nuevo,* a press that had published a pirated edition of *Poemas humanos,* had told me that Georgette and César had never been formally married, and because of this Georgette had no legal control over the estate. I think I blurted out, "Well, I really don't need your permission it turns out, as Gustavo Valcárcel told me you and Vallejo were never actually married!" At that point she jumped up, ran to the bedroom, and began bringing out shoeboxes of memorabilia, looking for the marriage certificate. She couldn't find it. But the next morning, of course, she was furious over my confrontation. I never saw her again.

When Barbara and I returned to the States in the spring of 1966 and moved to New York City, Grove Press expressed interest in the translation. I prepared a seventh draft, and after having it checked by readers, Dick Seaver, then the senior editor at Grove, offered me a contract—contingent on Mme. Vallejo's signature. I wrote to Maureen and asked her if there was anything she could do. She offered to go meet Georgette. Over the next six months, Maureen must have seen Georgette almost weekly, and she did this while taking care of her kids, teaching full-time, battling illness, and trying to save a floundering marriage.

Seaver was also working on Georgette, sending letter after letter to convince her that the translation Grove wished to publish was not the one I had sent her from Bloomington in 1964. Maureen and Johnny were inviting her out to the farm for holiday weekends and sending her back home with chickens and eggs. Since Seaver was getting nowhere, Maureen eventually had to mention that she was a friend of mine and that she had worked on the translation. Georgette protested that she had been betrayed, and once again it looked as if it was all off.

But Maureen kept after her, and one day Américo Ferrari, a Peruvian scholar who had written on Vallejo (and worked with Georgette on her French edition of Vallejo's poetry), appeared in the Grove offices and told Seaver that Mme. Vallejo had asked him to check the translation. Apparently he wrote her that it was publishable, because a week or so later, she wrote Seaver that she would sign a contract if Grove would include the following clause: when and if she found a better translation, Grove would have to destroy mine and publish the other. Seaver told me he'd had it with her.

I wrote again to Maureen, telling her that unless a signed contract were sent to Grove within a month, the whole project would be off. Maureen continued to plead with Georgette, who finally said that if Johnny would type up the contract she wanted, she would sign it. He did, she signed it, and a few weeks later Seaver called to tell me that while it was not their contract, Grove found it acceptable and their lawyer had determined it was legal. He wrote Mme. Vallejo, enclosing her part of the advance. Subsequently, Maureen wrote that Georgette called to complain that she had never intended to sign a legal contract; she considered the contract Johnny had typed up "only a gesture" that she accepted so that Maureen would not be "upset." Grove went ahead anyway, and *Human Poems* was published in the spring of 1968.

I ended my introduction to the Grove edition of *Human Poems* with the words "My work is done." I must have forgotten that I had begun several drafts of a translation of Vallejo's sheaf of poems on the Spanish Civil War, *España, aparta de mí este cáliz*, with Octavio Corvalán, a professor in the Spanish Department at Indiana University, when I was living in Bloomington in 1965. By starting this new translation project and leaving it unfinished, I had unconsciously prolonged my relationship with Vallejo.

In 1970 I took a job at the new California Institute of the Arts outside Los Angeles, and my present wife, Caryl, and I moved to the San Fernando Valley. There I returned to *España,* made a new draft, and once again found myself looking for someone to check it with. I was introduced to José Rubia Barcia, a Spanish poet and essayist in exile since the Spanish Civil War, who had been teaching at UCLA for years. While going over the draft with Barcia, I was so impressed with his honesty, scrupulousness, and literary intelligence that I suggested we work together as co-translators.

Grove Press published our completed translation of *Spain, Take This Cup from Me* in 1974. While José and I were working on these poems, I showed him the 1968 translation of *Human Poems,* which he carefully went over, penciling in the margins around two thousand queries and suggestions for changes. He felt that what I had accomplished was meaningful but that we could do a better job working together. We worked from roughly 1972 to 1977. The University of California Press brought out *César Vallejo: The Complete Posthumous Poetry* in 1978, including what had previously been called *Human Poems* along with *Spain, Take This Cup from Me.*

Over the years, initially stimulated by Vallejo, I had developed an affinity for a poetry that went for the whole, a poetry that attempted to become responsible for all the poet knows about himself and his world. I saw Vallejo, Arthur Rimbaud, Antonin Artaud, Aimé Césaire, and Vladimír Holan as examples of these poetics. All inducted and ordered materials from the subconscious as well as from those untoward regions of human experience that defy rational explanation. Instead of conducting the orchestra of the living, they were conducting the orchestra's pit.

In 1988 I arranged with Paragon House in New York City to bring out a selection of my translations and co-translations of these poets, to be called *Conductors of the Pit*. While making the Vallejo selection, I got involved, once again, in revising previous versions, this time the ones that I had done with José. Some of these changes today strike me as less effective than the Eshleman/Barcia translations they were based on, and I have again, and now clearly for the last time, revised this work. But I do understand my dilemma: given the contextual density of Vallejo's European poetry, there are often multiple denotative word choices, and no matter how closely I have tried to adhere to what I thought Vallejo had written, I have found, over the years, that my own imagination has played tricks on me. At the same time, I have often had to invent words and phrases in an attempt to match Vallejo's originality, and these back-and-forth movements, between adherence to standard Spanish and the matching of the coined and arcane, have occasionally become confused. And in continuing to read Vallejo scholarship over the years, from time to time I have picked up an interpretation of a particular word that has made me rethink my own translation of it.

Up until the late 1980s, all my translational attention to Vallejo had been confined to the European poetry, written between 1923 and 1938. However, I had been circling around his second book, *Trilce* (1922), for many years, realizing in the 1960s and '70s that since it was a much more difficult book to translate than *Poemas humanos*, I should leave it alone. In 1988 I decided that if I could work with a Peruvian, a translation of *Trilce* could be attempted. I teamed up with Julio Ortega (one of the few Peruvian writers in Lima in the 1960s who did not think I was a spy!), and we decided to do it together. We worked out a first draft of the book in the fall of 1989. Caryl and I moved to Boston for a month, and every morning I took a bus into Providence and climbed the hill to Julio's office at Brown University, where we would work for several hours. Once back in Michigan, I went over our work and realized that I often had questions about several words in a single line. While Julio would occasionally respond to my queries, it was clear by the end of 1990 that he had decided I should finish *Trilce* on my own. And by then I needed his, or someone's help, even more than I did in the beginning. There are still many words in this book that have gone uncommented on in Vallejo scholarship (or have been wildly guessed at), and while critics can generalize and address Vallejo in terms of themes and preoccupations, a translator must go at him word by word, revealing all his choices in English without being able to dodge a single one. This process is especially tricky in the case of *Trilce*, with its intentionally misspelled words (often revealing secondary puns), neologisms, and arcane and archaic words.

At this point I contacted Américo Ferrari, who had inspected my manuscript at Grove Press in the late 1960s and who was now teaching translation at a university in Geneva . Ferrari had brought out an edition of Vallejo's *Obra poética completa* in 1988, and I figured he knew more about Vallejo's poetry than anyone. He agreed to respond to my questions; I would write in English and he in Spanish. Ferrari was willing to go to the library and research words he thought he was familiar with but that my questions led him to doubt. We had a wonderful exchange, and about two years later, after translating up to thirty versions of the most complex poems, I had something that I thought was publishable. Marsilio Publishers brought out a bilingual edition of *Trilce,* with an introduction by Ferrari, in 1992. When it went out of print, Wesleyan University Press brought out a second edition, with around one hundred word changes, in 2000.

Once more I felt that my involvement with Vallejo had come to an end. The only poetry of his that I had not translated was *Los heraldos negros* (1918), his first book, which had always struck me as more conventional by far than *Trilce* or the European poetry. Much of it is rhymed verse, which presents, in translation, its own problems: a sonnet is a little engine of sound and sense, and if you rhyme it in translation, you inevitably have to change some or much of its meaning. If you translate it for meaning alone, there is a chance you will end up with atonal free verse.

But as Michael Corleone says midway through *Godfather III,* "just when you think you're out, they pull you back in!" In 2003 I began to realize that all the years I had spent on this body of work had brought me very close to a "Complete Poetry of César Vallejo," and that it would be appropriate to review all my previous translations and add to them a version of *Los heraldos negros.* Once I began to work on *The Black Heralds,* I found the poems in it more interesting than I had originally thought, and since they were relatively easy to render, I took some pleasure in what could be thought of as strolling on a level playing field rather than climbing a vertical wall. When I could rhyme certain words in a sonnet and not change the meaning, I did so, and I constantly made myself aware of sound possibilities, attempting to make the translations sound as rich in English as I could without distorting Vallejo's intentions. Efraín Kristal, a Latin American scholar at UCLA who has recently edited a Spanish edition of *Los heraldos negros,* went over my third draft and made some very useful suggestions. José Cerna-Bazán, a Vallejo scholar from northern Peru now at Carleton College in Minnesota, has inspected my *Trilce* version word for word and proposed around a hundred changes, many of which I have accepted. Assuming that Vallejo is not writing poems in his Montparnasse tomb, I now should be able to stick to my statement that my work is done.

With an overview in mind, it is worth noting that Vallejo's poetic development is quite unusual. Coming from the conventional, if well-written and passionate, rhymed verse in *Los heraldos negros,* the reader is completely unprepared for *Trilce,* which is still the most dense, abstract, and transgression-driven collection of poetry in the Spanish language. For Vallejo to have gone beyond *Trilce,* in the experimental sense, would have involved his own version of the made-up language that one finds at the end of Huidobro's *Altazor.* On one level, then, Vallejo took a step back from *Trilce* in his European poetry, but not as far back as the writing of *Los heraldos negros.* In moving from Lima to Paris, the poet hit the aesthetic honey head of the European colonial world just as it was being rocked by political revolution in Russia. Given the non-sequitur shifts in *Trilce*'s composition, it is possible to imagine Vallejo forming some sort of relationship with French Surrealism (the first *Manifesto* having appeared a year after he arrived). However, Vallejo had nothing but contempt for Surrealism, which he seems to have regarded pretty much as Artaud did: as an amusing parlor-game, more concerned with pleasure and freedom than with suffering and moral struggle.

Vallejo's development in his post-Peruvian poetry involves taking on an ontological abyss, which might be briefly described as follows: Man is a sadness-exuding mammal, self-contradictory, perpetually immature, equally deserving of hatred, affection, and indifference, whose anger breaks any wholeness into warring fragments. This anger's only redeeming quality is that it is, paradoxically, a weapon of the poor, nearly always impotent against the military resources of the rich. Man is in flight from himself: what once was an expulsion from paradise has become a flight from self, as the worlds of colonial culture and colonized oppressiveness intersect. At the core of life's fullness is death, the "never" we fail to penetrate, "always" and "never" being the infinite extensions of "yes" and "no." Sorrow is the defining tone of human existence. Poetry thus becomes the imaginative expression of the inability to resolve the contradictions of man as an animal, divorced from nature as well as from any sustaining faith and caught up in the trivia of socialized life.

I have thought more about poetry while translating Vallejo than while reading anyone else. Influence through translation is different from influence through reading the masters in one's own tongue. I am creating an American version out of a Spanish text, and if Vallejo is to enter my own poetry, he must do so through what I have already, as a translator, turned him into. This is, in the long run, very close to being influenced by myself, or better, by a self I have created *to mine*. In this way, I do not feel that my poetry reflects Vallejo's. He taught me that ambivalence and contradiction are facets of metaphoric probing, and he gave me permission to try anything in my quest for an authentic alternative world in poetry.

Human Poems redefines the "political" poem. With one or two exceptions, the poems in this collection have no political position or agenda in the traditional sense. Yet they are directly sympathetic, in a way that does not remind us of other poetries, with the human situation I have briefly described above. In fact, they are so permeated by Vallejo's own suffering as it is wedded to that of other people, that it is as if the dualisms of colonial and colonized, rich and poor, become fused at a level where the human animal, aware of his fate, is embraced in all his absurd fallibility. Whitman's adhesive bond with others comes to mind, but Whitman used his "democratic vista" to express an idealism that is foreign to the world Vallejo saw around him while growing up in Peru and to the even darker world he encountered as a poor man in Paris, where his already marginal existence imploded before the horrors of the Spanish Civil War.

I think the key lesson Vallejo holds today may be that of a poet learning how to become imprisoned, as it were, in global life as a whole, and in each moment in particular. All his poetry, including the blistering Eros that opens up a breach in the wall separating mother and lover in *Trilce*, urges the poet to confront his own destiny and to stew in what is happening to him—and also to believe that his bewildering situation is significant. To be bound to, or imprisoned in, the present, includes confronting not only life as it really is but also psyche as it really is not— weighing all affirmation against, in an American's case, our imperial obsessions *and* our own intrinsic dark.

YPSILANTI, MARCH–AUGUST 2005

APPENDIX: A CHRONOLOGY OF VALLEJO'S LIFE AND WORKS

STEPHEN M. HART

Screw yourself, Vallejo, your fate is to screw yourself!

FERNANDO IBÁÑEZ

1892 On March 16, César Abraham Vallejo is born at 96 Calle Colón (now Calle César Vallejo) in Santiago de Chuco, a small Andean town in northern Peru, in the Libertad district, the eleventh child of Francisco de Paula Vallejo Benites (1840–1924) and María de los Santos Mendoza Gurrionero (1850–1918). Although the date is based on André Coyné's original supposition,[1] it appears reasonable, despite the recent claim that Vallejo was born on March 7, 1892.[2] He is baptized at the local church in Santiago de Chuco on May 19.[3]

1900–1905 Vallejo attends primary school in Santiago de Chuco. As the *shulca*, or youngest, of the family, Vallejo is a cosseted child; when returning home from school, his mother sucks his toes to warm him up.[4]

1905–1908 Vallejo attends secondary school at the Colegio Nacional de San Nicolás in Huamachuco, a small town in the Libertad region. He is given the nickname *machetón* because his nose looks like a machete.[5] Vallejo creates a scandal in the village by disturbing the peace during a funeral wake, for which he is severely reprimanded.[6]

1910 On April 2, Vallejo enrolls in the Faculty of Humanities at La Libertad University in Trujillo but does not complete the year. He works for a while in the mines of Quiruvilca, an experience he will later use as a basis for his proletarian novel, *El Tungsteno*.[7]

1911 On April 11, Vallejo enrolls in the Faculty of Sciences at the Universidad Nacional Mayor de San Marcos in Lima, but he is unable to continue his studies for financial reasons. From May to December he is employed as a private tutor for the children of the wealthy mine owner Domingo Sotil. He stays on the Acobamba estate, where he meets Américo España, the Italian anarchist who may have kindled the revolutionary flame that would burn brightly in years to come.[8]

His first poem, "Soneto," dated November 1911, is published in the newspaper *El Minero Ilustrado* (Cerro de Pasco), no. 782 (6 December 1911).[9] Rather similar in tone and imagery to the section "Nostalgias imperiales" in *Los heraldos negros*, this sonnet contains early evidence of Vallejo's verbal ingenuity; line 7 concludes with the neologism *soledumbre*.

1912 Vallejo works as an assistant cashier on the sugar plantation Roma, near Trujillo, owned by the Larco Herreras, one of the two big families (the other being the Gildemeisters) who had come to monopolize the sugar industry in Peru after the War of the Pacific. The sight of hundreds of peons arriving at the sugar estate at the crack of dawn and working until nightfall in the fields, with only a fistful of rice to live on, made a lasting impression on Vallejo.

1913   In March, Vallejo reenrolls in the Faculty of Humanities at La Libertad University in Trujillo. He supports himself with a teaching job at the Centro Escolar de Varones in Trujillo.

1914   Vallejo enrolls for his second year at La Libertad and continues his job at the Centro Escolar.

1914–1916   Vallejo begins to publish poems in local newspapers, which he would subsequently use as drafts for *Los heraldos negros*.[10]

1915   Vallejo enrolls for his third year at La Libertad and also takes courses in law. He subsequently gets a post as teacher at the Colegio Nacional de San Juan and, while there, teaches Ciro Alegría, who would one day publish the novel *El mundo es ancho y ajeno* (1941). Alegría later said that he felt there was something profoundly "torn" in Vallejo's being: "From his whole being there flowed a deep sadness."[11]

On August 22, Vallejo's brother, Miguel, dies in Santiago de Chuco. Vallejo writes an elegy for him, "A mi hermano muerto . . ." (*Cultura Infantil*, no. 33 [August 1917]: 5), subsequently revised as "A mi hermano Miguel," the third poem of the "Canciones de hogar" section of *Los heraldos negros*.

On September 22, Vallejo is awarded a Bachelor of Arts in Philosophy and Letters at La Libertad University with a thesis titled "El Romanticismo en la poesía castellana," which is later published (Trujillo: Tipografía Olaya, 1915).

1915–1916   A number of Vallejo's poems, early drafts of *Los heraldos negros*, appear in local magazines.

1916   Vallejo continues studying law in Trujillo, supporting his studies by teaching at the Colegio Nacional. He begins a love affair with María Rosa Sandoval, who inspires a number of the early love poems; she dies tragically young (Espejo, 44–45) of tuberculosis.[12]

During this time Vallejo adopts the appearance of a literary dandy, wearing a smart suit and gloves and carrying a silver-capped cane (Izquierdo Ríos, 107, 150). His cousin catches him lying under a tree in the countryside surrounding Santiago de Chuco, banging his head and muttering: "I want to write. . . . I want to write" (Izquierdo Ríos, 50).

1917   Vallejo begins his third year of a law degree and continues to support himself by teaching. He reads foreign and local literary journals such as *Cervantes, Colónida, La Esfera,* and *España,* which would later inspire him to write avant-garde poetry.[13]

At a soirée organized for the painter Macedonio de la Torre on June 10, Vallejo recites "Los heraldos negros," which would be the eponymous poem of his first collection.

From July to December he has a passionate love affair with Zoila Rosa Cuadra (whom he nicknames "Mirtho"), a fifteen-year-old girl; Espejo Asturrizaga believes that "Setiembre," "Heces," "Yeso," "El tálamo eterno," and "El poeta a su amada" were inspired by this relationship (Espejo, 54–57). When the relationship deteriorates, Vallejo attempts suicide by shooting himself; the gun has only one bullet in the barrel, and he survives (Espejo, 56–57).

On September 22 the Lima magazine *Variedades* publishes an ironic review of "El poeta a su amada," saying the poem would be best accompanied by an accordion, and advising those living in Trujillo to tie the author of the poem to a railway track; the article is accompanied by a graphic cartoon.[14]

1918   In January, Vallejo begins postgraduate study in the Humanities Department at Universidad Nacional Mayor de San Marcos in Lima.

In February he strikes up a friendship with Abraham Valdelomar and as a result gradually begins to make a name for himself in Lima's literary circles. Later Valdelomar offers to write a foreword to Vallejo's collection of poems, but he falls ill and dies (on November 3, 1919) before he can follow through; Vallejo is moved by Valdelomar's premature death (Espejo, 84).

Vallejo is offered a teaching position at the prestigious Colegio Barrós in Lima in May. He takes over as head of the school on September 12, following the unexpected death of its director.

On August 8, Vallejo's mother dies of angina in Santiago de Chuco, an event that will inspire some of his most famous poems (*Trilce* XVIII, XXIII, XXVIII, LII, LVIII, LXV).

In October Vallejo begins a passionate affair with Otilia; Espejo Asturrizaga refuses to give her surname but states that she was the sister-in-law of a colleague at the Colegio Barrós. Espejo also surmises that the majority of the love poems in *Trilce* are based on that tempestuous affair (116–21), which would go on until August 1920. Espejo further speculates— based on lines 17–18 of *Trilce* X ("Y los tres meses de ausencia. Y los nueve de gestación")— that Otilia was pregnant when she left for San Mateo de Surco but that Vallejo would never know the truth (Espejo, 76).

1919   Vallejo is thrown out of the Colegio Barrós in May because of his scandalous affair with Otilia; he refuses to marry her (see *Trilce* XXVII) and as a result comes to blows with Otilia's brother-in-law (Espejo, 75). Vallejo now has no job and no money—an early indication of Vallejo's impetuous nature, his tendency to sacrifice security on the altar of personal desire.

On July 23, Vallejo's *Los heraldos negros* (Lima: Souza Ferreira, 1918) is released and becomes available in Lima's bookshops. The delay in distribution, caused by Valdelomar's dilatoriness in providing a foreword, allows Vallejo to introduce some later poems, such as "Enereida" and "Los pasos lejanos."[15]

In December Vallejo is invited, through an intermediary, to meet a young woman in a dark room who makes passionate love to him, but whose identity Vallejo never discovers (Espejo, 85).

1920   On July 10 Vallejo gives a poetry reading at his old school, the Colegio Nacional in Huamachuco. Because nobody claps afterward, Vallejo is said to have stated—with amazing egoism for the time—"Why don't you applaud me? I will be greater than Rubén Darío and one day will be proud to see America lying at my feet" (Espejo, 92). On July 18 Vallejo returns to Santiago de Chuco for the local celebrations of the patron of the village, Santiago (July 23– August 2, 1920).

On August 1 the commercial premises of Carlos Santa María in Santiago de Chuco are burned to the ground. A bystander is shot by the police, and two policemen are killed by the crowd in retaliation.[16] The Santa María family indicts Héctor M. Vásquez, Pedro Lozada, César Vallejo, and fifteen others. Legal accounts show that—despite an adroit campaign mounted by the Trujillo intelligentsia in defense of the poet—Vallejo was directly involved in the events leading up to the destruction of the Santa María premises.[17]

Vallejo flees to Antenor Orrego's house in Mansiche, just outside Trujillo. While in hiding he has a waking dream in which he witnesses his own death in Paris, surrounded by people he doesn't recognize (Espejo, 97–98). Obviously brought on by the stress of being hunted down by the police, this dream is remarkable because some of the details would be borne out by his death in Paris eighteen years later. The experience inspired what is arguably his most famous poem, "Black Stone on a White Stone."

On November 6 Vallejo is captured by the police and imprisoned in Trujillo Central Jail. While there he continues to write, composing some of the poems that would be collected in *Trilce* (I, II, XVIII, XX, XL, L, LVIII, LXI), as well as the short stories of *Escalas*.

On December 24 Vallejo's poem "Fabla de gesta" wins second prize (fifty libras) in the Poesía del Concurso. The first prize is later declared void.

1921 On February 26, thanks to a publicity campaign orchestrated by the University of Trujillo and influential figures such as the poet Percy Gibson, Vallejo is released on bail.

He moves from Trujillo to Lima on March 30; six months later he is appointed to a teaching post at the Colegio Nacional de Nuestra Señora de Guadalupe in Lima.

On November 15 Vallejo's short story "Más allá de la vida y la muerte" wins first prize (twenty libras) in the competition organized by the book club "Entre Nous."

1922 *Variedades* publishes "Mas allá de la vida y la muerte" on June 17.

In October *Trilce* is published by the Talleres Tipográficos de la Penitenciaría in Lima, with a foreword by Vallejo's literary mentor, Antenor Orrego. The book title is inserted in proofs to replace the title *Cráneos de bronce*. The collection elicits no reaction from local readership.

1923 On March 15 a collection of short stories, *Escalas*, is published by the Talleres Tipográficos de la Penitenciaría.

On May 16 Vallejo's novel *Fabla salvaje* is published by Colección de la Novela Peruana.

On June 17, with the lawsuit against him reopened in Trujillo, Vallejo embarks with Julio Gálvez (Antenor Orrego's nephew) on the steamboat *Oroya* en route to Paris.

On July 13 Vallejo and Galvez arrive in Paris, where, with the exception of a year or so in Spain, Vallejo would live until his death. His first three years in Paris are plagued by poverty: he sometimes sleeps on park benches and cannot afford to buy new clothes.[18]

On July 28 Vallejo meets Alfonso de Silva in the Legación Peruana; they become friends, and Vallejo accompanies Alfonso to various restaurants, where Alfonso plays violin for a few sous to pay for their meal. Silva would return to Lima in 1930; on hearing of his death years later (Silva died on May 7, 1937), Vallejo wrote his famous poem "Alfonso, estás mirándome, lo veo. . . ."[19]

On October 26 Vallejo publishes his first article in the Trujillo newspaper *El Norte*. Between 1923 and 1930, he would write thirty-seven articles for this newspaper.[20] As the articles show, Vallejo becomes gradually more immersed in the cultural scene in Paris, attending art exhibitions and concerts; conversing about art in cafés such as La Rotonde, Dôme, Coupole, Sélect, and La Régence; and visiting Versailles and Fontainebleau.[21]

1923–1929 Vallejo writes the poems that Georgette would later group under the title *Poemas en prosa* in her 1968 facsimile edition of Vallejo's poetry.

1924   On March 24 Vallejo's father dies in Santiago de Chuco.

In September the Costa Rican sculptor Max Jiménez generously allows Vallejo to stay in his studio at 3, rue Vercingétorix. It is there that Vallejo poses for the Spanish sculptor José de Creeft. In Vicente Huidobro's house Vallejo meets the Spanish poet Juan Larrea, and they strike up a friendship. Later Vallejo also meets Pablo Neruda, who offers the following portrait in his memoirs: "Vallejo was shorter than I, he was thinner and bonier. He was also more Indian than I, with very dark eyes and a high, domed forehead. He had a beautiful Incan face saddened by a certain undeniable majesty. Vain like all poets, he liked it when others referred to his Indian features."[22]

In October Vallejo has an intestinal hemorrhage and is hospitalized in the Hôpital de la Charité, an experience that inspires him to write "Las ventanas se han estremecido ..." (*Poemas en prosa*).

1925   In the spring Mariano H. Cornejo, the Peruvian ambassador in Paris, asks Vallejo to tutor his nephews and grandchildren. The post is short-lived, because one of Cornejo's nieces dies. Cornejo invites Vallejo to write an elegy for her, but despite the remuneration and favor offered in return, Vallejo declines, thereafter remaining an "unofficial writer," as he was to call himself.[23]

On March 16 Vallejo discovers that because of Pablo Abril de Vivero's intercession on his behalf, he has been awarded a grant of three hundred pesetas per month to study in Spain. He never intends to study there but travels to Madrid three times to claim the grant money (October 1925, July 1926, June 1927).

On June 2 Vallejo learns that he has been offered a monthly commission by the Bureau des Grands Journaux Ibéroaméricains, which assuages his financial worries for a time.

On July 17 Vallejo publishes his first article with the Lima magazine *Mundial*, for which he will have written 127 articles by 1930.[24]

1926   Vallejo meets Henriette Maisse in May, and they become lovers (their relationship would last for eighteen months). Vallejo lives with Henriette at the Hôtel de Richelieu, 20 rue Molière, in room 19 on the fourth floor.[25] Now the Hôtel Louvre-Rivoli, the building has a plaque commemorating the fact that Vallejo once lived there.

On June 7, the High Court in Trujillo issues a warrant for Vallejo's arrest.

In July the first issue of an avant-garde magazine edited by Vallejo and Juan Larrea, *Favorables-París-Poema*, is published in Paris.[26] On July 10 Vallejo publishes his first article in *Variedades*, a Lima magazine for which he will have written forty-one articles by 1930.[27]

In October the second (and, as it proved, final) issue of *Favorables-París-Poema* is published.[28]

In winter Vallejo notices a young girl, Georgette de Phillipart, sewing at the window of the apartment across the road from the Hôtel de Richelieu, where he is living with Henriette. Because she sees Vallejo gesticulating, Georgette at first believes that he is a deaf-mute. But one day she hears his voice and exclaims to her mother that "the neighbor across from us can speak!" From that point on Georgette's interest in her Peruvian neighbor grows.[29] Vallejo and Georgette, who is eighteen years old at the time (she was born on January 7, 1908),[30] exchange glances and then smiles; they begin to see each other in the Bois de Boulogne

(Domingo Córdoba, 213). Once Georgette's mother, Mme. Marie Travers, a seamstress, discovers what is going on, however, she attempts to put an end to the nascent love affair, regarding Vallejo as a "drôle d'étranger" (Domingo Córdoba, 213).

1927 On March 10 Vallejo travels to Spain. Henriette moves out of the Hôtel de Richelieu.

On May 5 Vallejo argues with Georgette and asks Henriette to come back to live with him, as he describes in a letter to Juan Larrea.[31] He leaves the Hôtel de Richelieu and goes with Henriette to live at the Hôtel Mary, 32 rue Sainte-Anne (Domingo Córdoba, 41).

In June Vallejo goes to Madrid, where he stays with Xavier Abril in his apartment on Calle de la Aduana. He meets Juan Domingo Córdoba, and they become good friends (Domingo Córdoba, 35). Domingo Córdoba travels with Vallejo back to Paris, staying in an apartment near the hotel where Vallejo and Henriette are living; while there, Domingo Córdoba witnesses a heated argument between Vallejo and Henriette (Domingo Córdoba, 43).

1927–1929 Vallejo begins studying Marxist theory and acquires books from L'Humanité, a left-wing bookstore in Paris. He reads works by Marx, Trotsky, Engels, Plekhanov, Luxembourg, Liebknecht, Lenin, Riazanov, Bukharin, Kurella, Stalin, and Lissargaray (Domingo Córdoba, 165–66). Initially—like many of the French Surrealists—a Trotskyist, Vallejo gradually begins to adopt a more hard-line Stalinist approach.[32] But he does not spend all his time studying. On one occasion, when drunk, Vallejo insults and nearly comes to blows with a group of Argentineans in a nightclub, and—when driving around in a coupé taxi with Domingo Córdoba and two of the More brothers[33]—he stands up and shouts obscenities at bystanders (Domingo Córdoba, 123–25).

1928–1935 Vallejo composes and types up the undated poems of *Poemas humanos.*[34]

1928 In July, suffering from poor health, Vallejo is advised by his doctor to go to the countryside to recuperate. Accompanied by Henriette and Domingo Córdoba, he stays in the house of Monsieur Nauty in Ris-Orangis (Seine-et-Oise), not far from Paris (Domingo Córdoba, 204–10).

On September 8, Vallejo learns that the Peruvian government has granted him free passage back to Peru. He accepts the money but spends it on a lavish tour of Europe, leaving on October 19, for Berlin. His itinerary is Paris-Berlin-Moscow-Budapest-Berlin-Paris; he arrives back in Paris on December 27.

On November 12 Georgette's mother dies, leaving Georgette with an inheritance of 280,000 francs (Domingo Córdoba, 144).

In late December Vallejo meets Georgette by chance in a charcuterie, and she tells him her mother has died. They decide to get back together. Vallejo asks Domingo Córdoba if he will act as go-between and persuade Henriette to leave. Domingo Córdoba refuses; instead, Georgette talks to her, putting an end to Henriette's involvement with Vallejo (Domingo Córdoba, 213–14).

On December 29 Vallejo, along with Armando Bazán, Juan J. Paiva, Eudocio Ravines, Jorge Seoane, and Demetrio Tello, set up a Peruvian Socialist Party cell in Paris and write to inform José Carlos Mariátegui—who had recently (October 7, 1928) founded the Peruvian Communist Party in Lima—of their actions.

1929   In January, Vallejo moves into Georgette's apartment. Georgette has a prophetic experience when Vallejo first stays overnight: when folding up his suit she feels as if she is folding up a dead man's clothes.[35] The following month they move to a new apartment on an adjoining street, at 11, avenue de l'Opéra.

On February 3 Vallejo begins publishing articles in *El Comercio,* Lima's most prestigious daily, for which he will write twenty-three articles by 1930.

In July Vallejo, Georgette, and Domingo Córdoba travel to Brittany to stay at Ploumanach (Côte-du-Nord). While there, Vallejo and Domingo Córdoba—neither of them strong swimmers—nearly drown while going for a swim in the sea (Domingo Córdoba, 188).

In August Domingo Córdoba accompanies Vallejo to a clinic, where Georgette has an abortion (Domingo Córdoba, 227–28).

On September 19 Vallejo sets off on his second trip to the Soviet Union, this time with Georgette. Their itinerary, which has something of the Grand Tour about it, is Paris-Berlin-Moscow-Leningrad-Prague-Cologne-Vienna-Budapest-Trieste-Venice-Florence-Rome-Pisa-Genoa-Nice-Paris. In Moscow Vladimir Mayakovsky takes Vallejo to see Eisenstein's *The Battleship Potemkin.* Vallejo and Georgette also visit Lenin's tomb in Red Square.

1930   On January 2 Vallejo sends Luis Alberto Sánchez three poems in a letter: "Piedra negra sobre una piedra blanca," "Altura y pelos," and one other (title not given) (Ángel Flores, "Cronologia de viviencias y ideas," 105–6).

In February the biweekly review *Bolívar,* established by Pablo Abril in Madrid, begins to publish Vallejo's "Un reportaje en Rusia," which will later form Vallejo's travelogue *Rusia en 1931: reflexiones al pie del Kremlin.*

On April 9, at Gerardo Diego's suggestion, the second edition of *Trilce* is published by José Bergamín in Madrid (Compañía Iberoamericana de Publicaciones). Bergamín writes a warm, insightful foreword.

In May Vallejo travels to Spain with Georgette. He meets up with Gerardo Diego, Rafael Alberti, and Pedro Salinas in the Café de Recoletos (Domingo Córdoba, 189). He receives fifteen hundred pesetas in royalties for the second edition of *Trilce* (Domingo Córdoba, 145). Vallejo goes with Domingo Córdoba to Salamanca to meet Miguel de Unamuno, although they fail to arrange an interview (Domingo Córdoba, 189).

On December 2, as a result of his political activities, Vallejo is expelled from France and is given until January 29, 1931, to leave. He and Georgette leave Paris on December 29 and move to Madrid, where they live in a modest house on Calle del Acuerdo.

1931   Vallejo begins writing for various newspapers such as *La Voz* and doing commissioned translations (such as Henri Barbusse, *Elevación* [Madrid: Ulises, 1931], and Marcel Aymé, *La calle sin nombre* [Madrid: Editorial Cenit, 1931]).[36] He joins the Spanish Communist Party and teaches Marxist-Leninist theory in clandestine cells.

On March 7 Vallejo's novel *El Tungsteno*—the last few chapters of which were typed on Domingo Córdoba's typewriter in Madrid in January (Domingo Córdoba, 134)—is published by Editorial Cenit in Madrid.

On April 14 King Alfonso XIII abdicates, and the Spanish Republicans come to power;

Vallejo is unimpressed and remarks to Georgette that a bloodless revolution is not a true revolution.[37]

Rusia en 1931 is published in July by Ediciones Ulises in Madrid. Reprinted twice in four months, the book becomes something of a best seller. José Macedo remembers how it was advertised everywhere in Madrid, on the Puerta del Sol, the Calle de Alcalá, and along the Gran Vía (quoted in More, 86). Vallejo does not make much money from the book, however, since the publishers refuse to pay him royalties for the second and third printings (Domingo Córdoba, 145).

On October 27–30 Vallejo attends the International Writers' Congress in Moscow as an invited delegate.

In November he begins writing a second book on the Soviet Union, "Rusia ante el Segundo Plan Quinquenal," which is rejected by various publishers. It will be published years after his death by La Editora Gráfica in Lima (1965).

1932 On January 25 Georgette goes to Paris to sell her apartment. She claims to have received two letters from Vallejo, who is still in Madrid, one of which is dated January 29, 1932, describing his work on *El arte y la revolución:* "Estoy corrigiendo *El arte y la revolución.* Me parece que es un libro muy, muy bien. Me gusta mucho."[38] This letter may be fictitious, since it is not reproduced and is used as the main evidence with which to rebut Juan Larrea's view that Vallejo was losing interest in politics; a consultation of the manuscripts of *El arte y la revolución* and *Contra el secreto profesional,* now held in the Biblioteca Nacional, suggests that the titles for the collections were coined by Georgette rather than Vallejo.[39]

Also in January, Vallejo goes with Federico García Lorca to see Camila Quiroga to discuss the possibility of having one of Vallejo's plays performed in Madrid, but has no success.[40]

On February 12 Vallejo crosses the border illegally and joins Georgette in Paris. He is told that he will be allowed to remain in France if he desists from political activity and reports to the prefecture monthly.

On August 12 and 20, Vallejo reports to the prefecture in Paris.

1933 Vallejo publishes "Un grand reportage politique: Que se passe-t-il en Amérique du Sud au pays des Incas?" in the magazine *Germinal* (June 3, 10, 17, 24).

On August 20 he reports for the third and final time to the prefecture, after which his residency in France is legalized, despite the fact that he does not appear to have fulfilled all requirements.

1934 Vallejo attends a left-wing demonstration against Croix de Feux in Paris on February 6.

On October 11 Vallejo and Georgette get married in Paris.

1934–1936 Vallejo writes two plays, *Colacho hermanos* and *La piedra cansada,* but is unable to interest a publisher.[41] Vallejo and Georgette move to a little hotel at 64, avenue du Maine, near rue de la Gaîté. They often have lunch at the Cercle François Villon, an association for unemployed intellectuals (*Aula Vallejo,* 141). They pawn many of Georgette's possessions during this period, including an antique mirror (More, 22–24). Vallejo frequents a nearby workingman's bistro called Le Lion, where the beer, always Vallejo's favorite drink, is very cheap.[42] He is such a regular customer that the proprietor lets him have beer for seventy centimes instead of eighty (More, 58).

1935 On December 25 Vallejo writes to Juan Larrea asking him to inquire whether José Bergamín has received—via Rafael Alberti—his offer of "my publishable book of poems"[43]—most likely the poems of *Poemas en prosa* and the undated poems of *Poemas humanos*.

1936 On February 28 Vallejo publishes "Récentes découvertes au pays des Incas," *Beaux-Arts*, no. 165: 1.

On July 16–18 the Spanish Civil War breaks out, and Vallejo is caught up in the cause. He begins writing articles in support of the Republic, often going to the Montparnasse train station to hear the latest news from the front line.

On September 11 Vallejo publishes "L'homme et Dieu dans la sculpture incaïque," *Beaux-Arts*.

On December 15 Vallejo leaves Paris to visit Barcelona and Madrid; while in Madrid he visits the front line. He begins writing the first drafts of the poems that will come together as *España, aparta de mí este cáliz*, often using an individual battle as inspiration for the poem. He returns to Paris on December 31.

1937 On July 4–8 Vallejo attends the Second International Writers' Congress for the Defense of Culture held in Valencia and Madrid (Ehrenberg called it a "moving circus"). As the official Peruvian delegate, he gives a speech in Madrid, "La responsabilidad del escritor," which is later published in *El Mono Azul*, no. 4.[44]

On September 4 Vallejo helps to found the Ibero-American Committee for the Defense of the Spanish Republic and its bulletin, *Nuestra España*. He is later sidelined because of his Trotskyist sympathies.[45]

From September 3 to December 8 Vallejo writes the dated poems of *Poemas humanos* and *España, aparta de mí este cáliz* (the Civil War Poems). He types them on René Mossisson's typewriter, in the latter's hotel room on Rue Daguerre (More, 69). Every day for three months, Vallejo reads Georgette the poems he has typed up during the day (*¡Allá ellos!*, 107).

1938 On March 13 Vallejo falls ill and takes to his bed. His symptoms become worrying (*¡Allá ellos!*, 117), and on March 24 he is transferred to the Clinique Générale de Chirurgie (Villa Arago). Although the doctors—including an eminent specialist, Dr Lemière— run various tests, they are unable to agree on the cause of his illness.

On April 15 (Good Friday), Vallejo dies at 9:20 A.M. in the Villa Arago clinic. The death certificate records intestinal infection as the cause of death, but this has not prevented incessant speculation as to the "real" cause of death, including malaria, syphilis, exhaustion, spiritual martyrdom—given the day he died—and even grief over the Spanish Civil War.[46] Georgette has a death mask of Vallejo created on April 16.

On April 18 Vallejo is buried in the Montrouge Cemetery; homilies are given by Louis Aragon, Antonio Ruiz Vilaplana, and Gonzalo More. The tombstone lists Vallejo's year of birth incorrectly as 1893.

Although she has lived with him for years, even Georgette is surprised to find the wealth of unpublished papers Vallejo leaves on his death.[47] These consist of:

> autographs of the posthumous poems, which Georgette would attempt to publish in 1978–1979 and later destroy;

typescripts of the posthumous poems, which Georgette would publish in facsimile in 1968 and donate to the Hogar Clínica San Juan de Dios;

manuscripts and typescripts of Vallejo's plays, which she would later publish in 1979, donating most to the Biblioteca Nacional and some to the Library of the Pontificia Universidad Católica del Perú;[48]

the typescript of "Rusia ante el segundo plan quinquenal," which would be published in 1965;

typewritten essays, which Georgette would edit and use to produce two collections, *El arte y la revolución* and *Contra el secreto profesional,* published in 1973; the typescripts were later donated to the Biblioteca Nacional.

1939 Georgette publishes *Poemas humanos* in Paris, an edition that included all the posthumous poems (including the war poems).[49]

1940 An edition of *España, aparta de mí este cáliz* overseen by Emilio Prados is published on February 9 by Editorial Séneca in Mexico City.[50]

1951 In May, Georgette travels on the steamboat *Reina del Pacífico* from Paris to Lima with Vallejo's manuscripts. As she steps off the boat in Callao, she is met by Raúl Porras Barrenchea, Sebastián Salazar Bondy, and others.[51] She remains in Lima.

1957–1958 Thanks to Porras Barrenchea's intervention, Georgette is granted a modest monthly allowance of twenty-seven hundred soles from the Ministry of Education.[52]

1965 *Rusia antes el segundo plan quinquenal* is published in Lima.

1968 Georgette publishes a facsimile edition of the typescripts of the posthumous poetry, now divided up as *Poemas humanos, Poemas en prosa,* and *España, aparta de mí este cáliz.* Her pension from the Ministry of Education is unexpectedly curtailed.[53]

1970 Georgette returns to Paris to oversee the transfer of Vallejo's remains to Montparnasse Cemetery (twelfth division, 4 North, No. 7), close to Baudelaire's grave, where Vallejo told Georgette he would like to be buried. Vallejo's birth date is now listed correctly as 1892; Georgette has a section from one of her poems—"j'ai tant neigé/pour que tu dormes"—inscribed on the tomb.[54] Vallejo's grave soon becomes a place of pilgrimage for poets.

1973 Georgette edits and publishes Vallejo's essays, *El arte y la revolución* and *Contra el secreto profesional,* in Lima. She subsequently donates the typescripts to the manuscripts section of the Biblioteca Nacional in Lima.

1974 With the proceeds from book royalties, Georgette purchases and moves into an apartment at no. 5241–301, Avenida Arequipa in Miraflores, Lima.[55]

1976–1978 Georgette has a number of problems with translators and editors who produce new editions of Vallejo's work in various languages.[56]

1978 The major English translation by Clayton Eshleman and José Rubia Barcia, *César Vallejo: The Complete Posthumous Poetry* (Berkeley and Los Angeles: University of California Press), is published and wins the prestigious National Book Award.

A copy of the Spanish edition of *España, aparta de mí este cáliz* is discovered by Pedro Lastra Salazar and Juan Gilabert in the Montserrat Monastery near Barcelona.[57]

1978–1979   Georgette attempts to publish the autographs of the posthumous poems with Ángel Rama in his Ayacucho Series, but the project falls through.[58]

1979   Georgette publishes Vallejo's drama.[59] The typescripts and manuscripts are shared between the Biblioteca Nacional and the Library of the Pontificia Universidad Católica del Perú.

Later that year Georgette is partially paralyzed and lives from now on at the Maison de Santé in Lima.

1983   Georgette donates some of Vallejo's belongings, including his passport, to the Library of the Pontificia Universidad Católica del Perú. She donates the typescripts of the posthumous poems to the Hogar Clínica San Juan de Dios, Lima.[60] Since there is no sign of the original autographs (or, indeed, of Vallejo's death mask), it must be assumed that Georgette destroyed them around this time.

1984   On December 5, Georgette dies in the Maison de Santé, Lima.

1995   After his momentous discovery of a photocopy of the original autographs of the posthumous poems among Ángel Rama's private papers in Montevideo, Juan Fló publishes an article describing the autographs.[61]

1997–2004   Fifteen volumes of Vallejo's complete works are published by the press of the Pontifica Universidad Católica del Perú, under the stewardship of Ricardo Silva-Santisteban and Salomon Lerner Febres. They include Vallejo's poetry, narrative, drama, correspondence, articles, and translations.

2003   An edition of the autographs is published by Tamesis and La Católica University Press: Juan Fló and Stephen Hart, eds., *Autógrafos olvidados* (London-Lima: Tamesis-La Católica, 2003).

NOTES

EPIGRAPH   This is how the Spanish journalist Fernando Ibáñez, later killed in the Spanish Civil War, used to greet Vallejo; Juan Larrea, ed., *Aula Vallejo 11–12–13* (Córdoba: Universidad Nacional, Facultad de Filosofía y Humanidades, 1974), 193; hereafter cited in text as *Aula Vallejo*.

1   André Coyné, "Apuntes biográficos de César Vallejo," *Mar del Sur*, 8 (November–December 1949): n.p.

2   Oswaldo D. Vásquez Vallejo, *Abraham Vallejo: ascendencia y nacimiento* (Trujillo: Universidad Nacional de Trujillo, 1992), 20.

3   Antenor Samaniego, *César Vallejo: su poesía* (Lima: Mejía Baca and P. L. Villanueva, 1954), 14–15.

4   Francisco Izquierdo Ríos, *César Vallejo y su tierra*, 3rd ed. (Lima: Villanueva, 1972), 151; hereafter cited in text as Izquierdo Ríos.

5   Izquierdo Ríos, *César Vallejo y su tierra*, 144.

6   Juan Espejo Asturrizaga, *César Vallejo: itinerario del hombre* (Lima: Mejía Baca, 1965), 24; hereafter cited in text as Espejo.

7   When I visited Santiago de Chuco in December 1981, however, I was told that Vallejo worked in Tamboras and not Quirulvica, which is a copper mine.

8   Esteban Pavlotich, "El paso de Vallejo por los Andes centrales del Perú," in *Aproximaciones a César Vallejo*, vol. 1, ed. Ángel Flores (New York: Las Américas, 1971), 133.

9   *César Vallejo: Soneto*, preliminary study by Edmundo Bendezú Aibar, edited and notes by Hugo Arias Hidalgo (Lima: Universidad Ricardo Palma Editorial Universitaria, 2003).

10 For a comparison of the early drafts with the final versions, see Ricardo Silva-Santisteban, ed., *César Vallejo: poesía completa*, 4 vols. (Lima: Pontificia Universidad Católica del Perú, 1997), vol. 1, 65–237; and *César Vallejo: poemas completos*, ed. Ricardo González Vigil (Lima: Petroperú, 1998), 37–161. See also Américo Ferrari, ed., *César Vallejo: obra poética* (Madrid: Colección Archivos, 1988), which has excellent notes.

11 "El César Vallejo que yo conocí," in *César Vallejo*, ed. Julio Ortega (Madrid: Taurus, 1974), 162.

12 Jesús Fernández Palacios, "Georgette, la mujer del retrato," *La palabra y el hombre* 76 (1990): 281.

13 Roberto Paoli, "En los orígenes de *Trilce*: Vallejo entre modernismo y vanguardia," in *Mapas anatómicos de César Vallejo* (Florence: Casa Editrice D'Anna, 1981), 31–50; Jorge Cornejo Polar, "Vallejo y la vanguardia: una relación problemática," in *Estudios de literatura peruana* (Lima: Banco Central de Reserva del Perú, 1998), 169–90.

14 Georgette de Vallejo, *¡Allá ellos, allá ellos, allá ellos!* (Lima: Zalvac, 1978), 10; hereafter cited in text as *¡Allá ellos!*

15 Coyné, "La fecha," 107n. 42; and Ángel Flores, "Cronología de vivencias e ideas," in *Aproximaciones a César Vallejo*, ed. Ángel Flores (New York: Las Américas, 1971), vol. 1, 43.

16 Germán Patrón Candela, *El proceso Vallejo* (Trujillo: Universidad de Trujillo, 1992), 160–63.

17 All the existing court proceedings were published in Patrón Candela, *El proceso Vallejo*. They indicate that Vallejo was at the front of the crowd that gathered in the main square that afternoon and was heard inciting others to take part in the mayhem. He was seen holding a revolver, and in much of the evidence for the prosecution, he is mentioned as the instigator. Three years later, after his initial imprisonment in Trujillo, Vallejo fled to Europe to escape prosecution. See Stephen Hart, "Was César Vallejo Guilty as Charged?" *Latin American Literary Review* 26, no. 51 (1998): 79–89.

18 Armando Bazán, *Dolor y poesía* (Lima: Biblioteca Universitaria, 1958), 42–48. Ernesto More recounts that when traveling on the subway Vallejo would refuse to sit down in order to avoid wearing out his pants, and before stepping off the train he would wait until the car had completely stopped so as to avoid wearing out his shoes. *Vallejo en la encrucijada del drama peruano* (Lima: Librería y Distribuidora Bendezú, 1968), 26–27; hereafter cited in text as More.

19 Ricardo González Vigil, *César Vallejo* (Lima: Editorial Brasa, 1985), 82–83.

20 See articles in César Vallejo, *Artículos y crónicas completos*, ed. Jorge Puccinelli, 2 vols. (Lima: Pontificia Universidad Católica del Perú, 2002).

21 Juan Domingo Córdoba Vargas, *César Vallejo del Perú profundo y sacrificado* (Lima: Jaime Campodonico, 1995), 45; hereafter cited in text as Domingo Córdoba.

22 Pablo Neruda, *Confieso que he vivido: memorias* (Buenos Aires: Losada, 1974), 93; my translation. This complimentary portrait of Vallejo contrasts with the rivalry Neruda clearly felt with Vallejo years later. When visiting Clayton Eshleman in New York City in 1966, Neruda made a point of saying that "Vallejo never wrote any poetry after he left Peru" (email from Clayton Eshleman to author, August 17, 2005).

23 "Una gran reunión latinoamericana," *Mundial*, no. 353 (March 18, 1927); see Vallejo, *Artículos*, 1: 396–99.

24 Vallejo, *Artículos*.

25 Fernández Palacios, "Georgette," 281.

26 Ibid.

27 Ibid.

28 Ibid.

29 Fernández Palacios, "Georgette," 282.

30 "Testimonio de la Escritura de Testamento Ortorgada por Georgette Maria Phillipart Travers Viuda de Vallejo" (September 7, 1979; Fs. 14,151); Hogar Clínica San Juan de Dios, Lima.

31 César Vallejo, *Correspondencia completa*, ed. Jesús Cabel (Lima: Pontificia Universidad Católica del Perú, 2002), 234.

32 Stephen Hart, "Was César Vallejo a Communist? New Light on the Old Problem," *Ibero-romania* 22 (1985): 95–120.

33 The two More brothers on this occasion were Carlos and Ernesto; Vallejo would get to know the third More brother, Gonzalo, later. Ernesto wrote a memoir about Vallejo— *Vallejo en la encrucijada del drama peruano* (Lima: Librería y Distribuidora Bendezú, 1968)—while Gonzalo gave a homily at Vallejo's funeral (see below).

34 Stephen Hart, "The Chronology of César Vallejo's *Poemas humanos:* New Light on the Old Problem," *Modern Language Review* 97, no. 3 (2002): 602–19.

35 Larrea, *Aula Vallejo*, 204.

36 Vallejo's translations have been republished; see Rosario Valdivia Paz-Soldán, ed., *César Vallejo: traducciones completas*, 2 vols. (Lima: Pontificia Universidad Católica del Perú, 2003).

37 de Vallejo, *¡Allá ellos!*, 40.

38 "I am correcting *El arte y la revolución*. I think that it's a very, very good book. I like it a lot." Georgette de Vallejo, "Apuntes biográficos sobre *Poemas en prosa* y *Poemas humanos*," in *Visión del Perú*, ed. Washington Delgado and Carlos Milla Batres (Lima: Editorial Milla Batres, 1969), 174. This sentence is also quoted by Flores, "Cronología de vivencias," 117.

39 Stephen Hart, "César Vallejo y sus espejismos," *Romance Quarterly* 49, no. 2 (2002): 114–15.

40   Vallejo describes the visit in a letter to Juan Larrea dated January 27, 1932; Vallejo, *Correspondencia completa*, 413.

41   de Vallejo, *¡Allá ellos!*, 86.

42   Felipe Cossío del Pomar, "Con César Vallejo en la otra orilla," *Cuadernos Americanos* 188, no. 3 (May-June 1973): 201.

43   Vallejo, *Correspondencia completa*, 439.

44   Vallejo, *Artículos*, 2: 967–73.

45   de Vallejo, *¡Allá ellos!*, 100–5.

46   Stephen Hart, "Vallejo's 'Other': Versions of Otherness in the Work of Cesar Vallejo," *Modern Language Review* 93, no. 3 (1998): 711–12. Vallejo's medical records have been published in *Acta Herediana: Revista de la Universidad Peruana Cayetano Heredia* 2, no. 12 (October 1991–March 1992): 75–87.

47   Anaïs Nin relates that Gonzalo More, one of Vallejo's very close friends, once told her that "Vallejo never showed his poetry, that he had tons and tons of it all over his room that nobody had ever read. And that he told in one poem, how he would die on All Saints' Day, and then that day came and he did die." *The Diary of Anaïs Nin (1934–1939)*, vol. 2 (New York: Harvest/HBJ, 1970), 295. The prophetic poem is most likely "Black Stone on a White Stone," which mentions a Thursday in autumn; however, Vallejo died on Good Friday rather than All Saints' Day.

48   Stephen M. Hart and Jorge Cornejo Polar, *César Vallejo: Research Bibliography* (Woodbridge: Boydell and Brewer, 2002), 19–21.

49   Georgette de Vallejo and Raúl Porras Barrenchea, eds., *Poemas humanos (1923–1938)* (Paris: Les Éditions del Presses Modernes au Palais-Royal, 1939).

50   Juan Larrea, ed., *César Vallejo: poesía completa* (Barcelona: Barral, 1978), 197.

51   Fernández Palacios, "Georgette," 285.

52   Ibid., 285–86.

53   Georgette de Vallejo, *César Vallejo: obra poética completa: edición con facsímiles* (Lima: Francisco Moncloa Editores, 1968); Fernández Palacios, "Georgette," 286.

54   Georgette Phillipart Travers de Vallejo, "Toi ma vie," ll.5–6, *Masque de Chaux: Máscara de cal* (Trujillo: Instituto de Estudios Vallejianos, 1997), 94.

55   Fernández Palacios, "Georgette," 287.

56   In the collection of manuscripts (mainly correspondence by and to Georgette) held at the Hogar Clínica San Juan de Dios, a picture emerges of Georgette's fraught negotiations with various translators and editors around the world. Letters are to various parties including G. de Cortanze, S. Yurkievich, E. Ballón Aguirre, T. Hermans, O. Giddle, G. Jenebelly, M. Vagenhende, A. Schellekens, J. F. Azaïs, R. Marty, H. Podesta, A. Miró Quesada, J. Wilson Izquierdo, E. Villanueva, J. C. Comín, among others. I am grateful to Hermano Alejandro Torres Espinoza for allowing me to see these manuscripts. Of interest also is Georgette's will dated September 7, 1979, naming Fernando Szyszlo as the executor.

57   *España, aparta de mí este cáliz. Poemas* (Barcelona: Ediciones Literarias del Comisariado, Ejército del Este, 1939). See Tomas G. Escajadillo, "Se encontró la primera edición de *España, aparta de mí este cáliz*," *Runa*, nos. 7–8 (July 1978): 15–17.

58 Juan Fló, "Introducción," in *César Vallejo: autógrafos olvidados,* ed. Juan Fló and Stephen Hart (London: Tamesis, 2003), 1–30.

59 Enrique Ballón Aguirre, ed., *César Vallejo: teatro completo,* 2 vols. (Lima: Pontificia Universidad Católica del Perú, 1979).

60 The typescripts are available for consultation by personal application to Hermano Alejandro Torres Espinoza, currently director of the Hogar Clínica San Juan de Dios.

61 Juan Fló, "Acerca de algunos borradores de Vallejo: reflexiones sobre el surgimiento de la novedad," *Nuevo Texto Crítico* 8 (1995–1996): 93–127.

BIBLIOGRAPHY

An expansive bibliography is provided in the RGV edition. Here I will mention only recent collections of Vallejo's complete poetry, as well as works and/or authors mentioned in my notes. Since RGV does not list translations of Vallejo's poetry in English, I have listed all the collections that I am aware of at this time.

WORKS BY VALLEJO

Ferrari, Américo, ed. *Obra poética*. Paris and Madrid: Colección Archivos de A.L.L.C.A. XXe siècle, 1988.

González Vigil, Ricardo, ed. *Obras Completas*. Vol. 1, *Obra Poética*. Lima: Banco de Crédito del Perú, 1991.

Hernández Novás, Raúl, ed. *Poesía completa*. Havana: Editorial Arte y Literatura and Casa de las Américas, 1988.

Larrea, Juan, ed. *Poesía completa*. Barcelona: Barral Editores, 1978.

Vallejo, Georgette de, ed. *Obra poética completa*. Facsimile edition. Colección Piedra negra sobre una piedra blanca. Lima: Francisco Moncloa Editores, 1968.

WORKS ON VALLEJO

Bazán, José Cerna. *Sujeto a cambio: De las relaciones del texto y la sociedad en la escritura de César Vallejo*. Trujillo: ABC Publicidad S.A.C., 2004.

Coyné, André. *César Vallejo y su obra poética*. Lima: Ed. Letras Peruanas, 1957.

Escobar, Alberto. *Cómo leer a Vallejo*. Lima: P. L. Villanueva Edit., 1973.

Espejo Asturrizaga, Juan. *César Vallejo: Itinerario del hombre*. Lima: Ed. Juan Mejía Baca, 1965.

Flores, Ángel. *Aproximaciones a César Vallejo*. 2 volumes. New York: Las Américas Publishing, 1971.

Franco, Jean. *César Vallejo: The Dialectics of Poetry and Silence*. London: Cambridge University Press, 1976.

Hart, Stephen. *Religión, política y ciencia en la obra de César Vallejo*. London: Tamesis Books Publishers, 1987.

Izquierdo Ríos, Francisco. *César Vallejo y su tierra*. Lima: Ed. Rímac, 1972.

Meo Zilio, Giovanni. "Neologismos en la poesía de César Vallejo." In *Lavori della Sezione Fiorentina del Grupo Ispanistico*. Florence: C.N.R., Casa Editrice G. D'Anna, 1967.

Neale-Silva, Eduardo. *César Vallejo en su fase trílcica*. Madison: University of Wisconsin Press, 1975.

Ortega, Julio. *La teoría poética de César Vallejo*. Providence: Editores del Sol, 1986.

Sharman, Adam, ed. *The Poetry and Poetics of César Vallejo: The Fourth Angle of the Circle.* Lewiston, NY: Edwin Mellen Press, 1997.

TRANSLATIONS OF POETRY COLLECTIONS BY VALLEJO IN ENGLISH

(excluding those by Clayton Eshleman, for which see acknowledgments)

Boyle, Peter, trans. *I Am Going to Speak of Hope: An Anthology of Selected Poems by César Vallejo.* Sydney, Australia: Consulate General of Peru, 1999.

Cardona-Hine, Álvaro, trans. *Spain, Let This Cup Pass from Me.* Los Angeles: Red Hill Press, 1972.

Dorn, Edward, and Gordon Brotherston, trans. *César Vallejo: Selected Poems.* Harmondsworth, England: Penguin Books, 1976.

———, eds. *The Sun Unwound: Original Texts from Occupied America.* Berkeley: North Atlantic Books, 1999. (An anthology including all the translations published in their 1976 book, above, with one additional poem.)

Fogden, Barry, trans. *The Black Heralds.* East Sussex, England: Allardyce, Barnett, Publishers, 1995.

Hays, H. R., trans. *Poems of César Vallejo.* New Directions Annual 15. New York: Meridian Books, 1955. (Eleven poems. These translations, along with thirty-five more, were reprinted in *Ironwood* 15 [1980].)

Higgins, James, trans. *César Vallejo: A Selection of His Poetry.* Liverpool: Francis Carnes, 1987.

Knoepfle, John, James Wright, and Robert Bly, trans. *Twenty Poems of César Vallejo.* Madison, Minnesota: Sixties Press, 1962.

Price, Richard, and Stephen Watts, eds. *César Vallejo: Translations, Transformations, Tributes.* Middlesex, England: Southfields Press, 1998.

saíz, prospero, trans. "Selections from César Abraham Vallejo's *Trilce.*" *Abraxas* 38/39 and 40/41 (1990/1991). (Fifty-two poems.)

Sarko, Mary, trans. *Spain, Take This Cup from Me.* Washington, D.C.: Azul Editions, 1995.

Schaaf, Richard, and Kathleen Ross, trans. *The Black Heralds.* Pittsburgh: Latin American Literary Review Press, 1990.

Seiferle, Rebecca, trans. *Trilce.* Riverdale-on-Hudson, NY: Sheep Meadow Press, 1992.

———, trans. *The Black Heralds.* Port Townsend, WA: Copper Canyon Press, 2003.

Smith, David, trans. *Trilce.* New York: Mushinsha-Grossman, 1973.

Smith, Michael, and Valentino Gianuzzi, trans. *Trilce.* Exeter, England: Shearsman Books, 2005.

———, trans. *Complete Later Poems, 1923–1938.* Exeter, England: Shearsman Books, 2005.

INDEX OF SPANISH TITLES AND FIRST LINES

INDEX OF ENGLISH TITLES
AND FIRST LINES

DESIGN
J.G. Braun

COMPOSITION
BookMatters, Berkeley

TEXT & DISPLAY
Scala

PRINTER/BINDER
Thomson-Shore, Inc.